Beginning Fedora Desktop

Fedora 28 Edition

Third Edition

Richard Petersen

Apress®

Beginning Fedora Desktop

Richard Petersen
Alameda, California, USA

ISBN-13 (pbk): 978-1-4842-3881-3   ISBN-13 (electronic): 978-1-4842-3882-0
https://doi.org/10.1007/978-1-4842-3882-0

Library of Congress Control Number: 2018954625

Managing Director, Apress Media LLC: Welmoed Spahr
Acquisitions Editor: Louise Corrigan
Development Editor: James Markham
Coordinating Editor: Nancy Chen

Cover designed by eStudioCalamar

Cover image designed by Freepik (www.freepik.com)

Distributed to the book trade worldwide by Springer Science+Business Media New York, 233 Spring Street, 6th Floor, New York, NY 10013. Phone 1-800-SPRINGER, fax (201) 348-4505, e-mail orders-ny@springer-sbm.com, or visit www.springeronline.com. Apress Media, LLC is a California LLC and the sole member (owner) is Springer Science + Business Media Finance Inc (SSBM Finance Inc). SSBM Finance Inc is a **Delaware** corporation.

For information on translations, please e-mail rights@apress.com, or visit http://www.apress.com/rights-permissions.

Apress titles may be purchased in bulk for academic, corporate, or promotional use. eBook versions and licenses are also available for most titles. For more information, reference our Print and eBook Bulk Sales web page at http://www.apress.com/bulk-sales.

Any source code or other supplementary material referenced by the author in this book is available to readers on GitHub via the book's product page, located at www.apress.com/9781484238813. For more detailed information, please visit http://www.apress.com/source-code.

Printed on acid-free paper

To my cousins
Carolyn, Maryann, and Gloria

Table of Contents

About the Author

Richard Petersen holds a MLIS in Library and Information Studies (UC Berkeley). He is the author of numerous books on C programming, UNIX, and Linux. Currently he is the publisher for Surfing Turtle Press, specializing on books for Fedora and Ubuntu Linux. His research background includes artificial intelligence applications to information retrieval. He has taught computer science programming and UNIX at UC Berkeley.

About the Technical Reviewer

Nick Vyzas is a senior engineer at ProxySQL, where he spends the majority of his time writing Python and C/C++, and providing SRE/MySQL DBA support and automation services. Over the last 15 years, his focus has been on open source software implementation and integration at various organizations, including Accenture, Pythian, and Percona. When he isn't glued to his Linux servers you'll find him at home in Athens with his wife Spyridoula, out fishing with friends, or travelling through random European cities. He takes his coffee very, very seriously.

Acknowledgments

I would like to thank all those at Apress who made this book a reality, particularly Louise Corrigan, the Apress open source editor who initiated and oversaw the project; Nancy Chen, the coordinating editor; and Jim Markham, the development editor, for their support and analysis, as well as management of such a complex project. I also want to thank Nikolaos Vyzas, the technical reviewer, whose analysis and suggestions proved very insightful and helpful. Special thanks to Linus Torvalds, the creator of Linux, and to those who continue to develop Linux as an open, professional, and effective operating system accessible to anyone.

Introduction

This book examines Fedora Linux 28 for the user. Though administrative tools are covered, the emphasis is on what a user would need to know to perform tasks. The focus here is on what users face when using Fedora, covering topics like installation, applications, software management, the GNOME and Plasma (KDE) desktops, additional desktops such as Cinnamon and Mate, shell commands, and both the Fedora administration and network tools. Desktops are examined in detail, including configuration options. Applications examined include Office Suites, editors, ebook readers, music and video applications and codecs, email clients, Web and FTP browsers, and VoIP and IM applications. This book is designed for the Fedora 28 desktop, with all the latest features of interest to users.

Part I focuses on getting started, covering Fedora information and resources, Fedora Live DVDs, Live USBs, installing and setting up Fedora, and basic use of the desktop as well as device access. The GNOME settings configuration tools such as power, background, screen, network, and display are examined. Also covered is software management using GNOME software, packages, DnfDragora, and the dnf command, along with repositories and their uses, including the RPM Fusion repository.

Part II keys in on applications such as office, mail, graphics, multimedia, Web, FTP, VoIP, IM, and social networking applications. This part includes coverage of the PulseAudio sound interface and music and video applications.

Part III covers the two major desktops—GNOME and Plasma (KDE)—discussing the new GNOME 3 features, including the activities overviews, the dash, and the top bar. Unique Plasma features like the dashboard and activities are also explored. In addition, the shell interface is examined, including features like history, filename completion, directory and file operations, among others. Additional desktops are also discussed, including XFCE, LXDE, Mate, LXQT, Sugar (SoaS), and Cinnamon.

Part IV deals with administration topics, first discussing system tools like the GNOME system monitor, the Disk Usage Analyzer, the Disk Utility storage manager, temperature monitors, and the SELinux configuration dialog. Then there is a detailed chapter on Fedora system administration tools, like those for managing users, authorization controls, and Bluetooth, along with service management, file system access, and printer configuration. The network configuration chapter covers a variety of network tasks, including configuration of wired and wireless connections, firewalls, and Samba Windows access.

PART I

Getting Started

CHAPTER 1

Fedora 28 Introduction

The Fedora release of Linux is maintained and developed by an open source project called the Fedora Project (`https://fedoraproject.org`). The release consists entirely of open source software. Development is carried out using contributions from Linux developers. The project is designed to work much like other open source projects, with releases keeping pace with the course of rapid online development. The Fedora Project features detailed documentation of certain topics, such as installation and desktop user guides, at `https://docs.fedoraproject.org` (see Table 1-1).

Table 1-1. *Fedora Sites*

Website	Description
`https://fedoraproject.org`	Fedora resources
`https://download.fedoraproject.org`	Fedora repository site, mirror link
`https://docs.fedoraproject.org/f28/install-guide/index.html`	Fedora installation guide
`https://docs.fedoraproject.org/f28/release-notes/index.html`	Fedora release notes
`https://docs.fedoraproject.org/fedora-project/project/fedora-overview.html`	Fedora project overview
`https://fedoraproject.org/wiki/FAQ`	Fedora FAQ
`https://docs.fedoraproject.org`	Documentation and support tutorials for Fedora releases
`https://ask.fedoraproject.org/en/questions/`	Ask Fedora site where you can submit question and see answers popular questions

(continued)

© Richard Petersen 2018
R. Petersen, *Beginning Fedora Desktop*, https://doi.org/10.1007/978-1-4842-3882-0_1

Table 1-1. (*continued*)

Website	Description
https://fedoramagazine.org/	*Fedora Magazine* with articles on latest developments and projects
https://getfedora.org/	Fedora download page
https://alt.fedoraproject.org/	Fedora download page for alternative download methods
https://admin.fedoraproject.org/ mirrormanager/	Fedora mirrors list
https://fedoraforum.org	User discussion support forum, endorsed by the Fedora Project; includes FAQs and news links
https://www.linuxfoundation.org/	The Linux Foundation, official Linux development
https://www.kernel.org/	Latest Linux kernels
https://www.redhat.com/	The Red Hat website
https://www.centos.org/	Community Enterprise Operating System CENTOS (Red Hat–based)

This chapter covers the information about the Fedora release, where to obtain information on it, and what versions are available for download. You can also download and try out the Fedora release on a Live Workstation DVD or USB drive without installing it.

Fedora Documentation

Documentation for Fedora can be found at https://docs.fedoraproject.org (see Table 1-1). The Fedora Installation Guide provides a detailed description of all install procedures. The Fedora System Administration Guide covers basic system configuration and package management, as well as advanced topics such as server and system monitoring. Several dedicated Fedora support sites are available that provide helpful information, including https://fedoraforum.org, https://ask.fedoraproject.org/en/questions/, and https://fedoraproject.org. The https://fedoraforum.org site is a Fedora Project–sponsored forum for end-user support. Here you can post questions and check responses for common problems. The Ask Fedora site lets you ask a question and view the responses to other user's questions. Questions are ranked by views, number of answers, and votes.

Your Firefox browser will already be configured with the Fedora start page at `https://start.fedoraproject.org`. There are buttons at the top of the page for Fedora Documentation, Help for Fedora Users, and Get Fedora. The Help for Fedora Users button opens the Ask Fedora site where you can ask questions; see `https://ask.fedoraproject.org/en/questions/`. The Firefox browser is also configured with bookmarks for accessing popular Fedora documentation and support sites. There are bookmarks for Fedora Project, Fedora Forum, Fedora Magazine, Fedora Docs, Planet Fedora, and Join Fedora. Check the Bookmarks sidebar's Fedora Project, User Communities, and Red Hat folders. The Red Hat folder displays entries for Red Hat, jBoss, OpenSource.com, and The Open Source Way (you may have to set the bookmarks sidebar to display it; choose Bookmarks ➤ Bookmarking Tools ➤ View Bookmarks Sidebar).

Fedora maintains detailed specialized documentation, such as information on understanding how udev is implemented or how SELinux is configured. For much of the documentation you must rely on installed documentation in `/usr/share/doc` or on the man and info pages, as well as the context help button for different applications running on your desktop. Websites for software such as GNOME, KDE, and LibreOffice.org provide extensive applicable documentation. For installation, you can use the Fedora installation guide at `https://docs.fedoraproject.org/f28/install-guide/index.html`.

Fedora 28

The Fedora versions of Linux are entirely free. You can download the most current version from `https://getfedora.org/` or `https://download.fedoraproject.org`. The `https://download.fedoraproject.org` address will link to the best available mirror for you. You can update Fedora using the GNOME Software's Updates tab to access the Fedora repository. Access is automatically configured during installation.

The Fedora distribution is also available online at numerous FTP sites. Fedora maintains download sites at `https://download.fedoraproject.org`, along with a mirror listing at `https://mirrors.fedoraproject.org`, where you can download the entire current release of Fedora Linux, as well as updates and additional software.

Fedora 28 Features

Fedora releases feature key updates to critical applications as well as new tools. The following information is derived for the official Fedora release notes. Consult these notes for detailed information about all new changes. You can find the release notes at `https://docs.fedoraproject.org/f28/release-notes/index.html`. A list of changes is available at `https://fedoraproject.org/wiki/Releases/28/ChangeSet`. Some of the more prominent features of the Fedora Workstation are listed here.

> Fedora provides the Mate and Cinnamon desktops. Mate is a traditional desktop based on GNOME 2, and Cinnamon is the Mint Linux desktop derived from GNOME 3, but with many traditional features, such as the panel and applets.

> GNOME Software has replaced PackageKit as the primary frontend software management application, (gnome-software). The DnfDragora software manager has replaced the older Yumex software manager.

> The System Status Area is combined into one menu showing sound volume, brightness, network connections, the current user, battery power, and buttons for settings, lock screen, and power off. The Switch User item is only shown if more than one user is set up for the system. Sound volume and screen brightness (laptops) are adjusted using sliders on the System Status Area menu.

> For systems with wireless devices, there is a WiFi entry in the System Status Area menu that expands to a menu with options to select a network, turn off the wireless device, and to open the GNOME Network system setting dialog at the WiFi tab (WiFi Settings).

> GNOME windows and workspaces can be displayed easily and accessed quickly from the overview.

> A search box at the top of the overview allows you to search directly for applications, installed and uninstalled. Uninstalled entries open GNOME Software to let you install the application. Search is also configured to search for files, GNOME Contacts,

Documents, and Keys, as well as to conduct a web search. Use the GNOME Settings Search dialog to select the applications that can be searched. You can also add other applications.

The GNOME Tweak Tool lets you perform common desktop configurations, such as placing your home folder on the desktop, changing the theme for icons and windows, changing and adjusting fonts, choosing startup applications, configuring how the date is displayed on the top bar, and setting up static (fixed number) workspaces.

Though GNOME workspaces are generated automatically (dynamic) from the overview, you can also use the GNOME Tweak Tool to set up static (fixed-number) workspaces instead.

The GNOME overview features a dash (Activities) that lists icons for your favorite applications and opened applications, letting you access them quickly. You can add applications to the dash. An Applications icon on the dash opens the applications overview. A search box at the top lets you search for applications and files. A Frequent button at the bottom lets you display only frequently accessed applications. A pager to the right lets you move through the icons by page.

In the GNOME-shell, notifications are displayed in the message tray at the top of the screen next to the calendar. Use the Super+m key to display it (Windows key+m), or click the date button at the center top of the screen.

On all GNOME windows, the toolbar and the title bar have been combined into a header bar, with a single close box on the right side.

The GNOME Files file manager (Nautilus) features a sidebar. You can quickly access any file system on removalbel devices, remote networks, and internal drives, as well as your home folders.

The GNOME Classic desktop lets you use a GNOME 2–like interface, but still operating on the same Fedora Workstation GNOME 3 desktop.

Fedora ISO Images

Fedora disks are released as a set of spins that collect software for different purposes. Currently, there are two major Fedora distribution spins available: the Fedora Workstation Live spin (GNOME Desktop) and the Fedora Server Live spin. The Fedora Server Live spin includes a collection of server software, but not the entire collection. It installs only the command-line interface. Spins are created with Revisor, which you can use to develop your own customized spins.

> **Fedora Live Workstation ISO:** The Fedora Workstation Live ISO, include GNOME desktop and applications.

> **Fedora Server ISO:** The Fedora Server Live ISO, designed for network servers. Installs only a command-line interface.

Fedora Custom Spins

Custom spins are also available and can be downloaded from `https://spins.fedoraproject.org` and `https://fedoralabs.org`. The official spins are listed at `https://fedoraproject.org/wiki/Releases/28/Spins`.

Fedora Spins:

> **Fedora 28 Plasma Spin:** Available for i686 and x86_64; includes Plasma desktop (KDE).

> **Fedora 28 XFCE Spin:** Features the XFCE desktop instead of GNOME.

> **Fedora 28 LXDE Spin:** Features the lightweight LXDE desktop instead of GNOME.

> **Fedora 28 LXQT Spin:** Features the lightweight LXDE desktop based on the Qt libraries.

> **Fedora Mate-Compiz Desktop Spin:** The Mate Desktop Environment. Mate is an updated version of the GNOME 2 interface.

> **Fedora Cinnamon Desktop Spin:** The Cinnamon Desktop Environment. Cinnamon is an original desktop developed by Linux Mint.

Fedora SoaS Desktop Spin: Sugar on a Stick spin for USB drives featuring the Sugar desktop (OLPC).

Fedora Labs Spins:

Fedora Astronomy Spin: Astronomy applications and tools.

Fedora Games Spin: Games available on Fedora.

Fedora Design Suite: Image applications available on Fedora.

Fedora Security Lab Spin: Fedora Security Lab spin, a safe environment for security testing and recovering a system.

Fedora Robotics Spin: Robotic simulation environment.

Fedora Science Spin: Scientific research.

Fedora Jam: Audio and music applications and tools.

Fedora Python Classroom: Python instruction tools.

Multimedia

Although licensed multimedia formats such as DVD are still excluded, open source formats are all included, including Vorbis, Ogg, Theora, and FLAC. Multimedia codecs with licensing issues can be directly downloaded with PackageKit, once you have configured DNF to use the RPM Fusion (`https://rpmfusion.org`) or Negativo17.org (`https://negative17.org`) repositories on your system. Use one or the other, not both. These repositories are *not* configured by default. For the RPM Fusion repository, install the `https://rpmfusion.org` configuration package for Fedora 28, which is available from that site.

Fedora Workstation Live ISO

The Fedora Workstation Live ISO lets you run Fedora on any computer using a DVD-ROM drive or a USB drive. The ISO image can be installed to either a DVD disc or a USB drive. You can save files to removable devices such as USB drives. You can temporarily install software, but the install disappears when you shut down. You can also mount partitions from hard drives on the system you are running the Workstation Live DVD or USB on. Find out more about Live discs at `https://fedoraproject.org/wiki/FedoraLiveCD`.

The Workstation Live ISO provided by Fedora includes a limited set of software packages. Servers are not included. For desktop support, you use GNOME. Other than these limitations, you have a fully operational Fedora desktop. The Workstation Live ISO enables Network Manager by default, automatically detecting and configuring your network connection. You have the full set of administrative tools, with which you can add users and change configuration settings while the Workstation Live ISO is running. When you shut down, the configuration information is lost.

You can log out, but this will display a login screen with a simple login dialog for automatic login and a language menu. The bottom panel of the login screen has menus for setting the language and keyboard. You can shut down or restart from the shutdown menu on the right side of the panel.

When you first boot, you can press the spacebar to display the boot options. These include booting up the Workstation Live ISO directly (the default), booting with basic video, verifying the disk media first, performing a memory test, or booting to another OS already on your hard disk. If you press nothing, the Workstation Live ISO starts up automatically. After your system starts up, you will be presented with the standard login screen for the live user. Click for user login. The GNOME desktop (see Figure 1-1) will then start up.

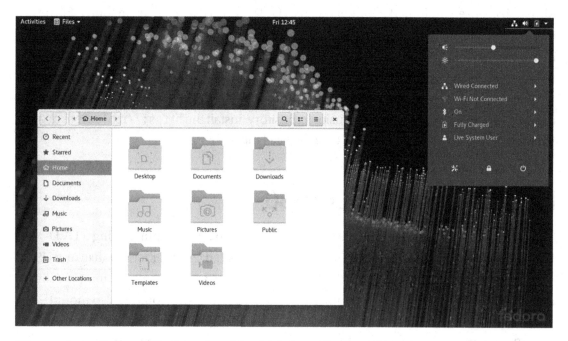

Figure 1-1. *Fedora Workstation Live ISO (run from a DVD disc or USB drive)*

Click the Activities button on the upper-left corner to enter the overview mode, where you can access windows, search for applications and files, and open applications (Applications icon on the dash, a favorites sidebar). From the dash, you can quickly open applications (see Figure 1-2). The dash contains, as its last icon, an Install to Hard Drive icon, which you can use to install Fedora on your hard drive.

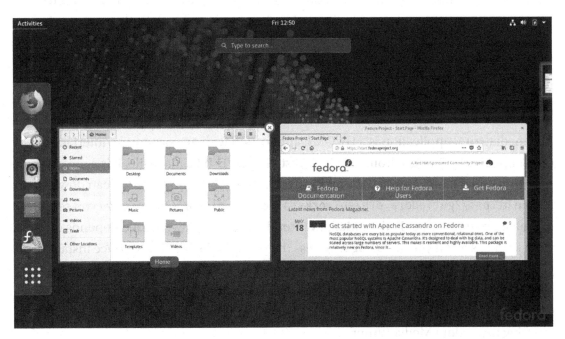

Figure 1-2. *Fedora Workstation Live DVD overview mode (Activities button)*

An easy way to save data from a Live session is to use a USB drive. On GNOME, the USB drive will appear as an entry on a file manager window sidebar. Double-click it to open a file manager window for the USB drive. You can then copy files generated during the session to the USB drive. Remember to eject the drive before removing it (click the eject button next to the USB drive entry on the file manager sidebar).

Installing Fedora from a Workstation Live ISO

The Workstation Live DVD can also be used as an installation disk, providing its limited collection of software on a system, that can be expanded and updated from Fedora online repositories (see Chapter 2). Later, you add packages from repositories. Double-click the Install to Hard Drive icon on the overview dash to start the installation (see Figure 2-4 in Chapter 2).

USB Live Drive

You can install a Fedora Workstation Live ISO image (or any Fedora spin) to a USB drive instead of a DVD disc. The procedure is not destructive. Your original data on the USB disk is preserved. To create a Live USB drive, you can either use the Fedora Media Writer application (mediawriter package), or the livecd-iso-to-disk command (livecd-iso-to-mediums package). A tutorial on using these tools to create USB Live drives is available at https://docs.fedoraproject.org/quick-docs/en-US/creating-and-using-a-live-installation-image.html.

Fedora Media Writer (mediawriter)

The mediawriter application is a GNOME application with an easy-to-use interface for creating a Live USB image from a Live Workstation DVD ISO image file. It is a cross-platform application with versions for Linux, Windows, and the Mac. You can download it from https://getfedora.org/en/workstation/download/. On this page you see a download button for the Fedora Media Writer. The version downloaded depends on what kind of system you are using to access the page. On Fedora Linux, once installed, you can start Fedora Media Writer from the applications overview to open the Fedora Media Writer window. Click Custom Image to open an ISO image you have downloaded. Check the Fedora Installation Guide ➤ Preparing for Installation for a detailed tutorial on using the Fedora Media Writer.

https://docs.fedoraproject.org/f28/install-guide/install/Preparing_for_Installation.html

livecd-iso-to-disk

You can also install Fedora Live images to a USB disk using the livecd-iso-to-disk command to install the image (part of the livecd-iso-to-mediums package). This is a command-line tool that you enter in a terminal window. Use the Live image and the device name of the USB disk as your arguments.

```
/usr/bin/livecd-iso-to-disk    Fedora-Workstation-Live-x86_64-28.1.1.iso
    /dev/sdb1
```

Each Live Workstation DVD also provides a livecd-iso-to-disk script in its LiveOS directory.

Live USB Persistence Storage

If you want to make changes to the Fedora OS on the USB Live version, set up an overlay memory segment on the USB drive. To do this, use the `--overlay-size-mb` option with the size of the overlay in megabytes. Be sure your USB drive is large enough to accommodate both the overlay memory and the DVD image. The following allows for 512MB of persistent data that will be encrypted:

```
livecd-iso-to-disk --overlay-size-mb 512 Fedora-Workstation-Live-x86_64-
28.1.1.iso /dev/sbd1
```

Persistent Home Directory

If you want to save data to a /home directory on the USB Live version, set up a home directory memory segment. To do this, use the `--home-size-mb` option with the size of the home directory segment in megabytes. Be sure your USB drive is large enough to accommodate the home memory and the DVD image, as well as a memory overlay, if you also want to enable changes to the operating system. Your /home directory memory segment will be encrypted by default, to protect your data in case it is lost or stolen. Upon creating your overlay, you will be prompted for a passphrase. Whenever you boot up your USB system, you will be prompted for the passphrase. The following allows for a 1024MB /home directory that will be encrypted:

```
livecd-iso-to-disk --home-size-mb 1024  Fedora-Workstation-Live-x86_64-
28.1.1.iso /dev/sbd1
```

If you do not want the data encrypted, add the `--unencrypted-home` option when creating the disk.

Combining the overlay and the /home memory would require a command such as the following. In all, about 3GB of disk space would be required.

```
livecd-iso-to-disk --overlay-size-mb 512 --home-size-mb 1024 Fedora-
Workstation-Live-x86_64-28.1.1.iso  /dev/sbd
```

Fedora Logo

The Fedora logo depicts an *f* encased in a blue circle (see Figure 1-3). The logo is designed to represent three features of the Linux community and development: freedom, communication, and infinite possibilities. The *f* stands for "freedom," which melds into the infinity symbol, both encased in a speech bubble evoking communication (voice). The logo, then, represents free and open software with infinite possibilities developed through global communication. The idea is to evoke the spirit and purpose of Linux development as one of infinite freedom given a voice. The logo incorporates the four basic ideals of Fedora: open, free, innovative, and forward vision. See `https://fedoraproject.org/wiki/Logo` for more details.

Figure 1-3. *Fedora logo*

Linux

Linux is a fast, stable, and open source operating system that features development tools, desktops, and a large number of applications, ranging from office suites to multimedia applications. Linux was developed in the early 1990s by Linus Torvalds, along with other programmers around the world. Technically, Linux consists of the operating system program, referred to as the *kernel*, which is the part originally developed by Torvalds. But it has always been distributed with a large number of software applications. Linux has evolved as part of the open source software movement. Currently, hundreds of open source applications are available for Linux from the Fedora software repository and the Fedora-compliant third-party repositories such as RPM Fusion (`https://rpmfusion.org`). Most of the GNOME and KDE applications are incorporated into the Fedora repository, using software packages that are Fedora-compliant. You should always check the Fedora repository first for the software you want.

Linux is distributed freely under a GNU General Public License, as specified by the Free Software Foundation, making it available to anyone who wants to use it. GNU (the acronym stands for "GNU's Not UNIX") is a project initiated and managed by the Free Software Foundation to provide free software to users, programmers, and developers. Linux is copyrighted, not public domain. However, a GNU public license has much the same effect as the software being in the public domain. The GNU General Public License is designed to ensure that Linux remains free and, at the same time, standardized.

Open Source Software

Most Linux software is developed as open source software. This means that the source code for an application is distributed free with the application. Programmers can make their own contributions to a software package's development, modifying and correcting the source code. Linux is an open source operating system. Its source code is included in all its distributions and is freely available. Much of the software provided for Linux is also open source projects, as are the KDE and GNOME desktops, along with most of their applications. The LibreOffice office suite is an open source project. You can find more information about the open source movement at https://opensource.org/.

Open source software is protected by public licenses. These licenses prevent commercial companies from taking control of open source software by adding a few modifications of their own, copyrighting those changes, and selling the software as their own product. The most popular public license is the GNU General Public License provided by the Free Software Foundation. This is the license that Linux is distributed under. The GNU General Public License (GPL) retains the copyright, freely licensing the software with the requirement that the software and any modifications made to it always be available for free. Other public licenses have also been created to support the demands of different kinds of open source projects. The GNU Lesser General Public License (LGPL) lets commercial applications use GNU licensed software libraries. The Qt Public License (QPL) lets open source developers use the Qt libraries essential to the KDE desktop.

Linux is currently copyrighted under a GNU public license provided by the Free Software Foundation, and it is often referred to as GNU software. GNU software is distributed free, provided it is distributed to others for free. GNU software has proved both reliable and effective. Many of the popular Linux utilities, such as C compilers, shells, and editors, are GNU software applications. Installed with your Linux distribution are the GNU C++ and Lisp compilers, Vi and Emacs editors, and BASH and TCSH shells. In addition, there are many open source software projects that are licensed under the GNU General Public License. Chapter 4 describes in detail the process of downloading software applications from online repositories and installing them on your system.

Under the terms of the GNU General Public License, the original author retains the copyright, although anyone can modify the software and redistribute it, provided the source code is included, made public, and provided free of charge. Also, no restriction exists on selling the software or giving it away free. One distributor could charge for the software, while another could provide it free of charge. Major software companies also provide Linux versions of their most popular applications. For example, Oracle provides a Linux version of its Oracle database.

Linux Documentation

The Linux Documentation Project (LDP) developed a complete set of Linux manuals, available at `https://www.tldp.org`. The documentation includes a user guide, an introduction, and administrative guides. These are available in text, PostScript, or web page format. You can also find briefer explanations, in what are referred to as HOWTO documents. The Linux documentation for your installed software is available in your `/usr/share/doc` directory. As previously noted, some Fedora-specific documentation is available at `https://docs.fedoraproject.org`. The `https://www.gnome.org` site holds documentation for the GNOME desktop, while `https://www.kde.org` holds documentation for the KDE desktop.

CHAPTER 2

Installation and Upgrade

This chapter describes the installation and upgrade procedures for Fedora Linux 28. Fedora uses the Anaconda installation program. Designed to be simple and fast, it installs a core set of applications. A Fedora Linux 28 installation guide is available online. First check the new Fedora installation guide at `https://docs.fedoraproject.org/f28/install-guide/`.

You can also link to this guide from the Fedora download page (right-side links) at `https://getfedora.org/`. Scroll to the bottom of the page and under the Support list click the "Installation Guide" link.

If you are upgrading your system from Fedora 27, check the section for upgrading at the end of this chapter. There are several methods you can use, including a direct upgrade from the online repositories. A clean install, if possible, is always recommended over an upgrade, as conflicts can occur with some software if configuration file formats and supporting software libraries change too much. You can only upgrade to Fedora 28 from a Fedora 27 install. If you want to upgrade from Fedora 26, you first have to upgrade to Fedora 27, before you can upgrade to Fedora 28.

Obtaining the DVDs

To obtain the current version of Fedora Linux, go to the Fedora Project download website at `https://getfedora.org`. There are large icons for Workstation, Server, and Atomic (cloud images). Click on the Workstation icon. You can also scroll to the bottom of the page and, under the Download list, click the Get Fedora Workstation link. On this same list is the Fedora Spins link, which lets you download alternate spins, such as the KDE and Mate versions. Also, under the Download list, the Alternative Downloads link opens the `https://alt.fedoraproject.org/` site with other methods for downloading, such as BitTorrent and Network installers, as well as other architectures such as ARM.

© Richard Petersen 2018
R. Petersen, *Beginning Fedora Desktop*, https://doi.org/10.1007/978-1-4842-3882-0_2

Fedora Linux 28 is also available on mirror sites. You can directly access a Fedora mirror site by entering the following URL: https://download.fedoraproject.org. You then need to navigate to the releases and the version directory (in this case 28) to find the Workstation directory, and then the architecture (x86_64) and media (iso) directories to where the Fedora Workstation iso image is kept (releases/28/x86_46/iso).

You can also access a specific mirror at the following URL: https://mirrors. fedoraproject.org/publiclist/. The current Fedora mirror and their addresses are listed there. The addresses include web and FTP addresses. You can use an FTP client such as gFTP or Filezilla to perform a direct download.

Basic Install of the Fedora Workstation

Once you download and burn the Fedora Workstation DVD, place it in your DVD drive and boot your system from it. The system starts up automatically and displays the following menu (see Figure 2-1). Once the installation program begins, you follow the instructions, screen by screen. Most of the time, you need only make simple selections. The installation program progresses through several phases. You perform some basic configuration, set up Linux partitions on your hard drive, configure your bootloader, then install the software packages.

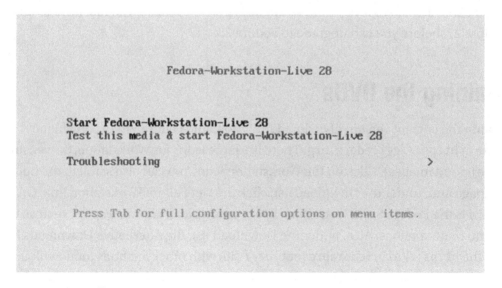

Figure 2-1. *Install menu*

By default, the first entry, Start Fedora Workstation Live 28, is selected. Press Enter to start Fedora. Should you need to add options directly to the boot command, press the Tab key. A command line is displayed on which you can enter the options (see Figure 2-2). Current options will already be listed. Use the Backspace key to delete and the arrow keys to move through the line. Press the ESC key to return to the menu.

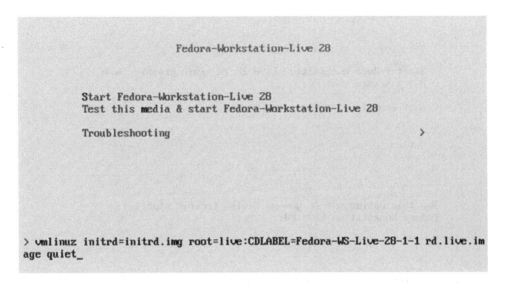

Figure 2-2. Install menu with boot options

For more startup options and testing, use the arrow key to move to the Troubleshooting entry. The Troubleshooting menu enables you to use the basic graphics mode, test the media, test the memory, and boot from a hard drive (see Figure 2-3). Use the arrow keys to move from one menu entry to the next, then press Enter to select the entry.

The first option (Start Fedora Workstation Live 28 in basic graphics mode) starts up with basic video. The second (Test This Media & Start Fedora Live) will test if your DVD/CD media is okay. The third (Run a Memory Test) performs a hardware memory test. The last (Boot from Local Drive) will boot a local OS on a connected hard drive, if there is one.

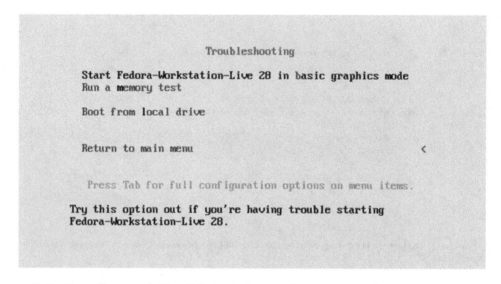

Figure 2-3.   *Install menu's Troubleshooting options*

When you first start the Live disk, you can choose whether to try Fedora or to install it (see Figure 2-4). If you want to install Fedora directly on your system, click the Install to Hard Drive icon to start the standard install procedure (Anaconda).

You can also install Fedora at any time while you are using the Fedora Workstation Live desktop. On the Activities dash, there is an icon showing the hard disk and Fedora logo image with the label Install to Hard Drive (see Figure 2-5).

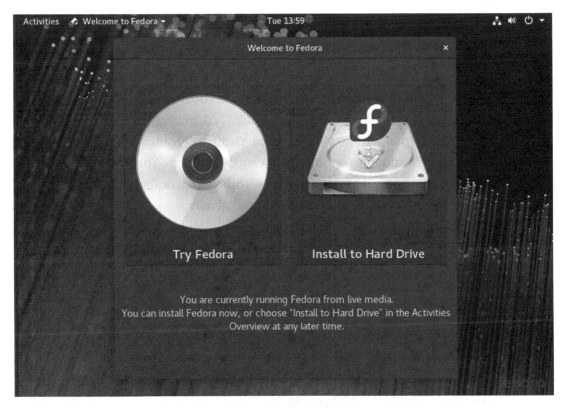

Figure 2-4. *Fedora Install window*

Figure 2-5. *Fedora Install icon on Fedora Workstation Live dash*

The install steps shown are as follows:

Language: Select your language.

Installation Summary: Configure your installation. The Fedora Live install has three options: Date & Time, Keyboard, and Installation Destination. A warning emblem is displayed on those options that require configuration. Ordinarily, only the Installation Destination option has a warning emblem. You cannot continue until all options with warnings are configured. Network configuration is performed automatically.

Date & Time: Select your city from the map or the pop-up menu or click the time zone on the map. This option may not have a warning on it but could still be incorrect. Be sure to check it.

Keyboard: Select and configure your keyboard, if you need to.

Installation Destination: Choose the hard drive to install on and set up your partitions. You have the option to manage your own. Once you finish configuring your installation summary items, the installation begins, showing a progress bar.

When the installation finishes, a simple Quit button will be displayed with a message to restart, to complete the installation. You can close at this point, to return to the Fedora Live Desktop, and then restart, to reboot to your installed system.

On reboot, you enter the Fedora Setup Agent procedure, where you can set the date and time and create a standard user, which you can use to log in as a normal user (not as root). More users can be created later. After setup, your login screen appears, and you can log in to your Fedora system.

You may have to update many of the applications installed from the DVD. Open GNOME Software to the Updates tab to start the update process. Applications and updates are downloaded from the Fedora repository and installed.

The installation process used on Fedora is a screen-based program that takes you through all installation steps as one continuous procedure. You can use the mouse or the keyboard to make selections. When you finish with a screen, click the Continue button at the bottom to move to the next screen. If you have to move back to the previous screen, click Back. You can also use Tab, the arrow keys, the spacebar, and Enter to make selections. You have little to do other than make selections and choose options.

Some screens provide a list of options from which you make a selection. The installation process will first install Linux on your system. It will then reboot and start a Setup process to let you set the time and date and create a user to log in as. The steps for each part of the procedure are delineated in the following sections.

As each screen appears in the installation, default entries will be selected, usually by the auto-probing capability of the installation program. Selected entries will appear highlighted. If these entries are correct, you can simply click Next to accept them and go on to the next screen.

The install program (Anaconda) will automatically detect and configure your video card so that it can run a graphical interface for the install procedure. If it has difficulty configuring the video card, you can choose to use a basic video driver instead, which means you can still use the graphical install. Choose Install Fedora in Basic Graphics Mode from the Troubleshooting menu.

Initial Setup

If your basic device and hardware configuration were appropriately detected, a Welcome screen is displayed, with a Continue button in the lower-right corner. Once you've completed a step, you click Continue to move on. In some cases, you can click a Back button to return to a previous step.

Tip   Your mouse will be automatically detected. If you have a USB mouse that is not being detected, try reinserting the USB connector several times. If you cannot use your mouse for some reason, you can use the Tab key to move to different components and buttons. Use the arrow keys to select and enter a list. Press the Enter key to click a selected button or entry. The Tab key will cycle through entries on a screen sequentially. To return to a button or component, just continue to press the Tab key.

On this screen, you are asked to select your language. A default language is already selected, usually English (see Figure 2-6).

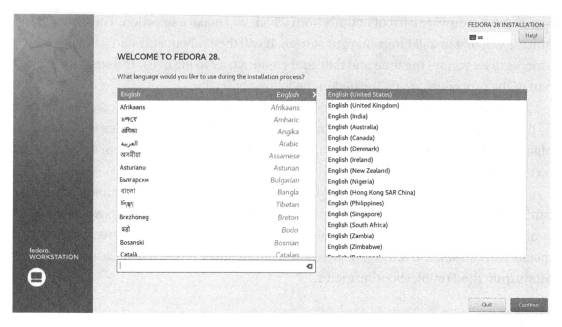

Figure 2-6. *Welcome and language selection*

You are then presented with an Installation summary screen with categories for Localization and System (see Figure 2-7). For Localization, you can configure the Date & Time and the Keyboard. For System, you can configure the Installation. A warning emblem appears on options that have to be configured, usually only the Installation Destination, although you should also check that the date and time are correct. A Quit button at the bottom-left of the screen lets you quit the installation. A Begin Installation button at the bottom-right remains grayed out as long as there are warnings. When all options are configured and the warning emblems disappear, this button becomes active, and you can click it to continue the installation.

For the Install DVD, the Installation Summary screen shows a Software category with Installation Source and Software Selection (see Figure 2-7). On the DVD install, Localization also has a Language Support icon. See the section "Software Installation Configuration with the Fedora Install DVD/CDs," later in this chapter.

Figure 2-7. *Installation Summary screen*

With warning emblems present, a warning appears at the bottom of the screen.

To check and configure your time, date, and time zone, click the Date & Time icon. On the Date & Time screen, you have the option of setting the time zone by using a map or pop-up menu to specify your location (see Figure 2-8). The selected city will appear as the pop-up menu selection. There is a switch that lets you turn off network time (the time obtained from NTP servers). A configure button next to this switch opens a dialog that lets you specify the NTP time servers to use. Click the Done button in the upper-left corner when you're finished.

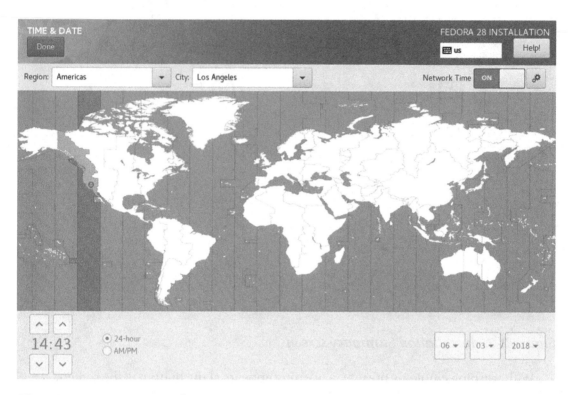

Figure 2-8. *Time zone selection*

On the Installation Summary page, click the Keyboard icon to configure your keyboard (see Figure 2-9). Keyboard layouts are listed on the left scroll box. Clicking the plus button at the bottom of this box lets you add another language layout. The Keyboard button displays an image showing all the keys. A text box to the right lets you test the keyboard. The Options button lets you specify which keys to use to switch layouts.

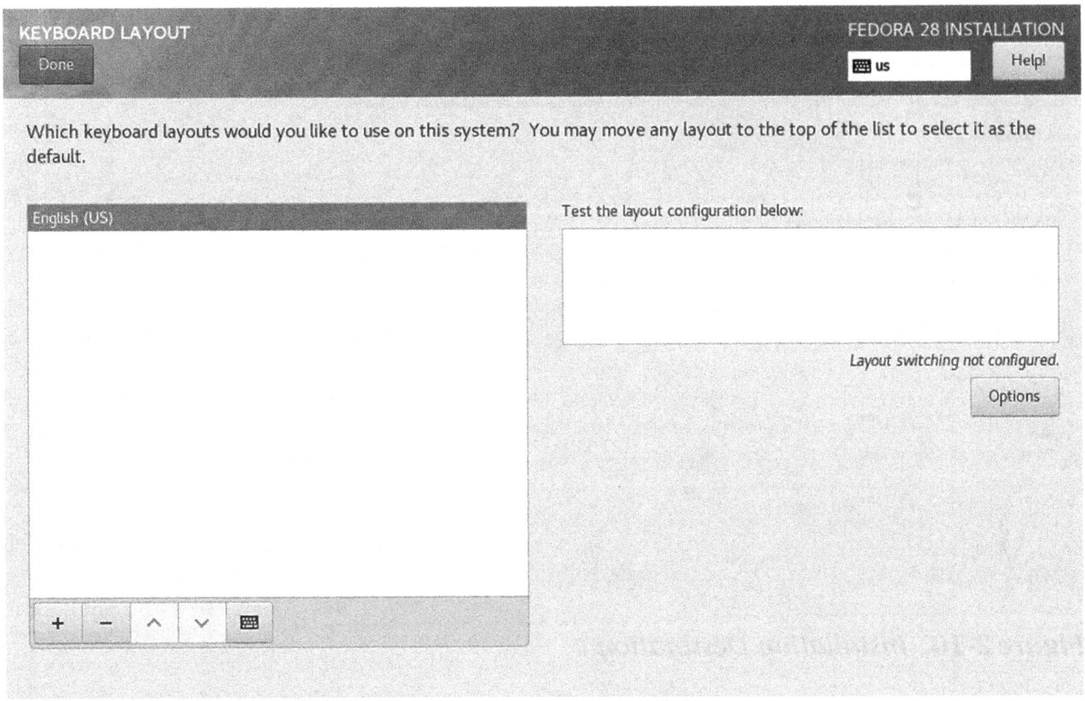

KEYBOARD LAYOUT

Done

FEDORA 28 INSTALLATION

⌨ us   Help!

Which keyboard layouts would you like to use on this system? You may move any layout to the top of the list to select it as the default.

English (US)

Test the layout configuration below:

Layout switching not configured.

Options

+   −   ⌃   ⌄   ⌨

Figure 2-9. *Keyboard selection*

On the Installation Summary screen, click the Installation Destination icon to open the Installation Destination screen, where you can choose the hard disk device on which to perform the installation (see Figure 2-10).

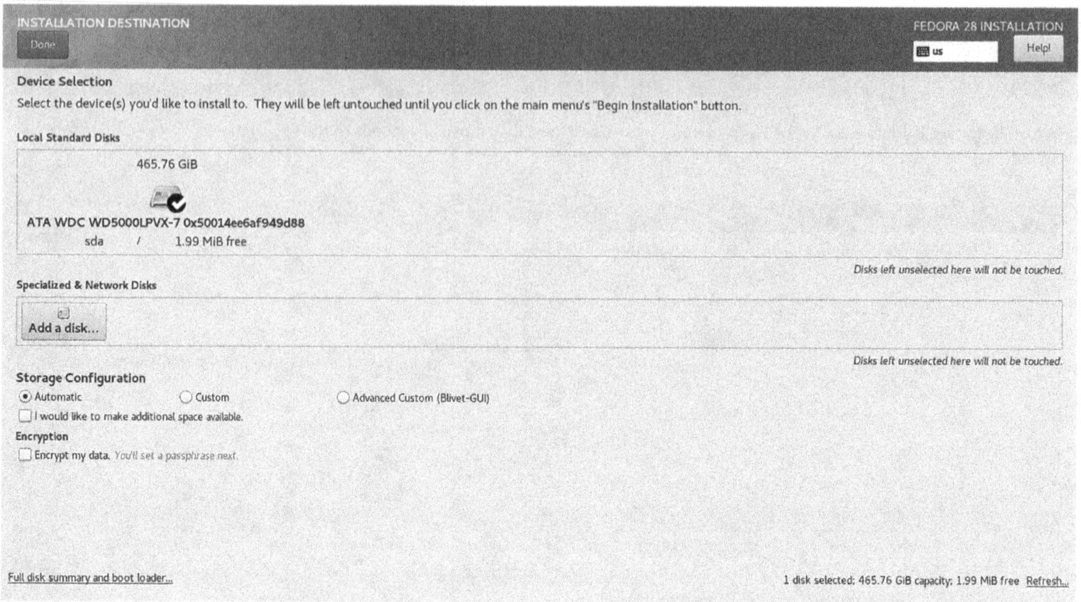

Figure 2-10. *Installation Destination*

The top icon bar shows your installation devices. The local drives are shown under the Local Standard Disks heading. If you have only a single local hard drive, that drive is automatically selected for you.

The Storage section lets you specify partitions on your hard drive and whether you want to encrypt it or not. Encryption sets a passphrase that you will be prompted for when you start up your system. Storage Configuration can be Automatic, Custom, or Advanced Custom. For a standard fresh install that overwrites your hard drive, using a standard set of partitions, simply choose the Automatic option. This is the default. The Custom and Advanced Custom options starts up the partitioner, which will let you create, edit, and delete partitions, as described in the next section. You can set your own size and type for your partitions. Use this option should you want to create added partitions or separate partition for certain system folders, such as the /var folder. You can also us the partitioner to preserve or reuse any existing partitions. You also have the option to free up additional space, should your hard drive have an operating system that you want to preserve, and has a large amount of unused space that can be freed up.

At the bottom of the screen, information is displayed about the selected disk. The Full Disk Summary and Options link opens with information about the device, as well as buttons to remove the device and install the bootloader. You can use this dialog to choose not to install the bootloader. If you have several hard disks, you can choose which one to install the bootloader on (should this be an issue). Usually, you install the bootloader on the same device as Fedora.

A check box at the bottom lets you encrypt the device.

When you have selected the device you want, click the Done button on the upper-left side of the screen.

Upon pressing Begin Installation from the Installation Summary screen, your installation begins with a progress bar at the bottom of the screen.

When installation finishes, a completion message is displayed at the bottom of the screen. The Fedora Workstation Live installation shows a Quit button that returns you to the Fedora Workstation Live Desktop (see Figure 2-11). You can then power off and restart your system to start up your new installation.

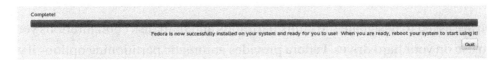

Figure 2-11. *Installation complete*

Manual Partitioning: Partitions, BTRFS, RAID, and Logical Volumes

On the Installation Destinations screen in the Storage Configuration section, you are given the option of customizing the disk partitioning. Click the Custom check box, and then click the Done button. This opens the Manual Partitioning screen (see Figure 2-12). The left-side scroll box lists the partitions as you create them. If your hard drive is blank, it will be empty. The button bar at the bottom of the scroll box has buttons for adding partitions, deleting them, and displaying information.

At the top right of the dialog is a Help button for the Help dialog. It is highly recommended that you read through the Help dialog, which provides a very detailed explanation of how to configure your partitions.

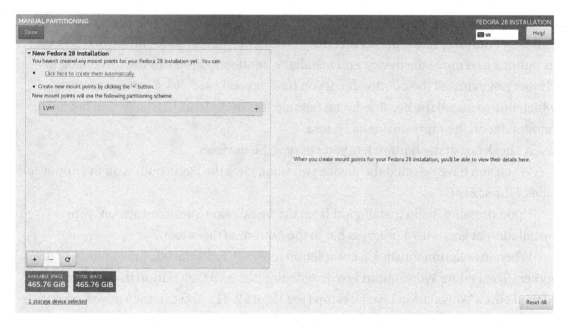

Figure 2-12. *Manual Partitioning dialog*

You are asked to designate the Linux partitions and hard disk configurations you want to use on your hard drives. Fedora provides automatic partitioning options if you just want to use available drives and free space for your Linux system. You can create specific partitions, configure RAID devices, or set up logical volumes (LVM).

No partitions will be changed or formatted until you leave the Manual Partitioning screen and, from the Installation Summary screen, you click the Done button. You can opt out of the installation any time until that point, and your original partitions will remain untouched. A default layout sets up a home partition, swap partition, a boot partition of type ext4 (Linux native) for the kernel, and an LVM partition that will hold all your applications and files, as well as a boot EFI partition if needed.

Initially, with no Linux partition set up and space available, you can click the Click Here to Create These Automatically link, to create a default set of Fedora partitions. These are a boot, root, home, and swap partitions (see Figure 2-13). The root and swap partitions are LVM volumes. The boot partition is a standard ext4 partition. This is the default set of partitions used, should you skip manual partitioning.

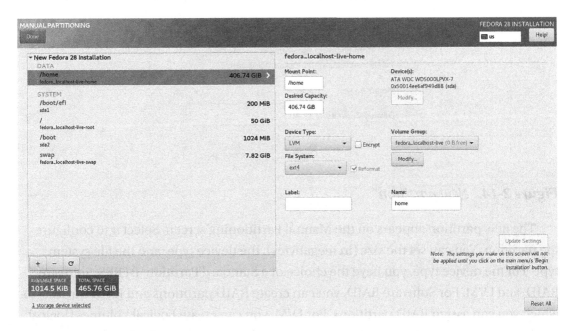

Figure 2-13. *Default partitions*

The side pane lists the partitions, showing the device name and size. The right pane shows the configuration for a selected partition. It displays the name, mount point, label, size, device type, file system, and encryption option. You can make changes to any of the entries. (No changes are actually made to the hard disk until you begin the software installation.)

Creating Partitions

To manually create a new partition, click the Plus button to display the Add a New Mount Point dialog, where you can choose the mount point and the size (see Figure 2-14). Mount points begin with a slash (/). If you enter a slash, a drop-down menu appears under the Mount Point text box. The common mount points for file systems are /, /boot, /home, /usr, and /var. If you have a root and boot system already configured, only the /home, /usr, and /var entries appear.

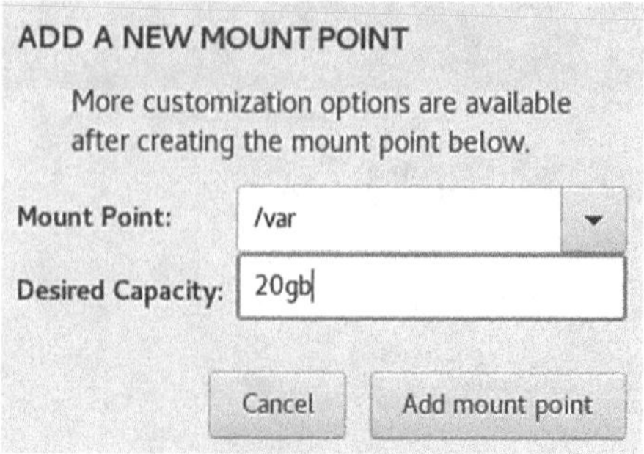

ADD A NEW MOUNT POINT

More customization options are available
after creating the mount point below.

Mount Point: /var

Desired Capacity: 20gb

Cancel   Add mount point

Figure 2-14. *New partition*

The new partition appears on the Manual Partitioning screen. Select it to configure the partition. You can set the size (in megabytes), the device type, and the file system type. For the device type, you have the choice of a Standard Partition, BTRFS, Software RAID, and LVM. For Software RAID, you can create RAID partitions and RAID devices, to which you can assign RAID partitions. For LVM, you can create Logical Volumes (logical partitions to which physical partitions are assigned) and a Volume Group (the group to which logical volumes are assigned). Physical volumes are set up for you.

There are several kinds of file systems supported during installation: ext2, ext3, ext4, swap, btrfs, xfs, and vfat. The ext2 and ext3 partitions are older forms of the Linux standard partition type, ext4.

To make configuration changes to any partition, select it and make the changes to its entries.

Logical Volumes

Fedora supports Logical Volume Management (LVM), which enables you to create logical volumes that you can use instead of hard disk partitions directly. LVM provides a more flexible and powerful way of dealing with disk storage, organizing physical partitions into logical volumes in which memory can be managed easily. Disk storage for a logical volume is treated as one pool of memory, though the volume may in fact contain several hard disk partitions on different hard disks. There is one restriction. The boot partition cannot be a logical volume. You still have to create a separate hard disk partition as your boot partition with the /boot mount point in which your kernel will be installed.

If you selected default partitioning, the /boot partition will have already been set up for you, along with an LVM volume partition for the rest of the system. A logical group will be set up with volumes for both the swap and root partitions. The logical group will be labeled with a name such as fedora. You can change these names by editing the logical group and volumes during installation. Click the Modify button to the right of the volume group entry.

Creating logical volumes is now a simple process of specifying the LVM device type and the volume group. The physical LVM partitions that logical volumes are based on are generated automatically by Fedora. For a particular LVM partition (logical volume), you will have a Volume Group entry in which you can specify the volume group it belongs to.

RAID and BTRFS

You also have the option of creating RAID devices. Such devices are for use with the Linux software RAID service, and shouldn't be used for your motherboard RAID devices, as these are automatically detected. If you have already decided to use the motherboard RAID support, you do not require Software RAID. Linux supports both motherboard/computer RAID devices (DMRAID), as well as its own Linux Software RAID. The RAID option is visible only if you have selected two or more hard disks.

BTRFS is the new file system format, still under development. If operates much like RAID devices, providing RAID0 (stripe), RAID (mirrors), and RAID10 (optimization) levels of support. You create the BTRFS sub-volumes, and the installer creates the BTRFS volume for you.

Advanced Custom (Blivet-GUI)

Choosing the Advanced Custom option on the Installation Destination screen, displays the Blivet-GUI disk configuration tool (see Figure 2-15). Blivet provides more detailed partitioning options.

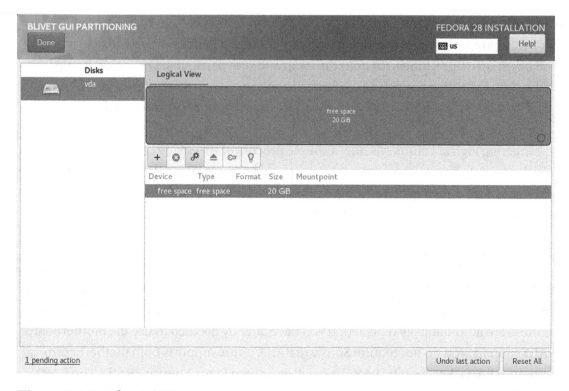

Figure 2-15. *Blivet-GUI*

GRUB on Restart

When you reboot, a GRUB bootloader briefly displays a startup message indicating which operating system on your disk will be started. The default is usually your Linux system. If Fedora is the only operating system on your system, GRUB will skip the startup message and the GRUB menu access and start Fedora immediately. Fedora 28 uses GRUB2. You can find out more about GRUB2 at https://fedoraproject.org/wiki/GRUB_2.

If you have encrypted your hard disk partitions, you are then prompted to enter the LUKS passphrase for them. A standard installation will prompt for the same passphrase for your swap and root partitions on your LVM file system. The prompt will use the physical partition name used for the LVM group, in this example, /dev/sda2. There are two prompts: one for the LVM volume for the root file system, and one for the LVM volume swap file system.

The startup screen then shows the progress of your boot procedures. If your graphics card supports kernel mode settings, the Plymouth bootup screen will be displayed; otherwise, a simple progress bar is shown. You can press the ESC key to see startup messages.

GNOME Initial Setup and GNOME Help

The first time you start up Fedora, the GNOME initial setup is run (see Figure 2-16). Click the Next button to continue to the next screen, Previous to go back. On the Privacy screen, you choose privacy options, location service, and automatic problem reporting (see Figure 2-17). On the Online Accounts screen you can configure online accounts such as Google, Facebook, and Microsoft (see Figure 2-18). If you do not want to configure your accounts at this time, just click the Skip button.

Figure 2-16. *GNOME initial setup*

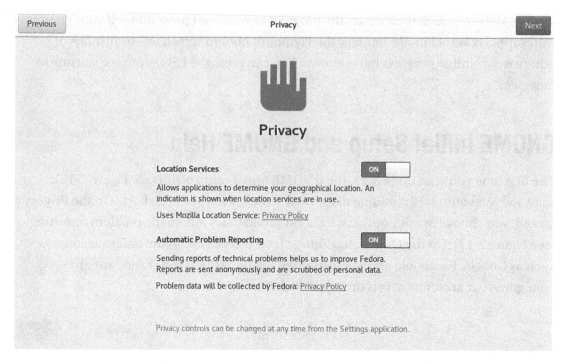

Figure 2-17. GNOME initial setup: Privacy

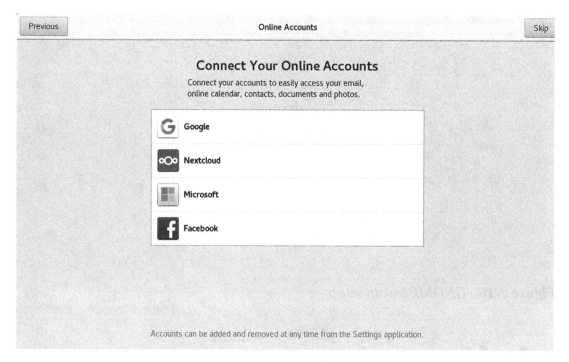

Figure 2-18. GNOME initial setup: Online Accounts

On the About You screen you create a user account, specifying the name and password (see Figure 2-19). You can click on the image to select an image from an image menu.

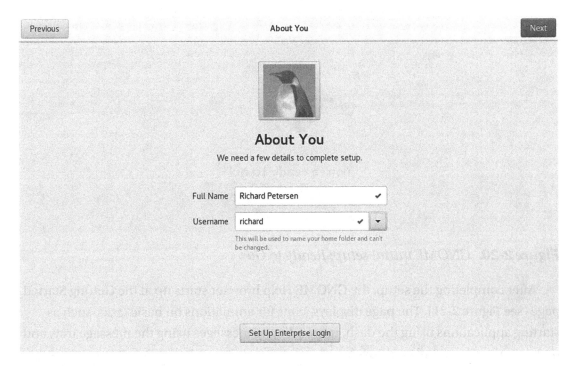

Figure 2-19. *GNOME initial setup: About You*

On the Ready to Go screen (see Figure 2-20), click on Start Using Fedora to start the desktop.

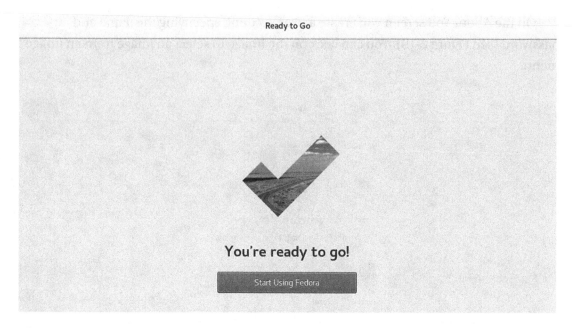

Figure 2-20. *GNOME initial setup: Ready to Go*

After completing the setup, the GNOME Help browser starts up at the Getting Started page (see Figure 2-21). The page displays icons for animations on basic tasks, such as starting applications using the dash, responding to messages using the message tray, and managing windows and workspaces.

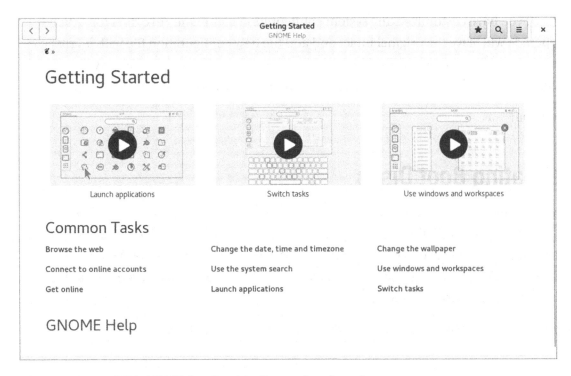

Figure 2-21. *GNOME Help: Getting Started animations*

Upgrading Fedora Linux

You can only upgrade an existing Fedora 27 system to Fedora 28. If you have Fedora 26, you first have to upgrade to Fedora 27. Be sure to back up your system, including the home, etc, and boot directories. You can use the dnf command to perform the upgrade. If not already installed, install the **dnf-plugin-system-upgrade** package. See https://fedoraproject.org/wiki/DNF_system_upgrade for details.

```
sudo dnf install dnf-plugin-system-upgrade
```

From a terminal window, you use the dnf system-upgrade command to perform the upgrade, specifying the release.

```
sudo dnf system-upgrade download --refresh --releasever=28
```

To remove unneeded files, use the autoremove option.

```
sudo dnf autoremove
```

If you have customized any system configuration files in the /etc directory, the upgrade will leave the original intact and add the new configuration file with a .rpmnew extension. You can then manually modify the new version to incorporate any custom changes. This process can be automated with the rpmconf command (rpmconf package).

```
rpmconf -a
```

Creating Boot Disks

You can use mkbootdisk to create a boot CD-ROM. Use the --iso option and the --device option with the name of an ISO image file to create (install the mkbootdisk package). You then use CD-ROM-burning software to create the CD-ROM from the image file. The following example creates a CD-ROM image file called mybootcd.iso that can be used as a boot CD-ROM:

```
mkbootdisk --iso --device mybootcd.iso  4.16.3-301.fc28.x86_64
```

Booting in Rescue Mode

If you are not able to boot or access your system, it may be due to conflicting configurations, libraries, or applications. In this case, you can boot your Linux system in a rescue mode and then edit configuration files with a text editor, remove the suspect libraries, or reinstall damaged software with dnf. To enter the rescue mode, run the Fedora Workstation Live DVD and then select Rescue a Fedora System from the Troubleshooting menu.

You will boot into the command-line mode with your system's files mounted at /mnt/sysimage. You will be notified that you can use the chroot command to set the / directory as the root. Issue the following command at the command-line prompt:

```
chroot /mnt/sysimage
```

Use the cd command to move between directories. Check /etc and /etc/sysconfig for your configuration files. You can use vi to edit your files and the less command to view them. To reinstall files, use the dnf install command. When you are finished, use the exit command.

If you have a command-line system, enter the following at the boot prompt:

```
linux rescue
```

Reinstalling the Bootloader

If you have a dual-boot system, where you are running Windows and Linux on the same machine, you may run into a situation where you have to reinstall your GRUB bootloader. This problem occurs if you have installed a new version of Windows after installing Linux. Windows will automatically overwrite your bootloader (alternatively, you could install your bootloader on your Linux partition instead of the MBR). You will no longer be able to access your Linux system.

All you have to do is reinstall your bootloader. First, in rescue mode as described in the previous section.

As noted in the preceding section, this boots your system in rescue mode. Then use `grub2-install` and the device name of your first partition to install the bootloader. At the prompt, enter

```
sudo grub-install /dev/sda1
```

This will reinstall your current GRUB bootloader, assuming that Windows is included in the GRUB configuration. You can then reboot, and the GRUB bootloader will start up.

You then have to create a new configuration file (`/boot/grub2/grub.cfg`), using the `grub2-mkconfig` command, as follows:

```
sudo grub2-mkconfig -o /boot/grub2/grub.cfg
```

If your Linux rescue disks are unable to access your system, you can use a Fedora Workstation Live DVD to start up Fedora and then manually mount your Fedora partitions. You will have to know your partition device names (use GParted). Once they are mounted, you can access the system files on the mounted partition and make any required changes.

CHAPTER 3

Usage Basics: Login, Desktop, and Help

To start using Fedora, you must know how to access your Fedora system and, once you are on the system, how to use and configure the desktop. A set of desktop GNOME Settings tools lets you easily configure such features as network access, desktop background, display resolution, and power usage. Access is supported through a graphical login. A simple screen appears with menus for selecting login options and your username.

GNOME Users

User access to the system is provided through accounts. To gain access to the system, you must have a user account set up for you. A system administrator creates the account, assigning a username and password for it. You then use your account to log in to and use the system. You can create other new user accounts, by using the system administration tool GNOME Users in GNOME Settings ➤ Details (accessible from the system-status-area menu). You can access these tools from any user account, provided you supply the administrative password. You had to provide a root user password when you installed your system. This is the administrative password required to access any administrative tool, such as the one for managing user accounts.

GRUB Start Menu and Boot Problems

When you boot up, the GRUB screen is displayed for a few seconds before the boot procedure begins. Should you want to start a different operating system or add options to your startup, you have to display the GRUB startup menu (see Figure 3-1). Do this by

43

© Richard Petersen 2018
R. Petersen, *Beginning Fedora Desktop*, https://doi.org/10.1007/978-1-4842-3882-0_3

pressing any key on your keyboard. The GRUB menu will be displayed and will list Linux and other operating systems you specified, such as Windows. Your Linux system should be selected by default. If not, use the arrow keys to move to the Linux entry, if it is not already highlighted, and press Enter.

To change a particular line, use the up/down arrow keys to move to the line. You can use the left/right arrow keys to move along the line. The Backspace key will delete characters and, simply by typing, will insert characters. The editing changes are temporary. Permanent changes can be made only by directly editing the GRUB configuration files. Fedora Linux uses GRUB2, which uses the configuration file /etc/default/grub. GRUB2 files are kept in the /etc/grub.d directory. Run as root the following grub2-mkconfig to apply changes made in /etc/default/grub:

```
grub2-mkconfig -o /boot/grub2/grub.cfg
```

See the GRUB2 page at https://fedoraproject.org/wiki/GRUB_2 for more information.

When your Fedora Linux operating system starts up, an Fedora Linux logo appears. You can press the Esc key to see the startup messages instead. Fedora Linux uses Plymouth with its kernel-mode setting ability to display a startup animation. The Plymouth Fedora Linux logo theme is installed by default.

For graphical installations, some displays may have difficulty running the graphical startup display known as the Plymouth boot tool. This tool replaces the Red Hat Graphical Boot tool but still uses the command rhgb. If you have this problem, you can edit your Linux GRUB entry and remove the rhgb term from the Linux line. Press the **e** key to edit a Grub Linux entry (see Figure 3-2). Then move the cursor to the Linux line and perform your edit. Use the Backspace key to delete. Then press Ctrl+x to boot the edited GRUB entry.

Your system will start up, initially using the text display for all the startup tasks, then shift to the graphical login.

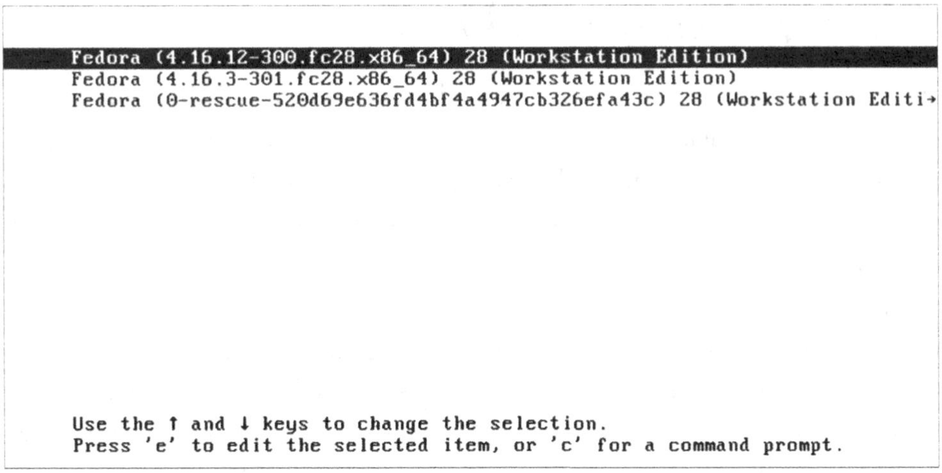

```
Fedora (4.16.12-300.fc28.x86_64) 28 (Workstation Edition)
Fedora (4.16.3-301.fc28.x86_64) 28 (Workstation Edition)
Fedora (0-rescue-520d69e636fd4bf4a4947cb326efa43c) 28 (Workstation Editi→




Use the ↑ and ↓ keys to change the selection.
Press 'e' to edit the selected item, or 'c' for a command prompt.
```

Figure 3-1. *GRUB menu*

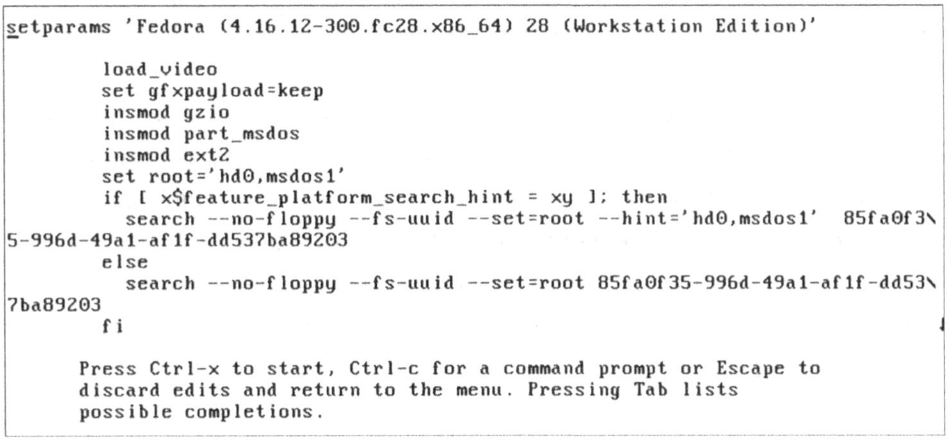

```
setparams 'Fedora (4.16.12-300.fc28.x86_64) 28 (Workstation Edition)'

        load_video
        set gfxpayload=keep
        insmod gzio
        insmod part_msdos
        insmod ext2
        set root='hd0,msdos1'
        if [ x$feature_platform_search_hint = xy ]; then
            search --no-floppy --fs-uuid --set=root --hint='hd0,msdos1'  85fa0f3\
5-996d-49a1-af1f-dd537ba89203
        else
            search --no-floppy --fs-uuid --set=root 85fa0f35-996d-49a1-af1f-dd53\
7ba89203
        fi                                                                      ↓

    Press Ctrl-x to start, Ctrl-c for a command prompt or Escape to
    discard edits and return to the menu. Pressing Tab lists
    possible completions.
```

Figure 3-2. *GRUB Edit window*

Should you have difficulty displaying your graphical interface, you can instead choose to boot up the command-line interface. From the command-line interface, you can make any needed configuration changes. To boot to the command-line interface from GRUB, edit the Linux line of the Linux GRUB entries, and add a 3 to the end of the line. The 3 indicates the command-line interface. In previous versions of Fedora Linux, the 3 indicated a run level. Now it refers to a systemd target.

The Display Manager: GDM

The graphical login interface displays a login window with a box listing a menu of usernames. When you click a username, a login box replaces the listing of users, displaying the selected username and a text box in which you then enter your password. Upon clicking the Sign In button or pressing Enter, you log in to the selected account, and your desktop starts up.

Graphical logins are handled by the GNOME Display Manager (GDM). The GDM manages the login interface, in addition to authenticating a user password and username, and then starts up a selected desktop. From the GDM, you can shift to the command-line interface with Ctrl+Alt+F2, and then shift back to the GDM with Ctrl+Alt+F1 (from a desktop, you would use the same keys to shift to a command-line interface and to shift back). The keys F2 through F6 provide different command-line terminals, as in Ctrl+Alt+F3 for the second command-line terminal. These terminals are known as TTY devices (teletypewriter), devices that only accept typed commands on a keyboard.

When the GDM starts up, it shows a listing of users (see Figure 3-3). A System Status Area at the top right of the screen displays icons indicating the status of the sound and battery. Clicking the icons displays the System Status Area menu, which shows the entries for sound adjustment, the battery status (if a laptop), and the status of your network connections. A power button at the bottom will display a power off dialog with options to Power Off and Restart. To shut down your system, click the Power Off button on the Power Off dialog.

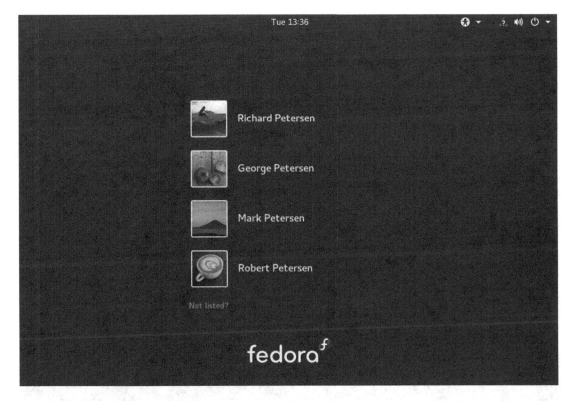

Figure 3-3. *The Fedora Linux GDM user listing*

At the top center of the screen is the date (day of the week) and time. Clicking on the time displays the calendar with the full date specified, and the notifications menu.

Next to the System Status Area icons is a menu for accessibility, which displays a menu of switches that let you turn on accessibility tools and such features as the onscreen keyboard, enhanced contrast, and the screen magnifier.

To log in, click a username from the list of users. You are then prompted to enter the user's password (see Figure 3-4). A new dialog replaces the user list, showing the username you selected and a Password text box in which you can enter the user's password. Once you enter the password, click the Sign In button or press Enter. By default, the GNOME desktop starts up. If the name of a user you want to log in as is not listed, click the Not Listed entry at the end, to open a text box, which prompts you for a username, and then the password.

A session button (gear icon) is displayed below the Password text box next to the Sign In button. Click that Session button to open a menu listing the installed desktops, then click the one you want to use (see Figure 3-5). The GNOME option is the main GNOME desktop, which runs under the new Wayland display server. You also have the choice to choose GNOME on Xorg, which runs under the older Xorg display server, or to choose GNOME Classic, which runs GNOME with older GNOME 2 features such as an Applications menu and a task bar. Though GNOME is the primary desktop for Fedora, it is possible to install and use other desktops, such as KDE (plasma-desktop), Xfce, and Mate. They are available on the Fedora Linux repository. Your installed desktops will appear as options on the Session menu.

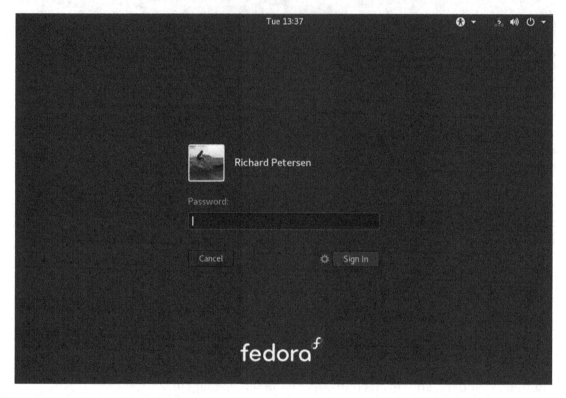

Figure 3-4. *GDM login*

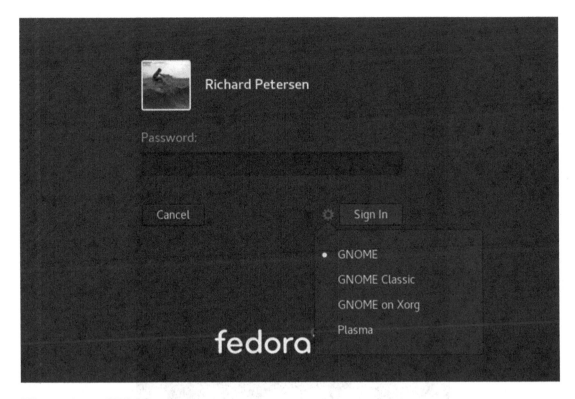

Figure 3-5. *GDM Session menu*

The System Status Area

Once you're logged in, the System Status Area is displayed on the right side of the top bar (see Figure 3-6). The area will include status icons for features such as sound and power. Clicking the button displays the System Status Area menu, with items for sound, brightness, wired and wireless connections, Bluetooth connections, the battery, and the current user, in addition to buttons at the bottom for opening GNOME Settings, activating the lock screen, and shutting down or rebooting the system. The sound and brightness items at the top include sliding bars with which you can adjust the volume and brightness. The Wired, WiFi, Bluetooth, Battery, and current user entries expand to submenus with added entries. The buttons at the bottom open separate dialogs for GNOME Settings, the lock screen, and poweroff and restart.

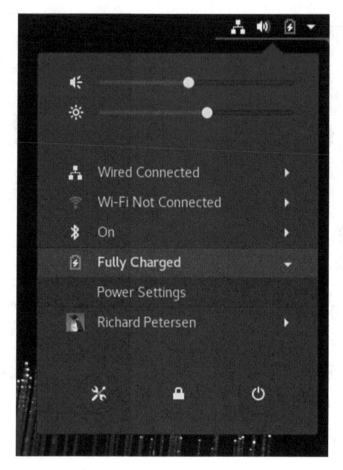

Figure 3-6. *System Status Area menu*

On systems that are not laptops, there will be no brightness slider or battery entry on the System Status Area menu. If the system also has no wireless device, the WiFi entry will also be missing. A system of this kind will only have a sound slider and a current user entry.

To log out or switch to another user, you click the current user entry to expand the menu to show Switch User and Log Out entries. The Log Out entry returns you to the GDM login screen. The Switch User entry suspends the current user and returns you to the GDM login screen, where you can log in as another user. If only one user is defined, there is no user entry, and, so, no Log Out entry, as there are no other users to log in.

For network connections, Fedora Linux uses Network Manager. Network Manager will detect available network connections automatically (see "Network Connections," later in this chapter).

Desktops

Several alternative desktop interfaces, such as GNOME and the K Desktop (KDE), can be installed on Fedora Linux. Each has its own style and appearance. It is important to keep in mind that the GNOME and KDE interfaces are two very different desktop interfaces, with separate tools for selecting preferences.

KDE

The K Desktop Environment (KDE) displays a panel at the bottom of the screen. The file manager operates much the same way as the GNOME file manager. There is a Settings entry in the main menu that opens the KDE Settings window, from which you can configure every aspect of the KDE environment, such as desktop effects, workspace appearance, and devices such as monitors and printers, and networking.

GNOME

Fedora Linux 28 uses the GNOME 3 desktop. It provides easy-to-use overviews and menus, along with a flexible file manager and desktop. GNOME 3 is based on the gnome-shell, which is a compositing window manager.

The screen displays a top bar, through which you access your applications, windows, and settings. Clicking the System Status Area button at the right side of the top bar displays the status user area menu, from which you can access buttons at the bottom to display the system setting dialog, lock the screen, and shut down the system (see Figure 3-7).

To access applications and windows, use the Activities overview mode. Click the Activities button at the left side of the top bar (or move the mouse to the left top corner, or press the Windows button). The overview mode consists of a dash listing your favorite and running applications, workspaces, and windows (see Figure 3-8). Large thumbnails of open windows are displayed on the Windows Overview (the desktop area). You can use the Search box at the top to locate an application quickly. Partially hidden thumbnails of your desktop workspaces are displayed on the right side. Initially, there are two. Moving your mouse to the right side displays the workspace thumbnails.

You can manually leave the overview at any time by pressing the Esc key or by clicking a window thumbnail.

The dash is a bar on the left side with icons for your favorite applications. Initially, there are icons for the Firefox web browser, files (the GNOME file manager), Mail, Rhythmbox, Shotwell, GNOME Software, GNOME Software, and the Applications overview, as depicted in Figure 3-9. The last icon opens an Applications overview that you can use to start other applications. To open an application from the dash, click its icon or right-click on the icon and choose New Window from the pop-up menu. You can also click and drag the icon to the Windows Overview or to a workspace thumbnail on the right side.

Figure 3-7. *The Fedora GNOME desktop*

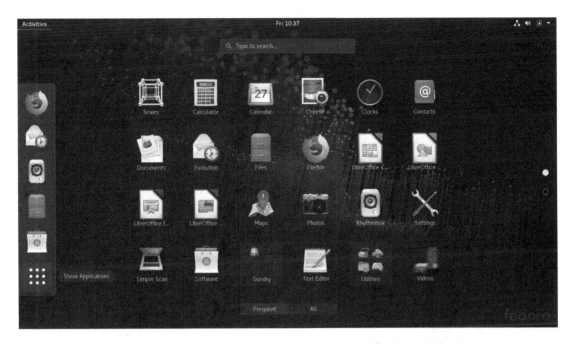

Figure 3-8. *GNOME Activities overview mode for applications*

You can access windows from the Windows Overview, which is displayed when you start Activities. The Windows Overview displays thumbnails of all your open windows. When you pass your mouse over a window thumbnail, a close box appears, at the upper-right corner, with which you can close the window. You can also move the window on the desktop to another workspace.

To move a window on the desktop, click and drag its title bar. To maximize a window, double-click its title bar or drag it to the top bar. To minimize, double-click the title bar again or drag it away from the top bar. To close a window, click its close box (upper right).

Two sub-folders are available on the applications overview: Utilities and Sundry. Utilities lists several tools, such as the text editor and system monitor, and Sundry lists additional administrative tools, such as `system-config-printer` and `firewall-config`. These sub-folders function like a submenu, overlaying the main overview with a sub-folder. You can use the GNOME Software Installed tab to create your own sub-folders and place application icons in them.

GNOME File Manager

You can access your home folder from the Files icon on the dash. A file manager window opens, showing your Home folder (see Figure 3-9). Your Home folder will already have default directories created for commonly used files. These include Documents, Downloads, Music, Pictures, and Videos. Your office applications will automatically save files to the Documents folder by default. Image and photo applications place image files in the Pictures directory. The Desktop folder will hold all files and directories saved to your desktop. When you download a file, it is placed in the Downloads directory.

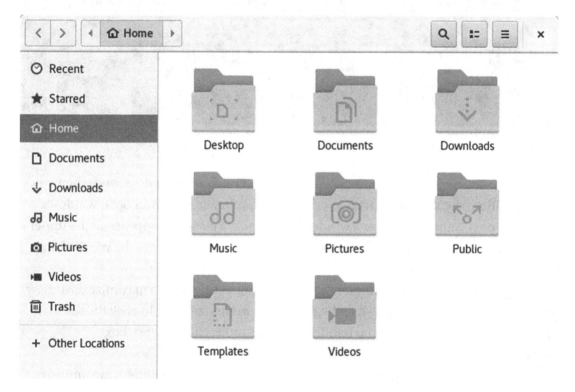

Figure 3-9. *File manager for the Home folder*

The file manager window displays several components, including a header bar, which combines the title bar and toolbar, and a sidebar. When you open a new directory, the same window is used to display it, and you can use the forward and back arrows to move through previously opened directories. The header bar displays navigation folder buttons that show your current folder and its parent folders. You can click a parent folder to move to it. The GNOME file manager also supports tabs. You can open several folders in the same file manager window. Click on the menu button on the right side of the title bar to display the file manager tools with buttons to add a new folder, tab, or bookmark, as well as zoom buttons for enlarging or reducing the size of the folder icons. You can also sort files and show hidden files.

GNOME Customization with the Tweak Tool: Themes, Fonts, Startup Applications, and Extensions

You can perform common desktop customizations using the GNOME Tweak Tool. Areas to customize include the desktop icons, fonts, themes, startup applications, workspaces, window behavior, and the time display. You can access the Tweak Tool from the Applications Overview ➤ Utilities. The GNOME Tweak Tool has tabs for Appearance, Extensions, Fonts, Keyboard and Mouse, Power, Startup Applications, Top Bar, Typing, Windows, and Workspaces (see Figure 3-10).

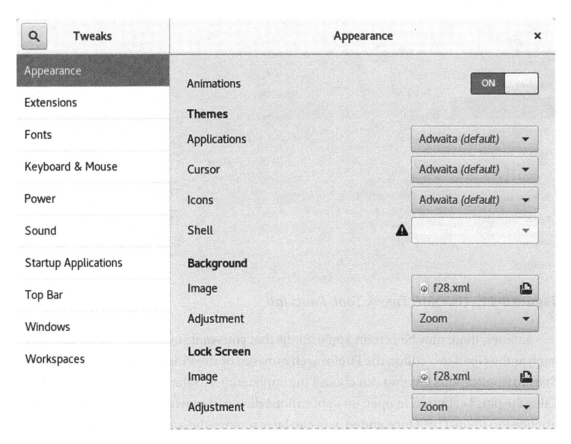

Figure 3-10. *GNOME Tweak Tool, Appearance tab (themes)*

The Appearance tab lets you set the theme for your windows, icons, and cursor. GNOME 3 uses the Adwaita Theme. This theme has a light and dark variant. The Global Light Theme is the default, but you can use the switch on the Appearance tab to enable the Global Dark Theme. The Global Dark Theme shades the background of windows to a dark gray, while text and button images appear in white.

As you add other desktops, such as Cinnamon, the available themes increase. There are many window themes to choose from, including Clearlooks, Mist, and Glider. For icons, you can choose among Oxygen (KDE), Mist (Cinnamon), and GNOME.

Desktop fonts for window titles, interface (application or dialog text), documents, and monospace (terminal windows or code) can be changed in the Fonts tab (see Figure 3-11). You can adjust the size of the font or change the font style. Clicking the font name opens a Pick a Font dialog from which you can choose a different font. The quality of text display can be further adjusted with Hinting and Antialiasing options. To simply increase or decrease the size of all fonts on your desktop interface, you can adjust the Scaling Factor.

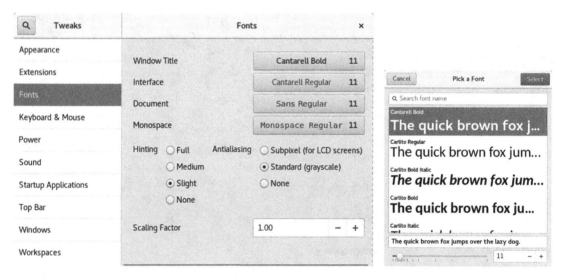

Figure 3-11. *GNOME Tweak Tool, Fonts tab*

At times, there may be certain applications that you want started up when you log in, such as the Gedit text editor, the Firefox web browser, or the Videos movie player. On the Startup Applications tab, you can choose the applications to start up (see Figure 3-12). Click the plus (+) button to open an applications dialog from which you can choose an application to start up. Once added, you can later remove the application by clicking its Remove button.

Figure 3-12. *GNOME Tweak Tool, Startup Applications tab*

For the GNOME Tweak Tool, extensions add different capabilities to the GNOME desktop. Installed extensions are listed on the Extensions tab of the Tweak Tool, where you can turn them on or off. Several extensions add GNOME Classic (GNOME 2) features to your GNOME 3 desktop (see Figure 3-13). Add the Applications menu and the Places menu to the top bar. The Applications menu organizes applications by the older and familiar menu categories such as Office and Sound & Video. The Applications menu replaces the Activities button, which you can still access as the last item on the Applications menu. The Places menu lists the default folders such as Documents and Pictures, along with Computer and Browse Network. The Window list extension adds a bottom bar showing the task bar applet for open windows and a window list applet to the right (see Figure 3-14).

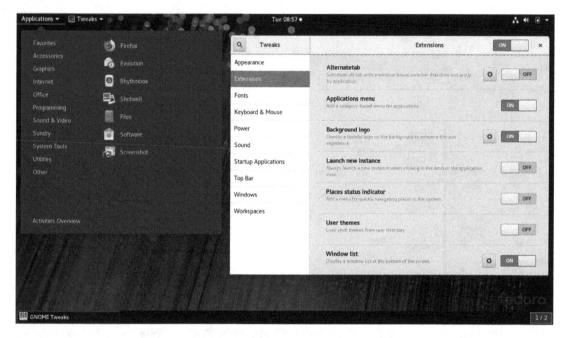

Figure 3-13. *GNOME Tweak Tool, Extensions tab*

Figure 3-14. *GNOME Tweak Tool, Window list extension*

Logging Out and Shutting Down GNOME

If you want to exit your desktop and return to the GDM login screen, or switch to a different user, you click the user entry in the System Status Area menu to expand to a menu with entries for Switch User and Log Out (see Figure 3-15). Click the Log Out entry to display a dialog that shows buttons for Cancel and Log Out. Click Log Out to log out of your account, exiting GNOME and returning to the login screen, where you can log in again as a different user or shut down the system. A countdown will commence in the dialog, showing how much time you have before it performs the logout automatically.

From the login screen, you can shut down the system: choose Power Off from the System Status Area menu on the lower right of the menu. This displays a power off dialog with options to restart or power off. A countdown will commence in the dialog, showing how much time you have before it performs the shutdown automatically.

The Switch User entry switches out from the current user and runs the GDM to display a list of users you can log in as. Click the name to open a password prompt and display a session button. You can then log in as that user. The sessions of users already logged will continue with the same open windows and applications that were running when the user switched off. You can switch back and forth between logged-in users, with all users retaining their session from where they left off. When you switch off from a user, that user's running programs will continue in the background.

Figure 3-15. *GNOME Log Out menu entry*

Network Connections

Network connections will be set up for you by Network Manager, which will detect your network connections automatically, both wired and wireless. Network Manager provides status information for your connection and allows you to switch easily from one configured connection to another, as needed. For initial configuration, it detects as much information as possible about the new connection.

Network Manager is user specific. Wired connections will be started automatically. For wireless connections, when a user logs in, Network Manager selects the connection preferred by that user. From a menu of detected wireless networks, the user can select a wireless connection to use.

Network Manager displays active network connections in the System Status Area: Wired for the wired connection and WiFi for a wireless connection. Each entry will indicate its status as connected or not connected. The Network Manager icon for these entries will vary according to the connection status: solid for an active connection and faded for a disconnected connection (see Figure 3-16). On wired systems that have no wireless devices, there is no WiFi network entry in the System Status Area menu.

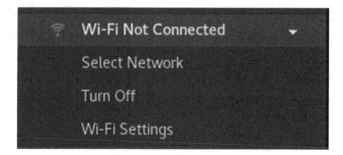

Figure 3-16. *Network Manager, wireless*

Network Manager Wired Connections

For computers connected to a wired network, such as an Ethernet connection, Network Manager automatically detects and establishes the network connection. Most networks use DHCP to provide such network information as an IP address and DNS server. With this kind of connection, Network Manager can connect automatically to your network whenever you start your system. Click the Wired entry in the System Status Area to expand the menu to show entries from which to connect or disconnect to wired networking and open the GNOME Network Settings dialog at the Wired tab (Wired Settings).

Network Manager Wireless Connections

With multiple wireless access points for Internet connections, a system could have several network connections to choose from. This is particularly true for notebook computers that access different wireless connections at different locations. Instead of manually configuring a new connection each time one is encountered, the Network Manager tool can configure and select a connection to use automatically.

Network Manager will scan for wireless connections, checking for Extended Service Set Identifiers (ESSIDs). If an ESSID identifies a previously used connection, it is selected. If several are found, the recently used one is chosen. If only new connections are available, Network Manager waits for the user to choose one. A connection is selected if the user is logged in.

Click the WiFi entry in the System Status Area to expand the menu to show entries from which to select a network, turn off wireless networking, and open the GNOME Network Settings dialog at the WiFi tab (WiFi Settings). Click the Select Network item to open a dialog that shows a list of all available wireless connections (see Figure 3-17).

Entries display the name of the wireless network and a wave graph showing the strength of its signal. To connect to a network, click its entry, then click the Connect button, to activate the connection. If this is the first time you are trying to connect to that network, you will be prompted to enter the password or encryption key (see Figure 3-18).

Figure 3-17. *Network Manager connections menu, wireless*

Figure 3-18. *Network Manager wireless authentication*

You can turn off wireless by clicking the Turn Off entry in the expanded WiFi section of the System Status Area (see Figure 3-19). When it's turned off, the entry label changes to Turn On. To reactivate your wireless connection, click the Turn On entry.

Figure 3-19. *Network Manager wireless on and off*

Settings WiFi and Network

On the GNOME Settings dialog, there is a WiFi tab for wireless configuration and a Network tab for wired, VPN, and proxy configurations. For WiFi, choose the Choose WiFi Settings from the expanded WiFi entries in the System Status Area, or click the WiFi tab in the Settings dialog, to open the WiFi tab (see Figure 3-20). On the WiFi tab, an Airplane Mode switch and a list of visible wireless connections are listed to the right. The currently active connection will have a checkmark next to its name. On the top-right bar is a switch for turning wireless on and off. A menu to the right of the switch list entries for connections to hidden networks, turning your computer's WiFi hotspot capability and listing previously accessed WiFi networks.

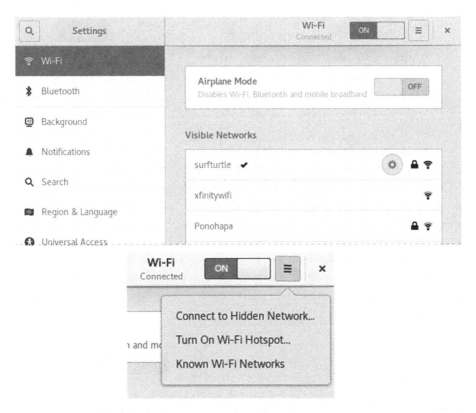

Figure 3-20. *Settings Network wireless connections*

Your current active connection will have a checkmark next to it and a gear button to
the right. Click the gear button to display a dialog with tabs for managing the connection.
The Details tab provides information about the connection (see Figure 3-21). The
Security, Identity, IPv4, and IPv6 tabs let you perform a detailed configuration of your
connection, as described in Chapter 10. The settings are fixed to automatic by default.
Should you make any changes, click the Apply button to have them take effect. The
Details tab has options both for connecting automatically and for providing availability
to other users. These are set by default. Should you not want to connect to the wireless
network automatically, be sure to uncheck this option. To remove a network's connection
information, click the Forget button on the Details tab.

Figure 3-21. *Settings Network wireless connection, Details tab*

The Identity tab has options for connecting automatically and for providing availability to other users. These are set by default. Should you not want to connect to the wireless network automatically, be sure to uncheck this option.

The Turn on Wi-Fi Hotspot entry in the wireless menu opens a dialog letting you set up your computer as a wireless router that other computers can connect through.

The Connect to Hidden Wi-Fi Network entry in the wireless menu lets you connect to a hidden network, not one visible. This opens the Connect to Hidden Wi-Fi Network window (see Figure 3-22), where you can enter the network name and security information.

Figure 3-22. *Connect to a Hidden WiFi Network*

For a wired connection, click the Network tab on GNOME Settings to display lists for Wired, VPN, and Network Proxy. The Wired list shows your current wired connections with on and off switched for each. A plus button at the top right of the Wired list lets you add more wired connections. Next to a connection's switch a gear button is displayed (see Figure 3-23). Clicking the gear button opens a configuration dialog with tabs for Details, Identity, IPv4, IPv6, and Security.

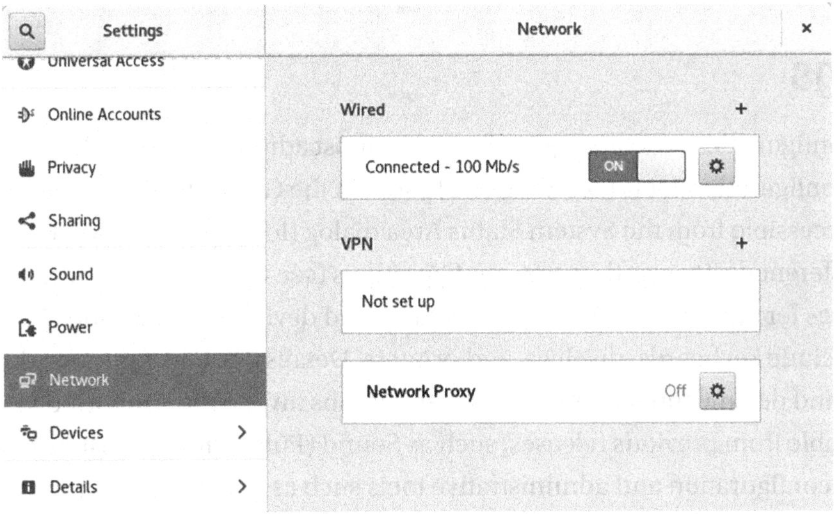

Figure 3-23. *Settings Network wired connection*

Clicking on the Network proxy gear button opens a Network Proxy dialog with Disabled, Manual, and Automatic options (see Figure 3-24). The Manual option lets you enter address and port information. For the Automatic option, you enter a configuration address.

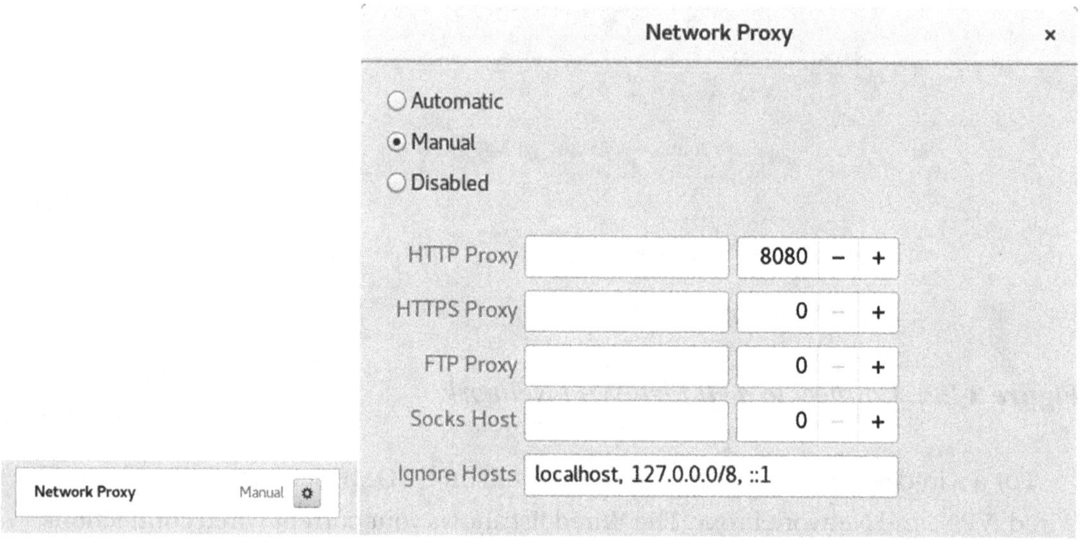

Figure 3-24. *Network proxy settings (Settings Network)*

To add a VPN connection, click the plus (+) button to the right of the VPN title to open Add VPN Dialog Network.

Settings

You can configure desktop settings and perform most administrative tasks using the GNOME configuration tools (see Table 3-1) listed in the GNOME Settings dialog, which is accessible from the System Status Area dialog (lower-left button). It displays tabs for different desktop and system configurations (see Figure 3-25). There are two subheadings for system administration (Details) and device configuration (Devices). Devices include keyboards, displays, and printers. Details has tabs for users, the date and time, and default applications. A few settings tabs invoke the supported system tools available from previous releases, such as Sound (PulseAudio). Most use the new GNOME 3 configuration and administrative tools such as Background, Privacy, Users, and Power (see Table 3-1).

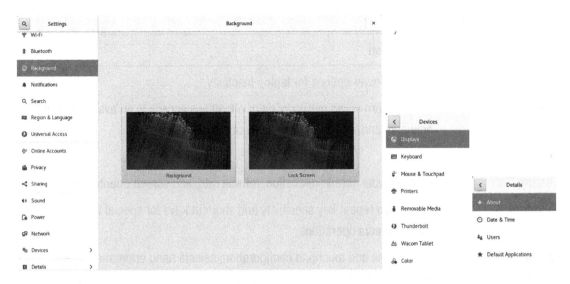

Figure 3-25. *GNOME system tools (settings)*

Table 3-1. *Settings*

Setting	Description
Personal	
WiFi	Lets you configure and manage wireless networks.
Bluetooth	Sets Bluetooth detection and configuration
Background	Sets desktop and screen lock backgrounds (wallpaper, color, and image)
Notifications	Turns on notifications for different applications
Search	Specifies the resources and locations searched by the GNOME overview search box
Region & Language	Chooses a language, region (formats), and keyboard layout
Universal Access	Enables features such as accessible login and keyboard screen
Online Accounts	Configures online accounts for use by email and browser applications
Privacy	Turns on privacy features, such as screen lock and purging trash
Sharing	Turns on sharing for media, remote login, and screen access
Sound	Configures sound effects, output volume, input volume, and sound application settings

(*continued*)

Table 3-1. (*continued*)

Setting	Description
Power	Sets the power options for laptop inactivity
Network	Lets you turn wired networks on or off; allows access to an available wired networks and specifies proxy configuration, if needed
Devices	
Displays	Changes your screen resolution, refresh rate, and screen orientation
Keyboard	Configures repeat key sensitivity and shortcut keys for special tasks, such as multimedia operations
Mouse & Touchpad	Sets mouse and touchpad configuration; selects hand orientation, speed, and accessibility
Printers	Turns printers on or off and accesses their print queues
Removable Media	Default applications for removable media
Wacom Tablet	Provides tablet options
Color	Sets the color profile for a device
Details	
About	Sets the hostname of your computer, displays hardware information, and assigns default applications for certain basic tasks
Date & Time	Sets the date, time, time zone, and network time
Users	Manages accounts
Default Applications	Default applications for different for user files

Background

With the Background dialog, you can set your background for both the desktop and screen lock backgrounds: wallpaper, picture, or color. You can access the Background dialog from the Settings Background tab (see Figure 3-26). The current backgrounds are shown for the desktop and the screen lock. Click one to open the background dialog, with tabs for Wallpapers, Pictures, and Colors (see Figure 3-27). The dialog is the same for both desktop and screen lock backgrounds. If you choose Wallpapers, the installed backgrounds are displayed. The Colors tab displays solid color images you can use instead. The Pictures tab displays images in your Pictures folder, which you can scroll through to select one to use for your background. To add your own image, first add the image to your Pictures folder. Then click the Pictures tab to display all the images in your Pictures folder. Once you make your selection, click the Select button at the upper right. You return to the main Background dialog, showing your new background. The background on your display is updated immediately.

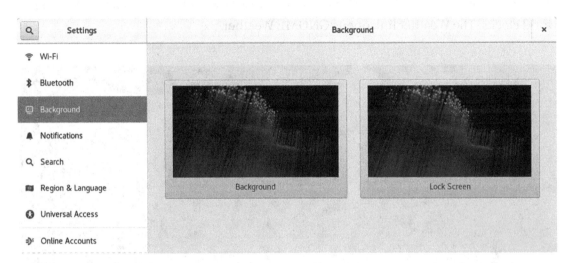

Figure 3-26. *Background*

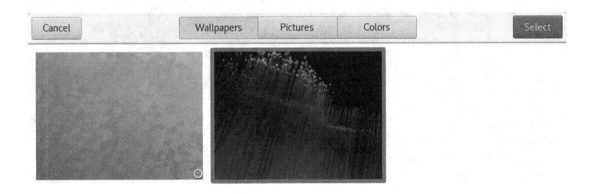

Figure 3-27. *Select Background*

Install the gnome-background-extra package to add a collection of GNOME backgrounds. You can download more GNOME backgrounds (wallpapers) from https://www.gnome-look.org/.

Date & Time

The Date & Time calendar and menu are located on the top bar at the center (see Figure 3-28). The dialog displays the current time and day of the week but can be modified to display 24-hour or AM/PM time. The calendar shows the current date, but you can move to different months and years using the month scroll arrows at the top of the calendar. The Add World Clocks link opens the GNOME Clocks tool for selecting world clocks. The Weather link opens GNOME Weather.

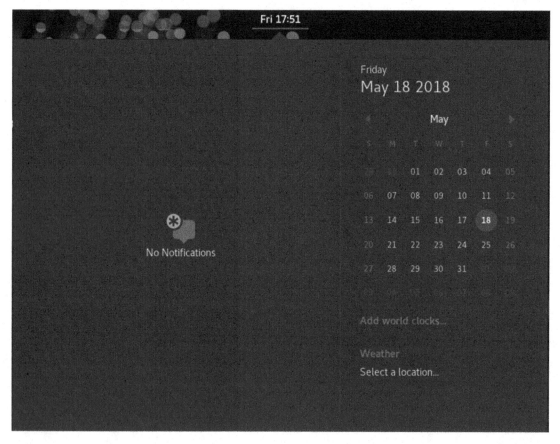

Figure 3-28. *Date & Time dialog*

You can further adjust the top bar time display using the GNOME Tweak Tool's Top Bar tab (see Figure 3-29). In the Clock section, there are options to show the date and seconds. For the Calendar, you can show week numbers.

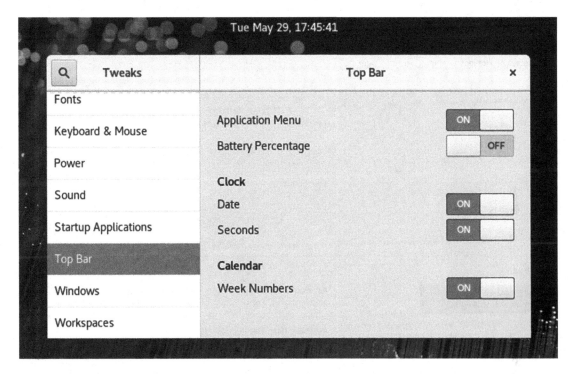

Figure 3-29. *GNOME Tweak Tool's Top Bar with clock options on*

Date & Time options are set using the Settings Details ➤ Date & Time tab. The Date & Time tab lets you set the time zone and time. Both are configured for automatic settings using Internet time servers (see Figure 3-30). The time zone or the time and date can be set manually by turning off the Automatic switches. Once turned off, the Date & Time and the Time Zone links become active.

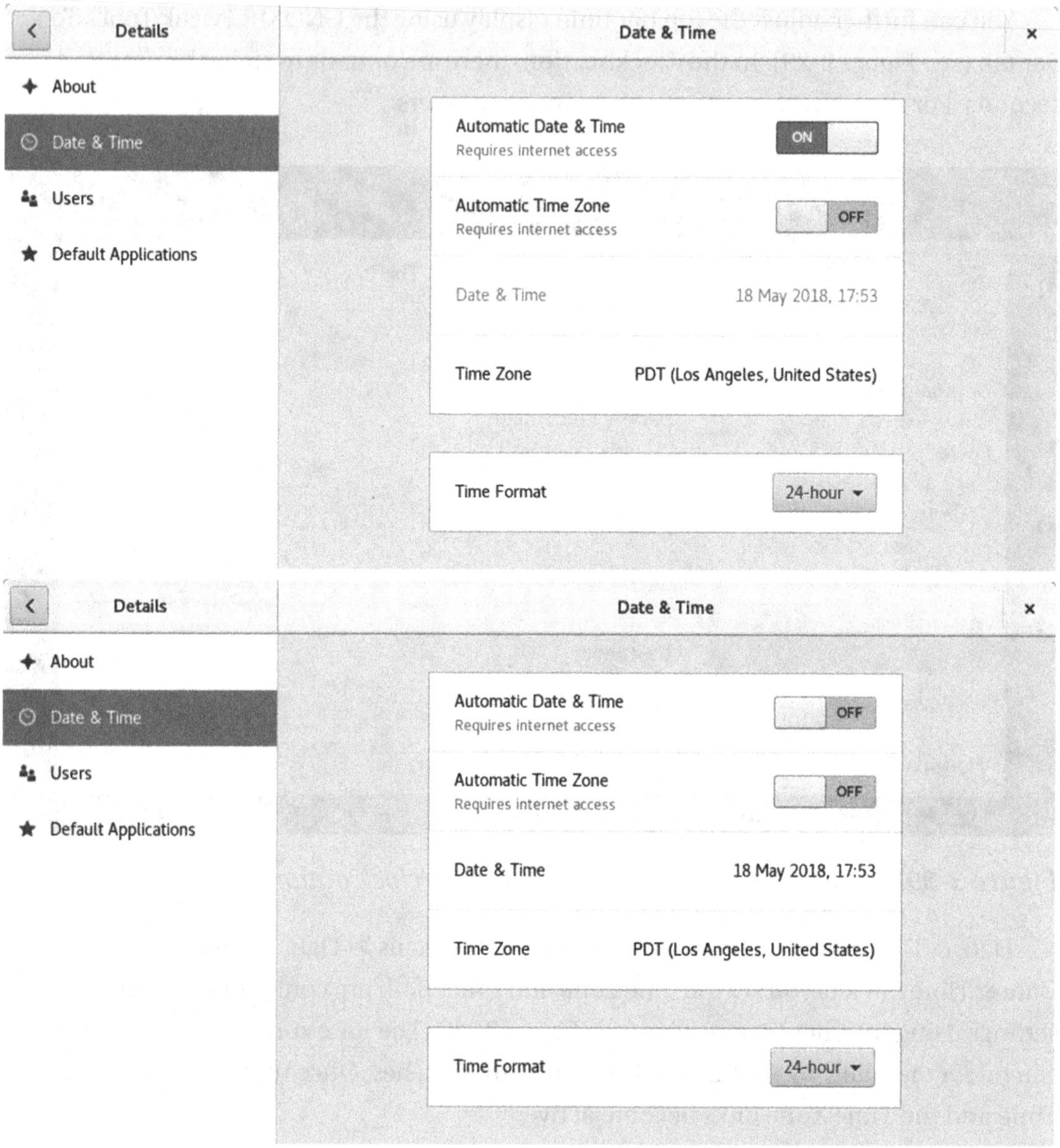

Figure 3-30. *Date & Time Settings dialog with automatic settings turned on (top) and off (bottom)*

The Date & Time link opens a dialog with settings for the hour, minutes, day, and year, with a menu for the month (see Figure 3-31). You can use the plus (+) and minus (-) buttons to sequentially change the values.

Figure 3-31. *Date & Time manual settings*

The Time Zone link opens a dialog with a map of the time zones and the current one selected (see Figure 3-32). Click a new time zone to change the zone.

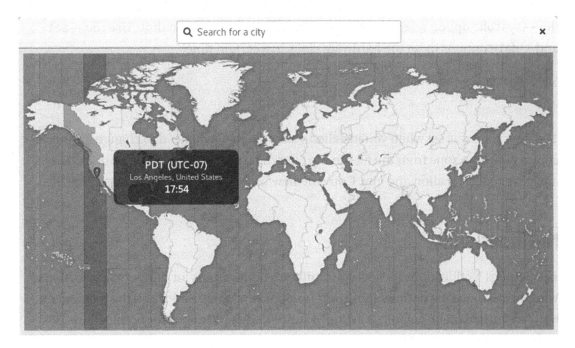

Figure 3-32. *Time Zone dialog*

You can set the system date and time either manually or by referencing an Internet time server. You could also use your local hardware clock. To set the system time manually, you use the date command. The date command has several options for adjusting both displaying and setting the date and time. Check the date man page for a detailed list, man date. You can set the time with the --set option and a string specifying the date. You use human readable terms for the time string, such as Mon or Monday for the day and Jul or July for the month. Hour, minute, and second can be represented by numbers separated by colons. The following sets the date to July 9, 8:15 AM 2018.

```
sudo date --set='Monday July 9 08:15 2018'
```

To just set the time you would enter something like:

```
sudo date --set='12:15:43'
```

To access the hardware clock, you use the hwclock command. The command will display the hardware clock time.

```
sudo hwclock
```

The --hctosys option will set the system clock using the hardware clock's time, and the --systohc option resets the hardware clock using the system time. Use the --set and --date options to set the hardware clock to a certain time.

```
sudo hwclock --systohc
```

The time zone was set when you installed your system. If you need to change it, you can copy a new time zone from the files in the /usr/share/zoneinfo subdirectories. They are arranged by location and city. Copy the new time zone to the /etc/localtime file.

Notifications

The Settings Notifications tab lets you configure notifications for different applications. You can also have the options show pop-up notices or show notices on the lock screen. Both are turned on by default. A listing of supported applications for notifications is displayed (see Figure 3-33).

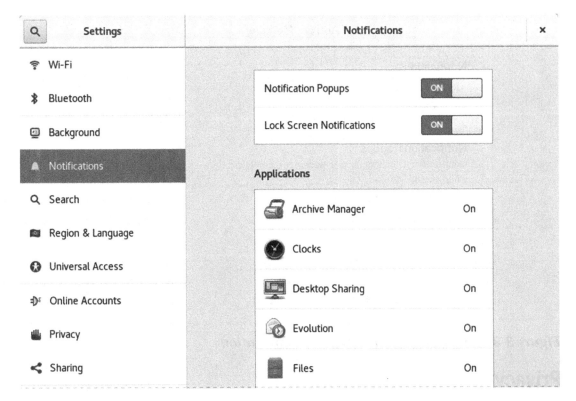

Figure 3-33. *Notifications dialog*

Click an application to display a dialog from which you can turn notifications for the application on or off, as well as set options such as sound alerts, pop-up notifications, and lock screen notification (see Figure 3-34).

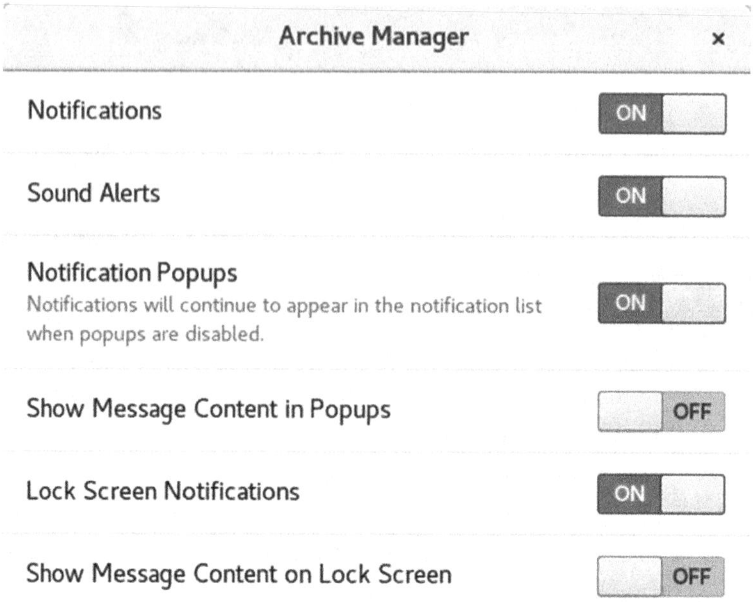

Figure 3-34. *Notification settings for an application*

Privacy

The Settings Privacy tab allows you to turn privacy features, such as the screen lock, usage and history logs, and the purging of trash and temporary files, on or off (see Figure 3-35). Screen Lock and Usage & History are turned on by default. The Purge Trash & Temporary Files and Location Services are turned off. Location Services allows your geographical location to be determined.

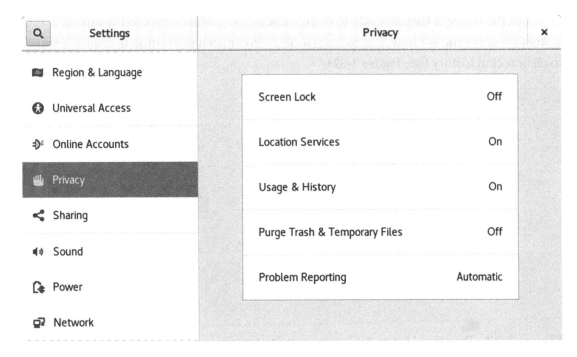

Figure 3-35. *Privacy*

Clicking the Screen Lock entry opens the Screen Lock configuration dialog, from which you can turn the Screen Lock on or off or set it to turn on after a period of idle time and allow or deny notifications on the Screen Lock screen (see Figure 3-36).

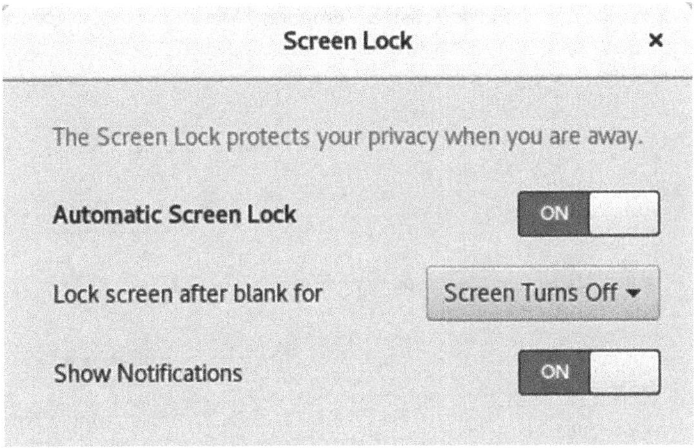

Figure 3-36. *Privacy, Screen Lock configuration*

Click the Usage & History entry to open a dialog from which you can turn usage history on or off and set how long to keep it. The entry also has a button that allows you to clear recent history (see Figure 3-37).

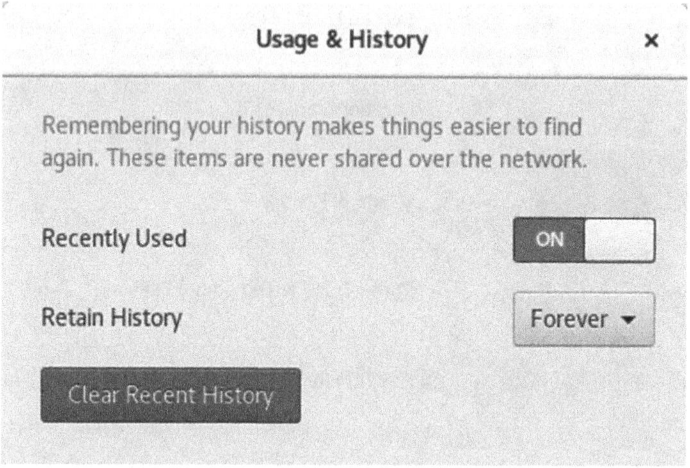

Figure 3-37. *Privacy, Usage & History configuration*

The Purge Trash & Temporary Files entry has options to automatically empty trash and remove temporary files (see Figure 3-38). You can also set a time limit for purging files. These options are turned off by default. The link also has buttons that allow you to empty trash and purge temporary files immediately.

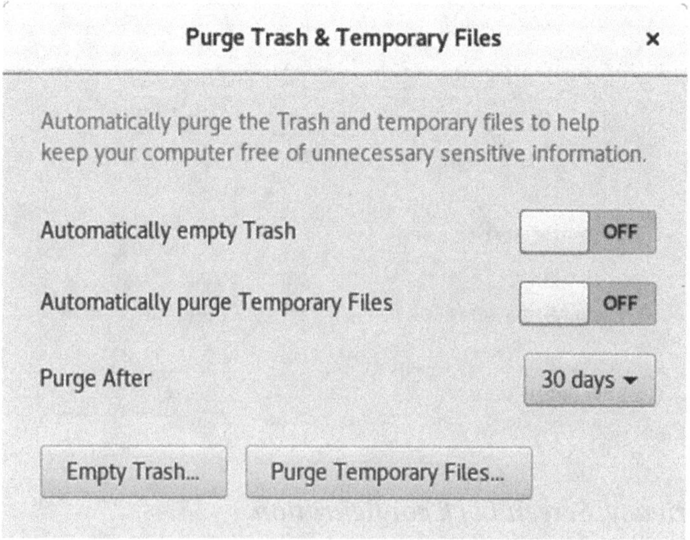

Figure 3-38. *Privacy, Purge Trash & Temporary Files configuration*

About (System Information)

The Settings Details ➤ About tab shows your hardware specifications (memory, CPU, graphics card chip, and free disk space), in addition to the hostname (device name) and the OS type (64- or 33-bit system) (see Figure 3-39). You can change the hostname here if you wish. A Check for Updates button is displayed, which opens GNOME Software to its Updates tab, allowing you to check for updates (see Chapter 4). If updates have been already detected an Install Update button is displayed instead.

Figure 3-39. *Details ➤ About*

You can also use the hostnamectl command with the set-hostname option in a terminal window to set the hostname.

```
sudo hostnamectl set-hostname richard-laptop
```

Just the hostnamectl command will display your hostname.

Default Applications

The Details ➤ Default Applications tab lets you set default applications for basic types of files: Web, Mail, Calendar, Music, Video, and Photos (see Figure 3-40). Use the menus to choose installed alternatives, such as Thunderbird instead of Evolution for Mail or Shotwell instead of Image Viewer for Photos.

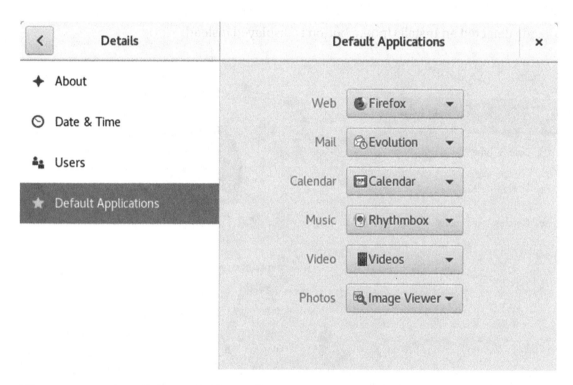

Figure 3-40. *Details ➤ Default Applications*

Using Removable Devices and Media

Fedora Linux supports removable devices and media, such as digital cameras, PDAs, card readers, and USB printers. These devices are handled automatically with device interfaces set up for them when needed. Removable media, such as CD and DVD discs, USB storage disks, and digital cameras, will be displayed as entries in the Removable Devices menu. On the Overview screen, when you click on the message number notice at the bottom of the screen, the Removable Devices icon is displayed. Clicking this icon displays a menu of all your removable devices, with an Eject button next to each entry. Click an entry to open the device in its associated applications, such as a file manager window for a USB drive. Be sure always to click the Eject button for device entry before removing a drive, such as a USB drive or removable disk drive. Removing the drive before clicking eject can result in incomplete write operations on the disk.

Removable storage devices and media will also appear in the file manager Devices sidebar with eject buttons that you can use instead of the message menu to eject the devices. For example, when you connect a USB drive to your system, it will be detected and can be displayed as a storage device with its own file system by the file manager.

Removable devices and media, such as USB drives and DVD/CD discs, can be ejected using Eject buttons in the Devices section of the file manager sidebar. The sidebar lists all your storage devices, including removable media. Removable devices and media will have an Eject button to the right. Just click the Eject button, and the media is ejected or unmounted. You can right-click the Device entry and, from a pop-up menu, choose the Eject entry.

The Settings Devices ➤ Removable Media tab lets you specify default actions for CD Audio, DVD Video, Music Player, Photos, and Software media (see Figure 3-41). You can select from menus the application to use for the different media. These menus also include options for Ask What To Do, Do Nothing, and Open Folder. The Open Folder option will open a window displaying the files on the disc. A button labeled Other Media opens a dialog that lets you set up an association for less used media such as BluRay discs and Audio DVD. Initially, the Ask What To Do option is set for all entries. Possible options are listed for the appropriate media, such as Rhythmbox Media Player for CD audio discs and Videos (Totem) for DVD-Video. Photos can be opened with the Shotwell photo manager.

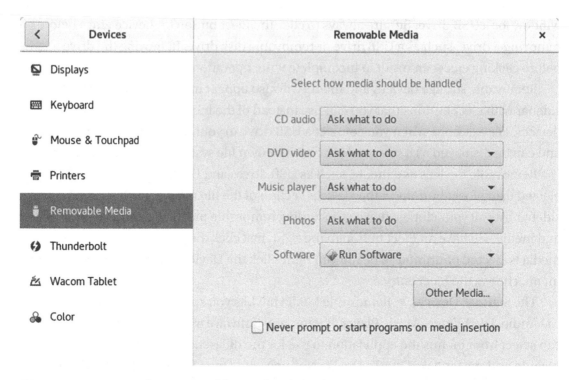

Figure 3-41. *Details, Removable Media defaults*

When you insert removable media, such as a CD audio disc, its associated application is automatically started, unless you change that preference. If you want to turn off this feature for a particular kind of media, you can select the Do Nothing entry from its application drop-down menu. If you want to be prompted for options, use the Ask What To Do entry. Then, when you insert a disc, a dialog with a drop-down menu for possible actions is displayed. From this menu, you can select another application or select the Do Nothing or Open Folder options.

You can turn the automatic startup off for all media by checking the box labeled Never Prompt or Start Programs on Media Insertion, which is at the bottom of the Removable Media tab.

Sharing

On the Sharing dialog, you can allow access to your account and your screen. A switch lets you turn all sharing on or off (see Figure 3-42). You can also choose what network device to use you if you have more than one.

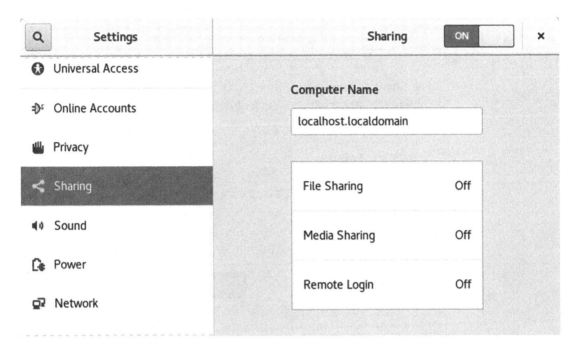

Figure 3-42. *Sharing*

Clicking the File Sharing entry opens a dialog from which you can allow access to your Public folder by other users. You can also require and set a password (see Figure 3-43). Media Sharing allows you to share the Music, Videos, and Pictures folders.

Figure 3-43. *Sharing, File and Media access by other users*

Power Management

For laptops and systems with remote battery devices such as mice, a power icon is displayed in the System Status Area (right side of the top bar). The System Status Area menu shows the current strength of the battery (see Figure 3-44). The entry expands to show a Power Settings entry, which you can use to open the Settings Power dialog.

Figure 3-44. *GNOME Power Manager menu*

The GNOME Power manager is configured with the Power tab, accessible as Power from Settings (see Figure 3-45). The dialog is organized into four sections: Battery, Devices, Power Saving, and Suspend & Power Off. On laptops, the Battery section shows the battery charge. The Devices section shows the strength of any remote devices, such as a wireless mouse. In the Power Saving section, you can set power saving features for your monitor, wireless devices, and network connections. When it's inactive for a period of time, you can choose to turn off the screen, as well as dim it whenever it is inactive. For laptops, you can also set the screen brightness. You can also choose to turn off Bluetooth, WiFi, and Mobile broadband. In the Suspend & Power Off section, you can turn on the automatic suspend for when a system remains inactive and when the power button is pressed.

Using the GNOME Tweak Tool's Power tab, you can further specify the action to take, such as suspend or shut down, when the laptop lid is closed.

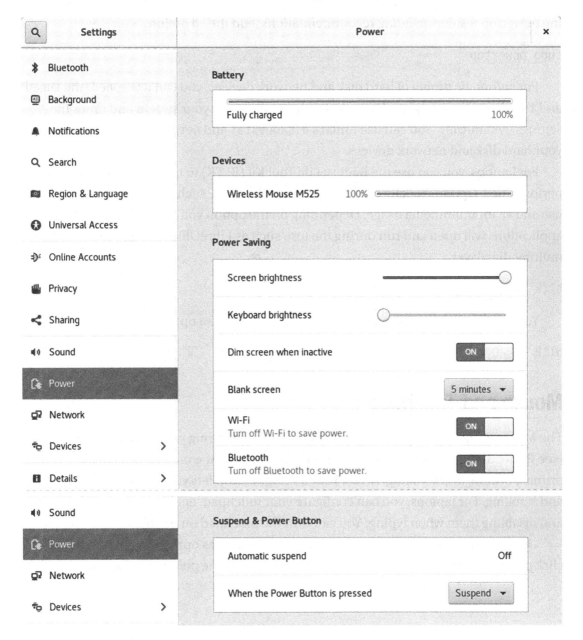

Figure 3-45. *GNOME Power manager*

powertop, tuned, and BLTK

For more refined power management, you can use the `powertop` and `tuned` tools. The `powertop` tool runs in a terminal window as the root user. It will detect and display information about the use of the CPU by running applications and connected devices. Recommendations are listed on how to configure the power usage. To display a listing of the powertop results including recommendations, add the `-d` option.

```
sudo powertop
```

For automatic tuning of hard disk and network devices, you can use `tuned` (the `tuned` and `tuned utils` packages). The `tuned` daemon monitors your system and tunes the settings dynamically. You can use tuned's `diskdevstat` and `netdevstat` tools to monitor your hard disk and network devices.

For laptops, you can use the Battery Life Tool Kit (BLTK) to test and analyze battery performance. Options specify different types of workloads, such as `-O` for office suite use and `-P` for multimedia usage. Depending on the option you specified, different applications will open and run during the test, such as LibreOffice Writer or the Totem multimedia player.

```
bltk -O
```

You can also run the test on desktop systems using an `-a` option.

```
bltk -a -O
```

Mouse and Touchpad

The Mouse & Touchpad tab is the primary tool for configuring your mouse and touchpad (see Figure 3-46). Mouse preferences allow you to choose the mouse's speed, the primary button, and scrolling. A Test Your Settings button lets you check clicks, speed, and scrolling. For laptops, you can configure your touchpad, enabling touchpad clicks and disabling them when typing. You can turn the touchpad on or off.

The GNOME Tweak Tool's Keyboard and Mouse tab has options to enable a middle-click paste for the mouse and to highlight the location of the pointer on the screen.

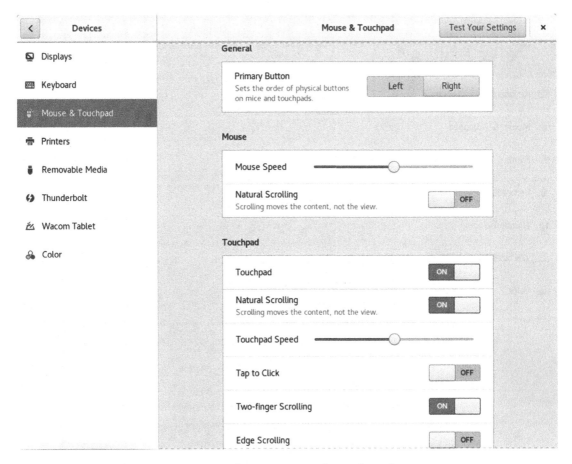

Figure 3-46. *GNOME system tools, mouse and touchpad*

Display (Resolution and Rotation)

The display drivers for Linux used on Fedora Linux support user-level resolution and orientation changes. Any user can specify a resolution or orientation, without affecting the settings of other users. The Settings Devices ➤ Displays tab provides a simple interface for setting orientation, resolution, and refresh rate for your monitor (see Figure 3-47). Click on an entry to display an appropriate menu listing possible configurations. From the resolution menu, you can set the resolution.

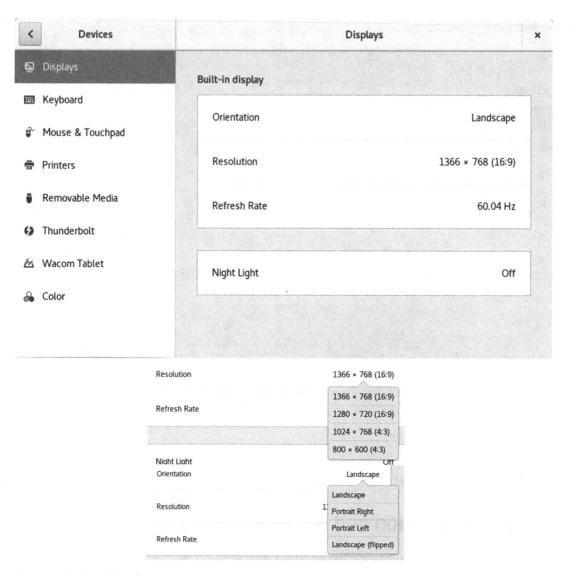

Figure 3-47. *Displays*

The graphics interface for your desktop display is implemented by the X Window System. The version used on Fedora Linux is X.org (x.org). X.org provides its own drivers for various graphics cards and monitors. You can find out more about X.org at www.x.org. X.org will automatically detect most hardware. The /etc/X11/xorg.conf file is no longer used for the open source drivers (nv and amd). Information such as the monitor used is determined automatically.

Universal Access

The Universal Access dialog in Settings lets you configure alternative access to your interface for your keyboard and mouse actions. Four sections set the display (Seeing), sound properties (Hearing), typing, and point-and-click features. Seeing lets you adjust the contrast and text size, and whether to allow zooming or use of screen reader (see Figure 3-48). Hearing uses visual cues for alert sounds. Typing displays a screen keyboard and adjusts key presses. Pointing and Clicking lets you use the keyboard for mouse operations.

Figure 3-48. *Universal Access*

Keyboard and Language

The Settings Keyboard dialog shows tabs for shortcuts (see Figure 3-49). You can assign keys to perform such tasks as starting the web browser. The plus button at the bottom of the screen lets you create custom shortcuts. The Reset All button resets the shortcuts to their default values. Click on an entry to set the shortcut. When the Set Shortcut dialog appears, type the keys for the shortcut, usually three. The keys appear on the next dialog with a Set button in the upper-right corner. The changed entry then appears on the Keyboard dialog with a delete box you can click to remove your shortcut setting. The plus button opens an Add Custom Shortcut dialog where you enter the name and command before setting the shortcut.

On the GNOME Tweak Tool's Keyboard & Mouse tab, you can click the Additional Layout Options button to display a dialog where you can specify the behavior of certain keys, such as the key sequence to stop the X server, the Caps Lock behavior, and the numeric keypad layout.

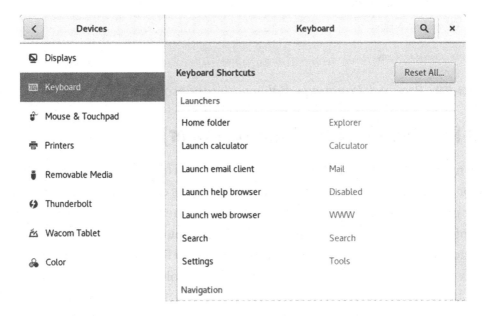

Figure 3-49. *Keyboard*

The Region & Language dialog lets you set the input source for the keyboard (see Figure 3-50). The current input language source is listed and selected. You can access the Region & Language dialog directly from Settings. Click the plus (+) button to open a dialog listing other language sources, which you can add. Click the Keyboard button to see the keyboard layout of your currently selected input source.

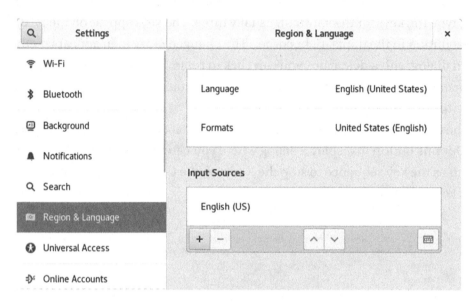

Figure 3-50. *Region & Language dialog with input sources*

Color Profiles (GNOME Color Manager)

You can manage the color for different devices by using color profiles specified with the Color tab accessible from Settings. The Color tab lists devices for which you can set color profiles. Click the menu button at the right of the device entry to display the color profiles for that device (see Figure 3-51). Your monitor will have a profile set up automatically. Click on a profile to display buttons to Set For All Users, Remove Profile, and View Details. Click the View Details button for the color profile information.

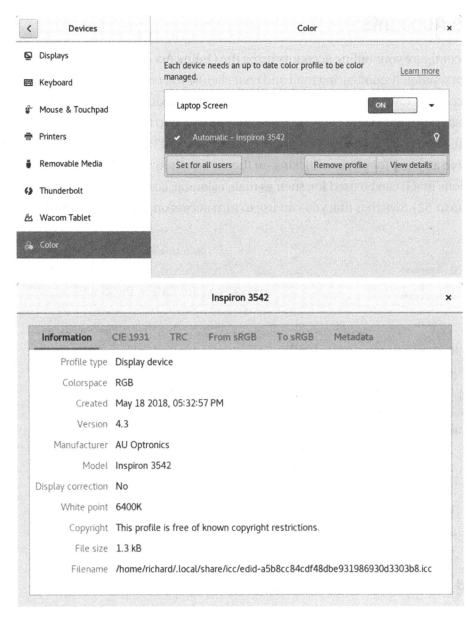

Figure 3-51. *Color management dialog*

Online Accounts

You can configure your online accounts using the Online Accounts dialog in Settings. Instead of separately configuring mail and chat clients, you can set up access once, using online accounts. Click on an entry to start the sign-in procedure. You are prompted to sign in using your email and password. Access is provided to Google, Facebook, Flickr, Microsoft, Microsoft Exchange, Nextcloud, Foursquare, and Pocket. Once access is granted, you will see an entry for service. Clicking on the service shows the different kinds of applications that it can be used for, such as mail, calendar, contacts, chat, and documents (see Figure 3-52). Switches that you can use to turn access on and off are provided.

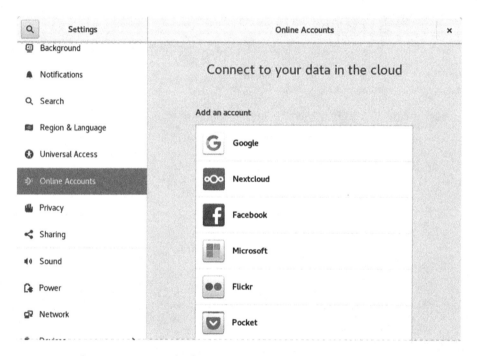

Figure 3-52. *Online Accounts dialog*

Accessing File Systems and Devices

When you attach an external storage device such as a USB, CD/DVD-ROM, or ESATA drive, it will be mounted automatically, and you will be prompted to open it in a file manager window. Be sure to unmount (eject) a drive before removing it, so that data will be written.

Your file systems and removable media appear as entries in the file manager sidebar (see Figure 3-53). External devices such as USB drives are mounted automatically and have Eject buttons next to their entries. Internal hard drive partitions not mounted at boot, such as Windows file systems, are not mounted automatically. Double-click the hard drive partition entry to mount them. An Eject button then appears next to the hard drive entry. You are also prompted to open the drive's file system in a new file manager window.

Figure 3-53. *Devices sidebar in the file manager window*

File systems on removable media will also appear automatically as entries directly on your desktop notifications dialog (see Figure 3-54). A notice briefly appears at the top of the screen that shows the name of the device. If you move your mouse to the notice, an Open with notice appears, which you can click to open the device. Should you not open the device at this time, you can later display it in the message tray. The message tray remains hidden, unless you access it manually by clicking the date button at the center of the top bar, or by pressing the Super key with the m key on the keyboard (Super+m, Super is the Windows key—see Figure 3-54). Clicking the device message opens it in a new file manager window.

When you eject a removable device, a notice briefly appears letting you know you can remove it (see Figure 3-55). A notice will also appear on the message tray.

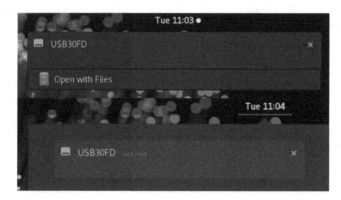

Figure 3-54. *Removable Devices notifications*

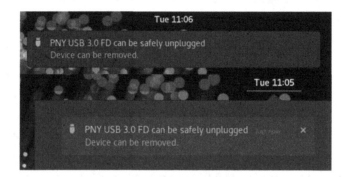

Figure 3-55. *Removable Devices notifications, Eject*

A DVD/CD-ROM is automatically mounted when you insert it into your DVD/
CD-ROM drive, displaying an entry for it in the file manage sidebar. The same kind of
access is also provided for card readers, digital cameras, USB drives, and external USB/
ESATA hard drives (hot-plugged). When you attach an external USB/ESATA drive, it will
be mounted automatically and opened in a file manager window. Be sure to unmount
(eject) the USB and external USB/ESATA drives before removing them, so that data will
be written.

If you have already configured associated applications for video and audio DVD/
CDs, or disks with images, sound, or video files, the disk will be opened with the
appropriate application, such as Shotwell for images, Rhythmbox for audio, and Movie
Player for DVD/video. If you have not yet configured these associations, you will be
prompted to specify which application you want to open it with.

To see network resources, click the Other Location entry in the file manager sidebar. The Networks section will list your connected network computers. Opening these networks displays the shares they provide, such as shared folders that you can have access to. Drag-and-drop operations are supported for all shared folders, letting you copy files and folders between a shared directory on another computer with a directory on your system. You first must configure your firewall to accept Samba connections before you can browse Windows systems on GNOME. Opening a network resource may require you to log in to access the resource.

Video Drivers

You can obtain the NVIDIA vendor graphics drivers from RPM Fusion (the nonfree repository). You can download and install them with DNF. RPM Fusion is the best repository for specialized kernel drivers and modules. Keep in mind, however, that due to open sourcing of some of the NVIDIA vendor driver software, the X.org open source versions are becoming almost as effective, especially for 2D display support. For normal usage, you might not need vendor driver support.

Installing the NVIDIA drivers can be a complex operation depending on what graphics card you have. The drivers are located on the RPM Fusion repository, not on Fedora. Check the RPM Fusion site for instructions on installing the NVIDIA drivers.

```
https://rpmfusion.org/Howto/Nvidia
```

For a simple install, a search on `nvidia` displays NVIDIA modules for each kernel version. The vendor graphic drivers use two packages, one for the supporting software and another for the kernel. The kernel modules are specific to the kernel you are using. Each time you update to a new kernel, you will require a new graphics kernel module created specifically for that kernel. This will be automatically downloaded and installed for you as a dependent package when you update your kernel (the RPM Fusion non-free repository must be active). The driver package is named `xorg-x11-drv-nvidia` and the kernel module generator is named `akmod-nvidia`.

```
xorg-x11-drv-nvidia
akmod-nvidia
```

You can use a dnf list command entered in a terminal window with nvidia* to list all NVIDIA packages.

```
dnf list nvidia*
```

You can then use the dnf install command to install the packages you need.

AMD drivers have been fully open sourced. You can download and install the driver from the Fedora repository. The name of the driver is amdgpu.

```
xorg-x11-drv-amdgpu
```

You could use a dnf command entered in a terminal window that references all the NVIDIA packages, by using an asterisk (*), for example:

```
dnf install nvidia*
```

If, once installed, your vendor driver fails (hangs or freezes), you must remove the vendor software packages. The easiest way to do this is to start up your system in the command-line mode. When the boot menu displays, edit the Fedora kernel line (press e) and add a 3 at the end of the linux line (see "GRUB Start Menu and Boot Problems," at the beginning of this chapter). You start up with the command-line interface. Log in as the root user and then use the dnf command to remove the vendor driver, such as NVIDIA. Use an asterisk (*) to select all the vendor packages. The following example will remove all the NVIDIA vendor packages.

```
sudo dnf remove nvidia*
```

When you restart, your system reconfigures automatically to the originally installed Xorg drivers.

Multimedia Support: MP3, DVD Video, and DivX

Due to licensing and other restrictions, the Fedora distribution does not include MP3, DVD video, or DivX media support. You cannot play DVD video disks or DivX files after installing Fedora. RPM Fusion (https://rpmfusion.org) and Negativo17.org (https://negativo17.org) provide the needed libraries and support files for these media formats. These are RPM packages that you can install with dnf, after first downloading and installing their repository configuration files. Use one or the other, not both. Their packages may conflict.

The commercial DVD-Video codec (DVDCSS) is available from the the Livna repository, `http://www.livna.org`.

DivX support can be obtained using the open source version of DivX, called Xvid (`xvid-core`). It's available on the RPM Fusion and Negativo17.or repositories and will play most DivX files.

Check `https://fedoraproject.org/wiki/Multimedia` for more information. There are many forbidden items that cannot be included with Fedora, due to licensing restrictions, including MP3 support, Adobe Reader, and NVIDIA vendor-provided drivers. Check `https://fedoraproject.org/wiki/ForbiddenItems` for details.

Terminal Window

The Terminal window allows you to enter Linux commands on a command line. It also provides you with a shell interface for using shell commands instead of your desktop. The command line is editable, allowing you to use the Backspace key to erase characters on the line. Pressing a key will insert that character. You can use the left and right arrow keys to move anywhere on the line, and then press keys to insert characters, or use backspace to delete characters (see Figure 3-56). Folders, files, and executable files are color-coded: black for files, blue for folders, green for executable files, and aqua for links. Shared folders are displayed with a green background.

The terminal window will remember the previous commands you entered. Use the Up and Down arrows to have those commands displayed in turn on the command line. Press the Enter key to re-execute the currently displayed command. You can even edit a previous command before running it, allowing you to execute a modified version of a previous command. This can be helpful if you need to re-execute a complex command with a different argument, or if you mistyped a complex command and want to correct it without having to re-type the entire command. The terminal window will display all your previous interactions and commands for that session. Use the scroll bar to see any previous commands you ran and their displayed results.

Figure 3-56. *Terminal window*

You can open as many terminal windows as you want, each working in its own shell. Instead of opening a separate window for each new shell, you can open several shells in the same window, using tabs. Use the keys Shift+Ctrl+t or click the Open Tab item on the File menu to open a new tab. A tab toolbar opens at the top of the terminal window with the folder name and a close button for each tab. Each tab runs a separate shell, letting you enter different commands in each (see Figure 3-57). You can right-click on the tab's folder name to display a pop-up menu to move to a different tab, or just click on a tab's folder name. You can also use the Tabs menu, or the Ctrl+PageUp and Ctrl+PageDown keys, to move to different tabs. The Tabs menu is displayed if multiple tabs are open.

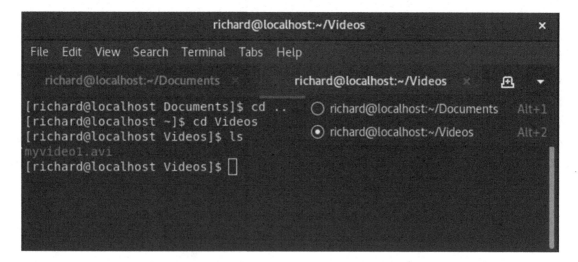

Figure 3-57. *Terminal Window with tabs*

The terminal window also supports desktop cut/copy and paste operations. You can copy a line from a web page and then paste it to the terminal window (you can use the Paste entry on the Terminal window's Edit menu or press Shift+Ctrl+v). The command will appear and then you can press Enter to execute the command. This is useful for command-line operations displayed on an instructional web page. Instead of typing in a complex command yourself, just select and copy from the web page directly and then paste to the Terminal window. You can also perform any edits on the command, if needed, before executing it. Should you want to copy a command on the terminal window, select the text with your mouse and then use Shift+Ctrl+c keys (or the Copy entry on the Terminal window's Edit menu) to copy the command. You can select part of a line or multiple lines, as long as they are shown on the terminal window.

You can customize terminal windows using profiles. A default profile is set up already. To customize your terminal window, select Preferences from the Edit menu. This opens a window for setting your default profile options with option categories on the sidebar for Global and Profiles. In the Profiles section there will be an Unnamed profile, the default. Click on the down menu button to the right to open a menu with the options to copy the profile or change the name. To add another profile, click on the plus button to the right of the Profiles heading to open a dialog to create a new profile. For profiles you create you have the added options to delete them and or to set one as the default. A selected profile displays tabs for Text, Colors, Scrolling, Command, and Compatibility (see Figure 3-58). On the Text tab, you can select the default size of a terminal window in text rows and columns.

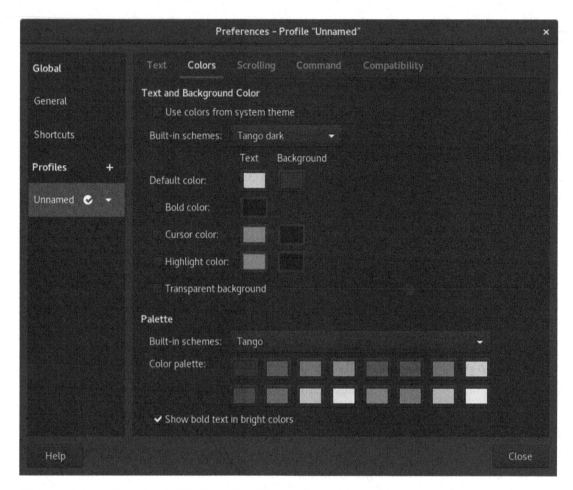

Figure 3-58. *Terminal Window Profile configuration*

Your terminal window will be set up to use a dark background with white text. To change this, you can edit the profile to change the background and text colors on the Colors tab. De-select the Use Colors from System Theme entry. This enables the Built-In Schemes menu from which you can select a Black on White display. Other color combinations are also listed, such as Black on Light Yellow and Green on Black. The Custom option lets you choose your own text and background colors. The colors on your open terminal window will change according to your selection, allowing you to see how the color choices will look. For a transparent background, choose the Use Transparent Background entry and then set the amount of shading (none is completely transparent and full shows no transparency).

The Scrolling tab specifies the number of command lines your terminal history will keep, as well as other scroll options such as the scroll speed and whether to display the scroll bar. These are the lines you can move back through and select to re-execute. You can unselect the Limit Scrollback option to set this to unlimited to keep all the commands.

You can create new profiles with customized preferences. To create a new profile, choose New Profile from the File menu to open the New Profile window where you can enter the profile name and select any profile to base it on. The default profile is chosen initially. Use the Change Profile submenu on the Terminal menu to change profiles.

To edit a particular profile, select Preferences from the Edit menu to open the Preferences window, and then click on the one you want in the Profiles section.

Command-Line Interface

When using the command-line interface, you are given a simple prompt into which you type a command. Even when you are using a desktop like GNOME, you sometimes need to execute commands on a command line. You can do so in a terminal window, which is accessed from the dash.

Linux commands make extensive use of options and arguments. Be careful to place your arguments and options in the correct order on the command line. The format for a Linux command is the command name followed by options, and then by arguments, as shown here:

```
$ command-name options arguments
```

An *option* is a one-letter code preceded by one or two hyphens, which modifies the type of action the command takes. Options and arguments may or may not be optional, depending on the command. For example, the ls command can take an option, -s. The ls command displays a listing of files in your directory, and the -s option adds the size of each file in blocks. You enter the command and its option on the command line as follows:

```
$ ls -s
```

If you are uncertain what format and options a command uses, you can check the command syntax quickly by displaying its man page. Most commands have a man page. Just enter the **man** command with the command name as an argument.

An argument is data the command may need to execute its task. In many cases, this is a filename. An argument is entered as a word on the command line that appears after any options. For example, to display the contents of a file, you can use the **more** command with the file's name as its argument. The **less** or **more** command used with the filename mydata would be entered on the command line as follows:

```
$ less mydata
```

The command line is actually a buffer of text you can edit. Before you press Enter to execute the command, you can edit the command on the command line. The editing capabilities provide a way to correct mistakes you make when typing a command and its options. The Backspace key lets you erase the character you just typed (the one to the left of the cursor), and the Del key lets you erase the character the cursor is on. With this character-erasing capability, you can backspace over the entire line if you want, erasing what you entered. Ctrl+u erases the whole command line and lets you start over again at the prompt.

You can use the Up Arrow key to redisplay your last executed command. You can then re-execute that command, or you can edit it and execute the modified command. This is helpful when you have to repeat certain operations, such as editing the same file. It is also helpful when you have already executed a command you entered incorrectly.

Running Windows Software on Linux: Wine

Wine is a Windows compatibility layer that allows you to run many Windows applications natively on Linux. The actual Windows operating system is not required. Windows applications will run as if they were Linux applications, and they can access the entire Linux file system and use Linux-connected devices. Applications that are heavily driver-dependent, such as graphic-intensive games, may not run. Others that do not rely on any specialized drivers may run very well, including Photoshop, Microsoft Office, and newsreaders like Newsbin. For some applications, you may also have to copy over specific Windows dynamic link libraries (DLLs) from a working Windows system to your Wine Windows System32 or System directory.

Once installed, Wine applications can be accessed from the Other overview. These applications include Wine configuration, the Wine software uninstaller, and the Wine file browser, as well as a Regedit registry editor, a notepad, and a Wine help tool.

To set up Wine, start the Wine Configuration tool. This opens a window with tabs for Applications, Libraries (DLL Selection), Audio (Sound Drivers), Drives, Desktop Integration, and Graphics. On the Applications tab, you can select the version of Windows an application is designed for. The Drives tab lists your detected partitions, as well as your Windows-emulated drives, such as drive C. The C drive is actually just a directory, `.wine/drive_c`, and not a partition of a fixed size. Your actual Linux file system will be listed as the Z drive.

Once configured, Wine will set up a `.wine` directory on the user's home directory. (The directory is hidden, so Show Hidden Files must be enabled in the file manager View menu to display it.) Within that directory will be the `drive_c` directory, which functions as the C drive that holds your Windows system files and program files in the Windows and Program File subdirectories. The System and System32 directories are located in the Windows directory. This is where you place any needed DLL files. The Program Files directory holds your installed Windows programs, just as they would be installed on a Windows Program Files directory.

To install a Windows application with Wine, double-click the application install icon in a file manager window, or right-click the application install icon and choose Open with Wine Windows Program Loader. Alternatively, you can open a terminal window and run the `wine` command with the Windows application as an argument. The following example installs the popular Newsbin program:

```
$ wine newsbin.exe
```

Icons for installed Windows software will appear on your Other overview. Just double-click an icon to start up the application. It will run normally within a Linux window, as would any Linux application.

Wine works on both `.exe` and `.msi` files installation files. You may have to make them executable by checking the file's Execute check box (from the Permissions tab on the Properties dialog).

Tip   Alternatively, you can use Crossover Office, the commercial Windows compatibility layer. This is a commercial product tested to run certain applications such as Microsoft Office. Check `https://www.codeweavers.com` for more details. Crossover Office is based on Wine, which CodeWeavers supports directly.

Help Resources

A great deal of support documentation is already installed on your system, in addition to being accessible from online sources. Table 3-2 lists Help tools and resources accessible on your Fedora Linux system.

Table 3-2. *Fedora Linux Help Resources*

Resource	Description
KDE Help Center	KDE Help tool, desktop interface for documentation on KDE desktop and applications, man pages, and info documents
GNOME Help Browser	GNOME Help tool, desktop interface for accessing documentation for the GNOME desktop and applications
/usr/share/doc	Location of application documentation
man command	Linux man pages, detailed information on Linux commands, including syntax and options
info *application*	GNU info pages, documentation on GNU applications
https://fedoraproject.org	Fedora Project site, with numerous documentation, FAQ, and help resources and links, with links to forums, newsgroups, and community websites
https://docs.fedoraproject.org	Online documentation, guides, HOWTOs, and FAQs for Fedora Linux
https://www.redhat.com	Red Hat Enterprise documentation, guides, HOWTOs, and FAQs; located under Support and Documentation; much of the Red Hat Linux documentation may be helpful
https://library.gnome.org	GNOME documentation site
https://fedoraforum.org	End-user discussion support forum, endorsed by the Fedora Project; includes FAQs and news links
https://fedorasolved.org	Solutions to common problems
https://ask.fedoraproject.org	Ask Fedora site, on which you can ask questions and search for previously answered questions

GNOME and KDE Help

Both the GNOME and KDE desktops feature Help systems that use a browser-like interface to display help files (Utilities ➤ Help). To start the GNOME Help browser, search for help on the Applications overview (see Figure 3-59). It opens with the GNOME desktop guide, showing links for desktop tasks and topics such as video, GNOME Settings, networking, and universal access. The Go menu's All Documents entry lists links for manuals for different applications, such as the Archive Manager, Empathy, Gedit, and the Totem movie player. The GNOME Help browser and the KDE Help Center also incorporate browser capabilities, including bookmarks and history lists for documents you view.

Both GNOME and KDE, in addition to other applications, provide context-sensitive help. Each KDE and GNOME application features detailed manuals that are displayed using their respective Help browsers. Also, system administrative tools feature detailed explanations for each task.

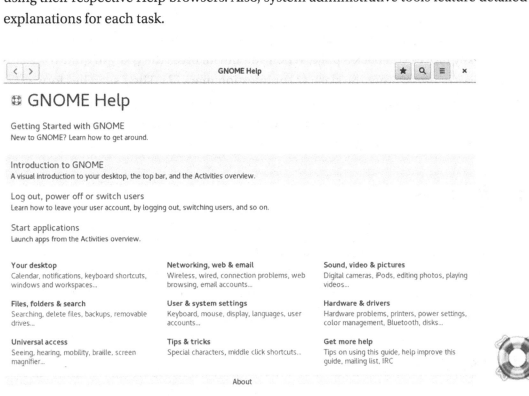

Figure 3-59. *GNOME Help browser*

Application Documentation

On your system, the /usr/share/doc directory contains documentation files installed by each application. Within each directory, you can usually find HOWTO, README, and INSTALL documents for that application.

The Man Pages

Each Linux command usually has a corresponding man page that describes its syntax, options, and examples of its use. A man page is a screen of text displayed from the command line, which you can access from a terminal window. To display a man page, enter the man command with the name of the command you want information about. The following example asks for information about the ls command:

```
$ man ls
```

Use basic keyboard keys to navigate the page. Press the spacebar to display the next page. The b key moves you back a page. When you finish, press the q key to quit. To perform a search, press either the slash (/) or question mark (?). The / searches forward, and the ? searches backward. When you press the /, a line opens at the bottom of your screen on which you enter a word to search for. Press Enter to activate the search. You can repeat the same search by pressing the n key.

The Info Pages

Some applications also provide info page documentation. The info pages are similar to man pages but tend to be more detailed. You can also access this documentation by entering the info command, to display a listing of applications. The info interface has its own set of commands. You can learn more about it by entering info info. The m command lets you search for an application by using a search pattern.

Web Resources

You can obtain documentation on Fedora from the Fedora Project site at https://docs.fedoraproject.org and from the Fedora forum at https://fedoraforum.org. The Ask Fedora Project site at https://ask.fedoraproject.org displays answers to common questions and lets you ask your own.

Most Linux applications are covered by the Linux Documentation Project. It shows you how to use the desktop and takes you through a detailed explanation of Linux applications. The GNOME and KDE websites also contain extensive documentation.

Shared Network Access for Windows (Samba): Samba

Shared Windows folders and printers on any of the computers connected to your local network are automatically accessible from your Fedora desktop. Supporting Samba libraries are already installed and will let you access directly any shared Windows folders. Currently, both Linux and Windows are in the process of transitioning from the older SMBv1 protocol (Server Message Block) to the more secure SMBv3 protocol. As a result, network browsing through the Linux file manager does not work currently. You can access Windows shares directly using the Connect to Server entry on the GNOME file manager's Other Locations window. Enter the `smb://` protocol and the name of the shared folder or that of the remote Windows system you want to access (see Figure 3-60). After being prompted to enter your password (see Figure 3-61), the particular shared folder or the shared folders on that host will be displayed (see Figure 3-62).

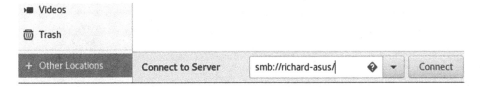

Figure 3-60. *Accessing Windows shared folders on GNOME*

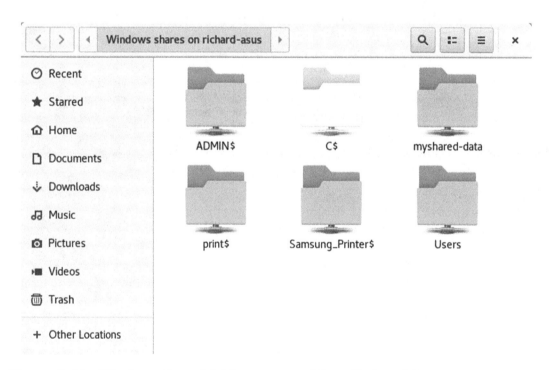

Figure 3-61. *Password for Samba Windows access*

Figure 3-62. *Windows shared folders, accessed from Fedora Linux*

Should you want to share a Linux folder on your Ubuntu computer with users on other Windows computers, you must install Samba and have the Server Message Block services enabled, using the smb and nmb daemons. Before you can use Samba, your network has to have a configured and running Samba server on a Linux system. If your network does not have a Samba server, you can install one on your Fedora workstation. The name of the Samba package is samba. You will have to use the dnf install command in a terminal window to install it. This will install an /etc/samba/smb.conf file, which you can use to configure Samba.

```
sudo dnf install samba
```

The names of the Samba servers are smb and nmb. Be sure to enable them. They are started automatically when you start up your system.

```
sudo systemctl enable smb
sudo systemctl enable nmb
sudo systemctl start smb
sudo systemctl start nmb
```

You will also have to create a Samba user for accessing any shared folders on your Fedora system. You can use the pdbedit command with the -a option to add a user (alternatively you can use the smbpasswd command, also with the -a option). This is a user you have set up on your Fedora system, usually your username. You are prompted to create a password, which you will use to access shares.

```
sudo pdbedit -a richard
new password:
re-type new password:
```

You will have to make sure that the firewall allows Samba access. You can use firewall-config to do this, as described in Chapter 14. A basic command-line operation is shown here.

```
sudo firewall-cmd --add-service=samba --permanent
```

You also have to make sure that SELinux allows Samba access. You can do this with policycoreutils-gui, as discussed in Chapter 12. The policycoreutils-gui package is on the RPMFusion repository, so you will have to configure that repository first, as discussed in Chapter 4. Use **the** dnf install command in a terminal window to install the package. You have to set the Samba options on the Boolean tab. There are several options, depending on the level of access you want to afford. Alternatively, you could use a simple command-line operation to allow access to your home directories. In this case, the shared Samba folder you are creating is your home folder, the same as your username.

```
sudo setsebool -P samba_enable_home_dirs on
```

To disable access, just turn it off.

```
sudo setsebool -P samba_enable_home_dirs off
```

Make sure your /etc/samba/smb.conf file has the workgroup entry set to the name of your Windows workgroup. The default name set up by Windows is workgroup.

```
workgroup = workgroup
```

You will may have to edit the file to change its entries. Use the sudo command and an editor such as nano or Leafpad in a terminal window. Be sure the editors are installed.

```
sudo nano /etc/samba/smb.conf
```

To add a particular shared folder, edit the /etc/samba/smb.conf file and add an entry for it. Be sure the folder already exits. If not, create it and set the permissions you want to give it. You will have to enter the full pathname for the folder (path), starting from the root directory, the Samba users (valid users) that can access the folder, and read/write permission (read only). The following are two samples of shared folders, one for a /mydocs folder and another for the Pictures folder of the user's home directory.

```
[mydocs]
path = /mydocs
valid users = richard
read only = no

[Pictures]
path = /home/richard/Pictures
valid users = richard
read only = no
```

Once you have made your changes, run the testparm command to see if the entry was added correctly.

Whenever you make changes to the smb.conf file, be sure to restart the Samba servers, smb and nmb.

```
sudo systemctl restart smb
sudo systemctl restart nmb
```

To see a list of your shares, use the `smbclient -L` command with your hostname (hostname of the Samba server).

```
smbclient -L richard-laptop
```

Accessing Samba shares from Windows is an issue for Windows 10. Upgrades to Windows 10 has disabled the SMBv1 network browsing capabilities of Windows, as it transitions to SMBv3 from SMBv1. You could try to manually re-enable SMBv1 browsing, but SMBv1 is being disabled due to security issues. It is not advisable to re-enable it. This means you cannot simply browse a Linux host currently, but you can still easily set up access to each Samba shared folder on that Linux host.

It is still easy to access your Samba Linux shares from Windows 10. You can simply add a new network location for it. It will then be accessible from a shortcut you can set up for it on your Windows file manager's This PC folder. To set up the shortcut, open the Windows file manager to any folder and right-click on the This PC entry in the sidebar to display a menu. Click on the Add a Network Location entry to open the Add Network Location wizard and click Next. Click on the Choose a Custom Network Location entry and click Next. In the text box labeled Internet or Network Address, enter the hostname of your Linux system that holds the shares you want to access, beginning with the two backward slashes and followed by a backward slash (you may have to also enter the name of one of the shared folders on that system).

```
\\richard-laptop\
```

You can then click the Browse button to open a dialog showing a tree of all the shared folders on that host. You can choose a share, or any of a share's subfolders. The file's pathname is automatically added to the address text box. Alternatively, you could enter the folder pathname in the text box directly with the subfolders separated by single backward slashes. If you are sharing your Linux home directories, then the shared folder is the name of the user's home folder, the username. Samples are shown here.

```
\\richard-laptop\richard
\\richard-laptop\richard\Pictures
\\richard-laptop\mydocs
```

Once the locations for your shared folders are set up in Windows, you can access them again quickly from their shortcuts in the This PC folder.

CHAPTER 4

Installing and Updating Software: DNF, GNOME Software, Packages, DnfDragora, and RPM

Fedora software is distributed through an online Fedora software repository. Table 4-1 lists Fedora software information and site locations. Software is added to your system by accessing software repositories with the DNF package manager. The DNF package manager replaces the YUM (Yellowdog Update, Modified) software package manager. Use the dnf command in place of yum. Options remain much the same, and you can still use the yum command instead. The commonly used Fedora software repositories are listed in Table 4-2.

Table 4-1. *Fedora Software Information and Sites*

Internet Site	Description
https://getfedora.org	Fedora distribution disks, download links for all formats
https://rpmfusion.org	RPM Fusion repository for third-party multimedia and driver Fedora-compliant software (Fedora Project extension)
https://fedoraproject.org/wiki/ForbiddenItems	Packages not included in the main Fedora software repository
https://fedoraproject.org/wiki/Multimedia	Information on multimedia packages available for Fedora
https://negativo17.org	Negativo17.org repository for third-party multimedia and driver Fedora-compliant software

© Richard Petersen 2018
R. Petersen, *Beginning Fedora Desktop*, https://doi.org/10.1007/978-1-4842-3882-0_4

Software applications, with all the needed programs, configuration files, and supporting library binaries, are combined into packages by the RPM Package Manager that will install all the components into the appropriate system folders. DNF manages all these RPM packages for your system, keeping track of updates and what collection of packages belong to different systems and collections such as your desktop or office suite. It also keeps track of dependencies, such as what supporting software an application may need. Multimedia applications may need sound support. To easily manage DNF operations you can use desktop frontends, such as GNOME Software, PackageKit, and DnfDragora. GNOME Software lets you manage software by topic, whereas Packages searches for particular RPM packages. DnfDragora does both.

Fedora provides only open source applications in its own repository. For proprietary applications such as NVIDIA's own graphics drivers, or multimedia applications that may have patent issues, you must use a third-party repository like RPM Fusion. The list of forbidden items for the official Fedora repository can be found at `https://www. fedoraproject.org/wiki/ForbiddenItems`. The list includes such items as the NVIDIA graphics drivers.

Software Repositories

For Fedora, you can add software to your system by accessing software repositories supporting DNF. In addition, many software applications, particularly multimedia ones, have potential licensing conflicts. By leaving such software in third-party repositories, Fedora avoids possible legal issues. Many of the popular multimedia applications, such as video and digital music support, can be obtained from third-party repositories using the same simple `dnf` commands you use with Fedora-sponsored software. The commonly used Fedora software repositories are listed in Table 4-2.

Table 4-2. *Fedora and Fedora-Compliant Software Repositories*

Internet Site	Description
https://download.fedoraproject.org	Links are provided to the best available mirror.
https://rpmfusion.org/Configuration	Fedora applications not included with the distribution, due to licensing and other restrictions, are provided. Go to the Configuration page to download the DNF configuration files.
https://negativo17.org	Negativo17.org repository for third-party multimedia and driver Fedora-compliant software.
https://get.adobe.com/flashplayer/	The Adobe repository. Select the Linux for YUM to download the Adobe YUM configuration file. Select YUM for Linux from the drop-down menu.
https://www.google.com/linuxrepositories/	Provides Google repositories for accessing Google software.

Most software is now located on the Internet-connected repositories. With the integration of DNF into your Fedora system, you can now think of that software as an easily installed extension of your current collection. You can find out more about how DNF is used on "Fedora Software Management Guide".

You could also browse many of these repositories and download packages individually, although this is not recommended, as you would lose the automatic updating support provided by DNF.

Fedora Software Repositories

The Fedora Linux distribution provides a comprehensive selection of software, ranging from office and multimedia applications to Internet servers and administration services. The complete set is available on the Fedora repository. During installation, DNF is configured on your system, to access the Fedora repository. Some third-party applications with licensing issues are not included, though Fedora-compliant versions are provided on associated software repositories.

For Fedora, you can update to the latest software from the Fedora DNF repository using GNOME Software or PackageKit's Package Updater. They are already configured to access the Fedora repositories.

RPM Fusion

Due to licensing restrictions, multimedia support for popular operations such as MP3, DVD, and DivX is not included with Fedora distributions. The Fedora Project associated site, RPM Fusion (`https://rpmfusion.org`), does provide support for these functions. Here, you can download support for MP3, DVD, and DivX software. This repository integrates support previously provided by Livna, Freshrpms, and Dribble. Fedora does include the generic X.org NVIDIA drivers, which will provide all the capabilities most people need. You do not have to use the NVIDIA proprietary drivers.

The Fedora-compliant repositories, such as RPM Fusion, will have Fedora-compliant DNF configuration files that you can download and install as an RPM package. You can then use the GNOME Software, PackageKit (Packages), DnfDragora, or the dnf command to select, download, and install software from the associated repository directly.

Adobe and Livna

Two smaller additional third-party repositories are often configured for desktop users: the Adobe repository and the Livna repository. The Adobe repository holds packages for the Linux version of the Adobe Flash software. (Two alternative Flash-compatible open source versions are already available, swfdec and gnash.) The Livna repository provides the commercial DVD video codec, libdvdcss. The repository contains only this one package. If you want to play commercial DVD video disks, you have to configure access to this repository so that you can install the codec.

Third-Party Linux Software Archives

Though almost all applications should be included in the Fedora software repository or its associated repositories, such as `https://rpmfusion.org`, you could download and install software from third-party software archives. Always check to see if the software you want is already in the Fedora or Fedora-associated repositories. If it is not available, you can download it from a third-party online site.

Several third-party repositories make it easy to locate and find information about an application. Of particular note are `https://www.sourceforge.net` and `https://www.linux-apps.com/`. Sites for Linux software are listed in Table 4-3, along with several specialized sites, such as those for commercial and game software. When downloading software packages, always check to see if the versions are packaged as RPM packages and if they are already available on the Fedora and RPM Fusion repositories.

Table 4-3. *Third-Party Linux Software Archives*

URL	Internet Site
`https://sourceforge.net`	SourceForge, open source software development site for Linux applications
`https://www.linux-apps.com/`	Linux software repository
`www.gnu.org`	GNU archive
`https://lgdb.org/`	Linux games
`https://www.fluendo.com`	Licensed multimedia codecs for Linux, including free MP3 code

Updating Fedora: GNOME Software and Software Update

New updates are continually being prepared for particular software packages. These are posted as updates that you can download from software repositories and install on your system. They include new versions of applications, servers, and even the kernel. Such updates may range from single software packages to whole components.

Updating your Linux system has become a very simple procedure, using the automatic update tools. For Fedora, you can update your system by accessing software repositories supporting the DNF (Dandified YUM) update methods. DNF uses RPM headers to determine which packages need to be updated.

If updates are detected, GNOME Software will display an update message in the message tray (see Figure 4-1). Clicking the entry button opens a dialog prompting you to restart and install the updates. Clicking the Restart & Install button immediately shuts down your system, then restarts, and, as part of the startup process, downloads and installs updates. Once installed, a message is displayed.

Figure 4-1. *Update notification message and icon*

To perform manual updates, you can use either GNOME Software to perform updates (the default), or you can use the older Package Updater. Package Updater is a graphical update interface for DNF (part of PackageKit), which performs all updates from the desktop. From a command line, you can perform updates using the dnf upgrade command.

Updating Fedora with GNOME Software Update

GNOME Software is the primary update tool for Fedora. You can view updates by using the Updates tab on GNOME Software (see Figure 4-2). The tab will display the number of updates. Clicking an update opens a dialog showing information about the update. Some entries, such as OS Updates, will have several packages that have to be updated (see Figure 4-3). When you are ready, click the Restart & Update button on the header bar to shut down your system and install the updates as it restarts.

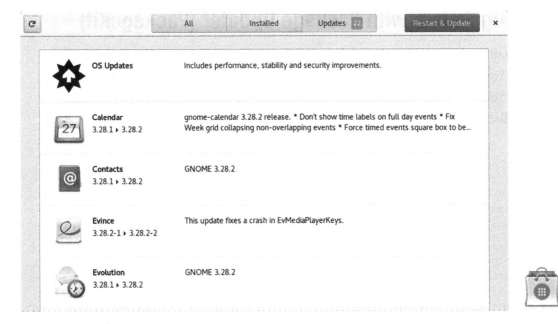

Figure 4-2. *GNOME Software Updates tab*

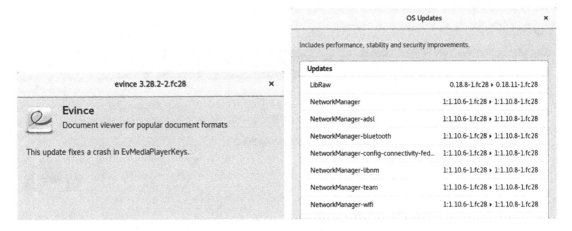

Figure 4-3. *GNOME Software: Update information dialog*

Updating Fedora with Package Updater (PackageKit)

If you install PackageKit (Packages), the Package Updater package will also have been installed. You can, if you wish, use it to update your system, instead of using GNOME Software. You can open Package Updater from the Applications overview. Package Updater displays the Package Updater dialog showing your updates (see Figure 4-4).

Figure 4-4. Software Update: Selected package with displayed description

The number of updates is shown at the top, along with Install Updates button on the right side of the title bar. To perform the updates, click the Install Updates button. If you want to review the updates and perhaps deselect certain updates, you scroll through the list of updates, selecting the ones you want more information on. All needed updates are selected automatically when Software Update starts up. The check boxes for each entry let you deselect particular packages you may not want to update. At the bottom of the dialog is an expandable entry name Details. This entry becomes active when you select a package. Expanding the Details entry display information about this package's update. The displayed information includes features such as the version and repository.

Click the Install Updates button to start updating. During the update, a status message is displayed at the bottom of the dialog for the different update stages along with a progress bar.

Update with the dnf Command

To perform a complete update of all your installed packages, you use the dnf command with the upgrade option.

```
sudo dnf upgrade
```

To update just a particular package, specify that package. The following would update an already installed Gnumeric package.

```
sudo dnf upgrade gnumeric
```

You can use the updateinfo option to see what packages need to be updated. With no option just a count of the kinds of updates is listed. With the --list option, the packages to be updated are shown. For details about each update, use the --info option.

```
dnf updateinfo
dnf updateinfo --list
dnf updateinfo --info
```

Automatic DNF Updates with dnf-automatic

If you want updates performed automatically, you can install the dnf-automatic package. This package installs timers and services for three automatic update options: notifyonly, download, and install. The download option notifies and downloads only. The install option notifies, downloads, and installs. To designate an option, you enable and start its timer. The three timers are:

```
dnf-automatic-notifyonly.timer
dnf-automatic-download.timer
dnf-automatic-install.timer
```

To choose the download and notify option, you would enter the following in a terminal window.

```
sudo systemctl enable dnf-automatic-download.timer
sudo systemctl start dnf-automatic-download.timer
```

To notify, download, and install, enable and start the install timer.

```
sudo systemctl start dnf-automatic-install.timer
```

To change from one option to another, be sure to disable the current one.

```
sudo systemctl disable dnf-automatic-install.timer
sudo systemctl enable dnf-automatic-notifyonly.timer
sudo systemctl start dnf-automatic-notifyonly.timer
```

Configuration for dnf-automatic is held in the /etc/dnf/automatic.conf file. The default entries for updates, download_updates and apply_updates, are overridden by the timer you have enabled. You can customize other entries such as those for email. Check the man page for dnf.automatic for configuration details.

Installing Software Packages

Installing software is an administrative function performed by a user with administrative access. Unless you chose to install all your packages during your installation, only some of the many applications and utilities available to Linux users were installed on your system. On Fedora, you can install or remove software from your system with the GNOME Software software manager or the dnf install command. You could also use the PackageKit (Packages) and DnfDragora package managers (not installed by default). Alternatively, you can install software as individual packages, with the rpm command or by downloading and compiling its source code. The procedure for installing software using its source code has been simplified to just a few commands, though you have a great deal of flexibility in tailoring an application to your specific system.

The dnf command remains the best way to access all available packages. GNOME Software and PackageKit do not detect and display all the packages available, such as the server software. They focus primarily on desktop applications.

An RPM software package operates like its own installation program for a software application. A Linux software application often consists of several files that must be installed in different directories. The program is most likely placed in a directory called /usr/bin; online manual files go in another directory; and library files go in yet another directory. In addition, the installation may require modification of certain configuration files on your system. The RPM software packages perform all these tasks for you. Also, if you later decide you don't want a specific application, you can uninstall packages to remove all the files and configuration information from your system.

The software packages on your install disk, as extensive as they are, represent only some of the software packages available for Fedora Linux. Most reside on the Fedora Software repository, a repository whose packages are available for automatic download using the GNOME Software application. Many additional multimedia applications and support libraries can be found at the RPM Fusion repository (https://rpmfusion.org) and, once configured, downloaded directly with DNF and GNOME Software. Table 4-2 lists several Fedora software repositories. Fedora and RPM Fusion are DNF-supported, meaning that a simple DNF configuration enables you to directly download and install software from those sites using the dnf command, GNOME Software, and any other software manager that supports DNF, such as PackageKit and DnfDragora. Fedora repository configuration was performed during the installation of your Fedora system. PackageKit and DnfDragora include repository configuration when installed. RPM Fusion provides DNF configuration files that you download and install manually from its website.

Managing Software with DNF

Downloading Fedora software or software from any Fedora repository is a simple matter of using the Dandified YUM (DNF) package manager (http://fedoraproject.org/wiki/Features/DNF). DNF uses many of the same commands and options as YUM, which it replaces. GNOME Software and Packages (PackageKit) provide desktop interfaces for the DNF package manager.

You can use the dnf command, in a terminal window or command-line interface, to access Fedora repositories and install new software. To use the dnf command, enter the dnf command with the install option on a command line. The package will be detected, along with any dependent software, and you will be asked to confirm installation. The download and installation is automatic. For query operations such as list, you do not need administrative access. But for actions such as install and remove, you do need administrative access, for which you use the sudo command. The following command installs Gnumeric:

```
sudo dnf install gnumeric
```

You can also remove packages, as well as search for packages and list packages by different criteria, such as those for update, those on the repository not yet installed, and those already installed. The following example lists all installed packages:

```
dnf list installed
```

The available option shows uninstalled packages.

```
dnf list available
```

To quickly to see if a package is available, you can use the list command. The list command works on a package name. Add the asterisk for a pattern search.

```
dnf list vsftpd
dnf list *ftp*
dnf list bind*
```

To search package descriptions, use the search command and a pattern.

```
dnf search wine
```

For details about a package, use the repoquery command with the -i option. The -l option lists the files the package will install.

```
dnf repoquery -i gnumeric
```

When removing a package, in some rare cases, the entire GNOME desktop, along with the GDM and Packages, could be selected and accidently removed. If this is the case, you should reinstall GNOME, GDM, and GNOME Software with dnf commands in a terminal window or by using the command-line interface. You might also have to reinstall graphics drivers. You can use group to install the entire GNOME desktop. The group list command displays groups.

```
sudo dnf group install gnome-desktop
sudo dnf install gdm
sudo dnf install gnome-software
```

GNOME Software (Software)

GNOME Software is the GNOME software management frontend for DNF. It is designed to be a cross-distribution package manager that can be used on any DNF-supported Linux distribution. GNOME Software performs a variety of different software tasks, including installation, removal, updating of software, as well as the management of system add-ons such as codecs, fonts, drivers, and desktop (shell) extensions. See `https://fedoraproject.org/wiki/Changes/AppInstaller` for more information.

GNOME Software is currently designed to install client and system applications. It does not install server software, such as the DNS name server or the Apache Web server. It also does not install many of the older system configuration tools, such as `system-config-samba`. To manage such software, you will have to install using the `dnf` command in a terminal.

To use GNOME Software, click the Software icon on the Activities dash or on the Applications overview. GNOME Software will start up by gathering information on all your packages. A window opens with three tabs at the top, for All, Installed, and Updates. You can install applications from the All tab which displays a collection of category buttons, a search button on the title bar you can click to display a search box, and several sets of picks to choose from (Editor, Recent Releases, Recommended Games, and Recommended Productivity Applications) (see Figure 4-5).

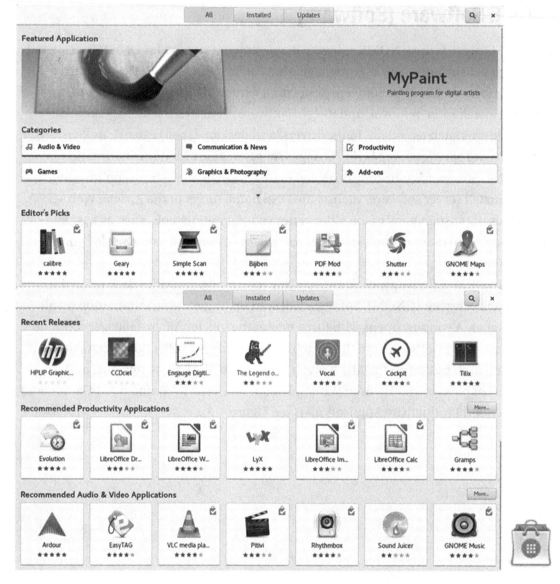

Figure 4-5. *GNOME Software*

The category buttons are Audio & Video, Games, Communication & News, Graphics & Photography, Productivity, and Add-ons. Click on any category button to open a dialog with subcategories. The Add-ons category covers enhancements to your desktop, such as codecs, fonts, drivers, and desktop (shell) extensions.

Categories allow you to further filter the selection using a Show menu. The Graphics & Photography category has filters such as Vector Graphics, Scanning, and Photography (Figure 4-6). A Sort menu lets you also sort items by name or·rating. The software in each category is listed as icons. A few featured packages are listed at the top. Packages already installed have a checkmark on a packet emblem displayed in the upper-right corner of the package icon.

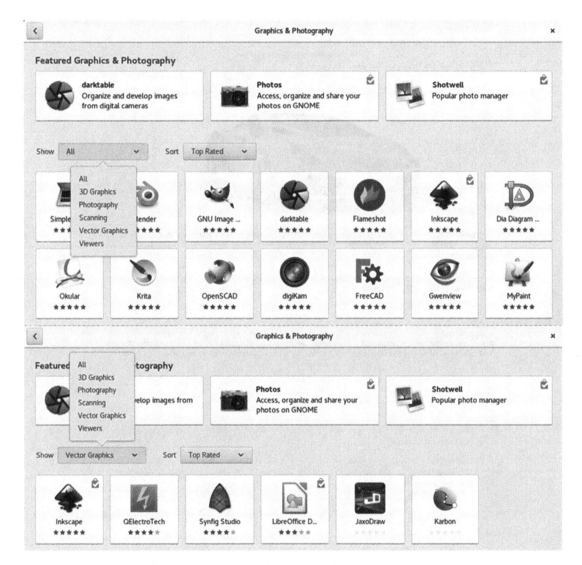

Figure 4-6. *GNOME Software: Graphics category*

Click a software icon to open its description page, which provides a brief description of the software and a link to its related website (see Figure 4-7). Uninstalled software displays an Install button below the software's name, and installed software shows a Remove button. To the right of the name is a star rating with the number of reviews.

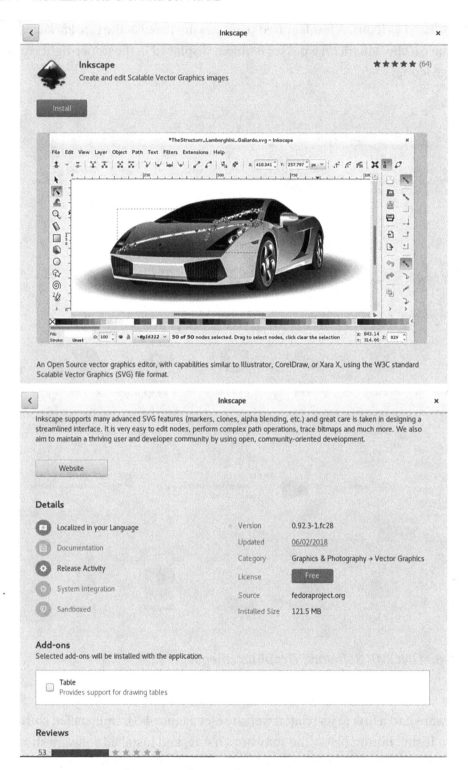

Figure 4-7.   *GNOME Software: Software descriptor page*

Click the Install button to install the software. As the software is installed, an Installing progress bar appears (see Figure 4-8). When it's complete, the Launch and Remove buttons are displayed below the name. You can use these to start or uninstall the software.

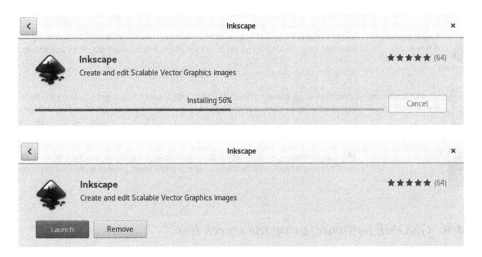

Figure 4-8. *GNOME Software: Installing software*

You can also search for a package using the search box on the All tab. Enter part of the name or a term to describe the package (see Figure 4-9). Results are listed, showing an icon, name, and description. Click on an entry to open its description page where you can perform possible actions such as install, remove, or launch.

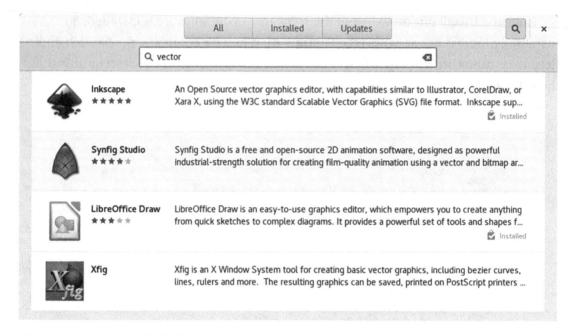

Figure 4-9. *GNOME Software: using the search box*

The Installed tab lists your installed software (see Figure 4-10). If the applications are located on the overview within a folder, that folder name is listed under the application name. The applications are organized into three sections: Applications, System Applications, and Add-ons. To remove an application, click its Remove button. You can also use the Installed tab to organize the applications overview, creating new category folders on the overview or moving applications into existing folders. Click on the check box at the right on the title bar on the Installed tab. Round check boxes will appear to the left of each software entry, which you can click to select that application (see Figure 4-11). Three buttons are listed at the bottom of the window, labeled Add to Folder, Move to Folder, and Remove from Folder. When you select an item, the possible buttons become active. Initially, most applications are not in folders, so when you select and application, only the Add to Folder button becomes active. Clicking on it opens an Add to Applications Folder dialog, which lists possible folder to move the application to. Clicking on the plus icon below the list opens a dialog where you can create a new folder with a name of your choosing. Click the Cancel button at the top right when you are finished. This feature lets you organize your Applications Overview using folders of your choosing.

Figure 4-10. *GNOME Software: Installed tab*

Figure 4-11. *GNOME Software: Installed tab, organize applications overview*

Using the Add-ons category, you can easily manage your fonts, graphics drivers, multimedia codecs, and any additional third-party apps or features you want installed on your system. Clicking on the Add-ons category on the All tab opens the Add-ons dialog with tabs for Codecs, Fonts, Hardware Drivers, Input Sources, Localization, and Shell Extensions (see Figure 4-12). Installed software will show an emblem with a checkmark in the top-right corner of their icons. To install or remove an add-on, click on its icon to open a description dialog. Installed add-ons will show a Remove button, and uninstalled ones will show an Install button.

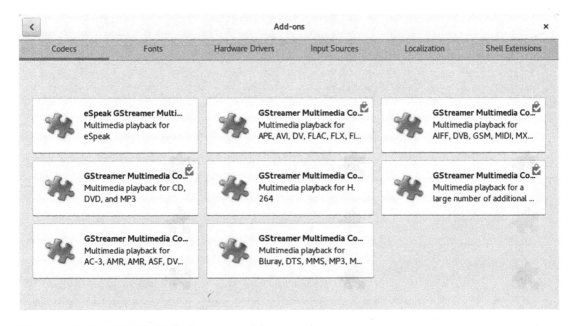

Figure 4-12. *GNOME Software: Add-ons tab*

The Shell Extensions tab shows extensions you can add to your desktop
(see Figure 4-13). You are warned to install them at your own risk. Clicking on the Shell
Extensions button allows you to turn on support for application indicators on the top
bar. The button then becomes an Extension Settings button, which you can use to
display the extensions you have installed and turn them on or off (see Figure 4-14).

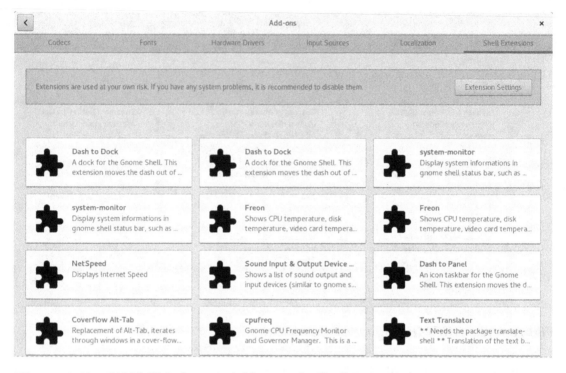

Figure 4-13. *GNOME Software: Add-ons tab, Shell Extensions*

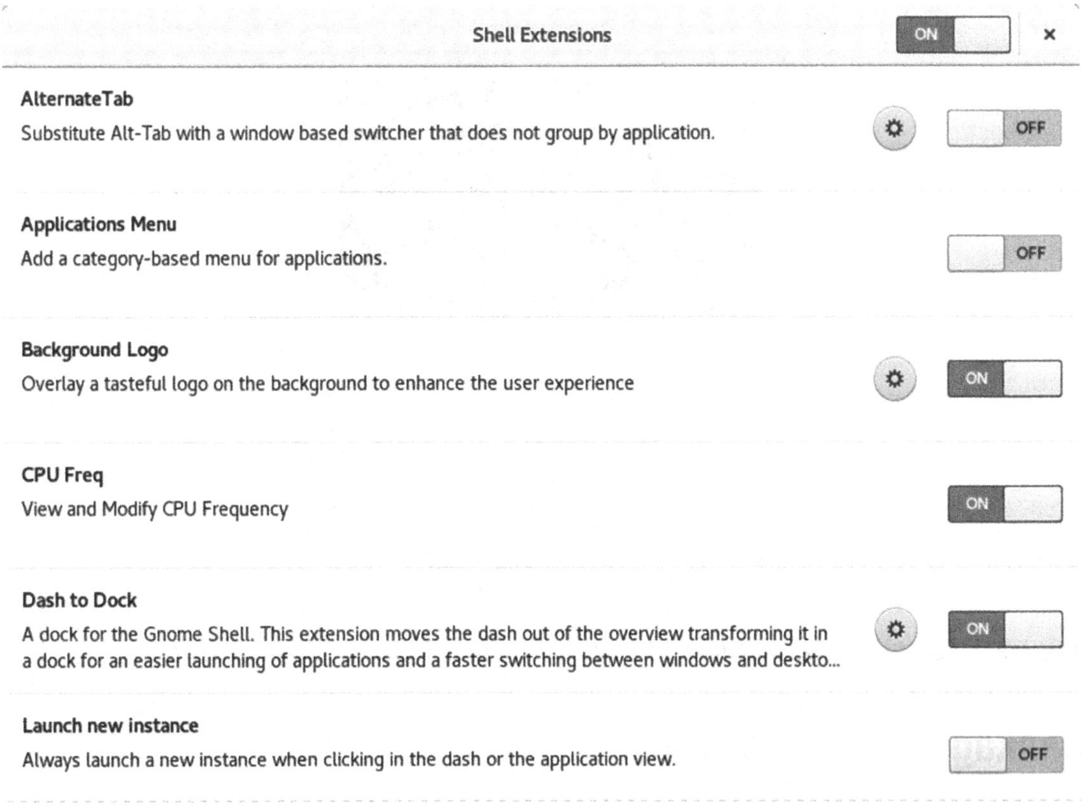

Shell Extensions		ON	×

AlternateTab
Substitute Alt-Tab with a window based switcher that does not group by application.

⚙ OFF

Applications Menu
Add a category-based menu for applications.

OFF

Background Logo
Overlay a tasteful logo on the background to enhance the user experience

⚙ ON

CPU Freq
View and Modify CPU Frequency

ON

Dash to Dock
A dock for the Gnome Shell. This extension moves the dash out of the overview transforming it in a dock for an easier launching of applications and a faster switching between windows and deskto...

⚙ ON

Launch new instance
Always launch a new instance when clicking in the dash or the application view.

OFF

Figure 4-14. *GNOME Software: Installed shell extension management*

Many of the shell extensions are designed to operate as indicators on the top bar. Others add features to the desktop, such as Dash to Dock, which adds a dash-like dock to the main screen, letting you start favorite applications directly from the desktop. Keep in mind that the extensions are not guaranteed to work. Some extensions are already installed but not turned on, such as the Applications menu, which can add the GNOME Classic applications menu to the top bar in place of the Activities button. Some of the extensions will have a configuration button you can click to display features you can set such as that for the Background Logo, which sets the position, size, opacity, and border of the Fedora logo on your desktop (see Figure 4-15). You can even change the logo. To remove the logo, just turn off the extension.

137

Figure 4-15. *GNOME Software: Installed Shell Extension Configuration*

PackageKit (Packages)

PackageKit is an older software management frontend for DNF. It is designed to be a cross-distribution package manager that can be used on any DNF-supported Linux distribution. See www.packagekit.org for more information. PackageKit provides a variety of applications for different software tasks, including installation, removal, updates, repository management, logs, and install of an individual RPM file (see Table 4-4). The primary PackageKit application is gpk-application, accessible as Packages. The gpk-update-viewer (Software Update) lets you examine and select updates. The gpk-log displays a list of all your previous install, removal, and update operations, including major updates and individual package installs (accessible on PackageKit from the Applications menu [top bar], as the Software Log menu item).

Table 4-4. *PackageKit Applications*

Application	Description
gpk-application	Packages
gpk-update-viewer	Updates your system with Package Updater
gpk-prefs	Configures repositories with Package Sources
gpk-log	Views history of updates and installs

To use PackageKit, click the Packages icon on the Applications overview. PackageKit will start up by gathering information on all your packages. A Software window opens with a search box at the top and packages listed below (see Figure 4-16). Before you install any packages, it is advisable to first refresh your software lists. This is a listing of software packages available on your enabled repositories. Select Refresh Package Lists from the PackageKit applications menu.

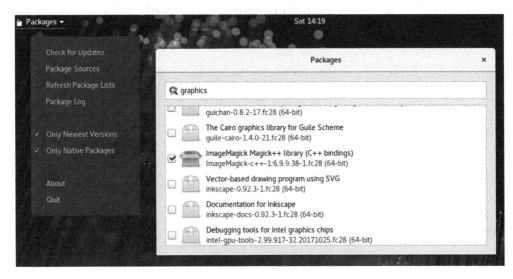

Figure 4-16. *PackageKit (Packages)*

Search for packages by entering the package name or descriptive term in the search box. Packages searches package descriptions, not just the filename. Uninstalled packages have faded package icons with an empty check box, and installed packages have a solid color with a checkmark in the check box.

To access information about a particular package, select it. A pane then opens at the bottom and displays a description of the software and a button bar to the right, with buttons to install the package (or remove if already installed),for the software's website (Homepage), and a list of installed files (Files). The Homepage button opens your browser to the package home page where you can find more detailed information about it. The Files button opens a window that lists all the files the package installs. This can be helpful for tracking down the command names and location of the configuration files.

To install a package, first click its check box (see Figure 4-17). The box is checked, and a plus sign (+) appears on the package icon. You can click several packages to select them for installation. Once you are ready to install, click the Apply Changes button (upper right). A progress bar will show the install task's progress. The PackageKit task messages are displayed at the top-center on the title bar. During the download phase, a Cancel button is displayed on the left side of the title bar, letting you cancel the install. Once the package is installed, the package icon color will change from faded to a solid color, and a checkmark will be displayed in its check box. If dependent or additional packages are required by the software you want to install, these are listed, and you are prompted to confirm their installation. Click Continue.

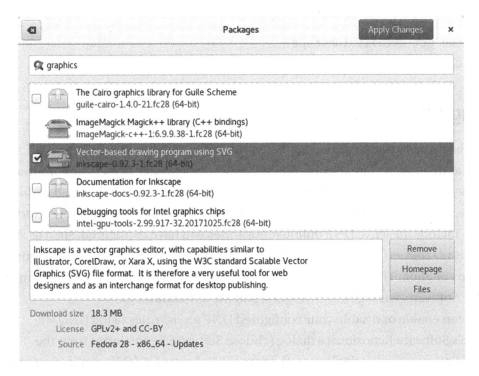

Figure 4-17. *Package information*

If you choose to remove an installed package, click its check box. The check box becomes empty, and a wastebasket image is displayed on the package icon. Then click Apply Changes to uninstall. Once the package is removed, the package icon color becomes faded. You could also just select it and click the Remove button in its description.

Instead of showing all your available packages, both installed and uninstalled, you can filter the package listings. Two filter options are available from the PackageKit GNOME applications menu. You can filter by newest versions and native packages. Native packages are those for your system architecture, such as 64-bit (x86_64) or 32-bit (i686).

PackageKit also has a CLI (command-line interface) version called pkcon. You can use the pkcon command in a terminal window to install and remove packages.

```
sudo pkcon install inkscape
sudo pkcon remove inkscape
```

The get-packages option lists all your packages and the get-files option lists all the files installed by a package. The get-details option displays the package description.

141

```
sudo pkcon get-packages
sudo pkcon get-details inkscape
sudo pkcon get-files inkscape
```

Managing Repositories

DNF is the primary package-management tool. When you install a package, DNF is invoked and automatically selects and downloads the package from the appropriate repository. After having installed your system, when you then want to install additional packages, GNOME Software and Packages will use DNF to install from a repository. This will include all active DNF online repositories you have configured, such as sites like https://rpmfusion.org, not just the Fedora and update repositories configured during installation. You can manage your repositories, enabling or disabling them, with GNOME Software, Packages, DnfDragora, and the dnf command.

You can enable or disable your configured DNF repositories using GNOME Software's Software Repositories dialog (choose Software Repositories from the GNOME Software application's menu). From the Software GNOME application's menu, select Software Sources. Click the Software Sources tab to see a list of your configured repositories (see Figure 4-18).

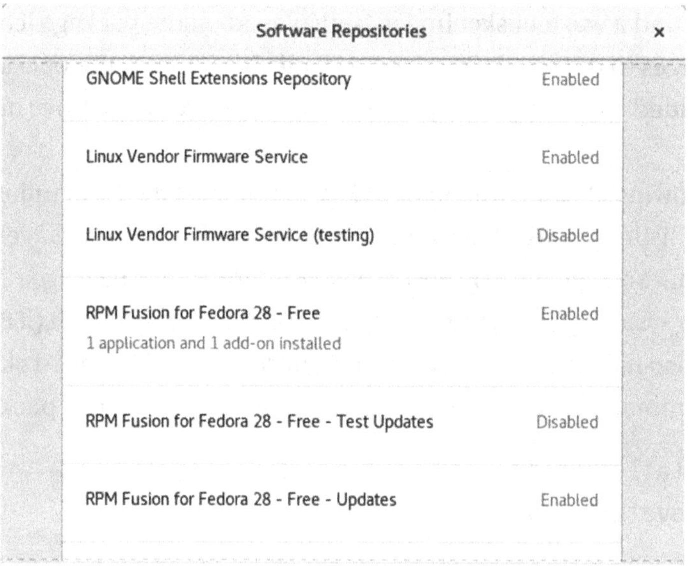

Figure 4-18. *Software Repositories: Configured software repositories (GNOME Software)*

The repositories listed have DNF configuration files in the /etc/yum.repos.d directory, holding information such as URLs, GPG keys, and descriptions. The Fedora repository names include the release number and the platform, such as x86_64 for the 64-bit version. Fedora and Fedora Update repositories will be enabled. If you want to see the package from just one repository, you can deactivate the others. For example, if you wanted to see only the RPM Fusion repository, you could deactivate all others, including Fedora. You can reactivate the other repositories later.

On GNOME Software's Software Sources dialog, all configured repositories are listed along with their status, disabled or enabled. To enable a disabled repository, click on its entry to display an Enable button, which you can click to enable the repository. For enabled repositories, a Disable button is shown, when their entry is clicked. Also, when you click a repository entry, the URL of its repository is displayed.

Repositories also have specialized repositories for development, debugging, and source code files. Here you find applications under development that may be useful, as well as the latest revisions. Some will have testing repositories for applications not yet completely validated for the current release. These applications might not work well. Source, Test, and Debug repositories will normally be disabled. Test is the development repository for a future release currently under development. The source repositories hold source code packages.

Fedora Linux designated certain repositories as third-party repositories, as listed at:

https://fedoraproject.org/wiki/Workstation/Third_Party_Software_Repositories

These include PyCharm (Python development environment), Google Chrome, the RPM Fusion NVIDIA graphics driver repository, and the RPM Fusion Steam client repository. When you first start GNOME Software, a notice asks you if you want to enable these repositories, as shown here.

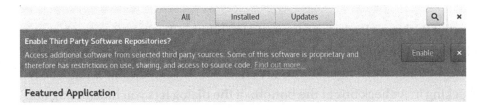

A Third Party Repositories section for those repositories is displayed at the top of the Software Repositories dialog. A Third Party Repositories noticeg at the top of the dialog has a Remove All button (see Figure 4-19), which you can click to remove these repositories, including their configuration files from /etc/yum.repos.d. Upon removal, the button becomes an Install button, which you can use to restore these repositories. The Remove and Install actions only affect these repositories, not any other third-party repositories you may have installed, such as Livna and the free and non-free RPM Fusion repositories.

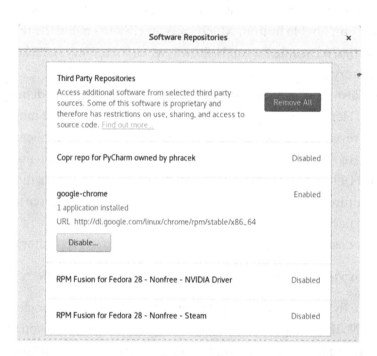

Figure 4-19. *Software repositories: Third-party repositories (GNOME Software)*

Using the Package's Package Sources dialog (choose Package Sources from the Packages application's menu), you can also enable and disable repositories (see Figure 4-20). Enabled repositories are checked. You can disable a repository by unchecking it. A check box at the bottom of the dialog lets you hide debug and development repositories, showing just the main repositories.

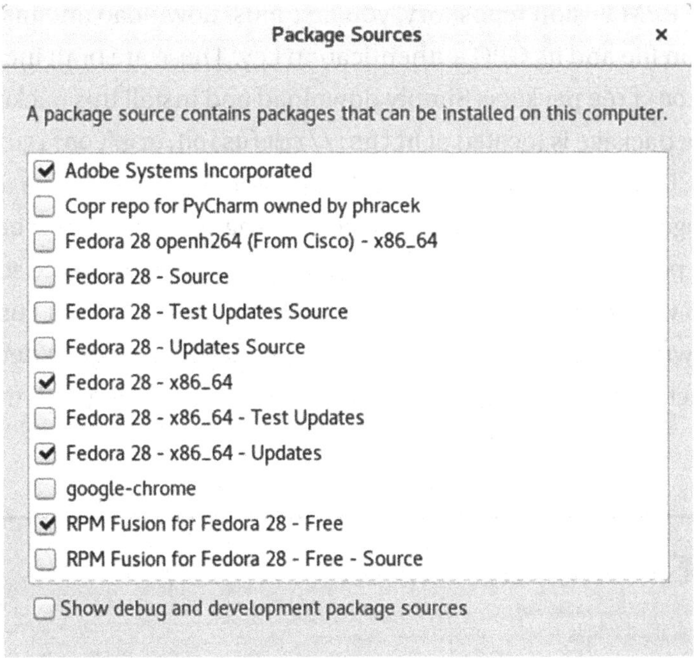

Figure 4-20. *Package Sources: Configured software repositories (Packages)*

You can also manage repositories using the dnf config-manager command with the --set-enabled and --set-disabled options. The following disables the RPM Fusion non-free repository.

```
sudo dnf config-manager --set-enabled rpmfusion-nonfree
```

You could later then enable it.

```
sudo dnf config-manager --set-enable rpmfusion-nonfree
```

To remove a repository, use the dnf remove command. This is a permanent removal.

Using the RPM Fusion Repository

The RPM Fusion repository (https://rpmfusion.org) holds popular third-party drivers and codecs. These include the vendor graphics drivers for Linux, when they become available, such as those provided by NVIDIA. Also included are multimedia codecs with licensing issues, such as MP3, AC3, and MPEG2 codecs, as well as MPEG4 and DivX (Xvid).

To access the RPM Fusion repository, you first must download and install both its DNF configuration file and its GPG authentication key. These are both included in RPM Fusion's `rpmfusion-free` package. Simply download and install this package using your web browser. The package is located at `https://rpmfusion.org/Configuration` (see Figure 4-21). Click the Configuration link at the top of the page to go to the Configuration page. There are free and non-free packages, with links for each. Be sure to install the free package first. The non-free package is optional. On the section titled "Graphical Setup via Firefox Web Browser," click the link labeled "RPM Fusion Free for Fedora 28" to download the `rpmfusion-free` configuration package. When you click the link, Fedora detects that it is a software package and opens a dialog with the option to install it directly.

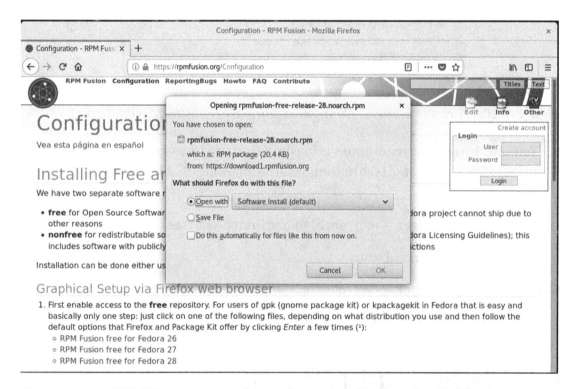

Figure 4-21. *RPM Fusion repository configuration file downloaded from rpmfusion.org*

After installing the free package, you can install the non-free package if you wish. Click the link labeled `RPM Fusion Nonfree for Fedora28`, listed under the second paragraph in the Graphical Setup section, then proceed with the install.

The page also tells you how to perform an installation of both free and non-free RPM Fusion configuration packages from the command line using the dnf command. The command is extensive and, instead of typing it on a command line in a terminal window, you can copy and paste the entire command from the web page to a terminal window. Click and drag the command on the web page to select it, then press Ctrl+c to copy it to the clipboard. Open a terminal window and press Ctrl+Shift+v to paste the command to the current command line. Then press Enter to run the command.

Once the repository is installed, you can open Software Sources to check that the RPM Fusion repository is enabled. On GNOME Software, select Software Repositories from its application menu to open the Software Repositories dialog and scroll down to the RPM Fusion for Fedora 28 entries. The ones for free and non-free should be enabled. On Packages, select Package Sources from its applications menu to open the Package Sources dialog, which should have the entries for Fedora 28 checked, both free and non-free.

With the RPM Fusion repository now enabled, you can use GNOME Software and Packages to search, select, and install any packages on its repository. Both RPM Fusion and the Fedora repositories have their packages intertwined on the GNOME Software and Packages software listings. When you first install the repository configuration, be sure to update your Packages package lists so that the new repository packages will be listed. From the Packages Applications menu, select Refresh Package Lists.

DnfDragora

DnfDragora is the replacement for the YUM Extender (dnf-yumex). It is an alternative desktop interface for managing software packages on your DNF repositories (see Figure 4-22). DnfDragora provides detailed package information and allows you to turn repositories on and off directly.

Figure 4-22. *DnfDragora (dnfdragora)*

DnfDragora displays three panes: a side pane for listing groups, a right pane for listing packages, and a bottom pane for display information about a selected package. A toolbar above the pane lets you organize and refine the display of your packages. The first menu button lets you choose to view all packages or to organize them by groups and display just those in the group (see Figure 4-23). The second menu lets you choose the type of packages you want displayed (All, Installed, To Be Updated, and Not Installed). For the searches you can search in package names, descriptions, summaries, or their filenames. Clicking a package displays detailed information about it, including a list of dependencies, files included with the package, a link to its repository, and the change log, if available. To install a selected package, click the Apply button at the bottom of the window.

Figure 4-23. *DnfDragora groups*

To manage your repositories, choose the Repositories entry from the File menu. The top pane lists your available repositories with checkmarks next to the ones that are enabled (see Figure 4-24). To enable other repositories, click their check boxes. Disable a repository, click its check box to remove the checkmark. Clicking on any repository entry displays details about the repository, such as the location of the cache it uses, if it is enabled, its gpgkey, the number of retries allowed, and the repository type.

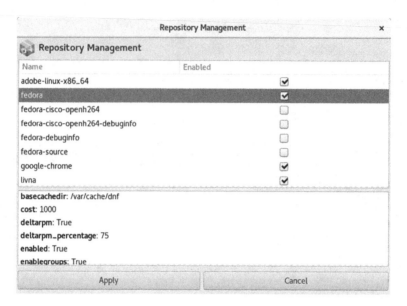

Figure 4-24. *DnfDragora Repository Management*

Installing Individual Packages with Your Browser

You can use your browser to download an individual package from a site directly. You should use this method only for packages not already available from DNF-supported repositories. This is true for certain packages, such as the RPM Fusion DNF configuration packages you need to install before you can access the RPM Fusion repository. You also have to install any needed dependent packages manually, as well as check system compatibility. Your Fedora web browsers will let you perform a download and install in one simple operation. A dialog opens that prompts you to open with the package installer, which invokes GNOME Software (see Figure 4-25, left). The package is downloaded, and you are asked if you want to install the file (see Figure 4-25, right). Subsequent dialogs show the installation progress.

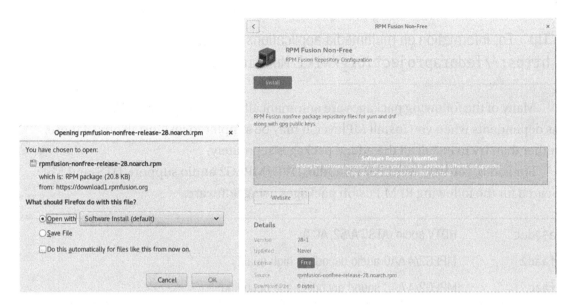

Figure 4-25. *Web browser package install*

On a GNOME desktop, packages that have already been downloaded can be installed with a simple right-click, then choose the install selection from the menu invoking GNOME Software, to perform the installation (`gnome-software`). As with the browser download, you are prompted to install the package.

Installing Some Popular Third-Party Software

For most third-party multimedia packages, you first install the DNF configuration file for a repository that carries them. Once configured, installation is a simple matter of using Software to search for and install packages. DNF downloads the package and performs the installation. It will also be careful to select the package for your architecture, such as x86_64 for 64-bit or i686 for 32-bit. DNF will ask for confirmation before installing, listing any dependent packages that will also have to be installed.

Multimedia Packages

For your third-party packages, you can use RPM Fusion, which carries collections of multimedia packages, including GStreamer and MPlayer. DVD/MPEG video players you might want include Xine, MPlayer, and VideoLAN. All support DVD, DVB, HDTV, H264, and MP3, provided the needed codecs are installed.

Tip   For information on multimedia applications available for Fedora, go to `https://fedoraproject.org/wiki/Multimedia`.

Many of the following packages are automatically selected and installed for you as dependents when you install MPlayer. It may be simpler to just install one of these, rather than try to install all the added packages separately.

For audio, you may want HDTV audio, DVD/MPEG2 audio support, DTS, and MP3. Search for the following RPM Fusion packages using Software.

a52dec	HDTV audio (ATSC A/52, AC3)
faad2	MPEG2/4 AAC audio decoding, high quality
faac	MPEG2/4 AAC sound encoding and decoding
libdca	DTS Coherent Acoustics playback capability
lame	MPEG1 and MPEG2 audio decoding

For video, you may want DVD video capability, MPEG and MPEG2 playback, DVB/HDTV playback, and H264 (HD media) decoding capability.

libdvbpsi	MPEG TS stream (DVB and PSI) decoding and encoding
vlc	DVD video playback capability, VideoLAN project
libdvdnav	DVD video menu navigation
libdvdcss	DVD video commercial decoding, Livna repo (`http://rpm.livna.org`)
x264	H264/AVC decoding and encoding (high-definition media)

For all GStreamer supported applications, you will want the bad and ugly packages.

gstreamer-plugins-bad	Not fully reliable codecs and tools for GStreamer, some with possible licensing issues
gstreamer-plugins-ugly	Reliable video and audio codecs for GStreamer that may have licensing issues

The Win32 codecs are not available on the Fedora repositories. Keep in mind that wmv files and Win32 codecs are already supported by the ffmpeg Linux codecs and will play on Totem and Dragon Player. You can download the Win32 codecs separately from the MPlayer website (www.mplayerhq.hu/MPlayer/releases/codecs).

Vendor Video Driver Support

You can obtain the NVIDIA vendor graphics drivers from RPM Fusion (the non-free repository). You can download and install them with DNF. RPM Fusion is the best repository for specialized kernel drivers and modules. Keep in mind, however, that due to open sourcing of some of the NVIDIA vendor driver software, the X.org and Nouveau open source versions are becoming almost as effective, especially for 2D display support. For normal usage, you might not need vendor driver support.

Installing the NVIDIA drivers can be a complex operation depending on what graphics card you have. The drivers are located on the RPM Fusion repository, not on Fedora. Check the RPM Fusion site for instructions on installing the NVIDIA drivers.

https://rpmfusion.org/Howto/Nvidia

For a simple install, a search on nvidia displays NVIDIA modules for each kernel version. The vendor graphic drivers use two packages, one for the supporting software and another for the kernel. The kernel modules are specific to the kernel you are using. Each time you update to a new kernel, you will require a new graphics kernel module created specifically for that kernel. This will be automatically downloaded and installed for you as a dependent package when you update your kernel (the RPM Fusion non-free repository must be active). The driver package is named xorg-x11-drv-nvidia, and the kernel module generator is named akmod-nvidia.

```
xorg-x11-drv-nvidia
akmod-nvidia
```

You can use a dnf list command entered in a terminal window with nvidia* to list all NVIDIA packages.

```
dnf list nvidia*
```

AMD drivers have been fully open sourced. You can download and install the driver from the Fedora repository. The name of the driver is amdgpu.

```
xorg-x11-drv-amdgpu
```

You can also install the drivers using GNOME Software's Add-ons Hardware Drivers tab (see Figure 4-26). Be sure that third-party repositories are enabled (Software Repositories dialog). Click on the driver you have determined that you need, such as the NVIDIA driver. This opens a GNOME Software software description dialog with an Install button and a description of the software including its version, its repository, and whether it is proprietary or free (License). Once you have installed the driver, the Install button changes to a Remove button. On the Hardware Drivers tab, a checkmark emblem appears on the upper-right corner of the driver icon, indicating that it is installed.

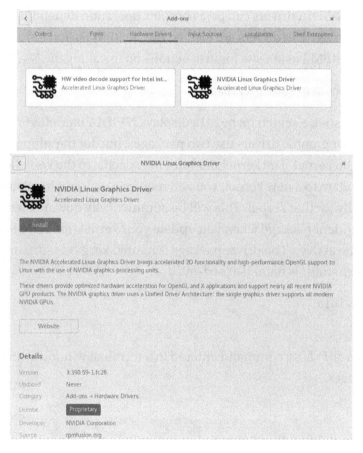

Figure 4-26. *Video Drivers install: GNOME Software Add-ons Hardware Drivers tab and install dialog*

Using Repositories

A few repositories provide much of the software you will normally require. The main Fedora software repository will most likely contain the software you want. Always check this repository first, before trying a third-party repository. Some specialized applications, such as vendor-supplied graphics drivers, as well as third-party multimedia support, can be located at `http://rpmfusion.org` and at `https://negativo17.org`. These repositories make up a set of software sites that you can use to provide most of the functionality users expect from a desktop system. All are DNF-compliant, with DNF configuration files designed for specific Fedora releases.

To see what packages are available, you can use your web browser to access the sites. Fedora and RPM Fusion provide `repodata` directories for detailed listings.

To use DNF on a software repository, DNF has to be configured to access them. This is a simple matter of listing the site's URL, both its web address and directory location. Configurations for repositories are placed in `repo` files located in the `/etc/yum.repos.d` directory on your Linux system. The `repo` files for Fedora are already installed. You must add `repo` files for RPM Fusion before you can access them with DNF. RPM Fusion provides RPM packages, free and non-free collections, named `rpmfusion-free-release-28.noarch.rpm` and `rpmfusion-nonfree-release-28.noarch.rpm`, on their website. When these are installed, they automatically set up the DNF configuration files. For RPM Fusion, these are `rpmfusion-free.repo` and `rpmfusion-nonfree.repo`, with corresponding update and development `repo` files.

The repository sites and their `repo` files are:

`https://download.fedoraproject.org`	The Fedora Repository, mirror link: Fedora-compliant software, `fedora.repo`
`https://download1.rpmfusion.org`	RPM Fusion: Repository for driver, multimedia, and other Fedora packages, `rpmfusion-free.repo` and `rpmfusion-nonfree.repo`
`https://negativo17.org/repos/`	negativo17.org: Repository for driver, multimedia, and other Fedora packages, `fedora-negativo17.repo`

Repository Repo Package Files

When you are installing packages, PackageKit, Yumex, and the dnf command automatically use the repo files to check your enabled repositories. One important exception to this rule is the initial install of the repository configuration files from third-party repositories. These configuration files (repo files) are usually contained in their own RPM packages. You download and install a repo package directly from the repository website, using your web browser. For example, the repo package for the RPM Fusion third-party Fedora DNF repository is rpmfusion-free-release-28.noarch.rpm. You download and install this package directly, using a web browser. Repository configuration files are located in the /etc/yum.repos.d directory and have the extension .repo.

Fedora Repository

The Fedora repository is already configured for use by DNF. To download any Fedora package, simply use GNOME Software, Packages, or enter the dnf command with the install option on a command line. The package will be detected, along with any dependent software, and you will be asked to confirm installation. The download and installation will be automatic. The first time you install a package from the Fedora repository, you are prompted to install the Fedora GPG key, used to authenticate the packages. Just click Yes to install the key.

A section of the following Fedora repo file (/etc/yum.repos.d/fedora.repo) lists several repository options. The name is Fedora, with releasever and basearch used to determine the release and architecture parts of the name. The mirrorlist option is used instead of baseurl, which is commented out (metalink provides mirror access, selecting the fastest available mirror). Again, the releasever is used to specify the release. The gpgkey used, RPM-GPG-KEY-fedora, is already installed in the /etc/pki/rpm-gpg directory. The skip_if_unavailable option is set to False so that the Fedora repository must always be checked.

```
[fedora]
name=Fedora $releasever - $basearch
failovermethod=priority
#baseurl=http://download.fedoraproject.org/pub/fedora/linux/
releases/$releasever/Everything/basearch/os/
```

```
metalink=http://mirrors.fedoraproject.org/metalink?repo=fedora-
$releasever&arch=$basearch
enabled=1
metadata expire=7d
repo-gpgcheck=0
type=rpm
gpgcheck=1
gpgkey=file:///etc/pki/rpm-gpg/RPM-GPG-KEY-fedora-$basearch
skip_if_unavailable=False
```

RPM Fusion

The https://rpmfusion.org site provides access to popular software for many software applications, including multimedia applications such as MPlayer, as well as those not included with Fedora, due to licensing issues. Several of the more popular packages include the vendor NVIDIA graphics drivers (when available). RPM Fusion specializes in configuring sometimes difficult drivers for compatibility with Fedora. For example, you can download the NVIDIA Linux driver directly from the NVIDIA website and try to install it on your Fedora system. But there can be complications, and the driver could require additional configuration. As an alternative, RPM Fusion provides a version of the driver that has already been configured for Fedora.

To configure DNF on your system to access https://rpmfusion.org, just install the rpmfusion-free-release and rpmfusion-nonfree-release packages for your version of Fedora. These will install the rpmfusion-free.repo and rpmfusion-nonfree.repo configuration files in the /etc/yum.repos.d directory, as well as download the RPM Fusion GPG key. You can install the GPG manually or just wait until you install a package from RPM Fusion, in which case, DNF will install it for you, after prompting for approval. Check the RPM Fusion configuration page at http://rpmfusion.org for details. The name of the package will be something like rpmfusion-free-release.

You can download and install the package directly with the rpm command from within a terminal window. Use a preceding sudo command for administrative access. The RPM Fusion site's configuration page provides a detailed example.

The GPG keys are included in the packages and installed automatically in the /etc/pki/rpm-gpg directory. They are named RPM-GPG-Key-rpmfusion-free-fedora and RPM-GPG-Key-rpmfusion-nonfree-fedora.

To see which packages are available on RPM Fusion, use your web browser to go to `https://download1.rpmfusion.org`. Here, you will find a listing of directories for each supported release. After selecting your release directory, you then choose your architecture, such as i386 (32-bit) or x86_64 (64-bit). Here, you will see a simple file listing of all available packages. Alternatively, on PackageKit, you could deselect all software sources except RPM Fusion, so that only the RPM Fusion packages are listed in the Software window.

Part of the `rpmfusion-free.repo` configuration file installed by the `rpmfusion-free-release` package is shown here. The configuration specifies the mirror list located at `http://mirrors.rpmfusion.org`.

```
[rpmfusion-free]
name=RPM Fusion for Fedora $releasever - Free
#baseurl=http://download1.rpmfusion.org/free/fedora/releases/$releasever/
Everything/$basearch/os/
metalink=https://mirrors.rpmfusion.org/metalink?repo=free-fedora-
$releasever&arch=$basearch
enabled=1
enabled-metadata=1
metadata expire=14d
gpgcheck=1
repo-gpgcheck=0
gpgkey=file:///etc/pki/rpm-gpg/RPM-GPG-KEY-rpmfusion-free-fedora-
$releasever
```

The corresponding part of the `rpmfusion-nonfree.repo` configuration file installed by the `rpmfusion-nonfree-release` package is shown here:

```
[rpmfusion-nonfree]
name=RPM Fusion for Fedora $releasever - NonFree
#baseurl=http://download1.rpmfusion.org/nonfree/fedora/
releases/$releasever/Everything/$basearch/os/
metalink=https://mirrors.rpmfusion.org/metalink?repo=nonfree-fedora-
$releasever&arch=$basearch
enabled=1
enabled-metadata=1
```

```
metadata expire=14d
gpgcheck=1
repo-gpgcheck=0
gpgkey=file:///etc/pki/rpm-gpg/RPM-GPG-KEY-rpmfusion-nonfree-fedora-$releasever
```

Livna (dvdcss)

The Livna repository (http://rpm.livna.org) provides access to one package, the commercial DVD video codec, called libdvdcss. Install the livna-release.rpm package. It contains the repository file, livna.repo.

```
[livna]
name=rpm.livna.org for $releasever - $basearch
#baseurl=http://rpm.livna.org/repo/$releasever/$basearch/ http://ftp-stud.
fht-esslingen.de/pub/Mirrors/rpm.livna.org/repo/$releasever/$basearch/
mirrorlist=http://rpm.livna.org/mirrorlist
failovermethod=roundrobin
enabled=1
gpgcheck=1
gpgkey=file:///etc/pki/rpm-gpg/RPM-GPG-KEY-livna
```

Adobe (Flash)

The Adobe repository provides access to the Adobe proprietary version of the Adobe Flash player for Linux. Adobe provides 32- and 64-bit software. The Fedora project Flash wiki explains the procedure in detail (see https://fedoraproject.org/wiki/Flash).

First, download the RPM package for the repository configuration. Select YUM for Linux.

```
https://get.adobe.com/flashplayer/
```

Then install the repository configuration package, called adobe-release. You can do this directly from the web browser by choosing to install and then clicking Yes, when prompted, to install the unsigned software, as the package key is not yet installed (it is included in the repository package). You could also first download the package, then install it with the following rpm command in a terminal window for the 64-bit version:

```
sudo su -c 'rpm -vhi adobe-release-x86_64-1.0-1.noarch.rpm'
```

159

This installs the /etc/yum.repos.d/adobe-linux-x86_64.repo file, shown here:

```
[adobe-linux-x86_64]
name=Adobe Systems Incorporated
baseurl=http://linuxdownload.adobe.com/linux/x86_64/
enabled=1
gpgcheck=1
gpgkey=file:///etc/pki/rpm-gpg/RPM-GPG-KEY-adobe-linux
```

Software Sources will list the repository as Adobe Systems Incorporated. You can then use GNOME Software and Packages to search for Flash and select the Flash package for installation. The Flash plugin package is flash-plugin and has the title "Adobe Flash Player".

The first time you install any package from the Adobe repository, you will be prompted to install its package key. A dialog will be displayed with the message "Do You Trust the Source of the Packages?". Click Yes to install the Adobe repository package key.

Alternatively, you can manually install the Adobe repository package key with the following command:

```
sudo su -c 'rpm --import /etc/pki/rpm-gpg/RPM-GPG-KEY-adobe-linux'
```

Restart Firefox to enable your Flash plugin. On the Tools ➤ Add-ons Plug-ins tab, you will find an entry for Flash.

Google

For Linux-compatible Google applications, you should configure access to the Google repository, which allows you to install applications such as Picasa from PackageKit. Google installs a separate repository file for each major application. Google Chrome has a google-chrome.repo file, and Google Earth has a google-earth.repo file. The signing key is installed automatically. Follow the instructions for the RPM at: https://www.google.com/linuxrepositories/.

Installation is performed using a terminal window. Click and drag to select the wget command on the browser.

```
wget https://dl-ssl.google.com/linux/linux_signing_key.pub
```

Then open a terminal window and press Ctrl+Shift+v to copy the command to that window. The signing key is then installed. Next, import the key with the following `rpm` command.

```
sudo rpm --import linux_signing_key.pub
```

A copy of the `google-chrome.repo` file follows:

```
[google-chrome]
name=google-chrome
baseurl=http://dl.google.com/linux/chrome/rpm/stable/x86_64
enabled=1
gpgcheck=1
gpgkey=https://dl.google.com/linux/linus/linux_signing_key.pub
```

DNF Configuration

DNF options are configured in the `/etc/dnf/dnf.conf` file, and the `/etc/yum.repos.d` directory holds repository (`repo`) files that list accessible DNF repositories. The repository files have the extension `.repo`. Check the `dnf.conf` man page for a listing of the different DNF options, along with entry formats. The `dnf.conf` file consists of different segments separated by bracket-encased headers, the first of which is always the main segment. Segments for different DNF server repositories can follow, beginning with the repository label encased in brackets. On Fedora, however, these are currently placed in separate repository files in the `/etc/yum.repos.d` directory. In addition to `dnf.conf`, DNF also supports an `/etc/dnf` directory that can hold additional configuration information.

/etc/dnf/dnf.conf

The `dnf.conf` file contains the main segment with settings for DNF options, as shown here:

```
[main]
gpgcheck=1
installonly_limit=3
clean_requirements_on_remove=True
```

gpgcheck is a repository option that is set globally for the repo files. It checks for GPG software signatures. The installonly_limit option limits the number of packages that can be installed concurrently. The clean_requirements_on_remove option checks for and removes unused dependent packages (packages installed only as dependencies).

There are also general DNF options, such as logdir, which lists the location of DNF logs, and pluginspath, which specifies the location of DNF plugins. You can elect to keep the downloaded packages with keepcache.

Repository Files: /etc/yum.repos.d

The repository entries in the repo files begin with a bracket-enclosed server ID, a single-word unique name. Repository-specific options govern the access of software repositories. These include gpgcheck, which checks for GPG software signatures; gpgkey, which specifies the location of the signature; metalink, which references fast links from a mirror list; and mirrorlist, which references a URL holding mirror sites. The repository-specific name option provides a name for the repository. The URL reference is then assigned to the baseurl option. There should be only one baseurl option, but you can list several URLs for it, each on its own line. With the mirrorlist option, you can just list a URL for a list of mirrors, instead of listing each mirror separately in the baseurl option. The URL entries often use special variables, releasever and basearch. The releasever obtains the release information from the distroverpkg option set in the main segment. The basearch variable specifies the architecture you are using, as determined by DNF, such as i386. The enabled option actually turns on access to the repository. By setting it to 0, you choose not to access a specific repository. The gpgcheck option specifies that you should perform a GPG authentication check to make sure the download is intact. The enabled option will enable a repository, allowing DNF to use it. You can set the enable bit to 0 or 1 to turn off or on access to the repository.

The gpgkey option provides an authentication check on the package to make sure you have downloaded the appropriate version. Downloads can sometimes be intercepted and viruses inserted. The GPG key check protects against such attacks. It can also check to make sure the download is not corrupt or incomplete. The Fedora public GPG key may already be installed on your system. If you have already used DNF, you have already downloaded it. The Fedora GPG key allows you to access Fedora packages. The RPM Fusion free and non-free repositories use their own public keys, referenced with the gpgkey option in their repos files. The keys for all these repositories will be installed in the /etc/pki/rpmgpg directory.

Managing DNF Caches

With the keepcache option enabled, DNF will keep its downloaded packages in the /var/cache/dnf directory. Should you want to save or copy any particular packages, you can locate them there. Caching lets you easily uninstall and reinstall packages without having to download them again. The package is retained in the cache. If caching is disabled, the packages are automatically deleted after they are installed.

Your cache can increase rapidly, so you may want to clean it out on occasion. If you just want to delete these packages, as they are already installed, you can use the clean packages option.

```
dnf clean packages
```

Manually Installing Packages with rpm

You can use the rpm command to install individual RPM packages that are not part of a DNF repository. Keep in mind that most software resides on DNF-supported, Fedora-compliant repositories. For such software, you use the dnf command or the Packages frontend. DNF has the advantage of automatically installing any dependent packages, whereas the rpm command, although it will detect needed packages, will not install them. Using only the rpm command, you would have to separately install any dependent packages in the correct order.

The rpm command is useful for packages that are not part of any DNF-supported repository, such as custom-made packages, and that have few or no dependent packages. You can also use the rpm command to bypass DNF, forcing installation of a particular package, instead of from DNF repositories.

The rpm command performs installation, removal, and verification of software packages. An RPM package is an archive of software files. Each archive has a name that ends with .rpm, indicating it is a software package that can be installed by the Red Hat Package Manager.

The rpm command uses a set of options to determine what action to take. The -i option installs the specified software package, and the -U option updates a package. With an -e option, rpm uninstalls the package. A q placed before an i (-qi) queries the system to see if a software package is already installed and displays information about the software (-qpi queries an uninstalled package file). The rpm command with no options provides a complete list of rpm options. A set of commonly used options is shown in Table 4-5.

Table 4-5. *rpm Command Options*

Option	Action
-U	Updates a package
-i	Installs a package
-e	Removes a package
-qi	Displays information for an installed package
-ql	Displays a file list for an installed package
-qpi	Displays information from an RPM package file (used for uninstalled packages)
-qpl	Displays the file list from an RPM package file (used for uninstalled packages)
-K	Authenticates and performs an integrity check on a package

The software package name includes information about the version and release date. In the next example, the user installs the xvidcore package using the rpm command. Notice that the full filename is entered. In most cases, you would install packages with the -U option, for update. If the package is not already installed, -U will install it. The following examples use the DivX xvidcore RPM packages downloaded from http://rpmfusion.org.

```
$ rpm -Uvh xvidcore-1.3.5-1.fc28.x86_64.rpm
```

To list the full name, you can use the ls command with the first few characters and an asterisk (*), as follows:

```
ls xvid*
```

You can also use the * to match the remainder of the name, as in the following:

```
ls xvidccore-1*.rpm
```

When RPM performs an installation, it first checks for any dependent packages. These are other software packages with programs the application you are installing has to use. If other dependent packages must be installed first, RPM cancels the installation and lists those packages. You can install those packages and then repeat the installation of the application. To determine if a package is already installed, use the -qi option with rpm. The -q stands for query. To obtain a list of all the files the package has installed, as

well as the directories it installed to, use the -ql option. To query package files, add the p
option. The -qpi option displays information about a package, and -qpl lists the files in
it. The following example lists all the files in the xvidcore package:

```
$ rpm -qpl xvidcore-1.3.5-1.fc28.x86_64.rpm
```

To remove a software package from your system, first use rpm -qi to make sure it is
actually installed, then use the -e option to uninstall it. As with the -qi and -e options,
you needn't use the full name of the installed file. You only need the name of the
application. In the following example, the user removes the DivX xvidcore package from
the system:

```
$ rpm -e xvidcore
```

Package Security Check

DNF automatically performs integrity and authentication checks on all software
downloaded from Fedora-compliant repositories, confirming that the package was
obtained from a valid source, and that it has not been modified. Each repository
configuration file in the /etc/yum.repos.d directory will have its gpgcheck option set
to 1. Should you want to turn off this check for a particular repository, you can set its
gpgcheck option to 0.

For packages not downloaded from a DNF repository, you may want to manually
check their integrity and authentication. To authenticate a package, you check its
digital signature. Packages are signed with encrypted digital keys that can be decrypted
using the public key provided by the author of the package. This public key has to be
downloaded and installed on the encryption tool used on your system. Fedora, along
with most Linux distributions, uses the GNU Privacy Guard (GPG) encryption tool. To
use a public key to authenticate an RPM package, you first must install it in the RPM
key database. For all RPM packages that are part of the Fedora distribution, you can use
the Fedora public key, placed during installation in the /etc/pki/rpm-gpg/ directory.
Here, you will find the RPM GPG keys for all your configured repositories, including
RPM Fusion.

The Fedora key is RPM-GPG-KEY-fedora-28-primary. Several keys are links to this key, such as RPM-GPG-KEY-28-fedora and RPM-GPG-KEY-fedora-28-x86_64. The RPM Fusion keys will have the same structure, with a primary key, such as RPM-GPG-KEY-rpmfusion-free-fedora-28-primary, and links to it, such as RPM-GPG-KEY-rpmfusion-free-fedora-28.

You must import the key to the RPM database before you can check Fedora RPM packages. The first time you use PackageKit to install a package, you will be prompted to import the GPG key. Once imported, you need not import it again. Alternatively, you can manually import the key, as follows:

```
rpm --import /etc/pki/rpm-gpg/RPM-GPG-KEY-fedora
```

If you have downloaded an RPM package from another site, you can also download and install its public key, with which you can authenticate that package. For example, there are public keys for both the RPM Fusion free and non-free Fedora DNF repositories. These are included in the RPM Fusion DNF configuration files, which you can download and install, such as rpmfusion-free-release-28.noarch.rpm for RPM Fusion repositories. The keys will be automatically installed with the configuration.

Once the public key is installed, you can check the package authentication using the rpm command with the -K option.

```
rpm -K xvidcore-1.3.5-1.fc28.x86_64.rpm
```

To see a list of all the keys you have imported, you can use the -qa option and match the gpg-pubkey* pattern. Using rpm with the -qi option and the public key, you can display detailed information about the key. The following example shows the Fedora public key:

```
$ rpm -qa gpg-pubkey*
gpg-pubkey-4f2a6fd2-3f9d9d3b
gpg-pubkey-db42a60e-37ea5438
```

You can manually check a package's integrity with the rpm command with the -K and the --nosignature options. A value called the MD5 digest measures the contents of a package. If the value is incorrect, the package has been tampered with. Some packages provide just digest values, allowing only integrity checks. In the next example, the user checks whether the xvidcore package has been tampered with. The --nosignature option says not to perform authentication, performing the integrity check only.

```
rpm -K --nosignature xvidcore-1.3.5-1.fc28.x86_64.rpm
```

Installing Source Code Applications

Some applications are available for Linux in source code format. These programs are stored in a compressed archive that you have to decompress and then extract. The resulting source code can then be configured, compiled, and installed on your system. Always check the README and INSTALL files that come with the source code to check the appropriate method for creating and installing that software. Be sure that you have installed all development packages onto your system. Development packages contain the key components, such as the compiler, GNOME and KDE headers and libraries, and preprocessors. You cannot compile the source code software without them.

Several tools you may need for installing and managing source code are already be installed. To install the full set of tool, use the groupinstall option with "Development Tools" and "C Development Tools and Libraries".

```
sudo dnf groupinstall "Development Tools"
sudo dnf groupinstall "C Development Tools and Libraries"
```

Extracting the Archive: Archive Manager (File Roller)

From the desktop, you can extract compressed archives with Archive Manager. Archive Manager is the Fileroller application. Archive Manager displays the top-level contents of the archive, which you can browse if you want, even reading such text files as README and INSTALL. You also can see which files will be installed. To extract the archive, click Extract.

Alternatively, on a command line (terminal window), you can use the tar command to extract archives. On the command line, enter the tar command with the xvjf options (j for bz2 and z for gz), as in the following:

```
tar xvjf freeciv-2.6.1.tar.bz2
```

Configure, Compile, and Install

Extracting the archive creates a directory with the name of the software, in this case, freeciv-2.3.4. Once it is extracted, you must configure, compile, and install the software, using command-line commands (terminal window).

Change to the software directory with the `cd` command.

```
cd freeciv-2.6.1
```

Run the command `./configure` to generate a compiler configuration for your particular system (creates a custom makefile used to compile the source code).

```
./configure
```

Compile the software with the `make` command.

```
make
```

Then install the program with the `make install` command.

```
make install
```

PART II

Applications

CHAPTER 5

Office Applications, Email, Editors, and Databases

Several office suites are now available for Fedora (see Table 5-1). These include professional-level word processors, presentation managers, drawing tools, and spreadsheets. The freely available versions are described in this chapter.

Table 5-1. *Linux Office Suites*

Website	Description
https://www.libreoffice.org	LibreOffice open source office suite
https://www.calligra.org	Calligra suite, for KDE
https://www.openoffice.org	Apache OpenOffice
https://www.codeweavers.com	CrossOver Office (Microsoft Office support)
https://www.scribus.net	Scribus desktop publishing tool

Linux provides many text editors that range from simple text editors to those with complex features such as spell checking, buffers, or complex searches. All generate character text files and can be used to edit Linux text files.

Fedora also provides a wide range of electronic mail applications, including desktop email applications featuring calendars and address books. Evolution and Thunderbird are the primary applications, both of which support GNOME Contacts. Newsreaders are also supported.

Fedora also supports several ebook readers, such as Calibre and FBReader, which run natively on Linux.

Fedora includes MySQL and PostgreSQL open source databases in its distribution, which can support smaller databases. Several database management systems are also available for Linux.

171

© Richard Petersen 2018
R. Petersen, *Beginning Fedora Desktop*, https://doi.org/10.1007/978-1-4842-3882-0_5

Office Applications

LibreOffice is currently the primary office suite supported by Fedora. Calligra is an office suite designed for use with KDE. CodeWeavers CrossOver Office provides reliable support for running Microsoft Office Windows applications directly on Linux, integrating them with KDE and GNOME. You can also download the Apache OpenOffice suite (originally, Oracle/StarOffice). For desktop publishing, especially PDF generation, you can use Scribus, a cross-platform tool available from the Fedora repository.

LibreOffice

LibreOffice is a fully integrated suite of office applications developed as an open source project and freely distributed to all. It is the primary office suite for Fedora, accessible from the Applications overview. LibreOffice is the open source and freely available office suite derived originally from OpenOffice. LibreOffice is supported by the Document Foundation, which was established after Oracle's acquisition of Sun, the main developer for OpenOffice. LibreOffice is now the primary open source office software for Linux. LibreOffice has replaced OpenOffice as the default office software for most Linux distributions.

LibreOffice includes word processing, spreadsheet, presentation, and drawing applications (see Table 5-2). Versions of LibreOffice exist for Linux, Windows, and MacOS. You can obtain information such as online manuals and FAQs, as well as current versions, from the LibreOffice website at `https://www.libreoffice.org`.

Table 5-2. *LibreOffice.org Applications*

Application	Description
Calc	LibreOffice spreadsheet
Draw	LibreOffice drawing application
Writer	LibreOffice word processor
Math	LibreOffice mathematical formula composer
Impress	LibreOffice presentation manager
Base	Database frontend for accessing and managing a variety of different databases

LibreOffice is an integrated suite of applications. You can open the writer, spreadsheet, or presentation application directly from the Applications overview. The word processing, spreadsheet, and presentations applications are also accessible from the Launcher: Writer, Calc, and Impress. You can also open existing office documents (Open button) and manage document templates. Buttons at the bottom of the dialog let you download new features and templates and access the LibreOffice website.

The LibreOffice Writer word processor supports standard word processing features, such as cut-and-paste, spell checking, and text formatting, as well as paragraph styles (see Figure 5-1). Context menus let you format text easily. Wizards (Letter, Web Page, Fax, and Agenda) let you generate different kinds of documents quickly. You can embed objects within documents, such as using Draw to create figures that you can then drag and drop to the Writer document. LibreOffice Writer is compatible with earlier versions of Microsoft Word. It will read and convert Word 2003 and earlier documents to a LibreOffice Writer document, preserving most features, including contents, tables, and indexes. Writer documents also can be saved as Word documents.

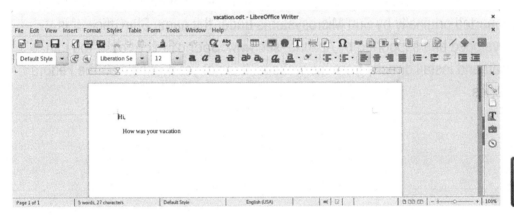

Figure 5-1. *LibreOffice: Writer word processor*

LibreOffice provides access to many database files. File types supported include ODBC (Open Database Connectivity), JDBC (Java), MySQL, PostgreSQL, and MDB (Microsoft Access) database files. You can also create your own simple databases. Check the LibreOffice Features ➤ Base page at `https://www.libreoffice.org/discover/base` for detailed information on drivers and supported databases.

LibreOffice Calc is a professional-level spreadsheet. With LibreOffice Math (LibreOffice Formula), you can create formulas that you can embed in a text document. With the presentation manager (LibreOffice Impress), you can create images for presentations, such as circles, rectangles, and connecting elements like arrows, as well as vector-based illustrations. Impress supports advanced features, such as morphing objects, grouping objects, and defining gradients. Draw is a sophisticated drawing tool that includes 3D modeling tools (LibreOffice Drawing). You can create simple or complex images, including animation text aligned on curves. LibreOffice also includes a printer setup tool with which you can select printers, fonts, paper sizes, and page formats.

Also for use on GNOME is Scribus, the open source desktop publishing tool (see Figure 5-2) at `www.scribus.net`. Scribus provides professional-level page layout capabilities for all Linux distribution, with color management and PDF generation.

Note   The former Oracle OpenOffice suite is now Apache OpenOffice. It is a fully integrated and Microsoft Office–compatible suite of office applications developed and supported originally by Sun Microsystems under the name StarOffice. It is now developed and supported by Apache; see `www.openoffice.org`. You can download and install directly from the website. It is not yet available on the Fedora repositories.

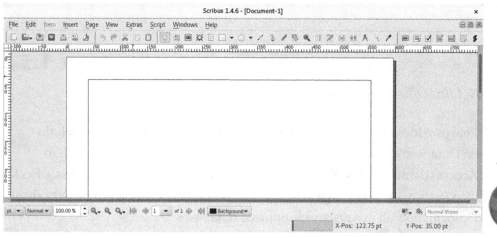

Figure 5-2. *Scribus desktop publisher*

Calligra

Calligra is an integrated office suite for the K Desktop Environment (KDE), consisting of several office applications, including a word processor, a spreadsheet, and graphics applications (`calligra` package). Calligra is the new version of KOffice, integrating many of the older applications provided by KOffice. Calligra allows components from any one application to be used in another, allowing you to embed a spreadsheet from Calligra Sheets or diagrams from Karbon in a Calligra Words document. It also uses the open document format (ODF) for its files, providing cross-application standardization. There is also a Windows version available. You can obtain more information about Calligra from `https://www.calligra.org`.

Currently, Calligra includes Calligra Sheets, Calligra Flow, Calligra Words, Karbon, Krita, Plan, Calligra Stage, Braindump, and Kexi (accessible from Office and Graphics; see Table 5-3). The contact application, Kontact, has been spun off as a separate project. Kontact is an integrated contact application including Kmail, Korganizer, Kaddressbook, and Knotes. Calligra Sheets is a spreadsheet; Calligra Stage is a presentation application; Karbon is a vector graphics program; and Calligra Words is a publisher-like word processor. Krita is a paint and image editor. Kexi provides database integration with Calligra applications, currently supporting PostgreSQL and MySQL.

Table 5-3. *Calligra Applications*

Application	Description
Braindump	Whiteboards for notes, images, and charts
Calligra Flow	Flowchart applications
Calligra Stage	Presentation application
Calligra Words	Word processor (desktop publisher)
Calligra Sheets	Spreadsheet
Karbon	Vector graphics program
Kexi	Database integration
Plan	Project management and planning
Krita	Paint and image-manipulation program
Kontact (separate project)	Contact application including mail, address book, and organizer

Calligra Sheets is the spreadsheet application, and it incorporates the basic operations found in most spreadsheets, with formulas similar to those used in MS Excel. You can also embed charts, pictures, or formulas using Krita and Karbon. With Calligra Stage, you can create presentations consisting of text and graphics modeled using different fonts, orientations, and attributes, such as colors. Karbon is a vector-based graphics program, much like Adobe Illustrator and LibreOffice Draw. It supports the standard graphic operations, such as rotating, scaling, and aligning objects. Calligra Words can best be described as a desktop publisher, with many of the features found in publishing applications. Although it is a fully functional word processor, Calligra Words sets up text in frames that are placed on the page like objects. Frames, like objects in a drawing program, can be moved, resized, and reoriented. You can organize frames into a frame set, having text flow from one to the other.

GNOME Office Applications

There are several GNOME applications that are used for Office tasks, including AbiWord, Gnumeric, Evince, and Evolution. These applications are located on the Fedora repository. A current listing of the common GNOME applications for Office related tasks is shown in Table 5-4. All applications implement the support for embedding components, ensuring drag-and-drop capability throughout the GNOME interface.

Table 5-4. *Office Applications for GNOME*

Application	Description
AbiWord	Cross-platform word processor
Gnumeric	Spreadsheet
Evince	Document viewer
Evolution	Integrated email, calendar, and personal organizer
Dia	Diagram and flowchart editor
GnuCash	Personal finance manager
Glom	Database frontend for PostgreSQL database
glabels	Label designer
Inkscape	Vector graphics and presentation creation

AbiWord is an open source word processor that aims to be a complete cross-platform solution, running on Mac, UNIX, and Windows, as well as Linux. It is part of a set of desktop productivity applications being developed by the AbiSource project (`www.abisource.com`).

Gnumeric is a professional-level GNOME spreadsheet meant to replace commercial spreadsheets. Gnumeric supports standard desktop spreadsheet features, including auto filling and cell formatting, and an extensive number of formats. Gnumeric also supports plugins, making it possible to extend and customize its capabilities easily.

Dia is a drawing program designed to create diagrams, such as database, circuit object, flowchart, and network diagrams. You can create elements along with lines and arcs with different types of endpoints, such as arrows or diamonds. Data can be saved in XML format, making it transportable to other applications.

GnuCash (`www.gnucash.org`) is a personal finance application for managing accounts, stocks, and expenses.

Running Microsoft Office on Linux: Wine and CrossOver

One of the concerns that new Linux users have relates to the kind of access they will have to their Microsoft Office files, particularly Word files. The major Linux Office suites, including Calligra, LibreOffice, and Oracle OpenOffice, all read and manage Microsoft Office files.

Wine (Windows Compatibility Layer) allows you to run many Windows applications directly, using a supporting virtual windows API. See the Wine website for a list of supported applications; see also `www.winehq.org`, the AppDB tab. Well-written applications may run directly from Wine, like the Newsbin newsreader. Each user can install a version of Wine with its own simulated C partition on which Windows applications are installed. The simulated drive is installed as `drive_c` in the `.wine` directory. The `.wine` directory is a hidden directory. It is not normally displayed with the `ls` command or the GNOME file manager (View ➤ Show Hidden Files). You can also use any of your Linux directories for your Windows application data files instead of the simulated C drive. These are referenced by Windows applications as the `z:` drive.

It is possible to install Microsoft Office on Fedora using Wine. Although there may be difficulties with the latest Microsoft Office versions, earlier versions, such as 2002, should work fine for the most part (see `www.winehq.org`, AppDB tab, search on Word). Applications are rated platinum, gold, silver, bronze, and garbage. Although effective, Wine support is not as stable as CrossOver.

CrossOver Office is a commercial product that lets you install and run most Microsoft Office applications (it has a silver rating). CrossOver Office was developed by CodeWeavers, which also supports Windows web browser plugins as well as several popular Windows applications, such as Adobe Photoshop. CrossOver features both standard and professional versions, providing reliable application support. You can find out more about CrossOver Office at `www.codeweavers.com`.

CrossOver can be installed either for private multiuser mode or managed multiuser mode. In private multiuser mode, each user installs Windows software, such as full versions of Office. In managed multiuser mode, the Windows software is installed once, and all the users share it. Once the software is installed, you will see a Windows Applications menu on the main menu, from which you can start your installed Windows software. The applications will run within a Linux window, but they will appear just as if they were running in Windows.

With VMware, you can run Windows under Linux, allowing you to run Windows applications, including Microsoft Office, on your Linux system. For more information, check the VMware website at `https://www.vmware.com`.

Another option, for users with high-powered computers that support virtualization, is to install the Windows OS on a virtual machine, using the Boxes virtual machine manager. You could then install and run Windows on the virtual machine and install Microsoft Office on it.

GNOME Documents

You can use the GNOME Documents application to access and search for local and cloud-based documents. Documents can be text (word processing), spreadsheets, presentations, or PDF files. Currently, both Google docs and Microsoft SkyDrive documents are supported. You have to enable access from the Online Accounts dialog on GNOME Settings.

GNOME Documents is accessible from the Applications overview. The Documents dialog shows tabs for both Documents and Collections. Documents lists your local and cloud-based documents (see Figure 5-3). The Documents GNOME applications menu lets you view the documents in a grid (icons) or as a list. Collections are categories you can set up to organize your documents. There are buttons at the right of the title bar for searching, sorting, and editing. Click the Search button to open a search box with a menu that lets you search for source (local or cloud), type, and search target (title or author).

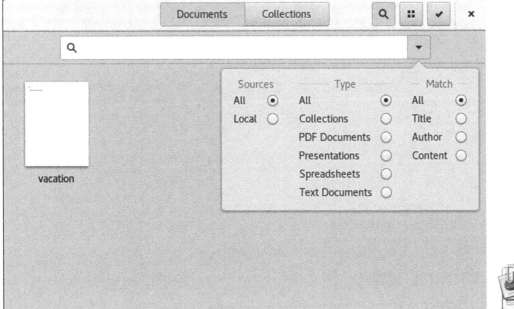

Figure 5-3. *GNOME Documents, with search*

Click the checkmark button at the top right to open a taskbar, which lets you open the document or print it (see Figure 5-4). In the list view, click the check box to the left of the document you want to perform the task on. In the grid view, a check box is displayed at the lower right of each icon. When you click a check box, the taskbar is displayed with buttons to open the document in the appropriate application, print the document, and delete it. The Properties button displays information about the document. The Collections button lets you place the document in a collection. When you're finished, click the Done button.

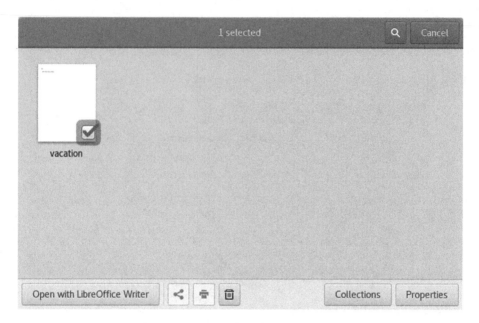

Figure 5-4. *GNOME Documents tasks*

Document Viewers and Scanning (PostScript, PDF, and DVI)

Although technically considered graphics applications, PostScript, PDF, DVI, and viewers are more commonly used with Office applications (see Table 5-5). Evince and Okular can display both PostScript (.ps) and PDF (.pdf) files. Evince is the default document viewer for GNOME. It is started automatically whenever you double-click a PDF file on the GNOME desktop. Okular is the default document viewer for KDE, with its overview icon as Okular.

Table 5-5. *PostScript, PDF, and DVI Viewers*

Viewer	Description
Evince	Document viewer for PostScript, DVI, and PDF files
Okular	KDE tool for displaying PDF, DVI, and PostScript files (replaces KPDF, Kghostview, and Kdvi)
Xpdf	X Window System tool for displaying PDF files only
Acrobat Reader for Linux	Adobe PDF viewer and ebook reader (`https://get.adobe.com/flashplayer/otherversions`)
Scribus	Desktop publisher for generating PDF documents
Simple Scan	GNOME Scanner interface for scanners (Graphics ➤ Simple Scan)
Yagf and cuneiform	OCR text conversion supporting multiple languages (install with `dnf`)

Okular, Evince, and Xpdf are PDF viewers. They include many of the standard Adobe Reader features, such as zoom, two-page display, and full-screen mode. Alternatively, you can use Acrobat Reader from Adobe to display PDF files. You can install it with Packages once you have enabled the Adobe repository (`https://get.adobe.com/flashplayer/otherversions/` as Linux and (Yum)). The package name is `flash-plugin`.

All these viewers can also print documents. To generate PDF documents, you can use LibreOffice Writer or the Scribus desktop publisher (`https://www.scribus.net`), and to edit PDF documents, you can use `pdfedit`.

Linux also features a professional-level typesetting tool, called TeX, commonly used to compose complex mathematical formulas. TeX generates a DVI document that can be displayed by DVI viewers, several of which are available for Linux. DVI files generated by the TeX document application can be viewed by Evince, Okular, and LibreOffice.

To scan documents directly, you can use Simple Scan, which you can save as JPEG, PNG, or PDF files. For OCR tasks, you can use cuneiform. Yagf provides a desktop frontend for cuneiform, allowing you to scan and convert text. You can choose from several languages.

Ebook Readers: FBReader and Calibre

On Fedora, you can use the Linux versions of Calibre and FBReader for ebooks (see Table 5-6). FBReader is an open source reader that can read non-DRM ebooks, including Mobipocket, HTML, EPUB, text, and RTF (install the fbreader-gtk package). The toolbar holds operations that move you through the text and configure your reader, adding books and setting interface preferences (see Figure 5-5). To see your selection of books, click the Library Tree icon on the left. You can organize text by author or tag. On the Options window, the Library tab lets you choose where your books are stored.

Table 5-6. *Ebook Readers*

Reader	Description
Calibre	Ebook reader and library, also converts various inputs to EPUB ebooks
Ebook reader (Ebook reader)	FBReader ebook reader, search under E-book reader (install with dnf)
Kindle Cloud Reader	Amazon Kindle ebook reader

About FBReader

FBReader is an e-book reader for Linux/Windows XP PDA/UMPC/desktop computer. FBReader supports several e-book formats: *ePub, fb2, chm, rtf, plucker,* etc. Direct reading from *zip, tar, gzip* and *bzip2* archives is also supported.

Figure 5-5. *FBReader ebook reader*

Calibre reads PDF, EPUB, Lit (Microsoft), and Mobipocket ebooks (see Figure 5-6). Calibre functions as a library for accessing and managing your ebooks. Calibre can convert many document files and ebooks to the EPUB format, the new open source standard used by Apple (iPad) and Amazon (Kindle). It can take as conversion input text, HTML, RTF, and ODT (LibreOffice), as well as ebooks.

Note   For older PDAs, you can use the pilot tools to access your handheld device, transferring information between it and your system. You can use the J-Pilot, KPilot, and GnomePilot applications to access your PDA from your desktop. The `pilot-link` package holds tools you can use to access your PDA. Check `www.pilot-link.org` for detailed documentation and useful links.

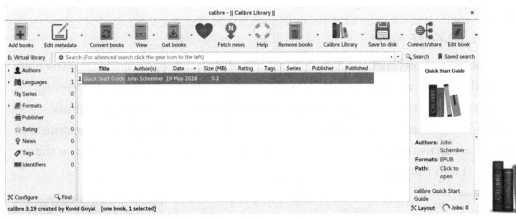

Figure 5-6. *Calibre ebook reader and converter*

GNOME Notes

The GNOME Notes (Bijiben) application lets you create and organize simple notes on your desktop. The Notes window lists your new and recent notes, showing the note title and the first few lines of text (see Figure 5-7). In the header bar, the search button opens a search box that lets you search for notes. The list button lets you switch between icon and list views. The check button lets you delete or organize your notes. A check box is displayed at the lower-right corner of the note icons. Clicking on that check box opens a taskbar at the bottom with buttons to delete the note, add it to a collection (notebooks), or email it. There is also a color button that you can use the background color.

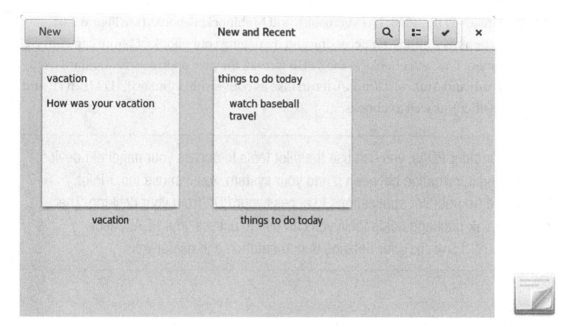

Figure 5-7. *GNOME Notes*

To create a new note, click the New button on the title bar to open a new text. The first line is the title of your note. Press the Enter key to move to the next line (see Figure 5-8). A color button lets you change the background color. The task menu (menu button) provides undo/redo functions, deletion, and email options. You can also add the note to a notebook. You can use notebooks to organize your notes. The share button lets you share the note with other users.

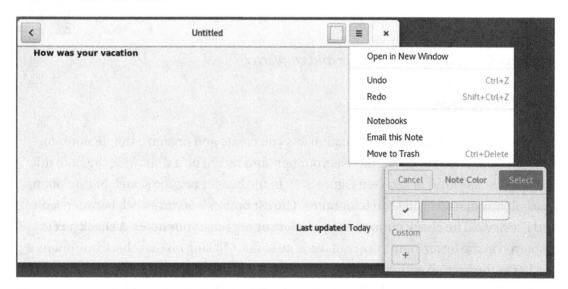

Figure 5-8. *GNOME Documents tasks*

Clocks

Two helpful tools are the clocks and weather applications. Clocks has four tabs: World, Alarm, Stopwatch, and Timer. The World tab displays the current time at any city and at your current location (see Figure 5-9). Click the New button to open a dialog in which you can add a city. To remove a city, click the check button to display a check box in the lower-right corner of each time icon. Check the ones you want to delete, and then click the Delete button. The Alarm tab works as an alarm clock. The Stopwatch tab operates a stopwatch, letting you mark laps. The timer counts down in time. You set the start amount.

Figure 5-9. GNOME Clocks, World tab

Weather

The weather tool lets you display the weather at any city. Click the Places button to open a dialog in which you can enter the name of a city. A partial entry is matched, giving you a listing of possible cities. Choose the one you want. A full image of the weather for that city is displayed, with the temperature and forecast for the next 24 hours, and a sidebar with the forecast for the next several days (see Figure 5-10). To see recently viewed cities, click the Places button to open a dialog where you can choose a city from the Recently Viewed list (see Figure 5-11).

Figure 5-10. *GNOME Weather*

Figure 5-11. *GNOME Weather: City with forecast*

Editors

The Fedora desktops (GNOME and KDE) support powerful text editors with full mouse support, scroll bars, and menus. These include basic text editors, such as Gedit and Kate, as well as word processors, such as LibreOffice Word, AbiWord, and KWord. Fedora also provides the cursor-based editors Nano, Vim, Emacs, and Leafpad. Nano is a cursor-based editor with an easy-to-use interface supporting menus and mouse selection (if it's run from a terminal window). Vim is an enhanced version of the vi text editor used on UNIX. These editors use simple, cursor-based operations to give you a full-screen format. Table 5-7 lists several desktop editors for Linux. Vim and Emacs have powerful editing features that have been refined over the years. Emacs, in particular, is extensible to a full-development environment for programming new applications. Later versions of Emacs and Vim—such as GNU Emacs, XEmacs, and Gvim—provide support for mouse, menu, and window operations.

***Table* 5-7.** *Desktop Editors*

Application	Description
Desktop	
KEdit	Text editor
Kate	Text and program editor
Words	Desktop publisher, part of Calligra
Gedit	Text editor
GNU Emacs	Emacs editor with X Window System support
XEmacs	X Window System version of Emacs editor
gvim	Vim version with X Window System support
AbiWord	Word processor (install with **dnf**)
OpenWriter	LibreOffice word processor that can edit text files
Command-Line Interface	
Vim	Vim version of vi
Emacs	Emacs command-line editor ·
Nano	Screen-based command-line interface editor (install with dnf)
Leafpad	Screen-based command-line interface editor with mouse support when run from a terminal window on desktop (install with dnf)

Text editors are often used in system administration tasks to change or add entries in Linux configuration files found in the /etc directory or in the user's initialization or application configuration files located in a user's home directory (dot files). You can use any text editor to work on source code files for any of the programming languages or shell program scripts.

GNOME Text Editor: Gedit

The Gedit editor is the basic text editor for the GNOME desktop. It provides full mouse support, implementing standard desktop operations, such as cut-and-paste to move text, and click-and-drag to select and move/copy text. It supports standard text-editing operations such as Find and Replace. You can use Gedit to create and modify your text files, including configuration files. Gedit also provides more advanced features, such as Print Preview and configurable levels of undo/redo operations, and it can read data from pipes. It features a plugin menu that provides added functionality, and it includes plugins for spell checking, encryption, email, and text-based web page display.

KDE Editor: Kate (KWrite)

The KDE editor Kate provides full mouse support, implementing standard desktop operations, such as cut-and-paste to move text, and click-and-drag to select and move/copy text. The editor is accessible from the Applications ➤ Utilities menu on the KDE desktop, and as KWrite on GNOME. Kate is an advanced editor, with such features as spell checking, font selection, and highlighting. Most commands can be selected by using menus. A toolbar of icons for common operations is displayed across the top of the Kate window. A sidebar displays panels for a file selector and a file list. With the file selector, you can navigate through the file system, selecting files to access. Kate also supports multiple views of a document, letting you display segments in their own windows, vertically or horizontally. You can also open several documents at the same time, moving among them with the file list. Kate is designed to be a program editor for editing software programming/development-related source code files. Kate can format the syntax for different programming languages, such as C, Perl, Java, and XML.

Leafpad

Leafpad is a very simple text editor that provides basic mouse support, letting you edit a file easily (install the leafpad package). It uses an interface similar to Windows Notepad, displaying a menu bar with the File, Edit, Search, and Options menu items. Features are limited to basic operations such as open, save, print, cut, copy, paste, find, and replace.

Nano

Several simple keyboard-based editors are available for Fedora that work on the command-line interface, such as nano and joe. The Nano editor is a simple screen-based editor that lets you visually edit your file, using arrow and page keys to move around the file (install the nano package). You use control keys to perform actions. Ctrl+x will exit and prompt you to save the file; Ctrl+o will save it. You start Nano with the nano command.

```
nano myreport
```

To edit a configuration file, you need administrative access, so you first have to use administrative access with the sudo command. Figure 5-12 shows the Nano editor being used to edit the GRUB configuration file, /etc/default/grub.

```
sudo nano /etc/default/grub
```

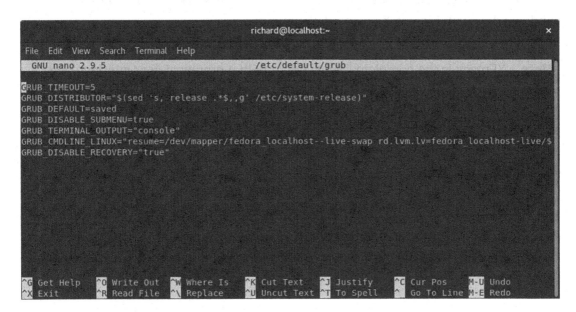

Figure 5-12. *Editing with Nano*

Emacs Editor

The Emacs editor is tailored for program development, enabling you to format source code according to the programming language you use. The versions usually included with Linux distributions are GNU Emacs and XEmacs. GNU Emacs is desktop-capable, with features such as menus, scroll bars, and mouse-based editing operations. You can find more information about Emacs at `www.emacs.org` and about XEmacs at its website at `www.xemacs.org`.

The Emacs editor operates much like a standard word processor. The keys on your keyboard represent input characters. Commands are implemented with special keys, such as the control (Ctrl) and alternate (Alt) keys. There is no special input mode, as in vi. You type in your text, and if you have to execute an editing command, such as moving the cursor or saving text, you use a Ctrl key. Such an organization makes the Emacs editor easy to use. You invoke the Emacs editor with the command `emacs`. You can enter the name of the file you want to edit, and if the file does not exist, it is created. In the following example, the user prepares to edit the file `mydata` with Emacs:

```
emacs mydata
```

The GNU Emacs editor supports basic desktop-editing operations such as selection of text with click-and-drag mouse operations, cut/copy/paste, and a scroll bar for moving through text. The Mode line and Echo areas are displayed at the bottom of the window, where you can enter keyboard commands.

Note   XEmacs is the complete Emacs editor with a graphical user interface and Internet applications, including a web browser, a mail utility, and a newsreader. XEmacs is available on the Fedora repository.

The Vi Editor: Vim and Gvim

The Vim editor included with most Linux distributions is an enhanced version of the vi editor. It includes all the commands and features of the vi editor. *Vi*, which stands for "visual," remains one of the most widely used editors in Linux. There are two versions of Vim available, `vim-minimal`, which is installed by default and provides vi editing capabilities, and `vim-enhanced`, which provides more advanced features such as Perl and Python interpreters, useful if you use vi to create Perl or Python scripts.

Keyboard-based editors like Vim and Emacs use a keyboard for two different operations: to specify editing commands and to receive character input. Used for editing commands, certain keys perform deletions, some execute changes, and others perform cursor movement. Used for character input, keys represent characters that can be entered into the file being edited. Usually, these two different functions are divided among different keys on the keyboard. Alphabetic keys are reserved for character input, while function keys and control keys specify editing commands, such as deleting text or moving the cursor. Such editors can rely on the existence of an extended keyboard that includes function and control keys.

Editors in UNIX, however, were designed to assume a minimal keyboard with alphanumeric characters and some control characters, as well as the Esc and Enter keys. Instead of dividing the command and input functions among different keys, the vi editor has three separate modes of operation for the keyboard: the command and input modes and a line-editing mode. In command mode, all the keys on the keyboard become editing commands; in the input mode, the keys on the keyboard become input characters. Some of the editing commands, such as `a` and `i`, enter the input mode. On typing `i`, you leave the command mode and enter the input mode. Each key now represents a character to be input to the text. Pressing Esc automatically returns you to the command mode, and the keys once again become editor commands. As you edit text, you are constantly moving from the command mode to the input mode and back again. With Vim, you can use the Ctrl+o command to jump quickly to the command mode and enter a command, and then automatically return to the input mode. Table 5-8 lists a basic set of vi commands to get you started.

Table 5-8. *Editor Commands*

Command	Description
h	Moves the cursor left one character.
l	Moves the cursor right one character.
k	Moves the cursor up one line.
j	Moves the cursor down one line.
Ctrl+f	Moves forward by a screen of text; the next screen of text is displayed.
Ctrl+b	Moves backward by a screen of text; the previous screen of text is displayed.
Input	*(All input commands place the user in input; the user leaves input with Esc.)*
a	Enters input after the cursor.
i	Enters input before the cursor.
o	Enters input below the line the cursor is on; inserts a new empty line below the one the cursor is currently on.
Text Selection (Vim)	
v	Visual mode; move the cursor to expand selected text by character. Once selected, press a key to execute an action: c change, d delete, y copy, : line-editing command, J join lines, U uppercase, u lowercase.
V	Visual mode; move cursor to expand selected text by line.
Delete	
x	Deletes the character the cursor is on.
dd	Deletes the line the cursor is on.
Change	Except for the replace command, r, all change commands place the user into input after deleting text.
cw	Deletes the word the cursor is on and places the user into the input mode.

(continued)

Table 5-8. (*continued*)

Command	Description
r	Replaces the character the cursor is on. After pressing r, the user enters the replacement character. The change is made without entering input; the user remains in the vi command mode.
R	First places into input mode, and then overwrites character by character. Appears as an overwrite mode on the screen but actually is in input mode.
Move	Moves text by first deleting it, moving the cursor to desired place of insertion, and then pressing the p command. (When text is deleted, it is automatically held in a special buffer.)
p	Inserts deleted or copied text after the character or line the cursor is on.
P	Inserts deleted or copied text before the character or line the cursor is on.
dw p	Deletes a word, and then moves it to the place you indicate with the cursor (press p to insert the word after the word the cursor is on).
yy or Y p	Copies the line the cursor is on.
Search	*The two search commands open a line at the bottom of the screen and enable the user to enter a pattern to be searched for; press Enter after typing in the pattern.*
/pattern	Searches forward in the text for a pattern.
?pattern	Searches backward in the text for a pattern.
n	Repeats the previous search, whether it was forward or backward.
Line-Editing Commands	Effect
w	Saves the file.
q	Quits the editor; q! quits without saving.

Although you can create, save, close, and quit files with the vi editor, the commands for each are not very similar. Saving and quitting a file involves the use of special line-editing commands, whereas closing a file is a vi editing command. Creation of a file is usually specified on the same shell command line that invokes the vi editor. To edit a file, type vi or vim and the name of a file on the shell command line. If a file by that name does not exist, the system creates it. In effect, entering the name of a file that does not yet exist instructs the vi editor to create that file. The following command invokes the vi editor, working on the file booklist. If booklist does not yet exist, the vi editor creates it.

```
$ vim booklist
```

After executing the vim command, you enter vi's command mode. Each key becomes a vi editing command, and the screen becomes a window onto the text file. Text is displayed screen by screen. The first screen of text is displayed, and the cursor is positioned in the upper-left corner. With a newly created file, there is no text to display. When you first enter the vi editor, you are in the command mode. To enter text, you must enter the input mode. In the command mode, a is the editor command for appending text. Pressing this key places you in the input mode. Now the keyboard operates like a typewriter, and you can input text to the file. If you press Enter, you merely start a new line of text. With Vim, you can use the arrow keys to move from one part of the entered text to another and work on different parts of the text. After entering text, you can leave the input mode and return to the command mode by pressing Esc. Once you've finished with the editing session, you exit vi by typing two capital Zs, ZZ. Hold down the Shift key and press Z twice. This sequence first saves the file and then exits the vi editor, returning you to the Linux shell. To save a file while editing, you use the line-editing command w, which writes a file to the disk. w is equivalent to the Save command found in other word processors. You first type a colon to access the line-editing mode and then type w and press Enter, :w.

You can use the :q command to quit an editing session. Unlike the ZZ command, the :q command does not perform a save operation before it quits. In this respect, it has one major constraint. If any modifications have been made to your file since the last save operation, the :q command will fail, and you will not leave the editor. However, you can override this restriction by placing a ! qualifier after the :q command. The command :q! will quit the vi editor without saving any modifications made to the file during that session (the combination :wq is the same as ZZ).

To obtain online help, enter the :help command. This is a line-editing command. Type a colon, enter the word help on the line that opens at the bottom of the screen, and then press Enter. You can add the name of a specific command after the word help. Pressing the F1 key also brings up online help.

As an alternative to using Vim in a command-line interface, you can use gvim, which provides X Window System–based menus for basic file, editing, and window operations.

The package vim is called the vim-X11 package, which includes several links to Gvim, such as evim, gview, and gex (open Ex editor line). To use Gvim, you can enter the gvim command at a terminal prompt. The standard vi interface is shown, but with several menu buttons displayed across the top, along with a toolbar with buttons for common commands like search and file saves. All the standard vi commands work as described previously; however, you can use your mouse to select items on these menus. You can open and close a file, or open several files, using split windows or different windows. The editing menu enables you to cut, copy, and paste text as well as undo or redo operations.

In the editing mode, you can select text with your mouse with a click-and-drag operation or use the Editing menu to cut or copy and then paste the selected text. Text entry, however, is still performed using the a, i, or o commands to enter the input mode. Searches and replacements are supported through a dialog window. There are also buttons on the toolbar for finding next and previous instances. You can also split the view into different windows to display parts of the same file or different files. Use the :split command to open a window, and use :hide to close the current one. Use Ctrl+w with the up and down arrow keys to move between them. On Gvim, you use entries in the Windows menu to manage windows. Configuration preferences can be placed in the user's .vimrc file.

Mail (Email) and News

Electronic mail utilities perform the same basic tasks of receiving and sending messages. Some mail clients operate on a desktop, such as KDE or GNOME. Others are designed to use a screen-based interface and can be run only from the command line (the terminal window). For web-based Internet mail services, such as Gmail and Yahoo, you can use a web browser instead of a mail client to access mail accounts provided by those services. Table 5-9 lists several popular Linux mail clients. Mail is sent to and from destinations using mail transport agents, such as Sendmail, Exim, and Smail.

Table 5-9. *Linux Mail Clients*

Mail Client	Description
Kontact (KMail, KAddressBook, KOrganizer)	Includes the K Desktop mail client, KMail; integrated mail, address book, and scheduler
Contacts	GNOME contact database synced with Online Accounts (currently supports only Google contacts)
Documents	GNOME documents for locating local and cloud-based documents; synced with Online Accounts (Google Docs and Microsoft SkyDrive)
Evolution	Email client
Thunderbird	Mozilla group standalone mail client and newsreader
Sylpheed	Gtk mail and news client (install with dnf)
Claws Mail	Extended version of the Sylpheed email client (install with dnf)
GNU Emacs and XEmacs	Emacs mail clients
Mutt	Screen-based mail client (install with dnf)
Mail	Original UNIX-based command-line mail client
Squirrel Mail	Web-based mail client (install with dnf)

Evolution

Evolution is the primary mail client for the GNOME desktop. Although it's designed for GNOME, it works equally well on other desktops. Evolution provides a mail client, calendar, and address book. The mailer supports several protocols (SMTP, POP, and IMAP), multiple mail accounts, and encryption. It also supports Pretty Good Privacy (PGP) and GNU Privacy Guard (GPG) encryption. Messages are indexed for easy searching. Junk mail filtering is provided. See the Evolution website (`https://wiki.gnome.org/Apps/Evolution`) for a complete description of its features.

You can access Evolution from the Applications overview. The Evolution mailer provides a simple desktop interface, with a toolbar for commonly used commands and a sidebar for shortcuts. A set of buttons on the lower left allows you to access other operations, such as the calendar and contacts. The mail screen is divided into two panes, one for listing the mail headers and the other for displaying the currently selected message (see Figure 5-13). You can click any header title to sort your headers by that category. Evolution also supports the use of virtual folders created by the user to hold mail that meets specified criteria. Incoming mail can be automatically distributed to a particular virtual folder.

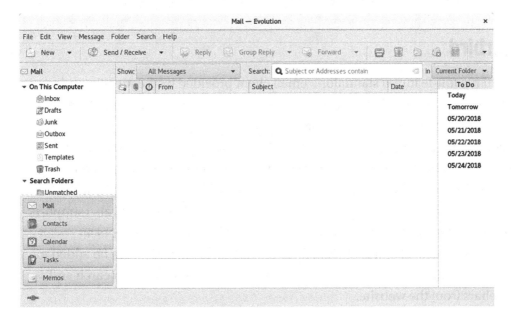

Figure 5-13. *Evolution email client*

To configure Evolution, select Preferences from the Edit menu (Edit ➤ Preferences). On the Evolution Preferences window, a sidebar shows icons for mail accounts, contacts, mail preferences, composer preference, network preferences, calendar and tasks, and certificates. The main accounts entry displays a list of current accounts. An Add button lets you add new accounts, and the Edit button allows you to change current accounts.

Numerous plugins are available to extend Evolution's capabilities. Most are installed and enabled for you automatically, including the SpamAssassin plugin for handling junk mail. To manage your plugins, select the Plugins entry in the Edit menu (Edit ➤ Plugin) to open the Plugin Manager. The plugins are listed in a left scroll window, and the configuration tabs for a selected plugin are on the right.

Evolution also supports contact operations such as calendars, contact lists, and memos. On the left-side pane, the bottom section displays buttons for these different functions: Mail, Contacts, Calendars, Tasks, and Memos. To see and manage your contacts, click the Contacts button on the left sidebar. The Calendar displays a browsable calendar on the left pane to move easily to a specific date. The right pane shows a daily calendar page by the hour, with sections for tasks and memos. You can set up several calendars, which you can access at the top of the right pane. A personal calendar is set up for you already. To add a new calendar, select Calendar from the New menu. This opens a New Calendar dialog, from which you can choose the type and name.

Thunderbird

Thunderbird is a full-featured standalone email client provided by the Mozilla project (`www.mozilla.org`). It is designed to be easy to use, highly customizable, and heavily secure. It features advanced intelligent spam filtering, as well as security features such as encryption, digital signatures, and S/MIME. To protect against viruses, email attachments can be examined without being run. Thunderbird supports both the Internet Message Access Protocol (IMAP) and the Post Office Protocol (POP). It also functions as a newsreader and features a built-in RSS reader. Thunderbird also supports the use of the Lightweight Directory Access Protocol (LDAP) for address books. Thunderbird is an extensible application, allowing customized modules to be added to enhance its capabilities. You can download extensions such as dictionary search and contact sidebars from the website.

Thunderbird provides integration with popular online mail services like Gmail, saved searches, and customized tags for selected messages. You can access Thunderbird from the Applications overview.

The Thunderbird interface uses a standard three-pane format, with a side pane for listing mail accounts and their mailboxes (see Figure 5-14). The top pane is the message list pane, and the bottom pane shows a selected message's text. Commands can be run using the toolbar, the tool menu (button at the right of the toolbar), or keyboard shortcuts. You can even change the appearance using different themes. Thunderbird also provides a Tasks tab and Calendar tab for scheduling events and noting dates. Upcoming tasks are listed on the main window on a sidebar on the right.

Figure 5-14. *Thunderbird email client*

To edit an email account, select the Preferences ➤ Account Settings from the menu opened by the menu button at the right of the toolbar. In the Account Settings window, you will see an entry for your mail account, with tabs for Server Settings, Copies & Folders, Composition & Addressing, Offline & Disk Space, Return Receipt, and Security. The Server Settings tab has entries for your server name, port, username, and connection and task configurations, such as when to check for messages. The Security tab shows a Manage Certificates button, which opens the Certificate Manager, from which you can select security certificates to use to digitally sign or encrypt messages.

Thunderbird provides an address book in which you can enter complete contact information, including email addresses, street addresses, phone numbers, and notes. Select the Address Book button on the toolbar to open the Address Book window.

GNOME Contacts

If you have enabled contacts for Online Accounts, you can use the GNOME Contacts application to manage and access those contacts (see Figure 5-16). Contacts are downloaded from the enabled online accounts. Currently, only Google is supported. You can then access and edit those contacts with the Contacts application, which is accessible from the Applications overview. First be sure to switch on Contacts in System Setting's Online Accounts (see Figure 5-15).

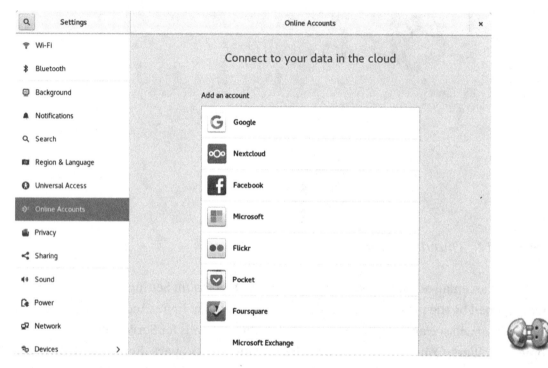

Figure 5-15. *Online Accounts contacts switch*

Contacts displays a sidebar listing your contacts. A search box lets you search for contacts. To add a contact manually, click the plus button (+) above the search box (see Figure 5-16). The selected contact shows the name, icon used, and the email address. The email entry is a mail button, which you can click to open your mailer to compose a message to be sent to that address.

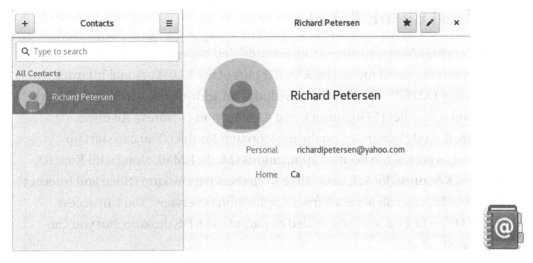

Figure 5-16. *GNOME Contacts*

To edit the contact information, click the edit button (pencil icon) at the top-right corner. You then can edit entries or provide additional information, such as the address, phone, links, website, birthday, and notes (see Figure 5-17). For each entry, you can classify whether it is work, home, or other. To remove a contact, click the Remove Contact button at the lower right. You can also remove the contact by clicking on its entry in the sidebar to display a check box, which, when clicked, displays a Remove button at the bottom of the sidebar.

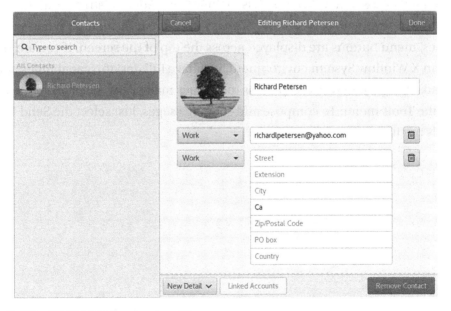

Figure 5-17. *GNOME Contacts edit*

The KDE Mail Client: KMail

The KDE mail client, KMail, provides a full-featured desktop interface for composing, sending, and receiving email messages. KMail is part of the KDE Personal Information Management suite (KDE-PIM), which also includes an address book (KAddressBook), an organizer and scheduler (KOrganizer), and a note writer (KNotes). All these components are directly integrated on the desktop into Kontact. You can start up KMail directly or as part of the Kontact applications (Mail). KMail, along with Kontact, KOrganizer, and KAddressBook, is accessible from the KDE Desktop Office and Internet menus. On GNOME, you can access it from Applications overview. You can access Kontact in the Office filter. KMail is installed as part of the KDE desktop, but you can install it separately.

To quickly set up a new email account, you can use the Account Wizard (Tools ➤ Account Wizard). A series of dialogs will prompt you to enter the account type, the account name and address, a login name and password, and the incoming and outgoing servers. For more detailed configuration, select the Configure Kmail entry in the Settings menu (Settings ➤ Configure Kmail).

Emacs Mail

The GNU version of Emacs includes a mail client, in addition to other components, such as a newsreader and editor. GNU Emacs is included on Fedora distributions. Check the Emacs website at `www.gnu.org/software/emacs` for more information. When you start GNU Emacs, menu buttons are displayed across the top of the screen. If you are running Emacs in an X Window System environment, you have full desktop capabilities and can select menus using your mouse. To access the Emacs mail client, select from the mail entries in the Tools menu. To compose and send messages, just select the Send Mail item in the Tools menu.

Command-Line Mail Clients

Several mail clients use a simple command-line interface. They are simple and easy to use but include an extensive set of features and options. Two of the more widely used mail clients of this type are Mail and Mutt. Mail is the mailx mail client that was developed for the UNIX system. It is considered a default mail client that can be found on all UNIX and Linux systems. Mutt is a cursor-based client that runs from the command line.

Mutt

Mutt has a cursor-based interface with an extensive set of features. You can find more information about Mutt from the Mutt website at `www.mutt.org`. Here, you can download recent versions of Mutt and access online manuals and help resources. The Mutt manual is located in the `/usr/doc` directory under `Mutt`. To use Mutt, enter the `mutt` command in a terminal window or on the command line.

Mail

The Mail utility was originally created for BSD UNIX and is called, simply, mail. Later versions of UNIX System V adopted the BSD mail utility and renamed it *mailx*. Now, it is simply referred to as Mail. Mail functions as a default mail client on most UNIX and Linux systems. It is installed on Fedora with the `mailx` package.

To send a message with Mail, type `mail` on the command line, in addition to the address of the person to whom you are sending the message. Press Enter, and you are prompted for a subject. Enter the subject of the message and press Enter again. At this point, you are placed in input mode. Anything you type is considered the contents of the message. Pressing Enter adds a new line to the text. When you finish typing your message, press Ctrl+d on a line of its own to end the message. You will then be prompted to enter a user to whom to send a carbon copy (cc) of the message. If you do not want to send a carbon copy, just press Enter. You will then see EOT (end of transmission) displayed after you press Ctrl+d.

You can send a message to several users at the same time by listing those users' addresses as arguments on the command line following the `mail` command. In the following example, the user sends the same message to `chris` and `aleina`:

```
$ mail chris aleina
```

To receive mail, you first enter the mail command and press Enter. This invokes a Mail shell with its own prompt and mail commands. A list of message headers is displayed. Header information is arranged into fields, beginning with the status of the message and the message number. The status of a message is indicated by a single uppercase letter, usually N for "new" or U for "unread." A message number, used for easy reference to your messages, follows the status field. The next field is the address of the sender, followed by the date and time the message was received, and then the number of lines and characters in the message. The last field contains the subject the sender gave to the message. After the headers, the Mail shell displays its prompt, an ampersand (&). At the Mail prompt, you enter commands that operate on the messages. An example of a Mail header and prompt follows:

```
$ mail
Mail version 8.2 01/15/2001. Type ? for help.
"/var/spool/mail/larisa": 3 messages 1 new 2 unread
 1 chris@turtle.mytrek. Thu Jun 7 14:17 22/554 "trip"
>U 2 aleina@turtle.mytrek Thu Jun 7 14:18 22/525 "party"
 U 3 dylan@turtle.mytrek. Thu Jun 7 14:18 22/528 "newsletter"
& q
```

Mail references messages either through a message list or through the current message marker (>). The greater-than sign (>) is placed before the current message. The current message is referenced by default when no message number is included with a Mail command. You can also reference messages using a message list consisting of several message numbers.

Use the R and r commands to reply to a message you have received. The R command entered with a message number generates a header for sending a message and then places you into input mode to type the message. The q command quits Mail. When you quit, messages you have already read are placed in a file called mbox in your home directory. Instead of saving messages in the mbox file, you can use the s command to save a message explicitly to a file of your choice. Mail has its own initialization file, called .mailrc, which is executed each time Mail is invoked, for sending or receiving messages. Within it, you can define Mail options and create Mail aliases.

Accessing Mail on Remote Mail Servers

Most new mail clients are equipped to access mail accounts on remote servers. Mail clients, such as Evolution, KMail, Sylpheed, and Thunderbird, enable you to set up a mailbox for such an account and access a mail server to check for and download received mail. You must specify what protocol a mail server uses. This is usually either the Post Office Protocol (POP) or the IMAP protocol (IMAP). Using a mail server address, you can access your account with your username and password.

For email clients, such as Mail and Mutt, that do not provide mail server access, you can use Fetchmail to have mail from those accounts sent directly to the inbox of your Linux account. All your mail, whether from other users on your Linux system or from remote mail accounts, will appear in your local inbox. Fetchmail checks for mail on remote mail servers and downloads it to your local inbox, where it appears as newly received mail. Enter `fetchmail` on the command line with the mail server address and any needed options. The mail protocol is indicated with the `-p` option and the mail server type, usually POP3. If your email username is different from your Linux login name, you use the `-u` option and the email name. Once you execute the `fetchmail` command, you are prompted for a password. The syntax for the `fetchmail` command for a POP3 mail server follows:

```
fetchmail -p POP3 -u username mail-server
```

You will see messages telling you if you have mail and how many messages are being downloaded. You can then use a mail client to read the messages from your inbox. You can run Fetchmail in daemon mode to have it check automatically for mail. You must include an option specifying the interval in seconds, for checking mail.

```
fetchmail -d 1200
```

To have Fetchmail run automatically, you can set the `START DAEMON` option to yes in the `/etc/default/fetchmail` file.

You can specify options, such as the server type, username, and password, in a .fetchmailrc file in your home directory. You can also include entries for other mail servers and accounts. Once Fetchmail is configured, you can enter fetchmail with no arguments; it will read entries from your .fetchmailrc file. You can also make entries directly in the .fetchmailrc file. An entry in the .fetchmailrc file for a particular mail account consists of several fields and their values poll, protocol, username, and password. The poll field refers to the mail server name. You can also specify your password, instead of having to enter it each time Fetchmail accesses the mail server.

Mailing Lists

Users on mailing lists automatically receive messages and articles sent to the lists. Mailing lists work much like a mail alias, broadcasting messages to all users on the list. Mailing lists were designed to serve specialized groups of people. Numerous mailing lists, as well as other subjects, are available for Linux. By convention, to subscribe to a list, you send a request to the mailing list address with a -request term added to its username. For example, to subscribe to gnome-list@gnome.org, you send a request to gnome-list-request@gnome.org.

You can use the Mailman program to manage your mailing lists automatically. Mailman is the GNU mailing list manager that is included with Fedora. You can find out more about Mailman at www.list.org.

Usenet News

Usenet is an open mail system on which users post messages that include news, discussions, and opinions. It operates like a mailbox to which any user on your Linux system can read or send messages. Users' messages are incorporated into Usenet files, which are distributed to any system signed up to receive them. Each system that receives Usenet files is referred to as a *site*. Certain sites perform organizational and distribution operations for Usenet, receiving messages from other sites and organizing them into Usenet files, which are then broadcast to many other sites. Such sites are called backbone sites, and they operate like publishers, receiving articles and organizing them into different groups.

To access Usenet news, you require access to a news server. A news server receives the daily Usenet newsfeeds and makes them accessible to other systems. Your network may have a system that operates as a news server. If you are using an Internet service provider (ISP), a news server is probably maintained by your ISP for your use. To read Usenet articles, you use a *newsreader,* a client program that connects to a news server and accesses the articles. On the Internet and in TCP/IP networks, news servers communicate with newsreaders using the Network News Transfer Protocol (NNTP) and are often referred to as NNTP news servers. You can also create your own news server on your Linux system to run a local Usenet news service or to download and maintain the full set of Usenet articles. Several Linux programs, called news transport agents, can be used to create such a server.

You read Usenet articles with a newsreader, such as KNode, Pan, Thunderbird, or tin, which enables you to select a specific newsgroup and then read the articles in it. A newsreader operates like a user interface, letting you browse through and select available articles for reading, saving, or printing. Most newsreaders employ a retrieval feature called *threads,* which pulls together articles on the same discussion or topic. Several popular newsreaders are listed in Table 5-10.

Table 5-10. *Linux Newsreaders*

Newsreader	Description
Pan	GNOME desktop newsreader (install with dnf)
KNode	KDE desktop newsreader
Thunderbird	Mail client with newsreader capabilities (X-based)
Sylpheed	GNOME Windows-like newsreader (install with dnf)
slrn	Newsreader (cursor-based) (install with dnf)
Emacs	Emacs editor, mail client, and newsreader (cursor-based) (install with dnf)
tin	Newsreader (command-line interface) (install with dnf)
kwooty	Binary only NZB-based news grabber (install with dnf)

Most newsreaders can read Usenet news provided on remote news servers that use the NNTP. Desktop newsreaders, such as KNode and Pan, have you specify the Internet address for the remote news server in their own configuration settings. Shell-based newsreaders such as tin obtain the news server's Internet address from the NNTPSERVER shell variable, configured in the .profile file.

```
NNTPSERVER=news.domain.com
export NNTPSERVER
```

There are few binary-based newsreaders for Linux that can convert text messages to binary equivalents like those found in `alt.binaries` newsgroups. There are some news *grabbers*, which are applications designed only to download binaries. The binaries are normally encoded with RAR compression, which can be decoded by Fedora. Binaries normally consist of several `rar` archive files, some of which may be incomplete. To repair them, you can use `par2`. Install the `par2cmdline` package. A binary should have its own set of `par2` files also listed on the new server that you can download and use to repair any incomplete `rar` files. The principle works much the same as RAID arrays using parity information to reconstruct damaged data.

The `slrn` newsreader is cursor-based. Commands are displayed across the top of the screen and can be executed using the listed keys. Different types of screens exist for the newsgroup list, article list, and article content, each with its own set of commands. An initial screen lists your subscribed newsgroups with commands for posting, listing, and subscribing to your newsgroups. When you start `slrn` for the first time, you may have to create a `.jnewsrc` file in your home directory. Use the following command: `slrn -f .jnewsrc -create`. Also, you must set the `NNTPSERVER` variable and make sure it is exported. The `slrn` newsreader features a utility called `slrn-pull` that you can use to download articles in specified newsgroups automatically.

Table 5-11. *Database Management Systems for Linux*

System	Site
LibreOffice Base	LibreOffice.org database: `https://www.libreoffice.org`
PostgreSQL	The PostgreSQL database: `www.postgresql.org` (install with dnf)
MariaDB	Advanced and fully open source version of MySQL (Fedora default) (install with dnf)
Derby	Apache JAVA-based database (install with dnf)
MongoDB	Document-based database (install with dnf)
Hadoop	Apache distributed database for very large data sets
SQLite	Simple SQL database (install with dnf)

Database Management Systems

Several database systems are provided for Fedora, including LibreOffice Base, MariaDB, Derby, and PostgreSQL. MariaDB is derived from MySQL but is fully open sourced. It is the default MySQL type database for Fedora. MariaDB is supported and developed by the original MySQL developers. The original MySQL is owned by Oracle and features commercial versions. You can still install the older noncommercial version of MySQL, if you wish. In addition, commercial SQL database software is also compatible with Fedora. Table 5-11 lists database management systems currently available for Linux.

Derby is a Java-based database developed by Apache. SQLite is a simple and fast database server requiring no configuration and implementing the database on a single-disk file. For small embedded databases, you can use Berkeley DB (db4).

In addition, Fedora also supports document-based non-SQL databases such as MongoDB and Hadoop. MongoDB is a document-based database that can be quickly searched. Hadoop is an Apache project for accessing very large data sets distributed across a network.

SQL Databases (RDBMS)

SQL databases are relational database management systems (RDBMSs) designed for extensive database management tasks. Many of the major SQL databases now have Linux versions, including Oracle, Informix, Sybase, and IBM. These are commercial and professional database management systems. Linux has proved itself capable of supporting complex and demanding database management tasks. In addition, many free SQL databases are available for Linux that offer much the same functionality. Most commercial databases also provide free personal versions.

LibreOffice.org Base

LibreOffice provides a basic database application, called LibreOffice Base, which can access many database files. You can set up and operate a simple database as well as access and manage files from other database applications. When you start up LibreOffice Base, you will be prompted either to start a new database or connect to an existing one. File types supported include ODBC (Open Database Connectivity), JDBC (Java), Adabas D, MySQL, PostgreSQL, and MDB (Microsoft Access) database files (install the unixodbc package). You can also create your own simple databases. Check the LibreOffice Base page at `https://www.libreoffice.org/discover/base/` for detailed information on drivers and supported databases.

MariaDB

MariaDB, included with Fedora, is a true multiuser, multithreaded SQL database server. MySQL is an open source product available free of charge under the GPL license. It is the default MySQL type database for Fedora. MariaDB is supported and developed by the original MySQL developers. MariaDB is designed to be fully compatible with MySQL. The original MySQL is owned by Oracle and features commercial versions. You can obtain current information on MariaDB from its website at `https://mariadb.org`. You can use the MySQL documentation for MariaDB that is available at `https://dev.mysql.com/doc/`.

PostgreSQL

PostgreSQL is based on the POSTURES database management system, although it uses SQL as its query language. PostgreSQL is a next-generation research prototype developed at the University of California, Berkeley. Linux versions of PostgreSQL are included in most distributions, including Red Hat, Fedora, Debian, and Ubuntu. You can find more information about it from the PostgreSQL website at `www.postgresql.org`. PostgreSQL is an open source project developed under the GPL license.

CHAPTER 6

Graphics and Multimedia

The Fedora repositories provide an extensive variety of graphic and multimedia applications, including image viewers, advanced image-manipulation programs like GIMP, music and CD players like Rhythmbox, and video players like Totem and VLC. Graphics tools available for use under Linux are listed in Table 6-2. Additionally, there is strong support for multimedia tasks from video and DVD to sound and music editing (see Tables 6-5 and 6-6).

Support for many popular multimedia codecs, specifically MP3, DVD, MKV, and DivX, are not included with the Fedora distribution, because of licensing and other restrictions. To play MP3, DVD, MKV, or DivX files, you must download and install support packages from third-party repositories. Precompiled RPM binary packages for many popular media applications and libraries, such as MPlayer and Xvid, are available on the RPM Fusion repository (see `https://rpmfusion.org`). RPM Fusion is an official Fedora repository that provides RPM Fedora–compatible packages for many multimedia and other applications that cannot be included with the Fedora distribution. These include MP3 support and DVD and DivX codecs. Current multimedia sites are listed in Table 6-1.

© Richard Petersen 2018
R. Petersen, *Beginning Fedora Desktop*, https://doi.org/10.1007/978-1-4842-3882-0_6

Table 6-1. *Linux Multimedia Sites*

Project/Site	Description
Fedora repository	Fedora Repository, which includes most GNU licensed multimedia applications: `https://fedoraprojet.org`
RPMFusion	Repository for drivers and multimedia applications and libraries that are not included with Fedora. This is an official extension of the Fedora project: `https://rpmfusion.org`
PulseAudio	PulseAudio sound interface, now the default for Fedora: `https://www.freedesktop.org/wiki/Software/PulseAudio/`
Advanced Linux Sound Architecture (ALSA)	The Advanced Linux Sound Architecture (ALSA) project for current sound drivers: `http://www.alsa-project.org`
Open Sound System	Open Sound System, drives for older devices: `http://www.opensound.com`
Design Suite	A Fedora Linux spin featuring Linux applications for graphic design and multimedia production: `https://labs.fedoraproject.org/en/design-suite/`

For the commercial DVD video codec, you still have to use the `http://rpm.livna.org` repository. Here you will find only one package, the `libdvdcss` package, for playing DVD video. Enable the Livna repository (`livna-release.rpm`) and then use PackageKit to install the `libdvdcss` package. You can also download it directly from `http://rpm.livna.org/repo/28/`.

Table 6-2. *Graphics Tools for Linux*

Tool	Description
Shotwell	GNOME digital camera application and image library manager `http://www.yorba.org/shotwell/`
Photos	GNOME photo viewer and organizer
Cheese	GNOME Web cam application for taking pictures and videos
Digikam	Digital photo management tool, works with both GNOME and KDE
KDE	
Gwenview	Image browser and viewer (default for KDE)
ShowFoto	Simple image viewer, works with DigiKam (`www.digikam.org`)
Spectacle	Screen grabber
KolourPaint	Paint program
Krita	Image editor (`www.calligra.org/krita`)
GNOME	
Eye of GNOME	GNOME Image Viewer
GIMP	GNU Image Manipulation Program (`www.gimp.org`)
Inkscape	GNOME Vector graphics application (`www.inkscape.org`)
Blender	3D modeling, rendering, and animation
Synfig Studio	2D modeling, rendering, and animation
Entangle	Camera and Computer linked photographic system
RawTherapee	Digital processing and raw image converter
LibreOffice Draw	LibreOffice Draw program
X Window System	
Xfig	Drawing program
ImageMagick	Image format conversion and editing tool

For those who want to install a multimedia system, such as for an HTPC, you can use the Korora Project spin (https://kororaproject.org). It includes Fedora as well as many free and non-free multimedia codecs and applications available from the RPM Fusion repository.

For those that wish to work primarily with graphics applications, you can install the Fedora Design Suite, a Fedora spin that installs available Fedora image applications such as Inkscape (vector graphics), Blender (3D modeling), and Darktable (virtual darkroom), as well as Scribus (desktop publishing), https://labs.fedoraproject.org/en/design-suite/.

Graphics Applications

The GNOME and KDE desktops support an impressive number of graphics applications, including image viewers, screen grabbers, image editors, and paint tools. These tools can be found in the Applications overview.

Photo Management: Shotwell, Cheese, and Photos

The Shotwell photo manager provides an easy and powerful way to manage, display, import, and publish your photos and images (https://wiki.gnome.org/Apps/Shotwell). It is the default photo manager for Fedora 28. See the Shotwell user manual for full details (Help ➤ User Manual, http://shotwell-project.org/doc/html/). You can open the Shotwell Photo Manager as Shotwell, using either the Applications overview or the Shotwell icon on the Activities sidebar.

You can import folders from cameras, folders (see Figure 6-1). Photo thumbnails are displayed in the main right pane. The View menu lets you control the thumbnail display, allowing you to sort photos, zoom, show photo filenames (Titles), or select by rating. You can adjust the size of the displayed thumbnails using a slider bar in the toolbar located at the bottom right of the Shotwell window. The small figure button to the left of the slider reduces thumbnails to their smallest size, and the large figure button to the right of the slider expands them to the largest size. To see a full-screen slideshow of the photos, choose the slideshow entry from the View menu (F5). The slideshow starts automatically. Moving your mouse to the bottom middle of the screen displays slideshow controls for pausing and stepping through photos (see Figure 6-2). The Settings button opens a dialog in which you can set the display time. To end the slideshow and return to the desktop, click the Full Screen button. The slideshow buttons are shown here.

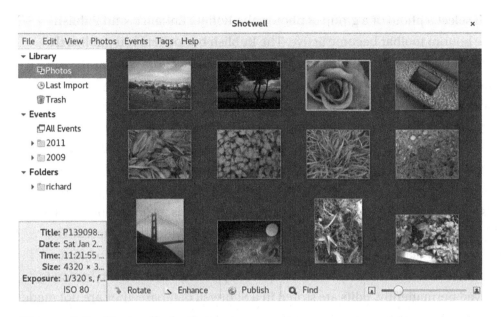

Figure 6-1. *Shotwell photo management*

Figure 6-2. *Shotwell slideshow controls*

Photos are organized automatically according to the time they were taken. Dates are listed under the Events entry in the left sidebar, arranged by year, month, and date. To name a photo, right-click it and choose Edit Title. This opens a dialog in which you can enter the name. You can also tag photos by placing them in groups, making them easier to access. To tag a photo, right-click it and choose Add Tags to open a dialog in which you can enter a tag name. The tag will show up as a label for the photo. You can access photos by tags by using the Tags entries in the left sidebar. For each photo, you can also set a rating indicated by five stars or fewer. You can also mark a photo as rejected. To rate a photo, right-click it and choose Set Rating, which then lists rating options in a submenu. Use the Show Photos button in the bottom toolbar to display photos by rating. You can select several photos at once by using click-and-drag, Ctrl-click, or Shift-click (as you do for files in a file manager window), then right-click to give them the same rating (Set Rating) or same tag (Add Tags).

When you select a photo or a group of photos, the Rotate, Enhance, and Publish buttons in the bottom toolbar become active. The Publish button lets you publish the photo on a web service: Facebook, Flickr, or Picasa. The Rotate button rotates the photo (from the Photos menu, you can also flip the photo horizontally or vertically). The Enhance button adjusts the photo automatically.

To perform more complex edits, select the photo and then choose View ➤ Fullscreen (F11) to open the photo in the Shotwell photo editor (see Figure 6-3). Move your mouse to the bottom of the screen to display the editing toolbar, which includes the Rotate, Crop, Red-eye, Adjust, and Enhance buttons. You can also enlarge or reduce the photo display by using the slider bar. The Crop button opens an adjustable border, with a menu for choosing the display proportions, such as HD video or postcard. The Adjust button opens a dialog for refined changes, such as exposure, saturation, tint, temperature, and shadows. The toolbar will keep disappearing. Click the Pin button to have it displayed permanently. Edits are stored in a Shotwell database; they are not made to the original photo. To revert to the original photo, right-click and choose Revert to Original or choose that entry from the Photos menu.

Figure 6-3. *Shotwell photo editing*

The Shotwell Preferences dialog (Edit ➤ Preferences) lets you set the background intensity, choose a photo library folder, and select a photo editor. To open a photo with an external photo editor, right-click the photo thumbnail and select Open with External Editor. Photos are stored in your Pictures directory under the Events subfolders, by year and then month. To open a photos folder, right-click and select Show in File Manager.

DigiKam (`www.digiKam.org`) is a KDE photo manager with many of the same features as F-Spot. A side panel allows easy access by album, date, tags, or previous searches. The program also provides image-editing capabilities, with numerous effects. The DigiKam configuration (Settings menu) provides extensive options, including image editing, digital camera support, and interface configuration.

Tip   The Windows version of Photoshop is supported by Wine. You can use Wine to install Photoshop CS on Fedora. Once started, Photoshop will operate like any Linux desktop application.

Cheese is a web cam picture-taking and video-recording tool (`www.gnome.org/projects/cheese`). You can snap pictures from your web cam and apply simple effects. You can open it from the Applications overview. Click the Photo button to manage photos and the Video button to record video. Icons of photos and video appear on the bottom panel, letting you select ones for effects or removal. The Effects pane shows effects that can be turned on or off for the current image. To save a photo, right-click its icon on the lower panel and select Save from the pop-up menu.

GNOME Photos is a simple image viewer and organizer for the images in your Pictures folder. GNOME Photos has three tabs: Photos, Albums, and Favorites (see Figure 6-4). It opens to the Photos tab. You can click a photo to open it, and then use arrow buttons to display the next or previous ones (see Figure 6-5). To return to the main window, click the left arrow button at the left side of the title bar. At the lower right is a button you can click to display zoom buttons to enlarge and reduce the photo. On an enlarged photo you can use the mouse to move around the photo. There are button at the right side of the title bar above the photo for favorite, edit, share, and menu. The favorite button (star) marks the photo as a favorite. The share button (network) lets you email the photo. The edit button (pencil) opens an editing dialog with an expandable sidebar for Crop, Colors, Enhance, and Filters. Click on an entry to show the options. Click the Done button at the upper right when you're finished.

Figure 6-4. *GNOME Photos: Photos tab*

Figure 6-5. *GNOME Photos: image display*

The menu has options to export, print, delete, or set as the background for your desktop or lock screen. You can also open it with Image Viewer. The Properties option opens the Properties dialog for the photo, displaying detailed information about the image and lets you give it a name (Title).

From the main window, you can choose several photos to work on by clicking the checkmark button at the top right. Check boxes appear on the lower-right corner of each image (see Figure 6-6). A menu at the top center lets you choose all or de-select all images. When you check a single image, a toolbar appears at the bottom that lets you print the image, check its properties, add it to an album, or tag it as a favorite. If you check several photos, you can add them to an album or mark them as favorites.

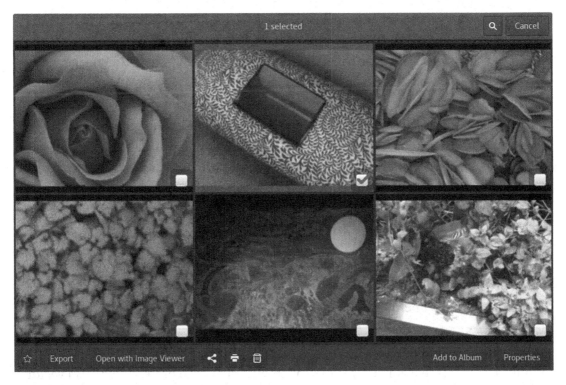

Figure 6-6. *GNOME Photos: selection*

You can use the search button to select a subset of photos, which you can then work on, displaying only that set of photos or clicking the checkmark button to work on just those.

When you open a photo, you can also tag it as a favorite by clicking the favorite button (star) at the right side of the title bar. On the Photos tab, favorite images show a star emblem in the lower-right corner of the image. To remove an image from favorites, open the photo and click its favorite button again.

Photos can be organized into albums. The albums are also displayed on the Photos dialog. When you add a photo to an album, you are prompted to choose an existing album or to create a new one.

GNOME Graphics Tools

Many powerful and easy-to-use graphic applications are available for use on GNOME. The Eye of GNOME is the GNOME image viewer accessible as Image Viewer. It lets you display images and provides rotation capability and zooming. You can display images in a slideshow. An image gallery toolbar lets you quickly choose an image.

GIMP is the GNU image-manipulation program, much like Adobe Photoshop. You can use GIMP for such tasks as photo retouching, image composition, and image authoring. It supports features such as layers, channels, blends, and gradients. GIMP makes effective use of the GTK+ widget set. You can find out more about GIMP and download the newest versions from its website at https://www.gimp.org. GIMP is freely distributed under the GNU Public License.

Note   The gPhoto project provides software for accessing digital cameras (http://www.gphoto.org). Several frontend interfaces are provided for a core library, called libgphoto2, consisting of drivers and tools that can access numerous digital cameras.

Inkscape is a GNOME-based vector graphics application for SVG (Scalable Vector Graphics) images (see Figure 6-7). It has capabilities similar to professional-level vector graphics applications such as Adobe Illustrator. The SVG format allows easy generation of images for web use as well as complex art. Though its native format is SVG, it can also export to the Portable Network Graphics (PNG) format. It features layers and easy object creation, including stars and spirals. A color bar lets you quickly change color fills.

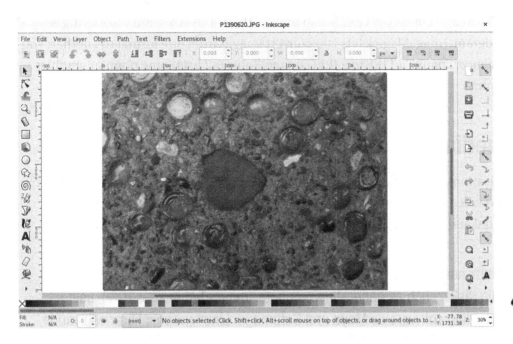

Figure 6-7. *Inkscape*

KDE Graphics Tools

The KDE desktop features the same variety of graphics tools found on the GNOME desktop. Many are available from the Fedora main repository. Most do not require a full installation of the KDE desktop. The KSnapshot program is a simple screen grabber for KDE. Gwenview is an easy-to-use image browser and viewer supporting slideshows and numerous image formats. It is the default viewer for KDE. KolourPaint is a basic paint program with brushes, shapes, and color effects; it supports numerous image formats. Krita is the Calligra professional image paint and editing application, with a wide range of features, such as the ability to create web images and modify photographs (formerly known as Krayon and KImageShop).

X Window System Graphic Programs

X Window System–based applications run directly on the underlying X Window System. These applications tend to be simpler, lacking the desktop functionality found in GNOME or KDE applications. Most are available on the Fedora repository. XPaint is a simple paint program that allows you to load graphics or photographs and then create

221

shapes, add text and colors, and use brush tools with various sizes and colors. Xfig is a drawing program. ImageMagick lets you convert images from one format to another; you can, for instance, change a TIFF to a JPEG image. Table 6-2 lists some popular graphics tools for Linux.

Multimedia

Many applications are available for both video and sound, including sound editors, MP3 players, and video players (see Tables 6-5 and 6-6). Linux sound applications include mixers, digital audio tools, CD audio writers, MP3 players, and network audio support.

Note   Linux has become a platform of choice for many professional-level multimedia tasks, such as generating computer-generated images (CGI), using such demanding software as Maya and Softimage. Linux graphic libraries include those for OpenGL, MESA, and SGI.

Information about many applications designed specifically for the GNOME or KDE user interface can be found at their respective software sites (`https://wiki.gnome.org/Apps` and `https://www.kde.org/applications/`). Precompiled binary RPM packages for most applications are at the Fedora or RPM Fusion repositories.

Codec Support with PackageKit

PackageKit is designed to work with GStreamer to detect and install needed codecs. Whenever you try to run a media file using a GStreamer-supported application such as the Totem movie player, and the codec is missing, GNOME Software is run to check for supporting codec packages and lets you install them (see Figure 6-8). A dialog lists the required packages (including any required additional plugins), and you are prompted to install them.

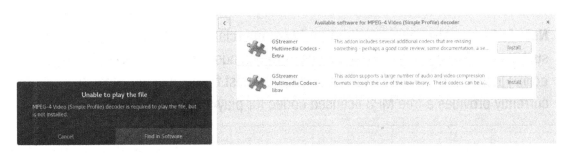

Figure 6-8. *Detecting and installing needed multimedia codecs*

If you have RPM Fusion support installed for DNF, GNOME Software, or Packages, will find and install multimedia codecs not included with the official Fedora release. For MP3, you can download the MP3 codec directly. There are also several multimedia codecs, such as MPEG2 (DVD video), MPEG4 (DivX), Dolby AC3 audio, and MPEG video playback.

For the commercial DVD video codec, you still must use the http://rpm.livna.org repository. Here, you will find only one package, the libdvdcss package, for playing DVD video. You can install repository support for rpm.livna.org by installing the livna-release package, which you can download from http://rpm.livna.org. Figure 6-9 shows the libdvdcss package available from the Livna repository.

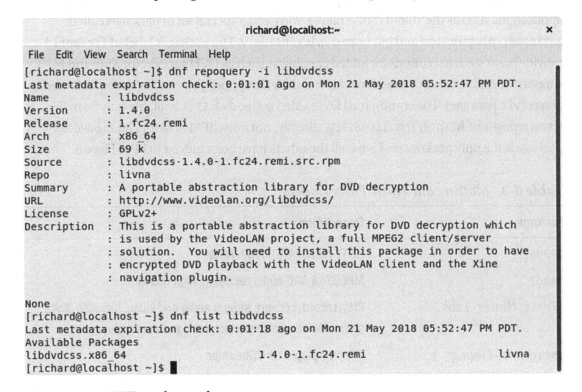

Figure 6-9. *DVD codec and support*

Note   You can also purchase third-party commercial and fully licensed codecs such as Window media or Dolby codecs from Fluendo (`https://www.fluendo.com`). Fluendo provides many licensed codecs, most for a small fee. Fluendo currently provides a free MP3 licensed codec for playing MP3 music files.

Third-Party Multimedia Codecs with License Issues

Fedora does not include any codecs or applications that may have licensing restrictions of any kind. These include multimedia codecs such as the DVD video decoder and the MP3 music decoder, as well as proprietary vendor graphics drivers like NVIDIA's own graphics driver. A list of forbidden items is located at `https://fedoraproject.org/wiki/ForbiddenItems`.

Many of these codecs are available from RPM Fusion; see `https://rpmfusion.org`. A listing of popular multimedia codecs available at these sites is shown in Table 6-3. Of particular interest may be the `a52dec`, `faad2`, and `lame` codecs for sound decoding, as well as the `xvidcore`, `x264`, and `libdvbpsi` for video decoding. For GStreamer-supported applications such as the Totem movie player, you need a special set of packages called `gstreamer-plugins-bad` and `gstreamer-plugins-ugly`. The packages labeled `freeworld` provide open source solutions for added capability, such as DVD support for Xine and MP3 support for Audacious. For extensive video and DVD support, you can install the VLC media player (`vlc` package). The commercial DVD video codec `dvdcss` is available only from the Livna repository, `http://rpm.livna.org`, directly, not from RPM Fusion. The `libdvdcss` package is the only package on Livna; all the others have been moved to RPM Fusion.

Table 6-3. *Multimedia Third-Party Codecs*

Package	Description
`a52dec`	HDTV audio (ATSC A/52, AC3)
`faad2`	MPEG2/ 4 AAC audio decoding, high quality
`ffmpeg, ffmpeg-libs`	Play, record, convert, stream audio and video. Includes digital streaming server, conversion tool, and media player
`gstreamer-ffmpeg`	`ffmpeg` plugin for GStreamer

(continued)

Table 6-3. (*continued*)

Package	Description
`gstreamer-plugins-bad`	Not fully reliable codecs and tools for GStreamer, some with possible licensing issues
`gstreamer-plugins-ugly`	Reliable video and audio codecs for GStreamer that may have licensing issues
`audacious-plugins-freeworld-mp3, -aac, -wma, -alac`	MP3, AAC, WMA, ALAC plugin packages for Audacious, among others
`lame`	MP3 playback capability, not an official MP3 decoder
`libdca`	DTS Coherent Acoustics playback capability
`libdvbpsi`	MPEG TS stream (DVB and PSI) decoding and encoding capability, VideoLAN project
`libdvdnav`	DVD video menu navigation
`libfame`	Fast Assembly MPEG video encoding
`libmad`	MPEG1 and MPEG2 audio decoding
`libmpeg3`	MPEG video audio decoding (MPEG1/2 audio and video, AC3, IFO, and VOB)
`libquicktime`	QuickTime playback
`mpeg2dec`	MPEG2 and MPEG1 playback
`twolame`	MPEG audio layer 2, MP2 encoding
`x264`	H264/AVC decoding and encoding (high definition media)
`xvidcore`	OpenDivx codec (DivX and Xvid playback)
`swftools`	Adobe Flash utilities for SWF files
`vlc`	DVD video playback capability, VideoLan project
`libdvdcss`	DVD-Video codec for commercial DVDs; available only from Livna site at `http://rpm.livna.org`

Obtaining the DVDCSS DVD Video Codec from Livna

The dvdcss decryption coded used to play back commercial DVD video disks is not included in the RPM Fusion repositories, free or non-free. Due to licensing issues, the dvdcss codec could not be included in the RPM Fusion repository. Instead, this codec remains the only software package still available on the Livna repositories. All other packages from Livna have been transferred to RPM Fusion and are no longer available on the Livna repository (beginning with Fedora 10). In effect this repository has only one package, the dvdcss DVD video decryption package.

To obtain the dvdcss decryption package, either download it directly from Livna and install it, or install the Livna repository YUM configuration package, and then use Packages to install the dvdcss package from Livna. The Livna website is located at http://rpm.livna.org.

You can install repository support for rpm.livna.org by installing the livna-release package, which you can download from http://rpm.livna.org. You can install directly from the website by using your web browser or run an rpm install command in a terminal window. The "How to Use rpm.livna.org" section on the website provides a link to download the livna-release package, as well as the following command-line alternative. Clicking the link, you will be prompted to open the package with the package installer. You will then be prompted to install the file.

The command-line install is shown here. The sudo command logs in as the administrative user, and the command to run is an rpm command to install (ivh) the livna-release.rpm package.

```
sudo rpm -ivh http://rpm.livna.org/livna-release.rpm
```

Once the file is installed, you can install the libdvdcss package using dnf in a terminal window (see Figure 6-9). The first time you install a package from Livna, you will be prompted to install its package key, asking if you trust packages from this repository. Click Yes to install the key.

The actual Livna libdvdcss package is located at: http://rpm.livna.org/repo/28/. There are x86_64 and i386 directories.

GStreamer

Many GNOME-based applications use GStreamer. GStreamer is a streaming media framework based on graphs and filters. Using a plugin structure, GStreamer applications can accommodate a wide variety of media types (`https://gstreamer.freedesktop.org`). Fedora includes several GStreamer applications, such as the Totem video player, which uses GStreamer to play DVDs, VCDs, and MPEG media. Rhythmbox provides integrated music management. Sound Juicer is an audio CD ripper.

GStreamer can be configured to use different input and output sound and video drivers and servers. You can make these selections using the GStreamer properties tool (install the `gnome-media-apps` package). Enter `gstreamer-properties` in a terminal window. The properties window displays two tabbed panels: one for audio and the other for video. The output drivers and servers are labeled Default Output, and the input drivers are labeled Default Input. There are pop-up menus for each, listing the available sound or video drivers or servers. For output, the AutoDetect option for a driver will use the default. You can change this to a specific device, such as using ALSA or OSS instead of PulseAudio.

GStreamer Plugins: The Good, the Bad, and the Ugly

Many GNOME multimedia applications such as Totem use GStreamer to provide multimedia support. To use such features as DVD video and MP3, you must install additional GStreamer plugins. You can find out more information about GStreamer and its supporting packages at `https://gstreamer.freedesktop.org`.

For version 1.0 and above, GStreamer establishes four support packages: the `base`, the `good`, the `bad`, and the `ugly`. The `base` package is a set of useful and reliable plugins. These are in the Fedora repository. The `good` package is a set of supported and tested plugins that meets all licensing requirements. This is also part of the Fedora repository. The `bad` is a set of unsupported plugins whose performance is not guaranteed and may crash but still meets licensing requirements. The `ugly` package contains plugins that work fine but may not meet licensing requirements, such as DVD support. The bad and ugly can be obtained from the RPM Fusion repositories:

> The `base`–Reliable, commonly used plugins

> The `good`–Reliable, additional, and useful plugins

The ugly–Reliable, but not fully licensed, plugins (DVD/MP3 support)

The bad–Possibly unreliable but useful plugins (possible crashes)

Another plugin for GStreamer that you may want to include is ffmpeg, gstreamer-ffmpeg (RPM Fusion repositories). ffmpeg provides several popular codecs, including ogg and 264. For Pulse (sound server) and Farsight (video conferencing) support, use their respective GStreamer plugins on the Fedora repository.

Packages will automatically detect the codec you will need to use for your GStreamer application. For commercial codecs such as MP3 or AAC, Packages will select the appropriate RPM Fusion package (with RPM Fusion enabled). This capability is provided by the gstreamer-plugin, installed during installation. For commercial DVD video, you can install the libdvdcss package from the Livna repository (http://rpm.livna.org).

To download and install the GStreamer plugin packages, just search for gstreamer on Packages. If you have enabled RPM Fusion or repository, you will also see entries for the ugly and bad packages. Alternatively, you could use the following dnf command to install all plugins at once. Be sure to include the asterisk (*) to match all the plugin packages. Your architecture (i586, i686, or x86_64) will be detected automatically.

```
dnf install gstreamer-plugins*
```

GStreamer MP3 Compatibility

To play MP3 and iPod song files and to configure other MP3 devices to work with GNOME applications such as Rhythmbox, you have to install MP3 support for GStreamer. MP3 support is not included with Fedora distributions because of licensing issues. Install the GStreamer gstreamer-plugins-ugly package, which contains most multimedia support codecs and applications that are not included with the distribution. This is a RPM Fusion package. Be sure that the RPM Fusion repository is configured for your system. The package will then appear in Packages, which you can then use to install it.

iPod

To play songs from your iPod, Fedora provides the libgpod library for GNOME. It allows player applications such as Rhythmbox, Banshee, and Amarok to use your iPod Touch and iPhone. GStreamer MP3 support is provided by the gstreamer-plugins-ugly package. To sync, import, or extract from your iPod, you can also use gtkpod.

Music Applications

Many music applications are currently available for GNOME, including sound editors, MP3 players, and audio players (see Table 6-4). You can use Rhythmbox, Banshee, GNOME Music, and Clementine to play music from different sources and the GNOME Sound Recorder to record sound sources. Several applications are also available for KDE, including the media player Amarok, a mixer (KMix), and a CD player (Kscd). Rhythmbox, Banshee, and Amarok provide access to the iPod iTouch and iPhone. For sound and music editing, you can use Audacity.

Table 6-4. *Music Players, Editors, and Rippers*

Application	Description
Rhythmbox	Music management (GStreamer); default CD player with iPod support
Sound Juicer	GNOME CD audio ripper (GStreamer)
Amarok	KDE4 multimedia audio player
Banshee	Multimedia player
Audacious	Multimedia player
Kscd	Music CD player
JuK	KDE4 music player (jukebox) for managing music collections
GNOME Music	GNOME Music player
GNOME CD Player	CD player
GNOME Sound Recorder	Sound recorder
XMMS	CD player
Clementine	Clementine music player (based on Rhythmbox)
Radio Tray	The RadioTray radio streaming player, works from the panel like an applet
Audacity	Professional multitrack audio editor
Ardour2	Digital Audio Workstation (DAW) and Hard Disk Recorder (HDR)
Rosegarden4	Audio/MIDI multitrack sequencer and score editor
FluidSynth	Software synthesizer
Qtractor	Audio/MIDI multitrack sequencer base on Qt toolkit

GNOME includes sound applications such as the GNOME CD player, Sound Juicer (Audio CD Extractor), GNOME Music, and Rhythmbox. Rhythmbox is the default sound multimedia player, supporting music files, radio streams, and podcasts (see Figure 6-10). In addition, you can use the Banshee and Clementine music players (similar to Rhythmbox), and the RadioTray radio streaming player (simple message tray access).

Figure 6-10. *Rhythmbox GNOME multimedia player*

GNOME Music is the new GNOME music player with tabs for Albums, Artists, and Songs (see Figure 6-11). GNOME Music accesses sound files in your Music folder. On the Songs tab, you can click on a file to play it. A toolbar opens at the bottom with buttons to control the playback. The button to the right opens a menu with shuffle and repeat options. At the top, click the Search button to search the list of sound files. To add files to the playlist, click the check button to display the check box next to each sound file, which you can check and then click the Add to Playlist button.

Figure 6-11. GNOME Music

KDE music applications include Amarok and JuK. Amarok is the primary multimedia player for the KDE desktop but will play on the GNOME desktop (see Figure 6-12). It includes access to Internet sources, local music files, and local devices such as Audio CDs. JuK (Music Jukebox) is the KDE4 music player for managing music collections.

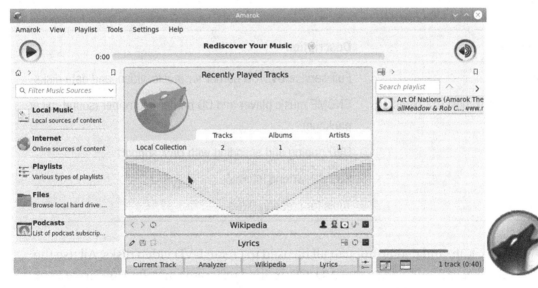

Figure 6-12. Amarok KDE multimedia player

Due to licensing and patent issues, Fedora does not install MP3 support by default. MP3 playback capability has been removed from multimedia players such as Rhythmbox and Banshee. The Fedora codec wizard will prompt you to install MP3 support when you first try to play an MP3 file, usually the GStreamer package and the free Fluendo MP3 codec. As an alternative to MP3, you can use Ogg Vorbis compression for music files (https://xiph.org/vorbis/).

Musicians should check the Fedora Musicians Guide for details on using Fedora applications for music development. Applications covered include Audacity (multitrack audio editor), Ardour (Digital Audio Workstation), Qtractor (multitrack sequencer), Rosegarden (audio and MIDI sequencer), FluidSynth (software synthesizer), LilyPond (music notation engraving), and GNU Solfege (music education).

Several DVD/CD ripper and writer programs can be used for CD music and MP3 writing (burners and rippers). These include Sound Juicer, Brasero (see Chapter 3), and K3b (see Table 6-5). GNOME features the CD audio ripper Sound Juicer. For burning DVD/CD music and data disks, you can use the Brasero DVD/CD burner. The Brasero DVD/CD burner is integrated into the GNOME file manager, the default file manager for the GNOME desktop. For KDE, you can use K3b.

Table 6-5. *DVD/CD Burners*

Application	Description
Brasero	Full-service DVD/CD burner for music, video, and data disks
Sound Juicer (audio CD extractor)	GNOME music player and CD burner and ripper (sound-juicer package)
ogmrip	DVD ripping and encoding with DivX support
K3b	KDE CD-writing interface
dvdauthor	Tools for creating DVDs

Brasero, K3b, and dvdauthor can all be used to create DVD video disks. All use the mkisofs, cdrecord, and cdda2wav DVD/CD-writing programs installed as part of your desktop. OGMrip can rip and encode DVD video. DVD video and CD music rippers may require additional codecs, for which the codec wizard will prompt you.

Burning DVD/CDs with GNOME (Brasero)

GNOME performs disk-burning operations using the Brasero Disc Burner application. Brasero is integrated into GNOME. The DVD/CD disk's GNOME desktop menu (right-click the DVD/CD disk's desktop icon) displays DVD/CD disk operations, such as burning data using a GNOME file manager window, copying disks, erasing them, and checking a disk.

Using the GNOME file manager to burn data to a DVD or CD is a matter of dragging files to an open blank CD or DVD and clicking the Write To Disk button. When you insert a blank DVD/CD, a window will open labeled CD/DVD Creator. To burn files, just drag them to that window. Click the Write To Disc button when you're ready to burn a DVD/CD. A Brasero Disc Burning Setup dialog will open, which will perform the actual write operation. You can also click the Properties button to open a dialog with burning options such as the burn speed.

The GNOME desktop also supports burning ISO images using Brasero. Just double-click the ISO image file or right-click the file and select Open with Brasero. This opens the Image Burning Setup dialog, which prompts you to burn the image. Be sure first to insert a blank DVD or CD into your DVD/CD burner.

You have the option of writing an ISO image to another disk. For the ISO image file, the Properties dialog lets you choose the folder to save the file. For copying to another disk, the Properties dialog lets you choose the burning speed and such options as using burnproof or performing a simulation first. Check Disc will check the integrity of the disk, with the option of using the disk's MD5 file, if available. The menu for DVD/CD RW disks will also display a Blank Disc entry, which will erase a disk.

For more complex DVD/CD burning options, you can use the Brasero DVD/CD burner application interface, called Brasero Disc Burner. Brasero supports drag-and-drop operations for creating audio CDs. In particular, it can handle DVD/CD read/write disks and can erase disks. It also supports multi-session burns, which add data to DVD/CD disks. Initially, Brasero displays a dialog with buttons for the type of project you want to create. You can create a data or audio project, create a DVD video disk, copy a DVD/CD, or burn a DVD/CD image file.

For a data project, the toolbar displays an Add button, which you use to select files and directories to be burned to your disk. You also can drag-and-drop files and folders to your data listing (right pane). You can choose to display a side panel (View menu), which will let you select files and directories.

Video Applications

Several projects provide TV, video, DivX, DVD, and DTV support for Linux. Most applications are already available from the Fedora and RPM Fusion repositories (http://rpmfusion.org). Be sure that the RPM Fusion DNF repository is configured for your system, and then use Packages or GNOME Software to install the applications. Aside from GStreamer applications, there are also several third-party multimedia applications you may want. All are available on the Fedora and RPM Fusion repositories.

Video and DVD Players

The default video player is GNOME Videos, whose interface has undergone a major change. The main dialog displays two tabs: Videos and Channels (see Figure 6-13). The Videos tab lists videos on your system and for those at specific sites on the Internet. Click the plus button at the left side of the header bar to display a menu for adding local or web videos. For a web video, you enter the video's web address.

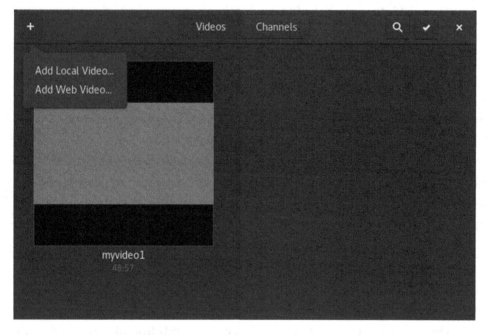

Figure 6-13. *GNOME Videos: Videos tab*

To play a video, click on it (see Figure 6-14). For full-screen viewing, click the expand arrows icon on the right side of the header bar. Move the mouse toward the bottom of the dialog to display viewing controls, including pause/play, repeat, sound volume, and skipping to the next or previous video. Click the back button (left side of the header bar) to return to the video listing. The menu button displays a menu with entries for video configuration such as aspect ratio, zoom, languages, subtitles, and screenshots. The Properties entry displays a Properties dialog listing technical video and audio information.

Figure 6-14. *GNOME Videos, playing a video*

To play several videos in sequence click on the checkmark button at the right side of the header bar to display check boxes at the corner of each video icon (see Figure 6-15). Click the check boxes of the videos you want to see, and then click the Play button on the lower-left corner of the dialog. To randomize the sequence, click the Shuffle button instead.

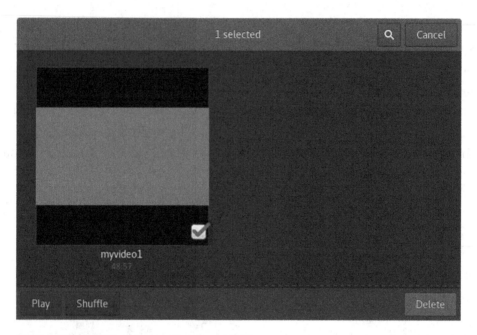

Figure 6-15. *GNOME videos, playing a video*

To remove a video, click the check icon at the right side of the header bar to display check boxes at the corner of each video icon. Click the check boxes of the videos you want to remove and then click the Delete button on the lower-right corner of the dialog.

The Channels tab list streaming services, such as Euronews, Apple Movie Trailers, and media on your system that you want to stream.

Clicking on the search icon opens a text box for searching for videos (see Figure 6-16). The resource searched is shown on the right side of the text box. Clicking on the resource name displays a menu with possible resources you can search, including your file system, YouTube, bookmarks, and supported streaming services.

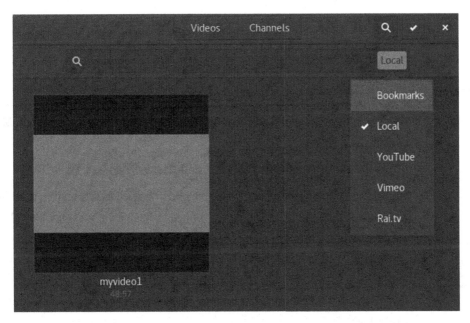

Figure 6-16. *GNOME Videos search*

From the GNOME Videos application menu on the top bar, you can select Preferences to open the Preferences dialog where you can set the enable plugins, configure the display color balance settings, and select the type of audio output (see Figure 6-17).

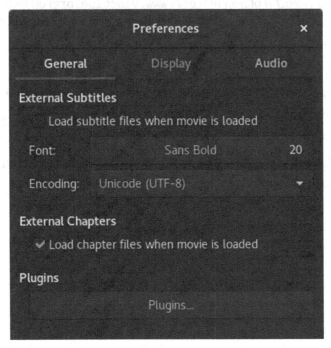

Figure 6-17. *GNOME Videos preferences*

Several popular video and DVD players are listed in Table 6-6.

Table 6-6. *Video Players*

Video Player	Description
Dragon Player	KDE multimedia player installed with KDE desktop but will play on the GNOME desktop (see Figure 6-18).
Kaffeine	KDE multimedia player (video and dvb) kaffeine package (see Figure 6-19).
MPlayer	Popular and capable multimedia/DVD players in use (RPM Fusion free repository). It is a cross-platform open source alternative to RealPlayer and Windows Media Player (www.mplayerhq.hu). MPlayer uses an extensive set of supporting libraries and applications like lirc, lame, lzo, and aalib, which are also available on the RPM Fusion repository. If you have trouble displaying video, be sure to check the preferences for different video devices and select one that works best.
Totem	GNOME movie player that uses GStreamer (see Figure 6-14). To expand Totem capabilities, you need to install added GStreamer plugins. The codec wizard will prompt you to install any needed media codecs and plugins.
VLC	The VideoLAN project (http://www.videolan.org) offers network-streaming support for most media formats, including MPEG-4 and MPEG-2. It includes a multimedia player, VLC, which can work on any kind of system (vlc package). VLC supports high-def hardware decoding (see Figure 6-20).
Kodi	Open source cross-platform integrated multimedia player incorporating a music, video, and TV player, a PVR for TV recording, video and music streaming, and photo viewing (formerly XBMC) https://kodi.tv/.
Xine	Multipurpose video engine and for Linux/UNIX systems that can play video, DVD, and audio discs. Many applications like Totem and Kaffeine use Xine support to play back DVD video. See http://xinehq.de for more information. For the Xine user interface, install the xine-ui package.

Figure 6-18. *KDE4 Dragon Player*

Figure 6-19. *Kaffeine*

Figure 6-20. *VLC Video Player (VideoLAN)*

Totem Plugins

The Totem movie player uses plugins to add capabilities such as Internet video streaming. Select the menu item Edit ➤ Plugins to open the Configure Plugins window (see Figure 6-21). Select the plugins you want. For added support, install the totem plugin packages.

```
totem-youtube
totem-lirc
```

The lirc package gives infrared remote control support. YouTube support is provided by the YouTube package.

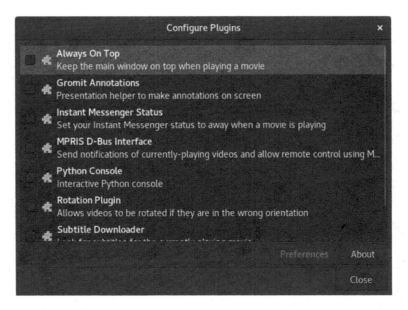

Figure 6-21. *Totem movie player plugins*

PiTiVi Video Editor

The PiTiVi video editor is an open source application that lets you edit your videos. It is accessible from the Applications overview as PiTiVi video editor. Check the PiTiVi website for more details (www.pitivi.org). You can download a quick-start manual from the Documentation page. PiTiVi is a GStreamer application and can work with any video file supported by an installed GStreamer plugin, including the ugly and bad plugins.

The PiTiVi window shows a Clip Library pane on the left and video playback for a selected video clip on the right (see Figure 6-22). To run a video clip, right-click its icon and select Play Clip. To add a video file to the library, click the Import Clips button on the toolbar. You can also drag-and-drop files directly to the Clip Library. The timeline at the bottom of the window displays the video and audio streams for the video clip you are editing, using a rule to show your position. To edit a video, drag its icon from the Clip Library to the timeline. To trim a video, you pass the mouse over the timeline video and audio streams. Trimming handles will appear that you can use to shorten the video. PiTiVi features ripple editing and rolling editing, splitting, and transitions.

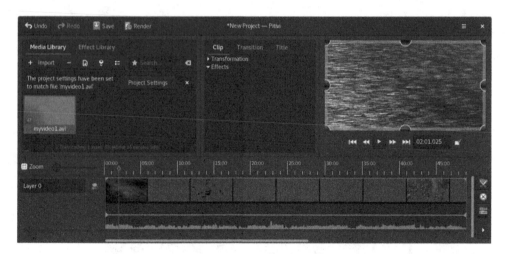

Figure 6-22. *PiTiVi video editor*

TV Players

The TV players that are provided on Fedora repositories are listed in Table 6-7.

Table 6-7. *TV Players*

TV Player	Description
Totem	Movie player that can access DVB stations using gnome-dvb. Choose Watch TV from the Movie menu. The Digital Television Assistant configures access to your DVB card. ATSC cards are not yet supported.
tvtime	TV player that works with many common video-capture cards, relying on drivers developed for TV tuner chips on those cards, such as the Conexant chips. It can only display a TV image. It has no recording or file playback capabilities. Check http://tvtime.sourceforge.net for more information.
Dragon Player	These are KDE multimedia players that will also play TV.
Kaffeine	KDE video recording and playback application on Linux systems. It can also play ATSC over-the-air digital broadcasts.
MythTV	Popular video recording and playback application on Linux systems. MythTV is available from the RPM Fusion free repository.
Kodi	Open source cross-platform integrated multimedia player with both TV viewing and PVR capabilities for TV recording (formerly XBMC) https://kodi.tv/.

Note To play DivX media on Fedora, use the Xvid OpenDivX codec `xvidcore`.

Xvid (DivX) and Matroska (mkv) on Linux

MPEG4 compressed files provide DVD-quality video with relatively small file sizes. They have become popular for distributing high-quality video files over the Internet. When you first try to play an MPEG4, the codec wizard will prompt you to install the needed codec packages to play it. Many multimedia applications such as VLC already support MPEG4 files.

MPEG4 files using the Matroska wrapper, also known by their file extension, `mkv`, can be played on most video players, including the VideoLan VLC player, Totem, Dragon Player, and Kaffeine. You will need HDTV codecs, such as MPEG4 AAC sound codec, installed to play the high-definition `mkv` file files. If needed, the codec wizard will prompt you to install them. To manage and create `mkv` files, you can install the `mkvtoolnix` packages and use the `mkvmerge` application.

You use the open source version of DivX, known as Xvid, to play DivX video (`libxvidcore` package). Most DivX files can be run using Xvid. Xvid is an entirely independent open source project, but it is compatible with DivX files. You can also download the XviD source code from `http://xvid.org`.

To convert DVD-Video files to an MPEG4/DivX format, you can use the `ffmpeg` libraries. Many DVD burners can use these to convert DVD video files to DivX/Xvid files.

Sound Settings

Your sound cards are detected automatically for you when you start up your system by ALSA, which is invoked by udev when your system starts up. Removable devices, like USB sound devices, are also detected. See Table 6-8 for a listing of sound device and interface tools.

Table 6-8. *Sound Device and Interface Tools*

Sound Tool	Description
KMix	KDE sound connection configuration and volume tool
Sound	GNOME Settings Sound, used to select and configure your sound interface
PulseAudio	PulseAudio sound interface, the default sound interface for Fedora Linux `https://www.freedesktop.org/wiki/Software/PulseAudio/`

In addition to hardware drivers, sound systems also use sound interfaces to direct encoded sound streams from an application to the hardware drivers and devices. Fedora Linux uses the PulseAudio server for its sound interface. PulseAudio aims to combine and consolidate all sound interfaces into a simple, flexible, and powerful server. The ALSA hardware drivers are still used, but the application interface is handled by PulseAudio. PulseAudio is installed as the default set up for Fedora Linux for both GNOME and KDE. PulseAudio provides packages for interfacing with applications like GStreamer and VLC.

PulseAudio is a cross-platform sound server, allowing you to modify the sound level for different audio streams separately. See `https://www.freedesktop.org/wiki/Software/PulseAudio/` for documentation and help. PulseAudio offers complete control over all your sound streams, letting you combine sound devices and direct the stream anywhere on your network. PulseAudio is not confined to a single system. It is network capable, letting you direct sound from one PC to another.

As an alternative, you can use the command-line ALSA control tool, `alsamixer` (`alsa-tools` package). This will display all connections and allow you to use keyboard commands to select (arrow keys), mute (m key), or set sound levels (Page Up and Down). Press the Esc key to exit. The `amixer` command lets you perform the same tasks for different sound connections from the command line. To actually play and record from the command-line, you can use the `play` and `rec` commands.

Volume Control

Volume control for different applications is displayed on the application's dialog as the speaker icon. You can click it to change your application's output sound volume using a sliding bar. The sliding sound bar on the system status area menu also lets you set the sound volume, as shown here.

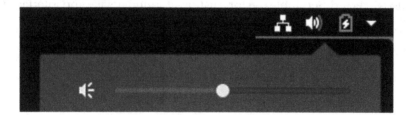

To perform volume control for specific devices like a microphone, you use the GNOME Settings Sound dialog.

Sound: PulseAudio

You configure sound devices and set the volume for sound effects, input, output, and applications using the GNOME Settings Sound dialog. The Sound dialog has four tabs: Output, Input, Sound Effects, and Applications (see Figure 6-23). Corresponding sound configuration is available on KDE, which also uses PulseAudio.

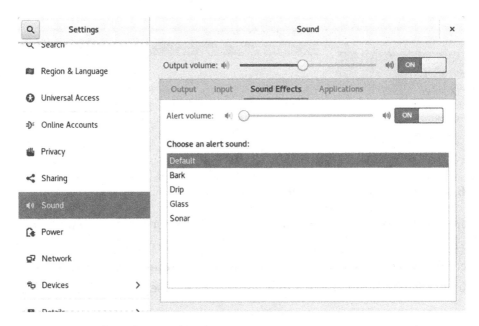

Figure 6-23. *Sound preferences*

Volume control is integrated into the Sound dialog. A sliding bar at the top of the dialog, above the tabs, lets you set the output volume.

The Sound Effects tab lets you select an alert sound, such as Drip or Sonar. A sliding bar lets you set the volume for your sound alerts, or turn them off by clicking the ON/OFF switch.

On the Input tab, you set the input volume for an input device such as a microphone. An ON/OFF switch lets you disable it. When speaking or recording, the input level is displayed (see Figure 6-24). If you have more than one input device, they will be listed in the "Choose a Device for Sound Input" section. Choose the one you want to configure.

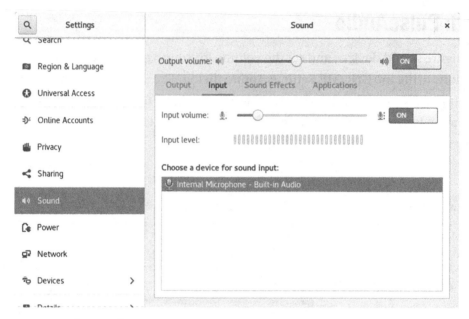

Figure 6-24. *Pulse preferences: Input*

On the Output tab, you can configure balance settings for a selected output device. If you have more than one device, it will be listed in the Profile menu. Choose the one you want to configure. The available settings will change according to the device selected. For a simple Analog Stereo Output, there is only a single balance setting (see Figure 6-25).

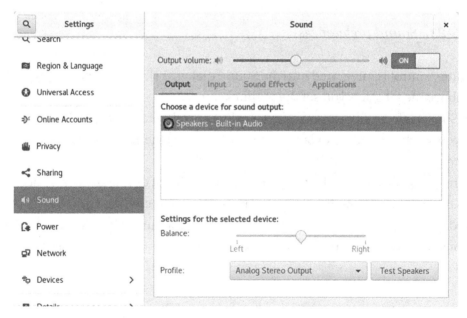

Figure 6-25. *Pulse preferences: Output*

The Applications tab will show applications currently using sound devices. You can set the sound volume for each (see Figure 6-26).

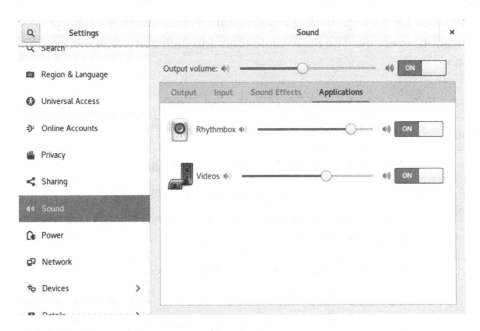

Figure 6-26. *Pulse preferences: Applications*

Sound devices that support multiple interfaces like analog surround sound 7.1 and digital SPDIF output, may have an extensive list of interface combinations in the Profile menu. The Input and Output tabs will then display configuration settings for the selected device. With Analog Surround 7.1 Output selected, the Output tab will show settings for Balance, Fade, and Subwoofer. Configuring digital output for SPDIF (digital) connectors is a simple matter of selecting the digital output entry on the Profiles menu.

Note   To find the actual name of the SPDIF output is not always obvious. You may need to run `aplay -L` in a terminal window to see what the name of the digital output device is on your system. It will be the entry with `Digital` in it.

PulseAudio Applications

For additional configuration abilities, you can also install the PulseAudio applications. Most begin with the prefix pa in the package name. PulseAudio tools are accessible from the Applications overview. The PulseAudio tools and their command names are shown in Table 6-9.

Table 6-9. *PulseAudio Commands (Command-Line)*

Sound Tool	Description
pacat	Plays, records, and configures a raw audio stream.
pacmd	Generates a shell for entering configuration commands.
pactl	Controls a PulseAudio server, changing input and output sources and providing information about the server.
padsp	PulseAudio wrapper for OSS sound applications.
pamon	Links to pacat.
paplay	Plays back audio. The -d option specifies the output device, the -s option specifies the server, and the --volume option sets the volume (link to pacat).
parec	Records and audio streams (link to pacat).
parecord	Records and audio streams (link to pacat).
pasuspender	Suspends a PulseAudio server.
pax11publish	Accesses PulseAudio server credentials.

PulseAudio Volume Control, pavucontrol

PulseAudio Volume Meter, pavumeter

PulseAudio Manager, paman

You can use the PulseAudio Volume Control tool to set the sound levels for different playback applications and sound devices (choose PulseAudio Volume Control on the Applications overview). The PulseAudio Volume Control applications will show five tabs: Playback, Recording, Output Devices, Input Devices, and Configuration (see Figure 6-27). The Playback tab shows all the applications currently using PulseAudio. You can adjust the volume for each application separately.

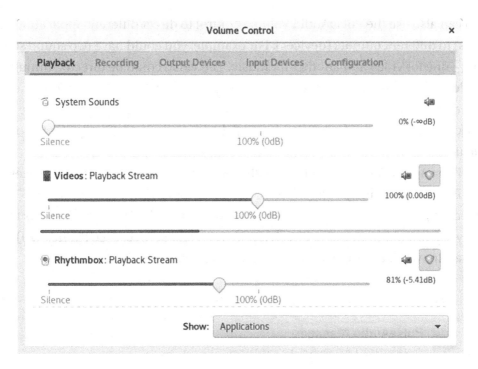

Figure 6-27. *PulseAudio volume control: Playback tab*

You can use the Output tab panel to set the volume control at the source and select different output devices, such as Headphones (see Figure 6-28). The volume for input and recording devices are set on the Recording and Input Devices tabs. The Configuration tab lets you choose different device profiles.

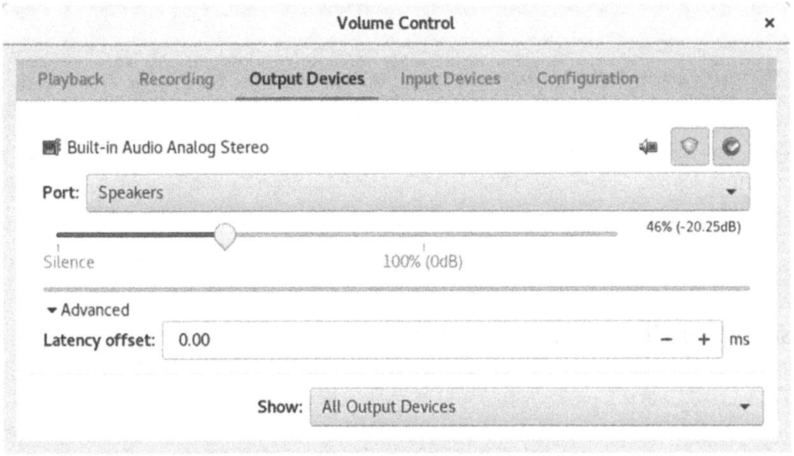

Figure 6-28. *PulseAudio volume control: Output Devices tab*

You can also use the PulseAudio Volume control to direct different applications (streams) to different outputs (devices). For example, you could have two sound sources running—one for video and another for music. The video could be directed through one device to headphones, and the music through another device to speakers, or even to another PC. To redirect an application to a different device, right-click its name in the Playback tab. A pop-up menu will list the available devices and let you select the one you want to use.

The PulseAudio Volume Meter tool will show the actual volume of your devices.

The PulseAudio Manager will show information about your PulseAudio configuration, accessible from the Applications overview. The Devices tab shows the currently active sinks (outputs or directed receivers) and sources (see Figure 6-29). The Clients tab shows all the applications currently using PulseAudio for sound.

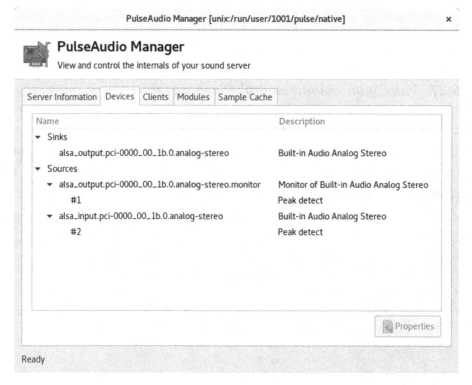

Figure 6-29. *PulseAudio Manager: Devices tab*

Simultaneous output creates a virtual output device to the same hardware device. This lets you channel two sources onto the same output. With PulseAudio Volume Control, you could then channel playback streams to the same output device, but using a virtual device as the output for one. This lets you change the output volume for each stream independently. You could have music and voice directed to the same hardware device, using a virtual device for music and the standard device for voice. You can then reduce the music stream or raise the voice stream.

.

CHAPTER 7

Internet Applications: Web and FTP

Fedora provides powerful web and FTP clients for accessing the Internet. Many are installed automatically and are ready to use when you first start up your Linux system. Linux also includes full Java development support, letting you run and construct Java applets. This chapter covers some of the more popular web, Java, and FTP clients available on Linux. Web and FTP clients connect to sites that run servers, using web pages and FTP files to provide services to users.

Web browsers and FTP clients are commonly used to conduct secure transactions, such as logging in to remote sites, ordering items, or transferring files. Such operations are currently secured by encryption methods provided by the Secure Sockets Layer (SSL). If you use a browser for secure transactions, it should be SSL-enabled. Most browsers, such as Mozilla and ELinks, include SSL support. For FTP operations, you can use the SSH version of ftp, sftp, or the Kerberos 5 version. Linux distributions include SSL as part of a standard installation.

Web Browsers

Most web browsers are designed to access several different kinds of information. Web browsers can access a web page on a remote website or a file on your own system. Some browsers can also access a remote news server or an FTP site. The type of information for a site is specified by the keyword http for websites, nntp for news servers, ftp for FTP sites, or file for files on your own system.

253

© Richard Petersen 2018
R. Petersen, *Beginning Fedora Desktop*, https://doi.org/10.1007/978-1-4842-3882-0_7

Popular browsers for Fedora include Firefox (Mozilla), Konqueror, Rekonq, GNOME Web (Epiphany), Chrome (Google), and Lynx (see Table 7-1). Firefox is the default web browser used on most Linux distributions, including Fedora. Rekonq is the KDE web browser, accessible from the KDE desktop, and Epiphany is the GNOME web browser. Chrome is the Google web browser. Lynx and ELinks are command-line-based browsers with no graphics capabilities, but in every other respect they are fully functional web browsers.

Table 7-1. *Web Browsers*

Website	Description
Firefox	The Mozilla project Firefox web browser; Fedora desktop default browser https://www.mozilla.org
Konqueror	KDE desktop web browser https://www.konqueror.org
Rekonq	KDE desktop web browser https://rekonq.kde.org
GNOME Web (Epiphany)	GNOME web browser https://wiki.gnome.org/Apps/Web
Chromium	Google Chrome web browser https://www.chromium.org
Lynx	Text-based command-line web browser https://lynx.isc.org
ELinks	Text-based command-line web browser https://elinks.or.cz

The Firefox Web Browser

Firefox is based on the Netscape core source code known as Mozilla (see Figure 7-1). In current releases, Fedora uses Firefox as its primary browser. The Mozilla project is an open source project based on the original Netscape browser code that provides a development framework for web-based applications, primarily the web browser and email client. The Mozilla project site is https://www.mozilla.org, and the site commonly used for plugin and extension development is https://www.mozdev.org. You can also sign up for a Firefox account which can then make your bookmarks available to the Firefox browsers on all your devices. Firefox calls this feature the pocket. So you can save a bookmark to your pocket on one of your Firefox browsers, and have it available on the Firefox browsers on all your devices.

Figure 7-1. *Firefox web browser*

Firefox is installed by default with icons on the dash and the Applications overview. When opened, Firefox displays the first tab. Firefox is designed to display tabs, each of which can display a complete web page, including the Firefox toolbar and sidebar. The tab title is shown at the top, and next to it is a plus button (+) you can click to add a new tab. You can also press Ctrl+t. You an easily switch from one page to another by click its tab. You can rearrange tabs by clicking and holding on a tab title and moving it to the right or left.

Within a tab, a navigation toolbar is displayed at the top, with an address bar (text box) for entering a URL address and a series of navigation buttons for accessing web pages. On the left side of the toolbar are the Next and Previous buttons for paging through previously accessed web pages, followed by a cancel button for loading a page (X). This becomes a refresh button when the page is fully displayed. Next to it is the Home button to move you to your home page.

When you enter a web page name in the address bar, Firefox performs a dynamic search on previously accessed pages and displays the pages in a drop-down menu, which you can choose from. Within the address bar to the right are buttons for recent history (down arrow), page actions (…), saving to the pocket (down arrow), and marking the page as a bookmark (star). The page actions button displays a menu for tasks such as bookmarking the page, saving to the pocket, and emailing the link.

Firefox provides a search bar (text box) where you can use different search engines for searching the Web, selected sites, or particular items. You have the option to display a search bar either to the right of the address bar or at the bottom of the recent history list. By default, the search bar is only shown at the bottom of the recent history list. It shows a list of icons for the different search services, showing the name of the one your mouse passes over. Upon clicking one, it moves you to that the page for the search service. To the right of the icon list is a gear icon, which you can click to open Firefox Preferences at the entry where you can choose to display the search bar in the toolbar instead. When on the toolbar, the search bar is displayed to the right of the address bar. A pop-up menu lets you select a search engine, showing small icons for the options. Currently included are Google, Bing, Amazon, and eBay.

To the right of the address bar are buttons for history-bookmarks, displaying the sidebar, and the Firefox menu. The history-bookmarks button displays a menu for accessing your bookmarks, history, downloads, and screenshots, as well as Firefox account supported features such as your pocket list and synced tabs.

To add a bookmark for a page, click the bookmark button on the right side of the address bar. This displays an Page Bookmarked dialog with a pop-up menu for folders and tags. The Folder menu is set to the Other Bookmarks folder by default. You can also select the Bookmarks Toolbar or the Bookmarks Menu. Clicking on the down button to the right expands a frame where you can edit your bookmark folders, adding new ones. Selecting Bookmarks on the history/bookmarks menu (accessible form the toolbar) displays the Bookmarks menu, showing a list of your bookmarks from which you can select one to view. Here you can also bookmark a page. The Show All Bookmarks entry at the bottom of the list opens the Library dialog where you can edit your bookmarks or delete bookmarks.

To search a current page for certain text, enter Ctrl+f. This opens a search toolbar at the bottom of Firefox from which you can enter a search term. You have search options to highlight found entries or to match character case. The Next and Previous buttons let you move to the next found pattern.

When you download a file using Firefox, the download is managed by the Download Manager. You can download several files at once. Progress is displayed download button on the toolbar, which you can click to see your downloads. You can cancel a download at any time or just pause a download, resuming it later.

Selecting History on the History/Bookmarks menu (accessible form the toolbar) displays the History menu, showing a list of your recently accessed web pages from which you can select one to view. You can also see recently closed tabs and Firefox windows. To clear your recent history, choose the Clear Recent History entry. The Show All History opens the Library dialog as the history entry, letting you edit, access, bookmark, or remove previous pages.

The Firefox menu lets you perform web page tasks such as zooming, opening new windows, printing and saving a page, and performing searches on a page. There are also administrative options such as Preference, Add-ons, and the Library. The Library dialog lets you manage all your history and bookmarks. On Preferences you can set your privacy and search options, as well as setting your home page, language, fonts, download location.

The Add-ons entry on the menu opens the Add-ons window with tabs for Get Add-ons, Extensions, Themes, and Plugins. Click the one you want to open a brief description and display the Add to Firefox button, which you click to open a download and install dialog. The Extensions tab lists installed Extensions with buttons for Preferences, Disable, and Uninstall for each. On the Plugins tab, you can disable or enable embedded applications, such as DivX, iTunes, QuickTime, and Skype. The Themes tab lets you choose a theme.

Firefox also supports profiles. You can set up different Firefox configurations, each with preferences and bookmarks. This is useful for computers like laptops that connect to different networks or are used for different purposes. You can select and create profiles by starting up the profile manager. Enter the `firefox` command in a terminal window with the `-P` option.

```
firefox -P
```

A default profile is already set up. You can create a new profile, which runs the profile wizard to prompt you for the profile name and directory to use. Select a profile to use and click Start Firefox. The last profile you used will be used again the next time you start Firefox. You have the option to prompt for the profile to use at startup, otherwise run the `firefox  -P` command again to change your profile.

GNOME Web (Epiphany)

GNOME Web, formerly known as Epiphany, is a GNOME web browser with a simple interface designed to be fast (see Figure 7-2). You can find out more about Epiphany at `https://wiki.gnome.org/Apps/Web`. Web works well as a simple browser with a clean interface. It is also integrated with the desktop, featuring a download applet that will continue after closing Web. Web also supports tabbed panels for multiple website access. Its applications menu lists options such as New Window, New Incognito Window, the import and export of bookmarks, History, and Preferences. For page-specific operations such as tabs, print, save, zooming, and find, click the menu button at the top right. You can install GNOME Web using GNOME Software and searching under Epiphany or Web. Install the GNOME Web package. Once installed, you can access it as Web.

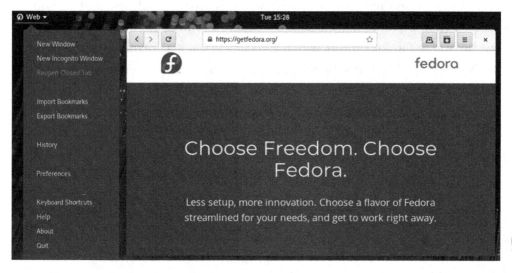

Figure 7-2. *Web (Epiphany) web browser*

Chromium

Google's Chromium web browser (`https://ww.chromium.org`) provides easy and very secure access to the Web with full Google integration. You can install it using GNOME Software, which will enable the Google repository from which it will be downloaded (`chromium`). You can access Chromium from the Applications overview as Chromium Web Browser. You are first prompted to enter your Google account email and password so that your online preferences and bookmarks can be used, but you can pass.

On Chromium, primacy is afforded to tabs. At the top of the Chromium window are your tabs for open web pages, with a square image button at the end of the tabs for opening a new tab (see Figure 7-3). Chromium features a simple toolbar with navigation buttons and a bookmark button (star icon). To close a tab, click the x button to the right of the tab title.

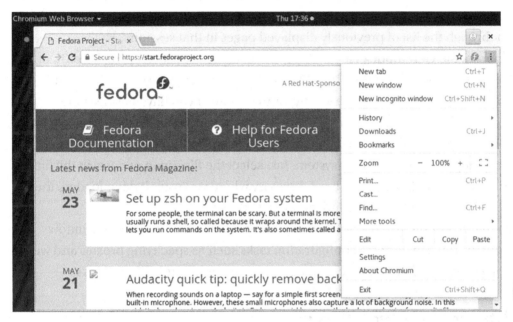

Figure 7-3. *Chromium Web browser*

To the right of the URL box, a menu button displays a drop-down menu for menu items for browser operations such as new tabs, print, zoom, history, bookmarks, and downloads. To configure Chromium, select Settings from this menu to open the Chromium Settings tab. Here you can set your home page, default search service, and themes. Click the Advanced on the sidebar (top-left menu icon) to expand the Settings dialog to let you manage passwords, languages, downloads, printing, and accessibility.

When you open a new tab, a thumbnail listing of recently closed and most visited sites is displayed. Clicking a thumbnail moves you to that site. On a new tab, the bookmark toolbar is also displayed, which you can use to access a site.

Konqueror: KDE Web and FTP Access

The KDE Konqueror is a full-featured web browser and an FTP client. It includes a box for entering either a pathname for a local file or a URL for a web page on the Internet or your intranet. A navigation toolbar can be used to display previous web pages. The Home button will always return you to your home page. When accessing a web page, the page is displayed as on any web browser. With the navigation toolbar, you can move back and forth through the list of previously displayed pages in that session.

You can set the view mode (View ➤ View Mode menu) to use KHTML, WebKit, or Embedded Advanced Text Editor. The editor displays the web page source code and allows you to edit a copy of the page locally, or to the site, if you have permission.

Konqueror also operates as an FTP client. When you access an FTP site, you navigate the remote directories as you would your own. The operations to download a file are the same as copying a file on your local system. Just select the file's icon or entry in the file manager window and drag it to the local directory where you want it downloaded, then select the Copy entry from the pop-up menu that appears.

To configure Konqueror, select Configure Konqueror from a Konqueror window Settings menu. You can perform configuration tasks such as specifying proxies and web page displays, choosing fonts to use, managing cookies, and setting bookmarks.

The KDE Rekonq Web Browser

Rekonq is the new web browser for KDE (see `https://rekonq.kde.org` for more details). Rekonq is based on the WebKit layout engine, like Chrome and Apple's Safari. A navigation bar lets you move through accessed pages on a tab, refresh a site, or enter the address of a new site (see Figure 7-4). On the right side of the navigation bar is a menu button that displays Rekonq browser operations such as open, save, print, panel display, help, and configuration. A bookmark navigation bar can be displayed.

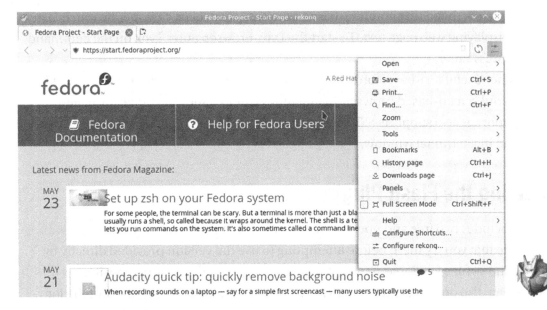

Figure 7-4. Rekonq web browser

Like Chrome, Rekonq is tab-based. Tabs can be reordered with a click-and-drag of their tab thumbnails. To close a tab, click its x button to the right of its name. You add new tabs by clicking the New Tab button to the right of an open tab. The new tab opens to the Favorites page. Should you ever want to return to the Favorites page, just open a new tab.

To configure Rekonq, select Configure Rekonq from the menu. The General tab specifies the page displayed on Rekonq at startup, the default being a new tab page. You can set it to your home page or to the last opened pages. Set your home page in the Home Page URL text box. The Tabs tab determines new tab behavior, such as displaying your Favorites page in a new tab or opening links in a new tab. Appearance is where you set the default font and font size. WebKit sets WebKit and Plugin settings, such as image loading, Java support, and storage use. Privacy controls your cache, cookies, and proxy settings.

Lynx and ELinks: Line-Mode Browsers

Lynx is a line-mode browser you can use without the X Window System. A web page is displayed as text only. A text page can contain links to other Internet resources but does not display any graphics, video, or sound. Except for the display limitations, Lynx is a fully functional web browser. You can also use Lynx to download files or access local pages. All information on the Web is still accessible to you. Because it does not require much of the overhead that graphics-based browsers need, Lynx can operate much faster, quickly displaying web page text. To start the Lynx browser, enter `lynx` on the command line and press Enter.

Another useful text-based browser shipped with most distributions is ELinks. ELinks is a powerful screen-based browser that includes features such as frame, form, and table support. It also supports SSL secure encryption. To start ELinks, enter the `elinks` command in a terminal window.

Enabling the Flash Plugin

Fedora includes two free and open source versions of Flash: `swfdec` and `gnash`. It is preferable that you try these before attempting to use the version provided directly by Adobe. The `swfdec` version is newer. Both are available on the Fedora repository.

You can also download and install the Adobe Flash plugin provided by Adobe for Linux. Adobe maintains a repository compatible with Fedora that contains the Flash plugin. Install the Adobe repository configuration package and then use `dnf` to download and install the Flash plugins. The Fedora project Flash wiki refers to an Ask Fedora page that explains the procedure in detail; see `http://fedoraproject.org/wiki/Flash`. Once the repository is configured, you can use `dnf` to install the Flash package. The Flash plugin package is `flash-plugin`.

```
sudo dnf install flash-plugin
```

The first time you install any package from the Adobe repository, you are prompted to install its package key. A dialog will be displayed with the message "Do You Trust the Source of the Packages?" Click Yes to install the Adobe repository package key.

Simply restart Firefox to enable your Flash plugin. On the Tools ➤ Add-ons Plugins tab, you will find an entry for Flash.

Java for Linux

To develop Java applications, use Java tools, and run many Java products, you use the Java Software Development Kit (SDK) and the Java Runtime Environment (JRE). The SDK is a superset of the JRE, adding development tools like compilers and debuggers. Sun (now owned by Oracle) has open sourced Java as the OpenJDK project and supports and distributes Linux versions. The JRE subset can be installed as java-1.8.0. The java-

`1.8.0-openjdk` package installs the Java 8 runtime environment, and `java-9-openjdk` installs both the JRE and the Java development tools for Java 9. Java packages and applications are listed in Table 7-2. Install with Packages or `dnf`.

Table 7-2. *Java Packages and Java Web Applications*

Application	Description
Java Development Kit, OpenJDK	An open source Java development environment with a compiler, interpreters, debugger, and more (include the JRE), `http://openjdk.java.net`, `java-9-openjdk`
Java Runtime Environment, OpenJRE (java-1.8.0)	An open source Java runtime environment, including the Java virtual machine, `java-1.8.0-openjdk` `http://openjdk.java.net`
Java Platform Standard Edition (JSE)	Complete Java collection, including JRE, JDK, and API,
GNU Java Compiler	GNU Public Licensed Java Compiler (GCJ) to compile Java programs

Several compatible GNU packages (Java-like) are provided that allow you to run Java applets using GNU free Java support. These include GNU Java compiler (`gcj`) and the Eclipse Java compiler (`ecj`).

BitTorrent Clients

GNOME and KDE provide very effective BitTorrent clients. With BitTorrent, you can download very large files quickly in a shared distributed download operation where several users participate in downloading different parts of a file, sending their parts of the download to other participants, known as peers. Instead of everyone trying to access a few central servers, all peers participating in the BitTorrent operation become sources for the file being downloaded. Certain peers function as seeders for those who have already downloaded the file but continue to send parts to those who need them.

For the Fedora desktop, you can install the GNOME BitTorrent client Transmission or qBitTorrent. For KDE, you can use the KTorrent BitTorrent client. To perform a BitTorrent download, you need the BitTorrent file for the file you want to download. The BitTorrent file for the Fedora DVD ISO image is `Fedora-Workstation-Live-x86_64-28.torrent`. When you download the file from the `https://torrent.fedoraproject.org/` site, you will be prompted to open it directly with Transmission or to save it to a file.

Transmission can handle several torrents at once. On the toolbar are buttons for starting, pausing, and removing a download. The Add button can be used to load a BitTorrent file (.torrent), thus setting up a download. You also can drag-and-drop a torrent file to the Transmission window. When you first open a torrent file, the Torrent Options window opens where you can specify the destination folder and the priority. The option to start the download automatically will be selected by default. Figure 7-5 shows Transmission with two BitTorrent operations set up, one of which is active. A progress bar shows how much of the file has been downloaded.

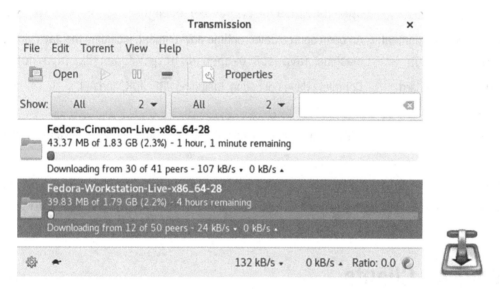

Figure 7-5. *Transmission BitTorrent client*

You could set up Transmission to manage several BitTorrent operations, of which only a few may be active, others paused, and still others complete but continuing to function as seeders. From the first drop-down menu, you can select All, Active, Downloading, Seeding, Paused, Finished, and Queued torrents. You can also choose those verifying and those that have errors. From the second menu, you can choose trackers, public or private torrents (privacy), and select by priority (high, normal, or low).

To remove a torrent, right-click it and select Remove. Choose Delete Files and Remove to remove what you have downloaded so far.

To see more information about a torrent, select it and then click the Properties button (see Figure 7-6). This opens a Properties window with tabs for Information, Peers, Trackers, Files, and Options. On the Information tab, the Activity section shows statistics such as the progress, times, and errors, and the Details section shows the origin, comment, and location of the download folder. Peers shows all the peers participating in the download. Trackers displays the location of the tracker, which is the server that manages the torrent operation. Files shows the progress of the file download (a torrent could download more than one file). The Options tab lets you set bandwidth and connection parameters, limiting the download or upload and the number of peers.

Figure 7-6. *Transmission BitTorrent client properties*

The qBitTorrent client is a feature-rich and simple to use cross-platform client available for Fedora (see Figure 7-7), `https://www.qbittorrent.org/`. It based on Qt (KDE) graphical user interface. A sidebar lets you access your torrents by status, as well as check errors and warnings. Use the toolbar to control torrents, add or remove torrents, pause or resume, and rearrange the list. To see information about a particular torrent, select it and use the buttons at the bottom of the window to display information, such as general statistics (progress and speed), peers, and trackers.

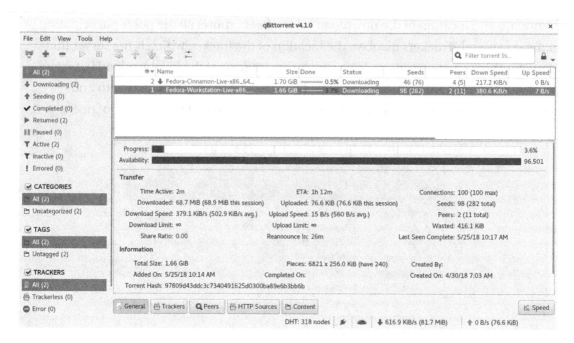

Figure 7-7. *qBitTorrent client*

FTP Clients

With File Transfer Protocol (FTP) clients, you can connect to a corresponding FTP site and download files from it. These sites feature anonymous logins that let any user access their files. Basic FTP client capabilities are incorporated into the Dolphin (KDE), Nemo (Cinnamon), and Caja (Mate) file managers. You can use a file manager window to access an FTP site and drag files to local directories to download them. Effective FTP clients are also now incorporated into most web browsers, making web browsers the primary downloading tool. Firefox, in particular, has strong FTP download capabilities.

Although file managers and web browsers provide effective access to public (anonymous login) sites, to access private sites, you may need a stand-alone FTP client like curl, wget, Filezilla, gFTP, lftp, or ftp. These clients let you enter usernames and passwords with which you can access a private FTP site. The stand-alone clients are also useful for large downloads from public FTP sites, especially those with little or no web display support. Popular Linux FTP clients are listed in Table 7-3.

Table 7-3. *Linux FTP Clients*

FTP Client	Description
Dolphin	KDE file manager
Nemo	GNOME file manager
gFTP	GNOME FTP client, gftp
ftp	Command-line FTP client
lftp	Command-line FTP client capable of multiple connections
curl	Internet transfer client (FTP and HTTP)
Filezilla	Linux version of the open source Filezilla ftp client

Network File Transfer: FTP

With File Transfer Protocol (FTP) clients, you can transfer extremely large files directly from one site to another. FTP can handle text and binary files. FTP performs a remote login to another account on another system connected to you on a network. Once logged in to that other system, you can transfer files to and from it. To log in, you must know the login name and password for the account on the remote system; however, many sites on the Internet allow public access using FTP. Such sites serve as depositories for large files that anyone can access and download. These sites are often referred to as FTP sites, and in many cases, their Internet addresses begin with the term ftp, such as ftp.gnome. org. These public sites allow anonymous FTP login from any user. For the login name, you use the word *anonymous*, and for the password, you use your email address. You can then transfer files from that site to your own system.

Several FTP protocols are available for accessing sites that support them. The original FTP protocol is used for most anonymous sites. FTP transmissions can also be encrypted using SSH2, the SFTP protocol. More secure connections use FTPS for TLS/SSL encryption. Some sites support a simplified version of FTP called File Service Protocol, FSP. FTP clients may support different protocols, such as gFTP for FSP and Filezilla for TLS/SSL. Most clients support both FTP and SSH2.

Web Browser-Based FTP: Firefox

You can access an FTP site and download files from it with any web browser. Browsers are useful for locating individual files, although not for downloading a large set of files. A web browser is effective for checking out an FTP site to see what files are listed there. When you access an FTP site with a web browser, the entire list of files in a directory is listed as a web page. You can move to a subdirectory by clicking its entry. You can easily browse through an FTP site to download files. To download a file, click the download link. This will start the transfer operation, opening a dialog for selecting your local directory and the name for the file. The default name is the same as on the remote system. On many browsers, you can manage your downloads with a download manager, which will let you cancel a download operation in progress or remove other downloads requested. The manager will show the time remaining, the speed, and the amount transferred for the current download.

GNOME Desktop FTP: Connect to Server

The easiest way to download files from an FTP site is to use the built-in FTP capabilities of the GNOME file manager, GNOME Files. The FTP operation has been seamlessly integrated into standard desktop file operations. Downloading files from an FTP site is as simple as dragging files from one folder window to another, where one of the folders happens to be located on a remote FTP site. Use the GNOME file manager (GNOME Files) to access a remote FTP site, listing files in the remote folder, just as local files are (see Figure 7-8). In a file manager's Location bar (Ctrl+l or Enter Location from the file manager Files applications menu), enter the FTP site's URL using the prefix `ftp://` and press Enter. A dialog opens prompting you to specify how you want to connect. You can connect anonymously for a public FTP site, or connect as a user by supplying your username and password (private site). You can also choose to remember the password.

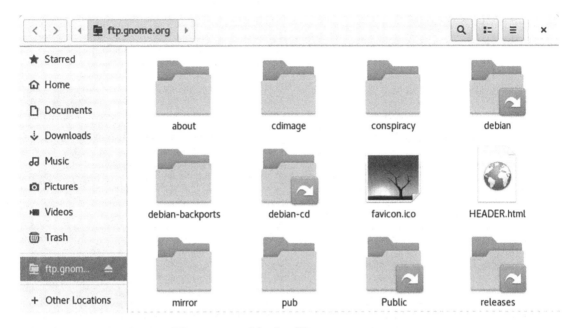

Figure 7-8. *GNOME FTP access with the file manager*

Folders on the FTP site will be displayed, and you can drag files to a local folder to download them. You can navigate through the folders as you would with any file manager folder, opening folders or returning to the parent folder. To download a file, just drag it from the FTP window to a local folder window. To upload a file, drag it from your local folder to the window for the open FTP folder. Your file will be uploaded to that FTP site (if you have permission to do so). You can also delete files on the site's folders if allowed.

You can also use the Connect to Server bar in the file manager (see Figure 7-9) to connect, which remembers your previous FTP connections. To access the Connect to Server bar, click on the Other Locations entry in any file manager sidebar. The Connect to Server bar is displayed at the bottom of the file manager window. It shows a text box for the server address, a menu button to display previous addresses, and a Connect button. Enter the server address. The address is remembered and added to the previous servers list. Then click the Connect button. A dialog opens letting you specify an Anonymous login or enter a username and password. Click the Connect button to access the site.

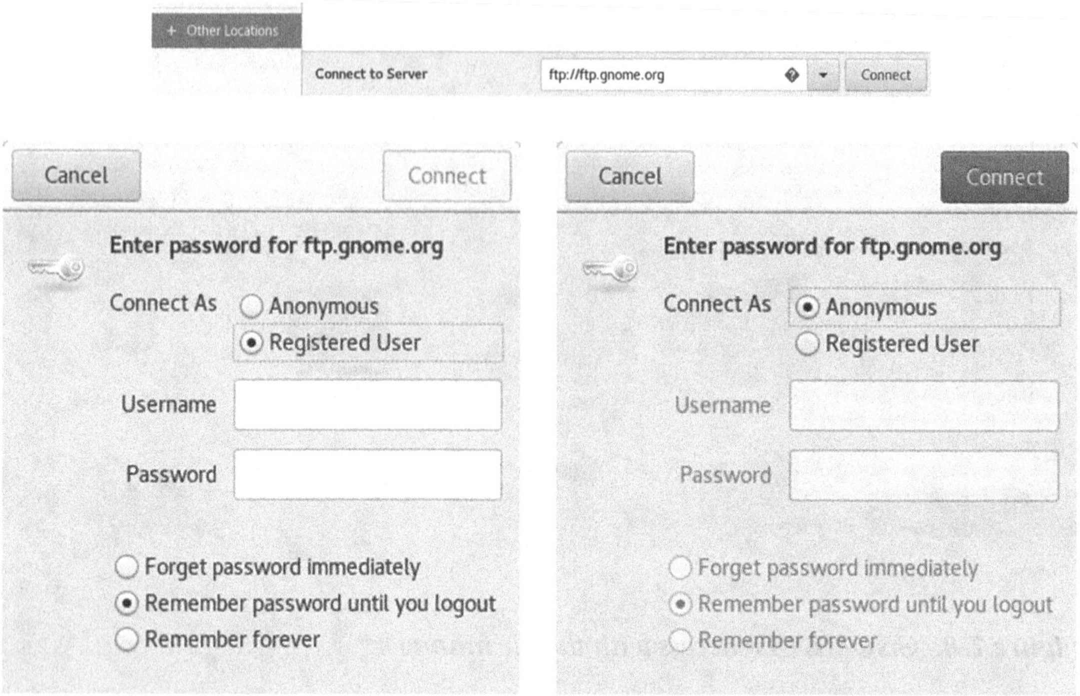

Figure 7-9. *GNOME FTP access with Connect to Server and the file manager*

The top directory of the remote FTP site will be displayed in a file manager window. Use the file manager to progress through the remote FTP site's directory tree until you find the file you want. Then, open another window for the local directory to which you want the remote files copied. In the window showing the FTP files, select those you want to download. Then click and drag those files to the window for the local folder. As files are downloaded, a dialog appears showing the progress.

The file manager window's sidebar will list an entry for the FTP site accessed. An eject button is shown to the right of the FTP site's name. To disconnect from the site, click this button. The FTP entry will disappear along with the FTP sites icons and file listings.

The KDE File Managers: Konqueror and Dolphin

On the KDE Desktop, the desktop file managers (Konqueror and Dolphin) have built-in FTP capability. The FTP operation has been seamlessly integrated into standard desktop file operations. Downloading files from an FTP site is as simple as copying files by dragging them from one directory window to another, with one of the directories located on a remote FTP site. On KDE, you can use a file manager window to access a remote FTP site. Files in the remote directory are listed just as your local files are. To download files from an FTP site, you open a window to access that site, entering the URL for the FTP site in the window's location box. Use the `ftp://` protocol for FTP access. Once connected, open the directory you want, and then open another window for the local directory to which you want the remote files copied. In the window showing the FTP files, select the ones you want to download. Then click-and-drag those files to the window for the local directory. A pop-up menu appears with choices for Copy, Link, or Move Select Copy. The selected files are then downloaded. Another window opens, showing the download progress and displaying the name of each file in turn, along with a bar indicating the percentage downloaded so far.

Filezilla

Filezilla is an open source FTP client originally implemented on Windows systems (`https://filezilla-project.org`). Use Packages to install it. Once installed, you can access it from the Applications overview. The interface displays a left and right pane for local and remote folders. You navigate through folder trees, with the files of a selected folder displayed below. To download a file, right-click a file in the Remote site pane (right) and select Download. To upload, right-click the file in the Local site pane (left) and select Upload. Text boxes at the top let you specify the host, username, password, and port. A Quick Connect drop-down menu will connect you to a preconfigured site.

To configure a remote-site connection, use the Site Manager (File ➤ Site Manager). In the Site Manager window, click the New Site button to create a new site connection. Four configuration tabs become active: General, Advanced, Transfer Settings, and Charset. On the General tab, you can specify the host, user, password, and account. The server type drop-down menu lets you specify a particular FTP protocol, such as SFTP for SSH encrypted transmissions or FTPS for TLS/SSL encryption.

gFTP

The gFTP program is a simpler GNOME FTP client designed to enable standard FTP file transfers. The package name for gFTP is `gftp`. You can access it from the Applications overview. The gFTP window consists of several panes. The top-left pane lists files in your local directory, and the top-right pane lists your remote directory. Subdirectories have folder icons preceding their names. The parent directory can be referenced by the double period entry (..) with an up arrow at the top of each list. Double-click a directory entry to access it. The pathnames for all directories are displayed in boxes above each pane. A drop-down menu to the far right lets you specify the FTP protocol to use, such as FTP for a standard transmission, SSH2 for SSH encrypted connections, and FSP for File Service Protocol transmissions.

Two buttons between the panes are used for transferring files. The left arrow button, <-, downloads selected files in the remote directory, and the right arrow button, ->, uploads files from the local directory. To download a file, click it in the right pane and then click the left arrow button, <-. When the file is downloaded, its name appears in the left pane, which is your local directory. Menus across the top of the window can be used to manage your transfers. A connection manager enables you to enter login information about a specific site. You can specify whether to perform an anonymous login or provide a username and password. Click Connect to connect to that site. A drop-down menu for sites lets you choose the site you want. Interrupted downloads can be restarted later.

wget

The wget tool lets you access web and FTP sites for particular directories and files. Directories can be recursively downloaded, letting you copy an entire website. The wget command takes as its option the URL for the file or directory you want. Helpful options include -q for quiet, -r for recursive (directories), -b to download in the background, and -c to continue downloading an interrupted file. One of the drawbacks is that your URL reference can be very complex. You must know the URL already. You cannot interactively locate an item as you would with an FTP client. The following would download the Fedora Workstation Live DVD in the background:

```
wget -b https://download.fedoraproject.org/pub/fedora/linux/releases/28/
Workstation/x86_64/iso/Fedora-Workstation-Live-x86_64-28-1.1.iso
```

Tip   With the GNOME wget tool (gwget package), you can run wget downloads using a GUI interface.

---

curl

The curl Internet client operates much like wget but with much more flexibility. With curl, you can specify multiple URLs on its command line. You can also use braces to specify multiple matching URLs, like different websites with the same domain name. You can list the different website hostnames within braces, followed by their domain name (or vice versa). You can also use brackets to specify a range of multiple items. This can be very useful for downloading archived files that have the same root name with varying extensions, such as different issues of the same magazine. curl can download using any protocol and will try to intelligently guess the protocol to use if none is provided. Check the curl man page for more information.

The `curl` client output to the standard output by default. Use the `-o` option to save the output to a file, and a `-O` to save it as the same name as the filename in the URL. The following example downloads the Fedora Workstation Live DVD with **curl**.

```
curl -O https://download.fedoraproject.org/pub/fedora/linux/releases/28/
Workstation/x86_64/iso/Fedora-Workstation-Live-x86_64-28-1.1.iso
```

ftp

The ftp client uses a command-line interface, and it has an extensive set of commands and options you can use to manage your FTP transfers. It is the original FTP client used on UNIX and Linux systems. See the ftp man page for more details. Alternatively, you can use `sftp` for more secure access. The sftp client has the same commands as ftp but provides SSH (Secure Shell) encryption. Also, if you installed the Kerberos clients (`krb5-clients`), a Kerberized version of FTP is set up, which provides for secure authentication from Kerberos servers. It has the same name as the FTP client (an `ftp` link to Kerberos FTP) and the same commands.

You start the ftp client by entering the command `ftp` at a shell prompt. If you want to connect to a specific site, you can include the name of that site on the command line after the `ftp` keyword. Otherwise, you have to connect to the remote system with the `ftp` command open. You are then prompted for the name of the remote system with the prompt "(to)." When you enter the remote system name, FTP connects you to the system and then prompts you for a login name. After entering the login name, you are prompted for the password. In the next example, the user connects to the remote system garnet and logs in to the robert account:

```
$ ftp
ftp> open
(to) garnet
Connected to garnet.berkeley.edu.
220 garnet.berkeley.edu FTP server ready.
Name (garnet.berkeley.edu:root): robert
password required
Password:
user robert logged in
ftp>
```

Once logged in, you can execute Linux commands on either the remote system or your local system. You execute a command on your local system in ftp by preceding the command with an exclamation point. Any Linux commands without an exclamation point are executed on the remote system. One exception exists to this rule. Whereas you can change directories on the remote system with the cd command, to change directories on your local system, you need to use a special ftp command called lcd (local cd). In the following example, the first command lists files in the remote system, while the second command lists files in the local system.

```
ftp> ls
ftp> !ls
```

The ftp program provides a basic set of commands for managing files and directories on your remote site, provided you have the permission to do so. You can use mkdir to create a remote directory and rmdir to remove one. Use the delete command to erase a remote file. With the rename command, you can change the names of files. You close your connection to a system with the close command. You can then open another connection if you want. To end the FTP session, use the quit or bye command.

```
ftp> close
ftp> bye
Good-bye
$
```

To transfer files to and from the remote system, use the get and put commands. The get command receives files from the remote system to your local system, and the put command sends files from your local system to the remote system. In a sense, your local system gets files from the remote and puts files to the remote. In the next example, the file weather is sent from the local system to the remote system using the put command.

```
ftp> put weather
PORT command successful.
ASCII data connection
ASCII Transfer complete.
ftp>
```

lftp

The lftp program is an enhanced FTP client with advanced features, such as the capabilities to download mirror sites and to run several FTP operations in the background at the same time.

It uses a command set similar to that for the ftp client. You use get and mget commands to download files, with the -o option to specify local locations for them. Use lcd and cd to change local and remote directories.

When you connect to a site, you can queue commands with the queue command, setting up a list of FTP operations to perform. With this feature, you could queue several download operations to a site. The queue can be reordered and entries deleted, if you wish. You can also connect to several sites and set up a queue for each one. The mirror command lets you maintain a local version of a mirror site. You can download an entire site or just update newer files, as well as remove files no longer present on the mirror.

You can tailor lftp with options set in the .lftprc file. System-wide settings are placed in the /etc/lftp.conf file. Here, you can set features such as the prompt to use and your anonymous password. The .lftp directory holds support files for command history, logs, bookmarks, and startup commands. The lftp program also supports the .netrc file, checking it for login information.

Social Networking: IM, VoIP, and Social Desktop

Fedora provides integrated social networking support for microblogging, IM (Instant Messenger), and VoIP (Voice over Internet Protocol). Instant messenger (IM) clients allow users on the same IM system to communicate anywhere across the Internet. With VoIP applications, you can speak over Internet connections, talking as if on a phone. The GNOME Maps application displays maps for cities, as well as your current location.

Instant Messenger: Empathy and Pidgin

Instant messenger (IM) clients allow users on the same IM service to communicate anywhere across the Internet (see Table 7-4). Currently, some of the major IM services are Microsoft Network (MSN), Yahoo, ICQ, and Jabber. Some use an XML protocol called XMPP, Extensible Messaging and Presence Protocol (https://xmpp.org).

Table 7-4. *Talk and Messenger Clients*

Client	Description
Ekiga	VoIP application
Skype	VoIP application (Partner repository)
Empathy	GNOME instant messenger
KDE empathy	KDE instant messenger client
Pidgin	Older instant messenger client
Jabber	Jabber IM service (gajim, psi, emacs, empathy)
Finch	Command-line cursor-based IM client
Hexchat	IRC client

Empathy

Fedora uses Empathy as the default IM application. Empathy is the GNOME replacement for Pidgin. There is also a KDE version, called KDE Empathy, which is the default IM application for the KDE desktop. Empathy is based on the Telepathy framework, which is designed to provide IM support to any application that wants an IM capability. All major IM services are supported, including Google Talk, AIM, Bonjour, MSN Messenger, Jabber (XMPP), ICQ, and Yahoo.

Empathy is accessible from the Applications overview (see Figure 7-10). Messages can be sent and received using the Empathy dialog and the message bar at the bottom of the screen. Empathy is integrated into the GNOME desktop, with its applications menu on the top bar. From the menu, choose Accounts to open the Messaging and VoIP Accounts dialog. Here, you can edit and add new accounts. Accounts are listed to the left. Information for a selected account is shown on the right. Click the plus button on the lower left to open the Adding New Account dialog. From a menu, you can choose from supported chat services, such as Facebook Chat, Jabber, Yahoo, and MSN. You enter your ID and password.

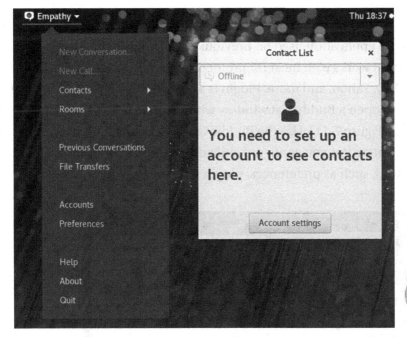

Figure 7-10. *Empathy IM client*

The login information will differ according to the chat service you choose. Facebook requires only a username and password. Others, such as MSN and AIM, have an advanced expansion set of entries from which you can specify the server and port. A drop-down menu on the Contact List window lets you select your status, such as Available, Busy, Away, Invisible, or Offline. You can specify a custom message for a particular status.

You can edit your configuration by clicking the Edit Connection Parameters on the Messaging and VoIP Accounts dialog. This opens the Online Accounts dialog with the service selected. You can then turn the chat service off, if you wish.

Telepathy provides IM support with connection managers, making IM services easy to maintain and add. Current connection managers include `telepathy-gabble` for Jabber/XMPP, `telepathy-idle` for IRC, `telepathy-butterfly` for MSN, `telepathy-salut` for local network (`link-local`) XMPP connections, `telepathy-sofiasip` for SIP, and `telepathy-haze` for Pidgin's Yahoo, AIM, and other support (`libpurple`; see `https://telepathy.freedesktop.org`).

Pidgin

Pidgin is the older IM application used on previous Fedora releases. Pidgin is a multi-protocol IM client that works with most IM protocols, including AIM, MSN, Jabber, Google Talk, ICQ, IRC, Yahoo, and more. Pidgin is accessible from the Applications overview. Pidgin will open a Buddy List window with menus for Buddies, Accounts, Tools, and Help (see Figure 7-11). Use the Buddies menu to send a message or join a chat. The Accounts menu lets you configure and add accounts. The Tools menu provides configuration features, such as preferences, plugin selection, privacy options, and sound.

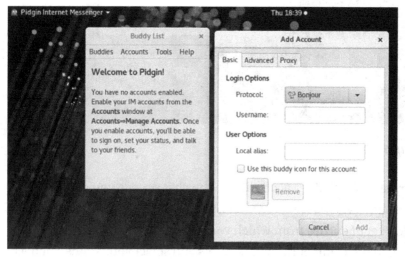

Figure 7-11. Pidgin's Buddy List

The first time you start Pidgin, the Add Account window is displayed with Basic, Advanced, and Proxy tabs for setting up an account. Later you can edit the account by selecting it in the Accounts window (Accounts ➤ Manage) and clicking the Modify button.

To create a new account, select Manage Accounts from the Accounts menu (Accounts ➤ Manage). This opens the Accounts dialog, which lists your current accounts. Click the Add button to open the Add Account dialog with a Basic, Advanced, and Proxy tabs. On the Basic tab, you choose the protocol from a pop-up menu that shows items such as AIM, Bonjour, Yahoo!, and IRC, and then enter the appropriate account information. You can also select a buddy icon to use for the account. On the Advanced tab, you specify the server and network connection settings. Many protocols will have a server entered already. The configuration entries for both the Basic and Advanced tabs will change, depending on the protocol. On the Proxy tab, you can enter specific proxy server host and connection information, should your network use a proxy.

To edit an existing account, click its entry in the Accounts menu and select Edit Account to open a Modify Account dialog with the same Basic, Advanced, and Proxy tabs. Make your changes and click Save. You can also select Accounts ➤ Manage Accounts to open the Accounts dialog, from which you can select the accounts you want to modify.

To configure your setup, select Preferences from the Tools menu (Tools ➤ Preferences) to open the Preferences dialog, from which you can set options for logging, sounds, themes, and the interface display. You can find out more about Pidgin at https://pidgin.im. Pidgin is a GNOME frontend that uses the libpurple library for its IM tasks (formerly libgaim). The libpurple library is used by many IM applications, including Finch.

Ekiga

Ekiga is GNOME's VoIP application. It provides Internet IP telephone and video conferencing support (see Figure 7-12); see https://www.ekiga.org. Ekiga supports the H.323 and SIP (Session Initiation Protocol) protocols. It is compatible with Microsoft's NetMeeting. H.323 is a comprehensive protocol that includes the digital broadcasting protocols, such as digital video broadcast (DVB) and H.261 for video streaming, as well as the supporting protocols such as the H.450 series for managing calls. You can access Ekiga from the Applications overview. Ekiga has panel status icons that display Online, Away, and Do Not Disturb.

Figure 7-12. *Ekiga VoIP*

To use Ekiga, you will need an SIP address. You can obtain a free address from https://www.ekiga.org. You first have to subscribe to the service. When you start Ekiga, the Ekiga Configuration Assistant prompts you to configure your connection (SIP address, callout account—if you wish, connection type, and audio and video devices). Here, you can provide contact information, your connection method, sound driver, and video device. Use the address book to connect to another Ekiga user. A white pages directory lets you search for people who are also using Ekiga.

Skype (VoIP)

Skype is one of the most popular VoIP applications. Skype provides a Fedora 16 i586 version that works on Fedora27. You can install Skype directly from the Skype website. To install Skype from the Skype website, go to the Skype Download page at https://www. skype.com/en/get-skype/.

On Fedora, your browser will display the download page for Linux. A button titled Get Skype for Linux RPM should be displayed. Click on it to download the skypeforlinux-64.rpm file and open it with GNOME Software. You can then install it. With the install, the sypeforlinux.repo file is also installed in the /etc/yum.repos.d directory, enabling access to the Skype repository and allowing you to update Skype as well as remove and reinstall with your software managers.

Once installed, you can access Skype from the Applications overview. You first sign into your account. A sidebar lets you perform searches, start chats and phone calls, and list contacts and notifications (see Figure 7-13).

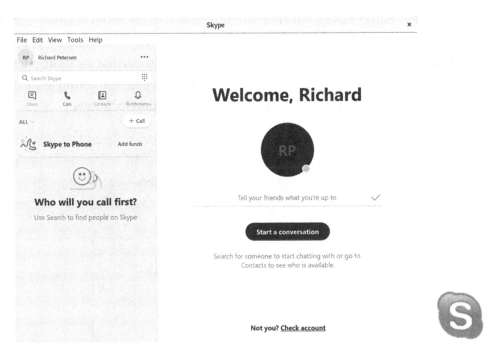

Figure 7-13. *Skype on Linux*

KDE Social Desktop

KDE provides a set of Internet applications as part of the KDE Social Desktop initiative. The social desktop is based on a web API called the Open Collaboration Services (OCS) that allows applications to interface easily with Internet services like blogging and Twitter (https://freedesktop.org/wiki/Specifications/open-collaboration-services). KDE provides a data engine for Plasma widgets supporting social desktop features. In effect, it establishes an open source method for social networking. In addition, the Geolocation data engine allows plasmoids to detect and respond to users' geographic locations. Currently, the social desktop supports plasmoids for microblogging, knowledge bases, messaging, and social networking.

Maps

GNOME Maps is a GNOME map utility that provides both street and satellite maps. It can also detect your current location or close to it (see Figure 7-14). From the task menu at the left, you can choose a street or satellite view. Use the zoom buttons, also at the left, or mouse scroll button to zoom in and out. To search for a location, enter the name in the search box, and options will be listed. To see your current location, click the Geolocation button to the left. To trace routes, click the route planner button to the right to open a dialog where you can enter the source and destination locations.

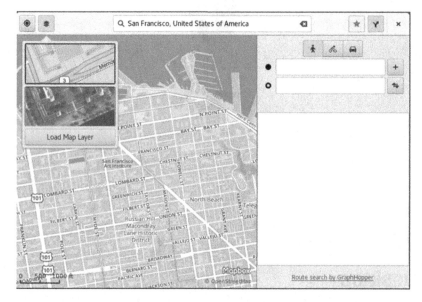

Figure 7-14. *GNOME Maps*

Note   It is also possible to download Google Earth for Fedora Linux at `https://www.google.com/earth/download/gep/agree.html`. Keep in mind that Google Earth is a proprietary product.

PART III

Desktops

CHAPTER 8

The GNOME Desktop

The GNU Network Object Model Environment, also known as GNOME, is a powerful and easy-to-use environment consisting primarily of a panel, a desktop, and a set of desktop tools with which program interfaces can be constructed. GNOME is designed to provide a flexible platform for the development of powerful applications. Currently, GNOME is supported by several distributions and is the primary interface for Fedora Linux. GNOME is free and released under the GNU Public License. GTK+ is the widget set used for GNOME applications. The GTK+ widget set is entirely free under the Lesser General Public License (LGPL). The LGPL enables developers to use the widget set with proprietary software, as well as free software (the GPL is restricted to free software).

For detailed documentation, check the GNOME documentation site at `https://help.gnome.org`. Documentation is organized by users, administrators, and developers. GNOME Help provides a complete tutorial on desktop use. For administrators, the "GNOME Desktop System Administration Guide" details how administrators can manage user desktops. Table 8-1 offers a listing of useful GNOME sites.

Table 8-1. *GNOME Resources*

Websites	Description
`https://www.gnome.org`	Official GNOME website
`https://help.gnome.org`	GNOME documentation website for users, administrators, and developers
`https://wiki.gnome.org/Personalization`	Desktop themes and background art
`https://wiki.gnome.org/Apps`	GNOME software applications
`https://developer.gnome.org`	GNOME developers site; see `http://help.gnome.org` for developer documentation

© Richard Petersen 2018
R. Petersen, *Beginning Fedora Desktop*, https://doi.org/10.1007/978-1-4842-3882-0_8

GNOME releases new versions on a frequent schedule. Fedora Linux uses GNOME 3.28.2. Key changes with GNOME 3.28 are described in detail at the following:

https://help.gnome.org/misc/release-notes/3.28/

The GNOME Desktop

GNOME is based on the gnome-shell, which is a compositing window manager (see Figure 8-1). The key components of the gnome-shell are a top bar, an Activities overview, and a notification/message tray feature. The top bar has a dialog for the date and time, a universal access menu, and a status area menu for sound volume, network connections, power information, and user tasks such as accessing settings and logging out. The Activities overview lets you quickly access favorite applications, locate applications, select windows, and change workspaces. The message tray and notification system notifies you of recent events, such as updates and recently attached USB drives. To the right of the Activities button is the Applications menu, which is a menu for the currently selected open application, such as the Files menu for a file manager window. Most applications have only a Quit entry, while others list key tasks.

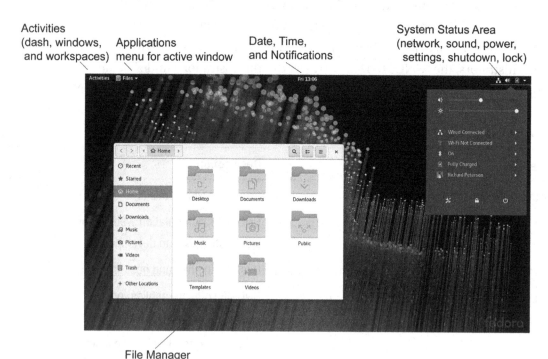

Figure 8-1. *GNOME Desktop*

You can configure desktop settings and perform most administrative tasks using the GNOME configuration tools (see Table 8-1) listed in the GNOME Settings dialog, accessible from the System Status Area menu (see Figure 8-2). Most use the GNOME 3 configuration and administrative tools such as Background, Lock Screen, Users, and Power.

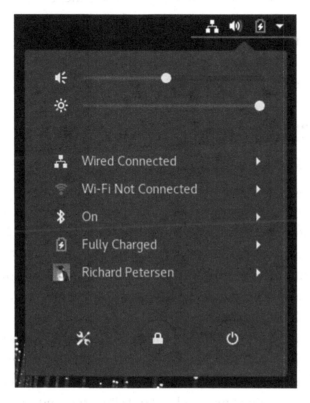

Figure 8-2. *System Status Area menu*

You can enhance the GNOME desktop by adding third-party extensions, as noted in Chapter 4 (see Figures 4-13, 4-14, and 4-15). These extensions are not guaranteed to work, though some are already installed and activated. Open the GNOME Software Add-ons category and click the Shell Extensions tab. First, enable the extensions. You will see icons with names and descriptions of different extensions, such as Dash to Dock which places a dash on the desktop instead of the Activities overview. Some extensions work as added items on the top bar, like system monitor. To manage installed extensions, click the Extension Settings button at the top of the Shell Extensions tab to pen a Shell Extension dialog where you can both turn extensions on or off and configure them if possible.

Top Bar

The screen displays a top bar, through which you access your applications, windows, and such system properties as sound and networking. Clicking the sound and power icons at the right of the top bar displays the system status area menu with options to set the sound level, screen brightness (laptop), wired and wireless connections, Bluetooth, and to shut down or lock the screen (see Figure 8-1). The center of the top bar has a button to display your clock and calendar. To the left is the Activities button, which displays an icon bar for favorite and open applications.

The System Status Area

Once logged in, the System Status Area is displayed on the right side of the top bar (see Figure 8-2). The area will include status icons for features such as sound and power. Clicking the button showing the sound, power, and down arrow icons displays the System Status Area menu, with items for sound, brightness, wired and wireless connections, the battery, the current user, in addition to buttons at the bottom for opening GNOME Settings, activating the lock screen, and shutting down or rebooting the system. The sound and brightness items feature sliding bars with which you can adjust the volume and brightness. The Wi-Fi, Battery, and current user entries expand to submenus with added entries. The buttons at the bottom open separate dialogs.

On systems that are not laptops, there will be no brightness slider or battery entry on the System Status Area menu. If the system also has no wireless device, the WiFi entry will also be missing. A system of this kind will only have a sound slider and a user entry.

To log out, you click the current user entry to expand the menu to show Switch User, Log Out, and Account Settings entries. The Log Out returns you to the login screen, where you can log in as another user. To switch to another user, click the Switch User entry to display the login screen. You can then log in as another user. When you log out or choose Switch User, you can then select the original user. When you log back in, your session is restored.

Activities Overview

To access applications and windows, you use the Activities Overview mode. Click the Activities button at the left side of the top bar (or move the mouse to the left corner, or press the super (Windows) key). The Activities Overview mode consists of a dash listing your favorite and running applications, thumbnails of open windows, and workspace thumbnails (see Figure 8-3). You can use the search box at the top center to locate applications and files. Partially hidden thumbnails of your desktop workspaces are displayed on the right side. Initially, there are two. Moving your mouse to the right side displays the workspace thumbnails.

Figure 8-3. *GNOME 3 activities overview*

You can manually leave the Activities Overview mode at any time by pressing the Esc key.

Dash

The dash is a bar on the left side with icons for your favorite applications (see Figure 8-4). Initially, on the Fedora Workstation version, there is the Firefox Web browser, the Evolution mail application, the Rhythmbox music player, the Shotwell photo manager, the file manager, and software. To open an application from the dash, click its icon, or right-click and choose New Window from the pop-up menu. You can also click-and-drag the icon to the windows thumbnail area or to a workspace thumbnail on the right side.

Favorites are always displayed on the dash. When you run other applications, they are also placed on the dash during the time they are running. To add a running application to the dash as a favorite, right-click the icon and choose Add to Favorites. You can later remove an application as a favorite by choosing Remove from Favorites. You can also add any application to the dash from the Applications Overview, by clicking-and-dragging its icon to the dash, or by right-clicking the icon and choosing Add to Favorites from the menu (see Figure 8-4).

Figure 8-4. *Overview dash with favorites and running applications*

Window Thumbnails

You access windows using the window thumbnails on the Activities overview. Thumbnails are displayed of all your open windows (see Figure 8-5). To select a window, move your mouse over the window's thumbnail. The selected window also shows an x (close) button at the top right of the window's thumbnail, which you can use to close the window directly. To access the window, move your mouse over it and click. This displays the window, exiting the overview and returning to the desktop.

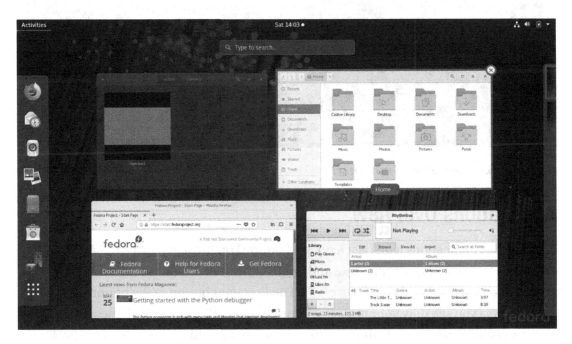

Figure 8-5. *Window thumbnails*

Moving your mouse to the right side of the screen displays the workspace selector showing workspace thumbnails, with the current workspace highlighted (see Figure 8-6). You can switch to another workspace by clicking its thumbnail. You can also move windows or applications directly to a workspace. If your mouse has a scroll wheel, you can press the Ctrl key and use the scroll wheel to move through workspaces, forward or backward.

Figure 8-6. *Workspace thumbnails*

Applications Overview

Clicking the Applications icon (last icon, grid button) on the dash opens the Applications Overview, from which you can locate and open applications. Icons for installed applications are displayed (see Figure 8-7). The Frequent button at the bottom of the overview lets you see only your most frequently used applications. Click the All button to see them all. A pager consisting of buttons, on the right side, lets you move quickly through the list of applications. You can move anywhere to a page in the list using the buttons. There are two special sub-folders: Utilities and Sundry. Clicking those icons opens another, sub-folders, showing applications in those categories, such as Tweak Tool and Backups in the Utilities overview. You can use the GNOME Software Installed tab to create your own sub-folders and place application icons in them. Click an application icon to open it and exit the overview. Should you return to the overview mode, you will see its window in the overview. The super key (Windows key) with the a key (super+a) will switch automatically from the desktop to the Applications Overview. Continuing to press it switches between the Applications Overview and the window thumbnails.

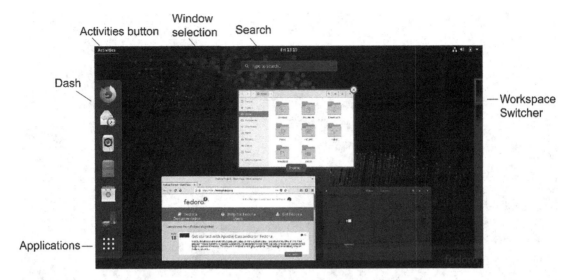

Figure 8-7. *Applications Overview*

You can also open an application by dragging its icon to a workspace thumbnail on the right side, starting it in that workspace.

Also, as previously noted, to add an application as a favorite on the dash, you can simply drag its icon from the Applications Overview to the dash directly.

Activities Search

The Activities search will search applications and files. Should you know the name of the application you want, you can simply start typing, and the matching results are displayed (see Figure 8-8). Your search term is entered in the search box as you type. The results dynamically narrow the more you type. The first application is selected automatically. If this is the one you want, just press Enter to start it. Results will also show Settings tools and recently accessed files, as well as uninstalled applications. From the result list you can click on an uninstalled application to open GNOME Software showing the application and an Install button, which you can click to install it.

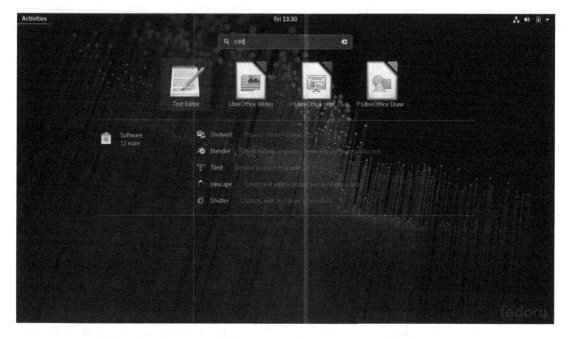

Figure 8-8. *Activities search box*

The search box for the Activities overview can be configured from the Settings Search tab (see Figure 8-9). Here, you can turn search on or off and specify which applications are to support searches. By default, these include Contacts, Documents, the Files file manager, Passwords and Keys, and the Firefox Web browser. To specify the folders to be searched, click the gear button on the lower right to open the Search Locations dialog with switches for currently supported folders, bookmarks, or other locations (see Figure 8-10). To add a folder of your choosing, go to the Other tab and click the plus button.

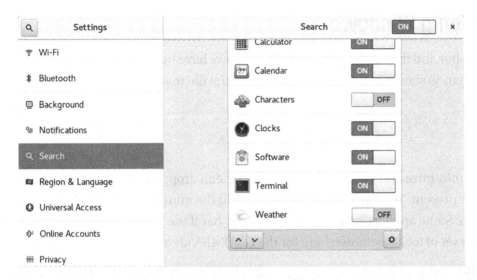

Figure 8-9. *Activities: Search configuration*

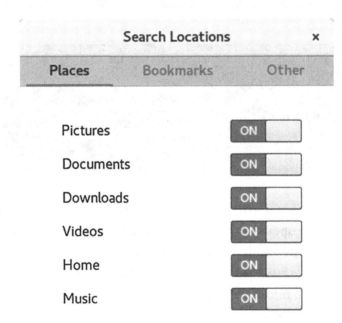

Figure 8-10. *Activities: Search Locations*

Managing Windows

The title bar and the toolbar for GNOME windows have been combined into a single header bar, as shown in the following image of the file manager.

The minimize and maximize buttons have been dropped, and a single close button is always present. You can use Tweak Tool to add the minimize and maximize buttons if you wish. Some applications change the header bar if the function changes, presenting a different set of tools, as shown here for the GNOME Videos application.

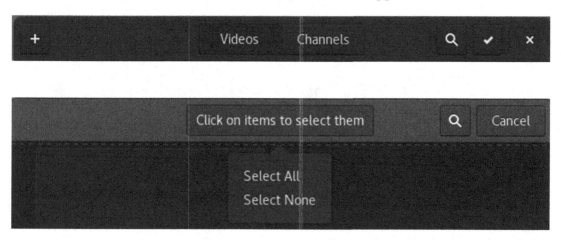

Windows no longer have maximize and minimize buttons. These tasks can be carried out by a dragging operation or by double-clicking the header bar. To maximize a window, double-click its header bar or drag the header bar to the top edge of the screen. To minimize, drag the title away from the top edge of the screen. You can also use a window's menu entries to maximize or minimize it. Right-click the header bar or press Alt+spacebar to display the window menu.

Open application windows also have an Applications menu on the left side of the top bar. For many applications, this menu holds only a Quit entry (see Figure 8-11). Others, such as the file manager, list key tasks, such as Bookmarks, Preferences, and Help. The Firefox web browser only lists a Quit button, whereas the GNOME file manager lists items such as New Window, Bookmarks, Preferences, and Help, as well as Quit.

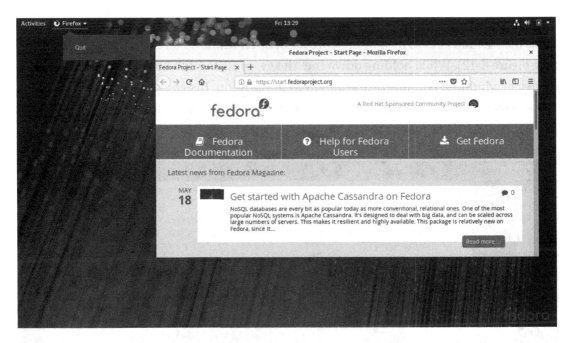

Figure 8-11. *Window with Applications menu*

To minimize an open window so that it no longer displays on the desktop, right-click the header bar and choose minimize. This will hide the window. You can then maximize the window later, using the window's thumbnails on the activities overview (Activities button).

To close a window, click its close box or choose Close from the Window menu (right-click on title bar). Many currently selected windows have an Applications menu in the top bar to the left. Should an application not have a close button, you can click the Applications menu button on the top bar and choose the Quit entry (see Figure 8-11).

To tile a window, click-and-drag its header bar to the left or right edge of the screen. When your mouse reaches the edge of the screen, the window is tiled to take up that half of the screen. You can do the same with another window for the other edge, showing two windows side by side.

To resize a window, move the mouse to the edge or corner until it changes to an edge or corner mouse, then click-and-drag.

The scroll bar to the right also features fine scrolling. When scrolling through a large number of items, you can fine scroll to slow the scrolling when you reach a point to search. To activate fine scrolling, click and hold the scroll bar handle, or press the Shift key while scrolling.

You can use the Window Switcher on the desktop to quickly search open windows. Press the Alt+Tab keys to display an icon bar of open windows on the current workspace (see Figure 8-12). While holding down the Alt key, press the Tab key to move through the list of windows. Windows are grouped by application. Instead of the Tab keys, you can use the forward and back arrow keys. For applications with multiple open windows, press the tilde (~) key (above the Tab key) to move through a list of the open windows.

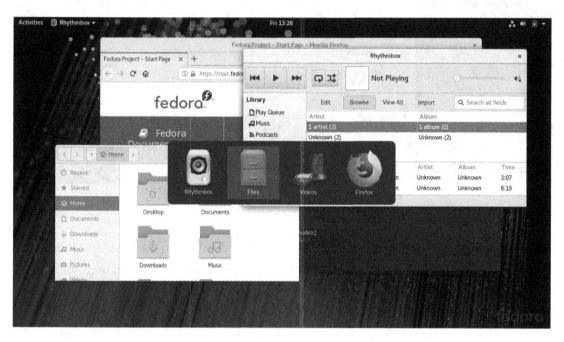

Figure 8-12.   *Window Switcher (Alt+Tab)*

On the GNOME Tweak Tool's Windows tab, you can configure certain windows' actions and components. Attached Modal Dialogs will attach a dialog that an application opens to the application's window (see Figure 8-13). You can use the switch to turn this feature off, allowing you to move a modal dialog away from the application window. Actions on the title bar (Titlebar Actions) are also defined, such as double-click to maximize and secondary-click to display the menu. There are also switches to display the Maximize and Minimize buttons on the title bar.

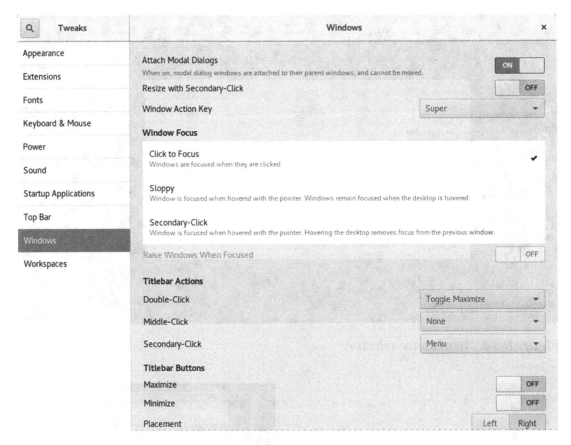

Figure 8-13. *GNOME Tweak Tool: Windows (dialogs and title bar)*

Workspaces

You can organize your windows into different workspaces. Workspaces are managed using the Workspace selector. In the overview, move your mouse to the right edge of the screen to display the workspace selector, a vertical panel showing thumbnails of your workspaces (see Figure 8-14). Workspaces are generated dynamically. The workspace selector will show an empty workspace as the last workspace (see Figure 8-15). To add a workspace, click-and-drag a window in the overview to the empty workspace on the workspace selector. A new empty workspace appears automatically below the current workspaces.

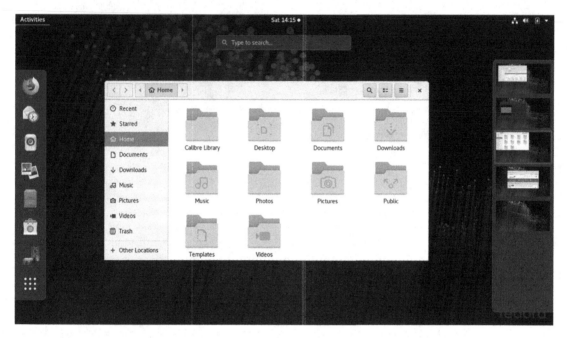

Figure 8-14. *Workspace selector*

Figure 8-15. *Adding workspaces*

To remove a workspace, close all its open windows or move the windows to other workspaces.

To move to another workspace, in the overview mode, move to the right edge to display the workspace selector, then click on the workspace you want. You can also use Ctrl+Alt with the up and down arrow keys to move to the next or previous workspaces.

To move a window to a workspace, on the Windows overview, click-and-drag the window to the workspace selector (right edge) and then to the workspace you want. You can also use the Window menu and choose Move to Workspace Down or Move to Workspace Up. You can also use Ctrl+Alt+Shift and the up or down arrow keys to move the window to the next workspace. Continue pressing the arrow to move it further should you have several workspaces.

You can use the GNOME Tweak Tool's Workspaces tab to change workspace creation from dynamic to static, letting you specify a fixed number of workspaces (see Figure 8-16).

Figure 8-16. *Static Workspaces: GNOME Tweak Tool Workspaces tab*

Notifications and Message Dialog

Notifications, such as software updates and removable device activation, are displayed in the message tray that is to the left of the calendar accessed from the top-center of the screen by clicking on the date. You can also press the super key with the m key to open the message tray. File systems on removable media will appear automatically as entries directly on your desktop notifications dialog (see Figure 8-17). A notice briefly appears at the top of the screen that shows the name of the device. If you move your mouse to the notice, an Open With notice appears, which you can click to open the device. Should you not open the device at this time, you can later display it in the message tray. When you eject a removable device, a notice briefly appears letting you know you can remove it. A notice will also appear on the message tray.

Figure 8-17. *Notifications*

GNOME Customization with Tweak Tool: Themes, Icons, Fonts, Startup Applications, and Extensions

You can perform common desktop customizations using the GNOME Tweak Tool. Areas to customize include the desktop icons, fonts, themes, startup applications, workspaces, window behavior, and the time display. You can access Tweak Tool from the Applications Overview ➤ Utilities. The GNOME Tweak Tool has tabs for Appearance, Desktop, Extensions, Fonts, Keyboard and Mouse, Power, Startup Applications, Top Bar, Typing, Windows, and Workspaces (see Figure 8-18).

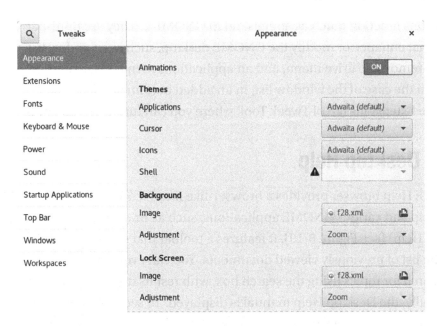

Figure 8-18. *GNOME Tweak Tool: Appearance tab (themes)*

The Appearance tab lets you set the theme for your windows, icons, and cursor. GNOME 3 uses the Adwaita Theme. This theme has a light and dark variant. The Global Light Theme is the default, but you can use the switch on the Appearance tab to enable the Global Dark Theme. The Global Dark Theme shades the background of windows to a dark gray, while text and button images appear in white.

Desktop fonts for window titles, interface (application or dialog text), documents, and monospace (terminal windows or code) can be changed in the Fonts tab. You can adjust the size of the font or change the font style. Clicking the font name opens a Pick a Font dialog from which you can choose a different font. The quality of text display can be further adjusted with Hinting and Antialiasing options. To simply increase or decrease the size of all fonts on your desktop interface, you can adjust the scaling factor.

At times, there may be certain applications that you want started up when you log in, such as the Gedit text editor, the Firefox web browser, or the Videos movie player. On the Startup Applications tab, you can choose the applications to start up. Click the plus (+) button to open an applications dialog from which you can choose an application to start up. Once added, you can later remove the application by clicking its Remove button.

Extensions function much as applets did in GNOME 2. They are third-party programs that enhance or modify the GNOME desktop, such as a window list, workspace indicator, a removable drive menu, and an applications menu. Extensions appear on the top bar or, in the case of the window list, in an added bottom bar. Installed extensions are listed on the Extensions tab of Tweak Tool, where you can turn them on or off.

GNOME Desktop Help

The GNOME Help browser provides a browser-like interface for displaying the GNOME Desktop Help and various GNOME applications, such as Brasero, Evince, and gedit (Utilities ➤ Help) (see Figure 8-19). It features a toolbar that enables you to move through the list of previously viewed documents. You can even bookmark specific items. You can search for topics using the search box, with results displayed in the drop-down menu. Initially, the Desktop Help manual is displayed. To see other help pages and manuals, choose All Help from the menu next to the close box (see Figure 8-20).

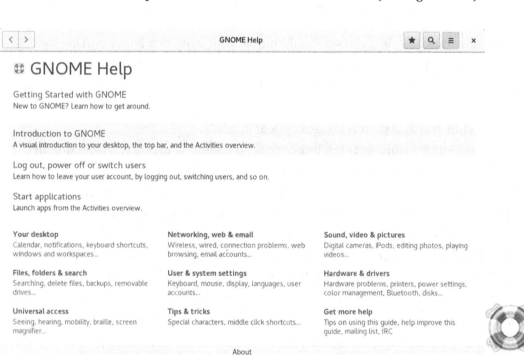

Figure 8-19. *GNOME Help browser*

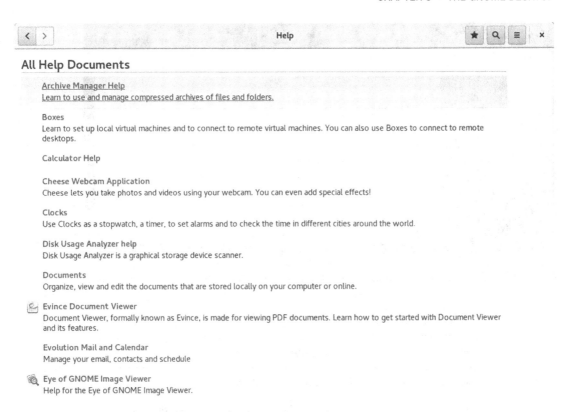

Figure 8-20. *GNOME Help: All Documents*

The GNOME Files File Manager

The GNOME file manager supports the standard features for copying, removing, and deleting items as well as setting permissions and displaying items. The name used for the file manager is Files, but the actual program name is still nautilus. When you select a file manager window, a Files menu appears as the Applications menu on the top bar to the left (see Figure 8-21). The Files menu has entries for opening a new file manager window, displaying the sidebar, the file manager preferences, displaying the file manager keyboard shortcuts, and help (see Table 8-2).

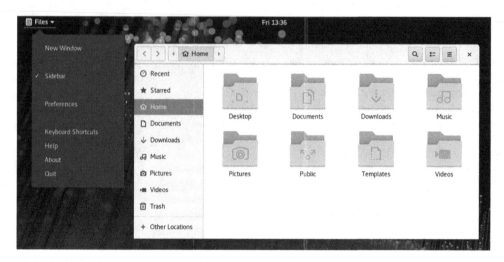

Figure 8-21. *File manager with Files applications menu*

Table 8-2. *File Manager GNOME Menu*

Menu Item	Description
New Window	Open a new file manager window
Sidebar	Toggle display of the file manager sidebar
Preferences	Open the file manager Preferences dialog
Keyboard Shortcuts	Display a dialog listing keyboard shortcuts
Help	Open GNOME desktop help
About	Current GNOME release
Quit	Close the file manager

Home Folder Subfolders

GNOME uses the Common User Directory Structure (xdg-user-dirs at
http://freedesktop.org) to set up subfolders in the user home directory. Folders
include Documents, Music, Pictures, Downloads, and Videos. These localized user
folders are used as defaults by many desktop applications. Users can change their folder
names or place them within each other using the GNOME file browser. For example,
Music can be moved into Videos or Documents into Pictures. Local configuration is

held in the `.config/user-dirs.dirs` file (`.config` is a hidden directory). System-wide defaults are set up in the `/etc/xdg/user-dirs.defaults` file. You can edit the local configuration using a text editor and change the directories for the current ones.

File Manager Windows

When you click the Files icon on the dash, a file manager window opens showing your home folder. The file manager window displays several components, including a toolbar and a sidebar (see Figure 8-22). The sidebar displays sections for folder, device, bookmark, and network items showing your file systems and default home folder subfolders. You can choose to display or hide the sidebar toolbar by selecting its entry in the View and Tools menu. The main pane (to the right) displays the icons or lists files and subfolders in the current working folder. When you select a file and folder, a status section at the bottom right of the window displays the number or name of the file or folder selected and the total size.

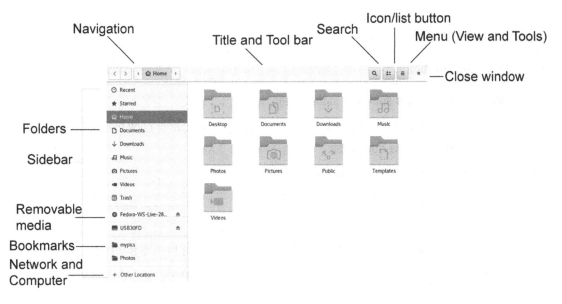

Figure 8-22. *File manager with sidebar*

When you open a new folder, the same window is used to display it, and you can use the forward and back arrows to move through previously opened folders (top left). As you open subfolders, the main toolbar displays buttons for your current folder and its parent folders, as shown here:

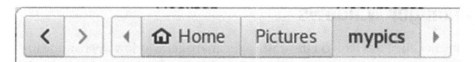

You can click a folder button to move to it directly. It also can display a location URL text box instead of buttons, from which you can enter the location of a folder, either on your system or on a remote one. Press Ctrl+l to display the text box. Press the Esc key to revert back to the folder location buttons.

You can click anywhere on the empty space on the main pane of a file manager window to display a pop-up menu with entries to create a new folder, open the current folder in a terminal window with a command line prompt, and open the file manager properties dialog (see Table 8-3).

Table 8-3. *File Manager Pop-Up Menu*

Menu Item	Description
New Folder	Creates a new subfolder in the current folder.
Paste	Pastes files that you have copied or cut, letting you move or copy files between folders or make duplicates.
Select All	Selects all files and folders in the current folder.
Properties	Opens the Properties dialog for the directory.

The file manager displays a dialog for folder creation (see Figure 8-23). Be sure to click the Create button once you have entered the folder name.

Figure 8-23. *File manager New Folder dialog*

File Manager Sidebar

The file manager sidebar shows file system locations that you would normally access: folders, devices, bookmarks, and network folders (See Figure 8-24). The Recent folder holds links to your recently used files. You can also mark files or folders as a favorites and have them listed by clicking the Starred entry on the file manager sidebar. Should you bookmark the current folder (the bookmark button on the file manager window's menu), a bookmark for it will appear on the sidebar. To remove or rename a bookmark, right-click its entry on the sidebar and choose Remove or Rename from the pop-up menu. The bookmark's name changes, but not the original folder name.

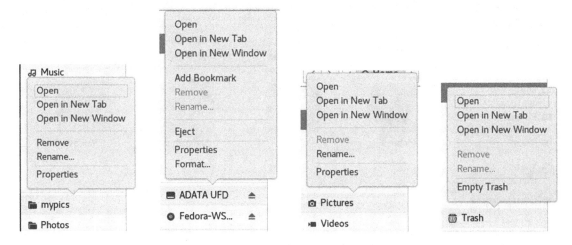

Figure 8-24. *File manager sidebar with menus for bookmarks, devices, folders, and trash*

Selecting the Other Locations entry on the sidebar displays entries for Computer and your networks. The Computer entry places you at the top of the file system, letting you move to any accessible part of it. In the Network section, you can access systems and shared folders on your network.

Tabs

The GNOME file manager supports tabs with which you can open several folders in the same file manager window. To open a tab, select New Tab from the Tools menu (see Figure 8-25) or press Ctrl+t. You can use the Tabs buttons to move from one tab to another, or to rearrange tabs. You can also use the Ctrl+PageUp and Ctrl+PageDown keys to move from one tab to another. Use the Shift+Ctrl+PageUp and Shift+Ctrl+PageDown keys to rearrange the tabs. To close a tab, click its close (x) button on the right side of the tab (see Figure 8-27) or press Ctrl+w. Tabs are detachable. You can drag a tab out to a separate window.

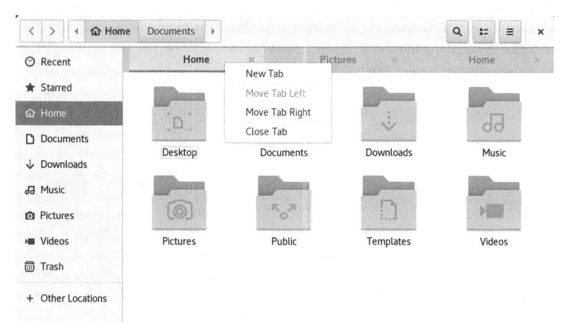

Figure 8-25. *File manager window with tabs*

Displaying and Managing Files and Folders

You can view a folder's contents as icons or as a detailed list, which you can choose by clicking the icon/list button between the search and menu buttons on the right side of the toolbar as shown here. This button toggles between icon and list views.

Use the Ctrl key to change views quickly: Ctrl+1 for icons and Ctrl+2 for list (there is no longer a Compact view). The List view provides the name, permissions, size, date, owner, and group. Buttons are displayed for each field across the top of the main pane. You can use these buttons to sort the list according to that field. For example, to sort the files by date, click the Date button; to sort by size, click Size. Click again to alternate between ascending and descending order.

Certain types of file icons display previews of their contents. For example, the icons for image files display a thumbnail of the image. A text file displays in its icon the first few words of its text.

You can click the menu button at the right of toolbar to display the file manager menu with entries for managing and sorting your file manager icons (see Table 8-4). The sort entries allow you to sort your icons by name (A-Z and Z-A), size, type, modification date, and access date. You can also reverse the order by name and modification date (see Figure 8-26).

Table 8-4. *File Manager Menu*

Menu Item	Description
New Folder button	Creates a new subfolder in the current folder
Bookmark button	Creates a bookmark for current folder
Tab button	Creates a new tab
Zoom In button	Enlarges icon size
Zoom Out button	Reduces icon size
Undo	Undoes the previous operation
Redo	Redoes an undo operation
A-Z	Sorts in alphabetic order
Z-A	Sorts in reverse alphabetic order
Last Modified	Sorts by last modified date
First Modified	Sorts by recent modified date
Size	Sorts by file size
Type	Sorts by file type
Show Hidden Files	Shows administrative dot files
Reload	Refreshes file and directory list

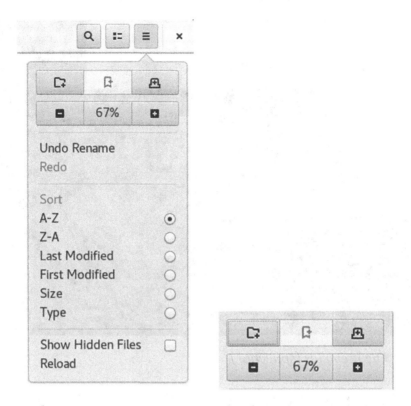

Figure 8-26. *File manager menu*

You can also bookmark the folder, create a new folder, and create a new tab. The top bar of the menu has buttons to create a new folder, create a bookmark for the current folder, and create a new file manager tab. Below that bar is a zoom bar, with zoom in and zoom out buttons, showing the zoom percentage between them. The zoom in button (+ button) enlarges your view of the window, making icons bigger. The zoom out button (- button) reduces your view, making them smaller. You can also use the Ctrl++ and Ctrl+- keys to zoom in and out.

Previews

The file manager supports previews for many different types of files. Select a file you want to preview, then press the spacebar. A dialog window opens, displaying the contents. Picture files show the image (see Figure 8-27). You can scroll through text and PDF files. Applications files such as LibreOffice files show information about the file. Video files are played, with controls to pause and to expand to full screen.

Figure 8-27. *File previews (spacebar)*

Navigating in the File Manager

The file manager operates similarly to a web browser, using the same window to display opened folders. It maintains a list of previously viewed folders, and you can move back and forth through that list using the toolbar buttons. The left arrow button moves you to the previously displayed directory, and the right arrow button moves you to the next displayed directory. Use the sidebar to access your storage devices (USB, DVD/CD, and attached hard drives). You can also access your home folders, trash, and recent files. From the sidebar Other Locations entry, you can also access mounted network folders. As noted, the Computer entry on the Other Locations section opens your root (top) system directory.

To open a subfolder, you can double-click its icon or right-click the icon and select Open from the menu (see Table 8-5). To open the folder in a new tab, select Open in New Tab.

Table 8-5. *The File and Folder Pop-Up Menu*

Menu Item	Description
Open With Application	Opens the file with its associated application. Directories are opened in the file manager. Associated applications are listed.
Open in New Tab	Opens a folder in a new tab in the same window.
Open in New Window	Opens a folder in a new file manager window.
Open With Other Application	Selects an application with which to open this file. An Open With dialog lists the possible applications.
Cut Copy	Cuts or copies the selected file.
Move To	Moves a file to the Home folder, desktop, or to a folder displayed in another pane in the File Manager window.
Copy To	Copies a file to the Home folder, desktop, or to a folder displayed in another pane in the File Manager window.
Rename (F2)	Renames the file.
Move To Trash	Moves a file to the Trash directory, where you can later delete it.
Compress	Archives the file using File Roller.
Send to	Emails the file.
Star	Marks file or folder as a favorite to be displayed by the starred entry in the sidebar.
Properties	Displays the Properties dialog.

To mark a file or folder as a favorite, right-click on it and choose Star from the pop-up menu. It can then be also accessed by clicking the starred entry on the sidebar.

You can open any folder or file system listed in the sidebar by clicking it. You can also right-click an entry to display a menu with entries to Open in a New Tab and Open in a New Window (see Table 8-6). The menu for the Trash entry lets you empty the trash. You can also remove and rename the bookmarks.

Table 8-6. *The File Manager Sidebar Pop-Up Menu*

Menu Item	Description
Open	Opens the file with its associated application. Folders are opened in the file manager. Associated applications are listed.
Open in a New Tab	Opens a folder in a new tab in the same window.
Open in a New Window	Opens a folder in a separate window, accessible from the toolbar with a right-click.
Remove	Removes the bookmark from the sidebar.
Rename	Renames the bookmark.

Entries for removable devices in the sidebar, such as USB drives, also have menu items for Eject and Safely Remove Drive. Internal hard drives have an Unmount option instead.

Managing Files and Folders

As a GNOME-compliant file manager, Files supports desktop drag-and-drop operations for copying and moving files. To move a file or directory, drag-and-drop from one directory to another. The move operation is the default drag-and-drop operation in GNOME.

To copy a file to a new location, press the Ctrl key as you drag-and-drop. When copying a large file or many files, an icon is displayed on the title bar to the right showing a circle chart and the progress of the copy operation. Clicking on the icon displays a menu showing the progress of the copy operation, with an x to the right you can click to cancel the copy, as shown here. When the copy process for a file is completed, the x becomes a checkmark. When the entire copy process is completed for all files, the icon shows a fully dark circle.

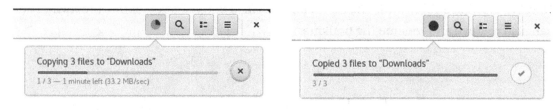

Renaming, Removing, and Compressing Files and Folders

You can also perform remove, rename, and compress operations on a file by right-clicking its icon and selecting the action you want from the pop-up menu that appears (see Table 8-5). For example, to remove an item, right-click it and select the Move To Trash entry from the pop-up menu. This places it in the Trash directory, where you can later delete it.

To rename a file, you can either right-click the file's icon and select the Rename entry from the pop-up menu or click its icon and press the F2 function key. The file manager displays a dialog file renaming (see Figure 8-28). When renaming a file, be sure to click the Rename button once you have entered the new name.

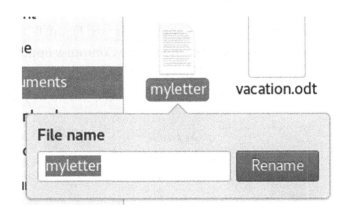

Figure 8-28. *File manager Rename dialog*

You can also change several filenames at once by selecting the files and then right-clicking and choosing Rename. A dialog opens listing the selected files and a text box for specifying the new names (see Figure 8-29). You can add to the name or choose the Find and Replace option to change a common part of the names. Clicking the Add button lets you choose from a list of possible automatic number formats to add. The added characters are encased in brackets in the text box, separated by commas, one for each filename. The Original File Name entry add the original filename specifier to the text box, should you remove it.

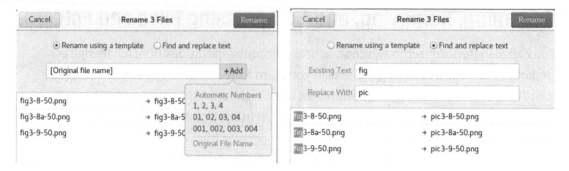

Figure 8-29. *Renaming several files at once with the file manager*

You can also rename a file by entering a new name in its Properties dialog box (Basic tab).

You can also compress and archive files and folders (see Figure 8-30). Select the files or folders to compress, right-click, and choose the Compress option. A dialog opens where you can specify the name of the compressed archive and the compression method. Choose the form of the archive from the list below the name (zip, tar, and 7z).

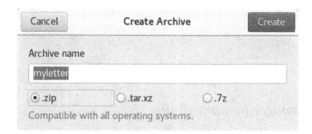

Figure 8-30. *File manager: Compress and Archive dialogs*

Grouping Files

You can select a group of files and folders by clicking the first item and then holding down the Shift key while clicking the last item, or by clicking and dragging the mouse across items you want to select. To select separated items, hold the Ctrl key down as you click the individual icons. If you want to select all the items in the directory, choose the Select All entry from the current folder's pop-up menu (see Table 8-3) or choose Ctrl+a. You can then copy, move, or delete several files at once.

Opening Applications and Files MIME Types

You can start any application in the file manager by double-clicking either the application or a data file used for that application. If you want to open the file with a specific application, you can right-click the file and select one of the Open With entries. One or more Open With entries will be displayed for default and possible application, such as Open With gedit for a text file. If the application you want is not listed, you can select Open With Other Application to access a list of available applications.

To change or set the default application to use for a certain type of file, you open a file's Properties dialog and select the Open With tab. Here, you can choose the default application to use for that kind of file. Possible applications will be listed, organized as the default, recommended, related, and other categories. Click the one you want and click the Set As Default button. Once you choose the default, it will appear in the Open With list for this file.

If you want to add an application to the Open With menu, click the Other Applications entry to list possible applications. Select the one you want and click the Add button. If there is an application on the Open With tab that you do not want listed in the Open With menu items, right-click it and choose Forget Association.

File and Directory Properties

In a file's Properties dialog, you can view detailed information on a file and set options and permissions (see Figure 8-31). A file's Properties dialog has three tabs: Basic, Permissions, and Open With. Folders will have an additional Local Network Share tab, instead of an Open With tab. The Basic tab shows detailed information, such as type, size, location, accessed, and date modified. The type is a MIME type, indicating the type of application associated with it. The file's icon is displayed at the top, with a text box showing the file's name. You can edit the filename in the Name text box. If you want to change the icon image used for the file or folder, click the icon image (next to the name) to open a Select Custom Icon dialog and browse for the one you want. The /usr/share/ pixmaps directory holds the set of current default images, although you can select your own images (click the Other Locations ➤ Computer entry to locate the pixmaps folder). In the pixmaps folder, click an image file to see its icon displayed in the right pane. Double-click to change the icon image.

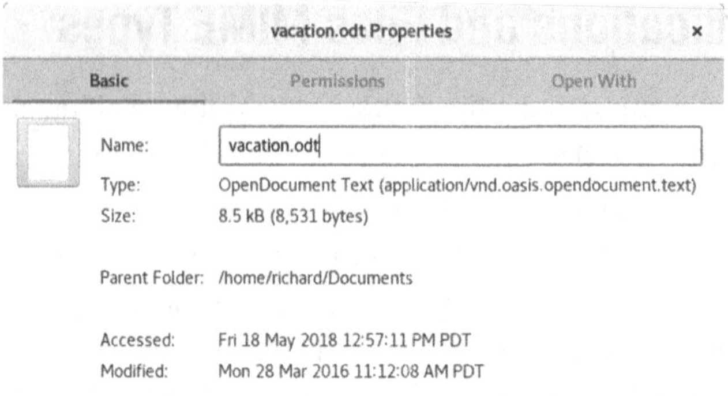

Figure 8-31. *File properties*

The Permissions tab for files shows the read, write, and execute permissions for owner, group, and others, as set for this file. You can change any of the permissions here, provided the file belongs to you. You configure access for the owner, the group, and others, using drop-down menus. You can set owner permissions as Read Only or Read and Write. For group and others, you can also set the None option, denying access. Clicking the group name displays a menu listing different groups, allowing you to select one to change the file's group. If you want to execute this as an application, you check the Allow Executing File as Program entry. This has the effect of setting the execute permission.

The Open With tab for files lists all the applications associated with this kind of file. You can select the one you want to use as the default. This can be particularly useful for media files, for which you may prefer a specific player for a certain file or a particular image viewer for pictures.

Certain kinds of files will have additional tabs, providing information about the file. For example, an audio file will have an Audio tab listing the type of audio file and any other information, such as a song title or the compression method used. An image file will have an Image tab listing the resolution and type of image. A video file will contain an Audio/Video tab showing the type of video file, along with compression and resolution information.

The Permissions tab for folders operates much the same way, with Access menus for Owner, Group, and Others. The Access menu controls access to the folder with options for None, List Files Only, Access Files, and Create and Delete Files. These correspond to the read and execute permissions given to directories. To set the permissions for all the files in the folder accordingly (not just the folder), click the Change Permissions for Enclosed Files button to open a dialog where you can specify the owner, group, and others permissions for files and folders in the folder.

File Manager Preferences

You can set preferences for your file manager in the Preferences dialog, accessible by selecting the Preferences item in any file manager window's application menu (Files ➤ Preferences).

The Views tab allows you to select how files are displayed by default, such as a list or icon view. You also can set default zoom levels for icon and list views.

Behavior lets you choose how to select files, manage the trash, handle scripts, and choose what information you want displayed in an icon caption, such as the size or date.

The List Columns tab lets you choose both the features to display in the detailed list and the order in which to display them. In addition to the already-selected name, size, date, and type, you can add permissions, group, MIME type, location, accessed, and owner.

The Preview tab lets you choose whether you to show thumbnail content displayed in the icons, search subfolders, or display the file count.

File Manager Search

Two primary search tools are available for your GNOME desktop: the GNOME dash search and the GNOME file manager search. With GNOME file manager, you enter a pattern to search. You can further refine your search by specifying dates and file types. Click the Search button (looking glass icon) on the toolbar to open a Search box. Enter the pattern to search, then press Enter. The results are displayed (see Figure 8-32). Click the menu button to the right to add file-type (What) and date (When) search parameters, or to search file text or just the filename. Selecting the When entry opens a dialog where you can specify the document's last use or modification, by day, week, month, or year. A calendar button to the right of the text box for the date opens a calendar to let you choose a specific date. The What entry displays a menu with different file categories such as music, Documents, folders, picture, and PDF.

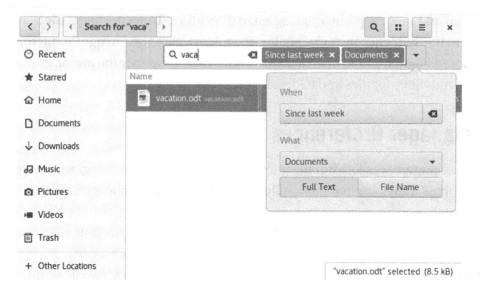

Figure 8-32. *GNOME file manager search*

GNOME Classic

As an alternative to the GNOME desktop, you can use the GNOME Classic desktop, which uses an interface similar to GNOME2 (see Figure 8-33). You can choose GNOME Classic from the session menu. GNOME Classic displays a top panel with Applications and Places menus. The System Status Area menu is the same. Also, application menus continue to be displayed on the top panel, after the Places menu. The bottom panel has a task bar and a workspace switcher menu. Icons for applications can be displayed on the desktop. The Applications menu is organized into submenus by category, such as Graphics, Office, and Sound & Video. The Activities Overview entry at the end of the Applications menu starts up the GNOME 3 overview interface. Windows show three buttons to the right on the title bar instead of one: the minimize, expand, and close buttons.

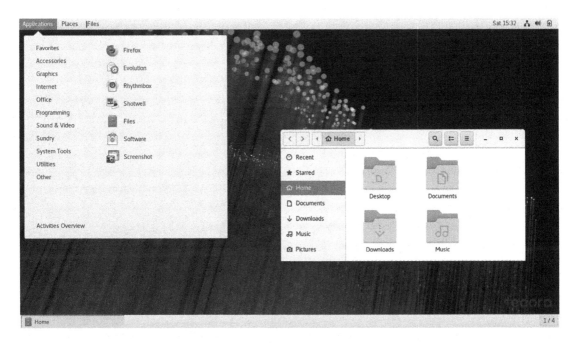

Figure 8-33. *GNOME Classic*

CHAPTER 9

Plasma Desktop: The K Desktop Environment (KDE)

Plasma is the desktop developed and distributed by KDE (the K Desktop Environment). It is often referred to as simply the KDE desktop. Plasma includes the standard desktop features, such as a window manager and a file manager, as well as an extensive set of applications that cover most Linux tasks. The KDE Plasma version of Fedora Linux is called the Fedora KDE Plasma Desktop and is available as a separate desktop DVD from `https://spins.fedoraproject.org/`. The Plasma desktop is developed and distributed by the KDE Project. KDE is open source software provided under a GNU Public License and is available free of charge along with its source code. KDE Plasma development is managed by the KDE Core Team. You can install it as an alternate desktop on a GNOME system by installing `plasma-desktop`.

The KDE software development and distribution is organized into three projects: Plasma, Applications, and Projects. KDE Applications include numerous applications written specifically for KDE Plasma are accessible from the desktop. These include editors, photo and image applications, sound and video players, and office applications. Some applications have the letter *K* as part of their name, for example, KOrganizer. On a system administration level, KDE provides several tools for managing your system, such as the Discover and Apper Software Managers, and the KDE system monitor. KDE applications also feature a built-in Help application. See `https://www.kde.org/applications/` for a list and descriptions of current applications.

© Richard Petersen 2018
R. Petersen, *Beginning Fedora Desktop*, https://doi.org/10.1007/978-1-4842-3882-0_9

KDE Frameworks provides support libraries designed to work with the Qt libraries that KDE plasma and applications depend on. Frameworks is designed to be cross-platform, enabling any KDE application to run on systems that support the Qt libraries. Frameworks can be used as a basis for any custom operating system, such as LXQt. KDE Framework packages have the prefix **kf5**, such as the `kf5-filesystem` that provides support for the KDE filesystem. Development for Plasma, Frameworks, and Applications proceed at different paces. The KDE Frameworks version used in Fedora 28 Plasma Desktop is 5.46.0, whereas the KDE Plasma version is 5.12.5.

Note   As as noted in Chapter 6 for GNOME, you can install the same third-party multimedia support and codecs on KDE from the RPM Fusion repository, as well as `dvdcss` support from the Livna repository.

Table 9-1. *KDE Websites*

Website	Description
`https://www.kde.org`	KDE website
`https://www.kde.org/plasma-desktop`	KDE Plasma desktop website
`https://www.kde.org/applications/`	KDE Applications website
`https://docs.kde.org`	KDE documentation site
`https://www.qt.io/`	Site for the Qt company
`https://store.kde.org`	KDE Plasma desktop themes
`https://mail.kde.org/mailman/` `listinfo/`	KDE mailing lists

KDE, initiated by Matthias Ettrich in October 1996, is designed to run on any UNIX implementation, including Linux, Solaris, HP-UX, and FreeBSD. The official KDE website is `https://www.kde.org`, which provides news updates, download links, and documentation. Several KDE mailing lists are available for users and developers, including announcements, administration, and other topics. Detailed documentation for the KDE desktop and its applications is available at `https://docs.kde.org`. Development support can be obtained at the KDE Techbase site at `https://techbase.kde.org`.

Most applications are available on the Fedora Linux repositories and can be installed directly from the Discover Software and Apper software managers. Various KDE websites are listed in Table 9-1. KDE uses as its library of GUI tools the Qt library, currently developed and supported by the Qt company, owned by Digia (`https://www.qt.io`). It provides the Qt libraries as open source software that is freely distributable, though a commercial license is also available.

KDE Plasma 5

The KDE Plasma 5 release is a major reworking of the KDE desktop. KDE Plasma 5.12.5 is included with the Fedora Linux 28 distribution. Check the Fedora Linux and KDE sites for detailed information on KDE 5.

```
https://www.kde.org/announcements/plasma5.0/
```

For features added with KDE Plasma 5.5, check:

```
https://www.kde.org/announcements/plasma-5.12.0.php
```

For features added with KDE Plasma 5.12.5 (current Fedora Linux KDE edition), check:

```
https://www.kde.org/announcements/plasma-5.12.5.php/
```

KDE development is organized into a plasma and applications releases. The plasma release covers the desktop interface (the Plasma desktop shell), and the applications release covers KDE applications. Plasma has containments and plasmoids (also called widgets). Plasmoids operate similarly to applets, small applications running on the desktop or panel. Plasmoids operate within containments. On KDE 5, there are two Plasma containments, the panel and the desktop. In this sense, the desktop and the panel are features of an underlying Plasma operation. They are not separate programs. Each has their own set of plasmoids.

Each containment has a toolbox for configuration. The desktop has a toolbox at the top left corner, and panels will have a toolbox on the right side. The panel toolbox includes configuration tools for sizing and positioning the panel. KDE also supports *activities*, which are multiple plasma desktop containments, each with their own set of active plasmoids (widgets) and open windows.

SDDM

KDE Fedora Linux uses the Simple Desktop Display Manager (SDDM) to manage logins. A login greeter is displayed at the center of the screen where you can select a user icon and enter a password (see Figure 9-1). Suspend, Restart, Shutdown, and Different User buttons are displayed below the login button. Use the Different User button to log in as a user not displayed in the user list.

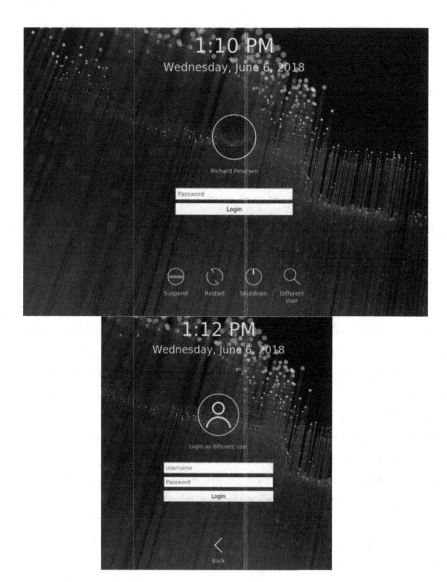

Figure 9-1. *SDDM Display Manager, login screen*

Upon choosing a user icon and entering the password, press Enter or click the login button at the right end of the password text box. Your KDE session then starts up.

If you have more than one desktop installed on your system, such as Cinnamon, Mate, or Xfce, then a Plasma menu item is displayed as one of the alternatives. Use this menu to choose a different desktop to log in to.

You can change the theme of the login greeter using the Login Screen (SDDM) entry in the Startup and Shutdown dialog (GNOME Settings ➤ Startup and Shutdown in the Workspace section). The theme section lists available theme. Currently, only Breeze is listed. To change the background image, click on a theme to display it in the Customize section to the right. Then click on the Background icon and choose the Load from File option from the pop-up menu. On the Advanced tab, you can choose the default user, the desktop for your session, and whether to automatically log in. You can also choose a cursor theme and an alternative desktop (session). You can also manually configure SDDM using the /etc/sddm.conf file.

The Plasma Desktop

One of KDE's aims is to provide users with a consistent integrated desktop (see Figure 9-2). Plasma provides its own window manager (KWM), file manager (Dolphin), program manager, and desktop and panel (Plasma). You can run any other X Window System–compliant application, such as Firefox, in Plasma, as well as any GNOME application. In turn, you can also run any KDE application, including the Dolphin File Manager in GNOME. The Plasma 5 desktop features the Plasma desktop shell with new panel, menu, widgets, and activities. Keyboard shortcuts are provided for many desktop operations, as well as plasmoid (widget) tasks (see Table 9-2).

Table 9-2. *Plasma Keyboard Shortcuts*

Keys	Description
Alt+F1	Kickoff menu
Alt+F2	Krunner, command execution, entry can be any search string for a relevant operation, including bookmarks and contacts, not just applications
Up/Down arrows	Move among entries in menus, including Kickoff and menus
Left/Right arrows	Move to submenus menus, including Kickoff and Quick Access submenus menus
Enter	Select a menu entry, including a Kickoff or QuickAccess
PageUp, PageDown	Scroll up fast
Alt+F4	Close current window
Alt+F3	Window menu for current window
Ctrl+Alt +F6	Command Line Interface
Ctrl+Alt +F8	Return to desktop from command line interface
Ctrl+r	Remove a selected widget
Ctrl+s	Open a selected widget configuration's settings
Ctrl+a	Open the Add Widgets window to add a widget to the desktop
Ctrl+l	Lock your widgets to prevent removal, adding new ones or changing settings
Alt+Tab	Cover Switch or Box Switch for open windows
Ctrl+F8	Desktop Grid
Ctrl+F9	Present Windows Current Desktop
Ctrl+F10	Present Windows All Desktops
Ctrl+F11	Desktop Cube for switching desktops

To configure your desktop, you use the System Settings dialog (Computer| System Settings), which lists icons for dialogs such as Workspace Theme, Font, Icons, Applications Style Desktop Behavior, Search, Application Style, Window Management, Driver Manager, and Bluetooth. Workspace Theme lets you choose desktop, cursor, and splash themes. Desktop Behavior is where you can set desktop effects and virtual desktops. Windows Management controls window display features like window switchers, title bar actions, and screen edge actions.

The desktop supports drag-and-drop and copy-and-paste operations. With the copy-and-paste operation, you can copy text from one application to another. You can even copy and paste from a Konsole terminal window.

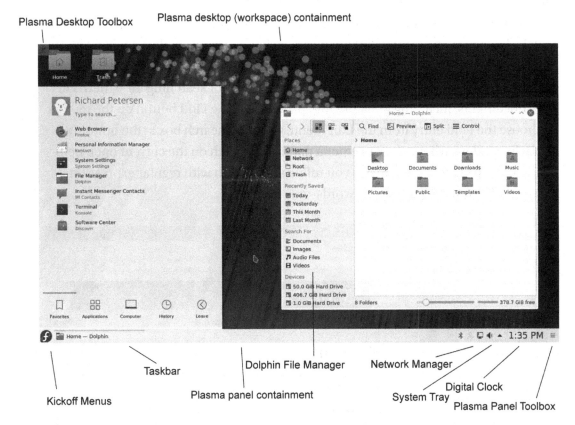

Figure 9-2. *The Plasma desktop*

The KDE Help Center

The KDE Help Center provides a browser-like interface for accessing and displaying KDE Help files and Linux Man and info files (see Figure 9-3). It may not be installed by default. Install the khelpcenter package. The same documentation is available at https://docs.kde.org. You can start the Help Center by searching for "help" in the search box of the Kickoff Applications menu. The Help window displays a sidebar that holds two tabs, one listing contents and one providing a glossary. The main pane displays currently selected document. A help tree on the contents tab in the sidebar lets you choose the kind of Help documents you want to access. Here you can choose KDE manuals, Man pages (UNIX manual pages), or info documents (Browse info Pages), or even application manuals (Application Manuals). Online Help provides links to KDE websites such as the KDE user forum and the KDE tech base sites. Click the Table of Contents button to open a listing of all KDE help documents, which you can browse through and click on to open.

A navigation toolbar enables you to move through previously viewed documents. KDE Help documents contain links you can click to access other documents. The Back and Forward buttons move you through the list of previously viewed documents. The KDE Help system provides an effective search tool for searching for patterns in Help documents, including Man and info pages. Click the Find button on the toolbar or choose the Find entry from the Edit menu, to open a search box at the bottom of the Help window, where you can enter a pattern to search on the current open help document. The Options menu lets you refine your search with regular expressions, case-sensitive queries, and whole words-only matches.

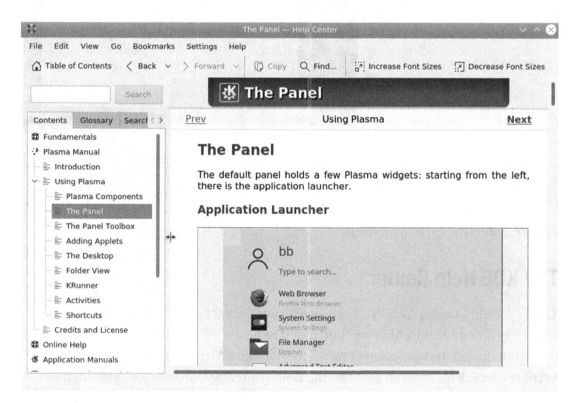

Figure 9-3. *KDE Help Center*

Desktop Backgrounds (Wallpaper)

The background (wallpaper) is set from the desktop menu directly. Right-click on the desktop to display the desktop menu and then select Configure Desktop to open the Desktop Settings dialog (see Figure 9-4).

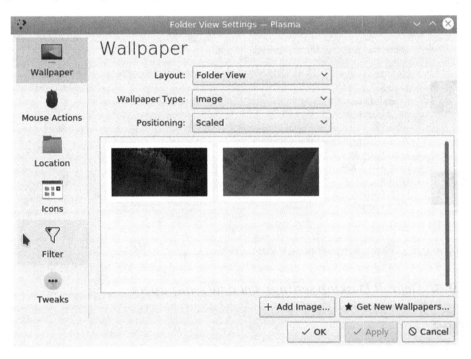

Figure 9-4. *Default Desktop settings, wallpaper*

You can also select Desktop Settings from the activities menu in the upper-left corner of the desktop. The background is called wallpaper in Plasma and can be changed in the Wallpaper tab. You can select other wallpapers from the wallpaper icons listed or select your own image by clicking the Open button.

You can add more wallpaper by clicking the Get New Wallpaper button to open a Get Hot New Stuff dialog, which lists and downloads wallpaper posted on the www. kde-look.org site (see Figure 9-5). Each wallpaper entry shows an image, description, and rating. Buttons at the upper right of the dialog let you view the entries in details (list) or icon mode. You can refine the wallpaper listing by size (category), newest, rating, and popularity (most downloads). Click the Install button to download the wallpaper and add it to your Desktop Setting's Wallpaper tab. The wallpaper is downloaded and the Install button changes to Uninstall. To remove a wallpaper, you can select installed wallpapers to find the entry quickly. You can also search by pattern for a wallpaper.

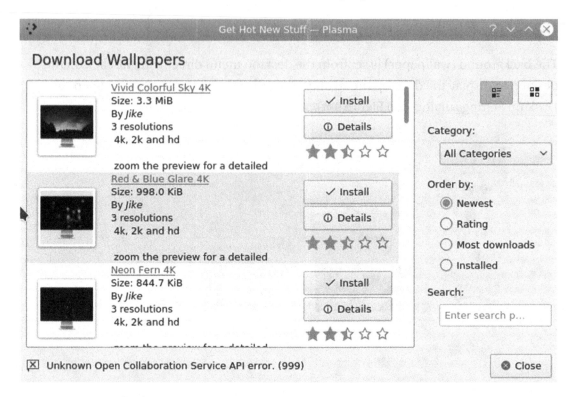

Figure 9-5. *Default Desktop settings, get new wallpapers*

Themes

For your desktop, you can also select a variety of different themes, icons, and window decorations. A theme changes the entire look and feel of your desktop, affecting the appearance of desktop elements, such as scroll bars, buttons, and icons. Themes and window decorations are provided for workspaces. Access the System Settings dialog from the Kickoff Computer menu or the Applications ➤ Settings menu. On the System Settings dialog, click the Workspace Theme icon in the Appearance section. The Workspace Theme dialog lets you choose overall look and feel, cursor themes, desktop themes, and a splash screen (startup) themes. The Desktop Themes tab lists installed themes, letting you choose the one you want. Click the Get New Themes button to open a Get Hot New Stuff dialog, listing desktop themes from https://store.kde.org (see Figure 9-6). Click a theme's Install button to download and install the theme.

For window decorations, you use the Application Style dialog, Window Decorations tab, where you can select window decoration themes. Click the Get New Decorations button to download new decorations. Icons styles are chosen using the Icons dialog, Icons tab, where you can choose the icon set to use and even download new sets (Get New Themes).

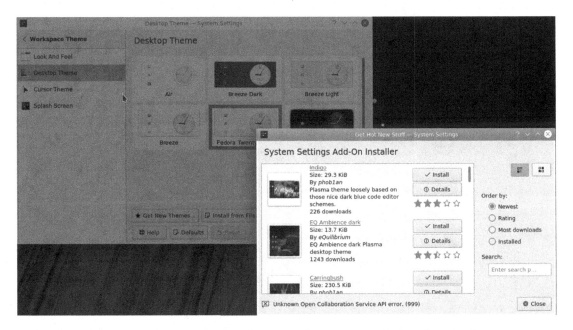

Figure 9-6. *System Settings ➤ Workspace Theme ➤ Desktop Theme, Get New Themes*

Leave Plasma

To leave Plasma, click the Leave tab on the Kickoff menu (see Figure 9-7). Here you will find options to log out, lock, switch user, suspend, shut down, and restart. There are Session and System sections. The Session section has entries for Logout, Lock, and Switch User. The System section lists the system-wide operations: Shut Down, Reboot, Hibernate, and Suspend. When you select a leave entry, a dialog for that action appears on the desktop, which you then click. The Shut Down entry will display the Shutdown and Logout dialog with the Shutdown button selected (see Figure 9-8). The Logout option displays the same dialog with the Logout button selected. The Switch User option displays a dialog with the currently logged in users to choose from, along with a plus button for a new login.

Figure 9-7.   The Kickoff menu includes the Leave tab

The Lock and Switch User display manager (SSDM) screens display both a button for the current user and a plus button for starting a new session (Switch User shows the icon for the user you selected). The new session button displays the login screen with its list of users to log in as.

If you log out and more than one user is logged in from a previous Switch User operation, then the Log Out display manager screen will show a logged in user button and a plus button. Use the plus button to display the main login screen.

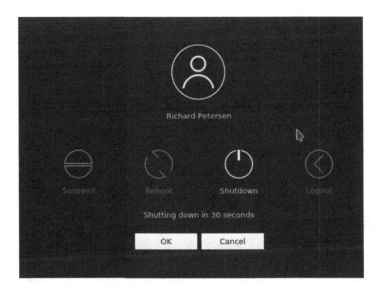

Figure 9-8. *Shutdown and Logout dialog*

If you have installed the Application Dashboard widget, you can click the logout, shutdown, and restart button on the lower left. For a complete selection, choose the Power/Session category on the right (see Figure 9-9).

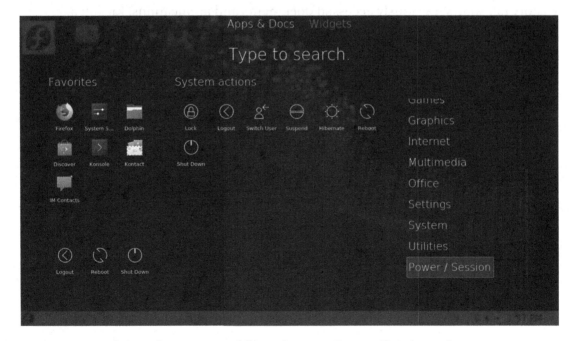

Figure 9-9. *The Application Dashboard menu, Power/Session tab*

You can also press your computer's power button or right-click anywhere on the desktop and select the Leave entry from the pop-up menu, to open a leave dialog with the Logout button selected, as shown here. Buttons to the left let you choose between the suspend, reboot, and shutdown operations.

If you just want to lock your desktop, you can select the Lock Screen entry (Lock on the Kickoff and Application Dashboard menus), and your screen saver will appear. To access a locked desktop, click on the screen and a box appears prompting you for your login password. When you enter the password, your desktop reappears.

Kickoff Menus

The Kickoff application launcher (see Figure 9-10) organizes menu entries into tabs that are accessed by icons at the bottom of the Kickoff menu. There are tabs for Favorites, Applications, Computer, History, and Leave. You can add an application to the Favorites tab by right-clicking on the application's Kickoff entry and selecting Add to Favorites. To remove an application from the Favorites menu, right-click on it and select Remove from Favorites. The Applications tab shows application categories. Click the Computer tab to list all your fixed and removable storage. The History tab shows previously accessed documents and applications. Kickoff also provides a search box where you can search for a particular application instead of paging through menus. As you move through sub-tabs, they are listed at the top of the Kickoff menu, below the search box, allowing you to move back to a previous tab quickly. Click on a tab name to move directly to that tab.

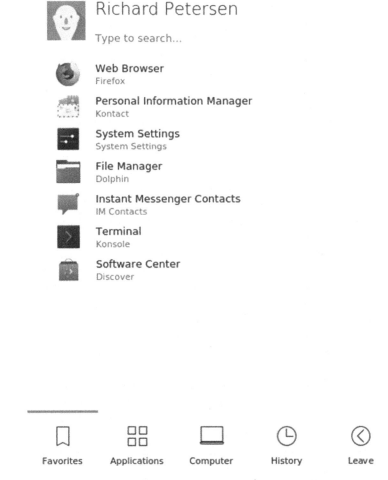

Richard Petersen

Type to search...

Web Browser
Firefox

Personal Information Manager
Kontact

System Settings
System Settings

File Manager
Dolphin

Instant Messenger Contacts
IM Contacts

Terminal
Konsole

Software Center
Discover

Favorites   Applications   Computer   History   Leave

Figure 9-10. *The Kickoff menu includes the Favorites tab*

The Computer menu has Applications, Places, and Removable Storage sections (see Figure 9-11). The Applications section has an entry for System Settings and Run Command (Krunner). The Places section is similar to the Places menu in GNOME, with entries for your home folder, root folder, network, and the trash. The root folder is the same as the system folder on GNOME, the top-level directory in the Linux file system. The Removable Storage section shows removable devices like USB drives and DVD/CD discs.

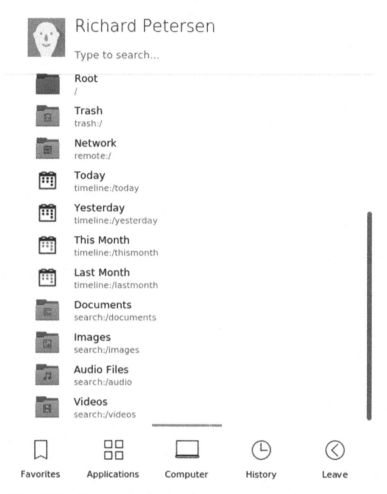

Figure 9-11. *The Kickoff menu includes the Computer tab*

The Applications menu has most of the same entries as those found on GNOME (see Figure 9-12). You can find entries for categories such as Internet, Graphics, and Office. These menus list both GNOME and KDE applications you can use. However, some of the menus contain entries for alternate KDE applications, like KMail on the Internet menu. Other entries will invoke the KDE version of a tool, like the Terminal entry in the System menu, which will invoke the KDE terminal window, Konsole. There is no Preferences menu.

Figure 9-12.   *The Kickoff menu includes an Applications tab*

Application Dashboard Menus

You can install the Application Dashboard as a desktop or panel widget. The Application Dashboard menu launcher displays menu entries on a full-screen dashboard, showing sections for applications, favorites, logout/shutdown options, and categories (see Figure 9-13). Press the Esc key to leave the dashboard without making a selection. You can add an application to the Favorites section by right-clicking on the application's icon and selecting Add to Favorites. To remove an application from the Favorites section, right-click on it and select Remove from Favorites. The Applications section shows categories to the right and the icons for a selected category to the left. There are also categories for recent applications and documents. The Power/Section category lists the complete set of leave options, including lock, suspend, and new session. The All Applications category lists all your applications under alphabetic headings (see Figure 9-14).

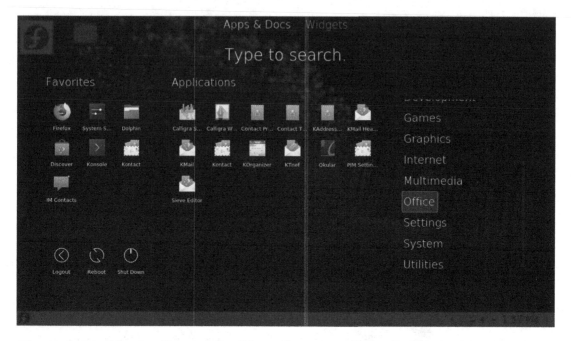

Figure 9-13. *The Application Dashboard menu, Office tab*

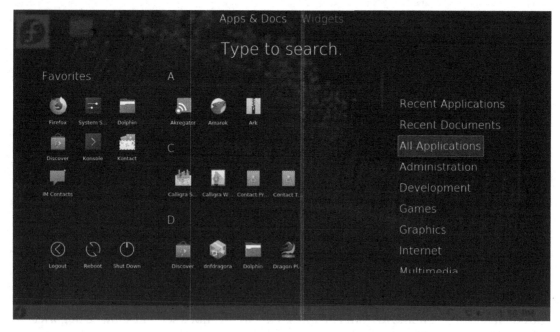

Figure 9-14. *Application Dashboard menu, All Applications tab*

Krunner

For fast access to applications, bookmarks, contacts, and other desktop items, you can use Krunner. The Krunner widget operates as a search tool for applications and other items such as bookmarks. To find an application, enter a search pattern; a listing of matching applications is displayed. Click on an application entry to start the application. You can also place an icon (application launcher) for an entry on the desktop by simply clicking and dragging its entry for the list to the desktop. For applications where you know the name, part of the name, or just its basic topic, Krunner is a very fast way to access the application. To start Krunner, press Alt+F2, Alt+space, or right-click on the desktop to display the desktop menu and select Run Command. Enter the pattern for the application you want to search for and press Enter. The pattern "software" or "package" would display an entry for Discover Software. Entering the pattern "office" displays entries for all the LibreOffice applications, as well as additional office applications you can install (see Figure 9-15).

Clicking the Settings button at the left opens the Configure Search dialog, which lists plugins for searching applications, widgets, and bookmarks, as well as providing capabilities such a running shell commands, opening files, and spell checking. The Clear History button deletes earlier search results. You can also configure Krunner search using the Plasma Search tab on System Settings Search (Workspace section).

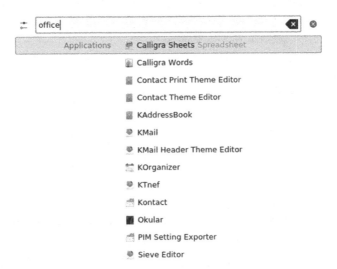

Figure 9-15. *Krunner application search*

Removable Devices: Device Notifier

Installed on the system tray to the right is the Device Notifier. When you insert a removable device like a CD/DVD disc or a USB drive, the New Device Notifier briefly displays a dialog showing all your removable devices, including the new one. The Device Notifier icon is displayed on the system tray. You can click on the New Device Notifier any time to display this dialog. Figure 9-16 shows the New Device Notifier displayed on the panel and its panel icon. The New Device Notifier is displayed only if at least one removable device is attached.

Removable devices are not displayed as icons on your desktop. Instead, to open the devices, you use the New Device Notifier. Click on the Device Notifier icon in the panel to open its dialog. The device is unmounted initially with an unmount button displayed. Click on this button to mount the device. An eject button is then displayed, which you can later use to unmount and eject the device. Opening the device with an application from its menu will mount the device automatically. Clicking on the eject button for a DVD/CD disc will physically eject it. For a USB drive, the drive will be unmounted and prepared for removal. You can then safely remove the USB drive.

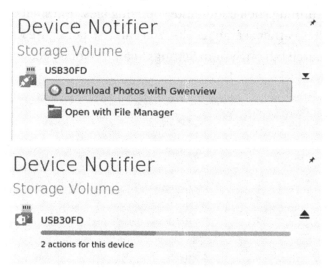

To open a device, click on its entry in the Device Notifier, like one for your DVD/CD disc or your USB drive (see Figure 9-16).

Removable media are also displayed on the File Manager window's side pane. You can choose to eject removable media from the file manager instead of from the Device Notifier by right-clicking on the removable media entry and selecting Safely Remove from the pop-up menu.

Figure 9-16. *Device Notifier and its panel widget icon*

Network Connections: Network Manager

On Plasma, the Network Manager plasma widget provides panel access for Network Manager. This is the same Network Manager application but adapted to the Plasma interface. The widget icon image changes for wireless only and wired connections. Clicking on the widget icon in the panel opens a dialog listing your current available wireless and wired connections. When you pass the mouse over an active connection, a Disconnect buttons appear (see Figure 9-17). For entries not connected, Connect buttons are displayed. To rescan your available connections, click the rescan button (circle) located to the right of the Available Connections heading. Clicking on a connected entry opens tabs for Speed and Details (see Figure 9-18).

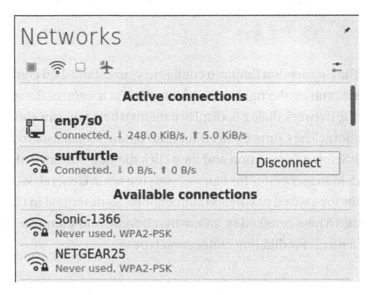

Figure 9-17. *Network Manager connections and panel icons*

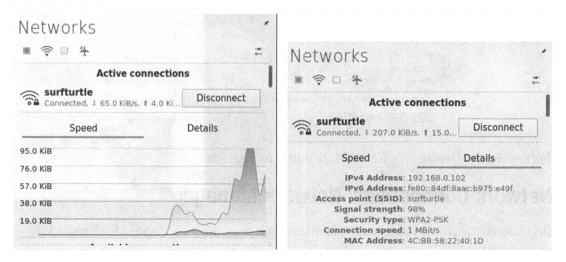

Figure 9-18. *Plasma Network Manager connection information: speed and details*

The toolbar at the top of the network plasma widget has buttons for wireless and airplane mode connections (shown below). Check boxes next to each connection icon show if it is enabled. Clicking on the check box for a connection will enable or disable the connection. Disabled connections have an empty check box and a red icon.

You can use the Connection Editor to configure your established connections. Either click the Settings button on the right side of the toolbar at the top of the network dialog or right-click on the network dialog to display a menu where you can choose Configure Network Connections. The Connection editor then opens, which lists your connections (see Figure 9-19). Select a connection and then click the Edit button on the toolbar to open the Network Manager editor for Plasma, with the same General, Wired, Security, and IPv4/IPv6 tabs for a wired or wireless connections, as described in Chapter 15 (see Figure 9-17). To add a new connection manually, click the Add button on the Connection editor to display a menu for different connection types.

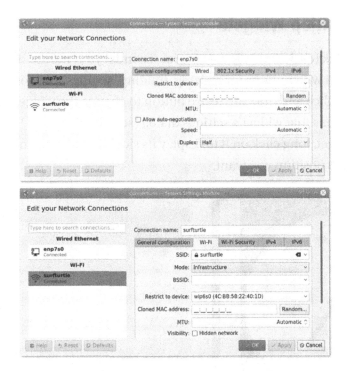

Figure 9-19. *Plasma connection editor and Plasma Network Manager*

Desktop Plasmoids (Widgets)

The Plasma desktop supports plasmoids. Plasmoids are integrated into the desktop on the same level as windows and icons. Just as a desktop can display windows, it can also display plasmoids. Plasmoids can take on desktop operations, running essential operations, even replacing, to a limited extent, the need for file manager windows. The name for plasmoids used on the desktop is widgets. The tools and commands on the desktop that manage plasmoids, refer to them as widgets. For that reason, they will be referred to as widgets.

Managing Desktop Widgets

When you long click (click and hold for several seconds) your mouse on a widget, its sidebar is displayed with buttons for resizing, rotating, settings, and removing the widget (see Figure 9-18). Click and drag the resize button to change the widget size. Clicking the Settings button opens that widget's settings dialog (see Figure 9-20).

To move a widget, long click on it to display its sidebar and while holding the click, drag the icon to the position you want.

Figure 9-20. *Clock Widget with task sidebar and configuration dialog*

To add a widget (plasmoid) to the desktop, right-click anywhere on the desktop and select Add Widgets from the pop-up menu. This opens the Widgets dialog at the left side of the desktop that lists widgets you can add (see Figure 9-21). Clicking on the Categories button opens a pop-up menu with different widget categories like Date and Time, Online Services, and Graphics. Double-click or drag a widget to the desktop to add it to the desktop. You can enter a pattern to search for a widget using the search box located at the top of the dialog.

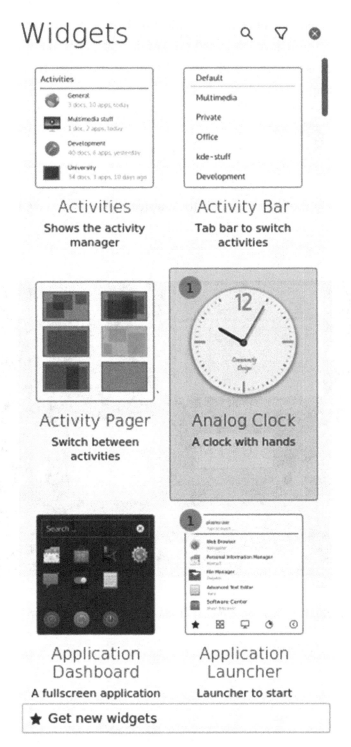

Figure 9-21. Adding a widget using the Widgets dialog

To remove a widget, long click on the widget to display its toolbar, and then click on the red Remove button at the bottom of the toolbar. When you remove a widget, a notification message is displayed with an Undo button, as shown here. Clicking on the Undo button will restore the widget.

Figure 9-22 shows the folder, digital clock, notes, calculator, and CPU monitor widgets. The desktop folder widget is just a folder widget set initially to the desktop folder.

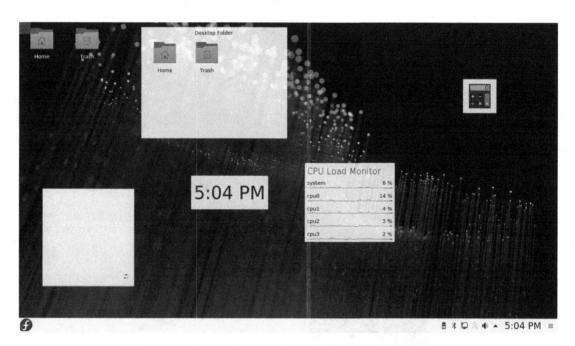

Figure 9-22. *Folder, calculator, digital clock, CPU load monitor, and notes widgets*

Folder and Icon Widgets

You can place access to any folders on the desktop by simply dragging their icons from a file manager window to the desktop (see Figure 9-23). A small menu will appear that includes options for the Icon and Folder View widgets. The Folder View option sets up a Folder View widget for the folder showing icons for subfolders and files. The Icon entry creates an Icon widget. The icon and folder view widgets are shown here.

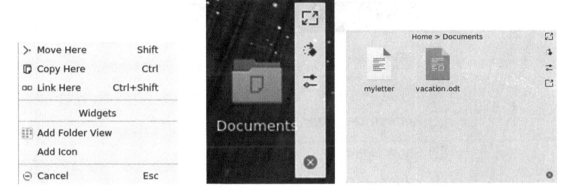

Figure 9-23. *Folder and Icon widgets*

For any Folder View widget, you can use that widget's settings dialog to change the folder it references. A Folder View widget has options for showing the desktop folder, a folder on your Places list, or a specific folder. You can also specify a title. You can easily create a Folder View widget for your home folder.

Activities

The Plasma desktop is designed to support multiple activities. Activities are different plasma containments, each with its set of widgets. An activity is not the same as virtual desktop. Virtual desktops affect space, displaying additional desktops. An activity has its own set of widgets (widgets) and windows, displaying a different set of widgets and windows for each activity. In effect, each activity has a different desktop and set of virtual desktops. Technically, each activity is a Plasma containment that has its own collection of widgets and windows. You can switch to a different activity (containment) and display a different collection of widgets and windows on your desktop.

An activity is often tailored for a certain task. You could have one activity for office work, another for news, and yet another for media. Each activity could have its own set of appropriate widgets, like clock, calculator, notes, and folder widgets for an office activity. A media activity might have a Media Player widget and media applications open.

Multiple activities are managed using the Activities Manager, which is accessed through the Activities entry on the desktop toolbox menu or the Activities widget, which you can install on the panel or desktop. Both are shown here.

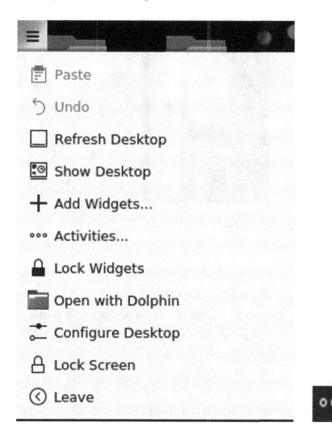

Files and folders can be attached to an activity, displaying them only on that activity. Right-click on the folder or file icon in the File Manager and choose the Activities submenu to choose an activity. Windows are set by default to display on the activity they are opened on. The window switcher is configured to work only on the current activity. The setting is configured in the Window Management dialog (Workspace section of the System settings dialog). On the Task Switcher tab, the Filter Windows By section has Activities checked and Current Activity selected.

To add an activity, click the Activities entry in the toolbox or desktop menus. If you have added and Activities widget to the panel, you can click the Activities button. The Activities Manager is displayed listing your activities on the left side of the screen (see Figure 9-24). A default activity icon for your desktop will already be displayed. Click the Create Activity button (plus button) to add a new activity. A Create a New Activity window opens with entries for the name and description (see Figure 9-25). Click on the Icon image to open a dialog where you can choose an icon for your activity. On the Other tab, you can choose not to track usage and to set up a keyboard shortcut for the activity. Click the Create button to add the new activity. An activity entry then appears on the Activity Manager. To switch to another activity, click its icon.

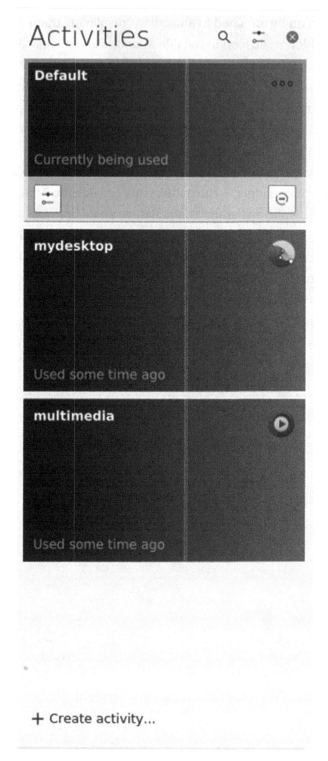

Figure 9-24. *Activity toolbar and icons*

Moving the mouse over an activity icon displays Configure and Stop buttons. The Configure button opens the Activity Settings dialog for that activity, which is the same as the create dialog, with Name, Description, and Icon settings. The Stop button deactivates the activity and places it at the bottom of the Activity Manager under the Stopped Activities heading. To start a stopped activity, simply click its icon in the Stopped Activities list.

To remove an activity, first stop it, then move your mouse over the activity icon in the Stopped activities section (see Figure 9-26). A remove button appears to the right of the activity entry. Click it to remove the activity. You are prompted to confirm the deletion.

Figure 9-25. *Create an activity*

To add widgets to an activity, first click the activity to make it the current activity, and then click the Add Widgets button to display the Widgets dialog. Widgets you add are placed in the current activity.

To switch from one activity to another, first display the Activities Manager by choosing Activities from the desktop toolbox menu (right-click on desktop) or the Activates button on the panel (if installed). Then click on the Activity icon you want. The new activity becomes your desktop (see Figure 9-27). To change to another activity, open the Activities Manager again and click the activity icon you want. Your original desktop is the first icon (Default).

355

Figure 9-26. *Stop Activity icons*

Figure 9-27. *Activity Manager and screen of selected activity*

To move easily between activities, you can add the Activity bar widget, either to the panel or to the desktop. On the panel, the Activity bar displays buttons for each activity. Click to move to a different activity. On the desktop, the Activity bar displays a dialog with an arrow button for moving from one activity to another.

Windows

A Plasma window has the same functionality you find in other window managers and desktops. You can resize the window by clicking and dragging any of its corners or sides. A click-and-drag operation on a side extends the window in that dimension, whereas a corner extends both height and width at the same time. The top of the window has a title bar showing the name of the window, the program name in the case of applications, and the current directory name for the file manager windows. The active window has the title bar highlighted.

To move the window, click the title bar and drag it where you want. Right-clicking the window title bar displays a pop-up menu with entries for window operations, such as minimize, maximize, and moving the window to a different desktop or activity. The More Actions submenu includes closing or resizing the window, the shade option to roll up the window to the title bar, and full screen. Menus, icons, and toolbars for the particular application are displayed in the window.

You can configure the appearance and operation of a window by selecting the Window Manager Settings from the More Actions submenu in the Window menu (right-click the title bar). Here you can set appearance (Window Decoration), button and key operations (Actions), the focus policy, such as a mouse click on the window or just passing the mouse over it (Focus), and how the window is displayed when moving it (Moving). All these features can be configured also using the System Setting's Window Behavior tool in the Workspace section.

Opened windows are shown as buttons on the Plasma taskbar located on the panel. The taskbar shows buttons for the different programs you are running or windows you have open. This is essentially a docking mechanism that lets you change to a window or application by clicking its button. When you minimize a window, it is reduced to its taskbar button. You can then restore the window by clicking its taskbar button. A live thumbnail of a window on the taskbar is displayed as your mouse passes over its taskbar button, showing its name, desktop, and image.

Taskbar buttons also function as progress bars, showing the progress of copy and download operations. Music and video players also show basic multimedia controls, such as pause, start, next, and previous.

To the right of the title bar are three small buttons for minimizing, maximizing, or closing the window (down, up, and x symbols). You can switch to a window at any time by clicking its taskbar button. You can also maximize a window by dragging it to the top edge of the screen.

From the keyboard, you can use the Alt+Tab key combination to display a list of current open windows. Holding down the Alt key and sequentially pressing Tab moves you through the list.

A window can be displayed as a tile on one half of the screen. Another tile can be set up for a different window on the other side of the screen, allowing you to display two windows side by side on the full screen (see Figure 9-28). You can tile a window by dragging it to the side of the screen (over the side edge to the middle of the window). A tile outline will appear. Add a second tile by moving a window to the other side edge. You can add more windows to a tile by moving them to that edge. Clicking on a window's taskbar button will display it on its tile.

The same process works for corners. You can tile a window to a corner by moving it to that corner. You can then have four tiled windows open at each corner. You could even have server windows open on the same corner, displaying the one you want by clicking its taskbar icon.

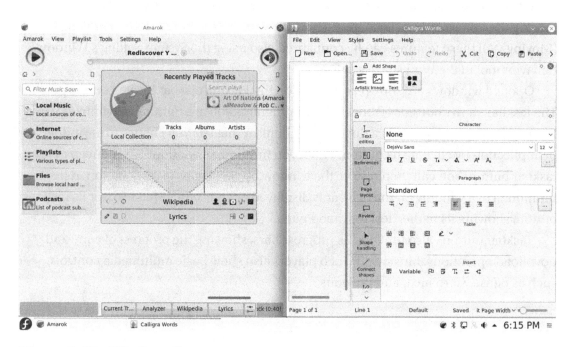

Figure 9-28. *Window tiles*

Applications

You can start an application in Plasma in several ways. If an entry for it is in the Kickoff Applications menu or Application Dashboard, you can select that entry to start the application. You can right-click on any application entry in the Applications menu to display a pop-up menu with Add to Panel and Add to Desktop entries. Select either to add a shortcut icon for the application to the desktop or the panel. You can then start an application by single-clicking its desktop or panel icon.

An application icon on the desktop is implemented as a desktop widget. Performing a long click on the application icon on the desktop displays a sidebar with the icon for the widget settings. This opens a Settings window that allows you to specify a keyboard shortcut.

You can also run an application by right-clicking on the desktop and selecting the Run Command (or press Alt+F2 or Alt+space), which will display the Krunner tool consisting of a box to enter a single command. Previous commands can be accessed from a pop-up menu. You need only enter a pattern to search for the application. Results will be displayed in the Krunner window. Choose the one you want.

Virtual Desktops: Pager

The Plasma desktop supports virtual desktops, extending the desktop area on which you can work. You could have a web browser running on one desktop and be using a text editor in another. Plasma can support up to 16 virtual desktops. To use virtual desktops, add the Pager widget to your panel or desktop. On the panel, you can use the panel editor (toolbox, right side) to move it to the location you want on the panel. The panel and desktop pagers are shown here.

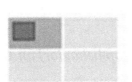

The Pager widget represents your virtual desktops as miniature screens, showing small squares for each desktop. It works much like the GNOME Workspace Switcher. To move from one desktop to another, click the square for the destination desktop. The selected desktop will be highlighted. Just passing your mouse over a desktop image on the panel will open a message displaying the desktop number along with the windows open on that desktop.

If you want to move a window to a different desktop, first open the window's menu by right-clicking the window's title bar. Then select the To Desktop entry, which lists the available desktops. Choose the one you want.

You can also configure Plasma so that if you move the mouse over the edge of a desktop screen, it automatically moves to the adjoining desktop. You need to imagine the desktops arranged next to each. You enable this feature by enabling the Switch Desktop on Edge feature in the System Settings ➤ Desktop Behavior ➤ Screen Edges tab. This feature will also allow you to move windows over the edge to an adjoining desktop.

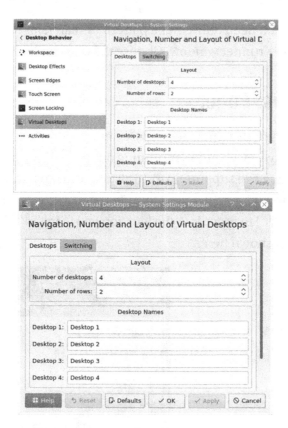

Figure 9-29. *Virtual desktop configuration (desktop behavior) and Pager widget icon*

To change the number of virtual desktops, right-click on the Desktop Pager widget, select the Configure Desktops entry in the pop-up menu to open the Virtual Desktops dialog, and choose the Desktops tab, which displays entries for your active desktops. You can also access the Virtual Desktops dialog from System Settings ➤ Desktop Behavior in the Workspace section (see Figure 9-29). The text box labeled Number of Desktops controls the number of active desktops. Use the arrows or enter a number to change the number of active desktops. You can change any of the desktop names by clicking an active name and entering a new one.

To change how the pager displays desktops on the pager, right-click on the pager and choose Pager Settings to open the Pager Settings dialog (see Figure 9-30). Here you can configure the pager to display numbers or names for desktops, or show icons of open windows.

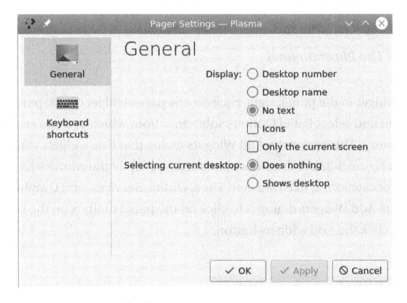

Figure 9-30. *Pager Settings dialog*

Tip   Use the Ctrl key in combination with a function key to switch to a specific desktop: for example, Ctrl+F1 switches to the first desktop and Ctrl+F3 to the third desktop.

Plasma Panel

The Plasma panel, located at the bottom of the screen, provides access to most Plasma functions (see Figure 9-31). The panel is a specially configured Plasma containment, just like the desktop. The panel can include icons for menus, folder windows, specific programs, and virtual desktops. These are widgets that are configured for use on the panel. At the left end of the panel is a button for the Kickoff menu, a KDE *K* icon.

To add an application to the panel, right-click on its entry in the Kickoff menu to open a pop-up menu and select Add to Panel.

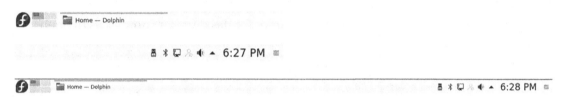

Figure 9-31. *The Plasma panel*

To add a widget to the panel, right-click on any panel widget on the panel to open a pop-up menu and select Panel Options submenu, from which you can select the Add Widgets entry. This opens the Add Widgets dialog that lists widgets you can add to the panel (see Figure 9-32). A drop-down menu at the top of the window lets you see different widget categories, like Date and Time, Online Services, and Graphics. Another way to open the Add Widgets dialog is to click on the panel toolbox on the right side of the panel and click the Add widgets button.

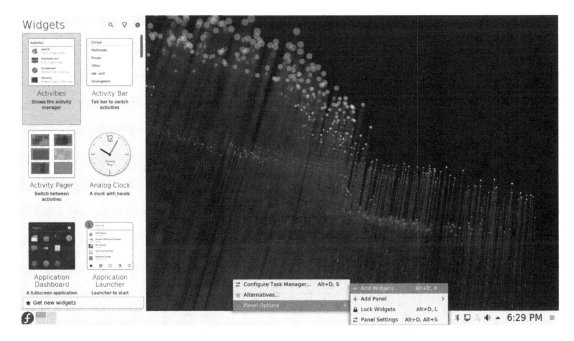

Figure 9-32. *Plasma Add Widgets for panel*

The Plasma panel supports several kinds of Windows and Tasks widgets, including the taskbar (Task Manager) and system tray. To the right of the system tray is the digital clock. The system tray holds widgets for desktop operations like update notifier, the clipboard, Bluetooth, device notifier, sound settings (kmix), media player (if a multimedia player is active), and network manager, as shown here.

The pop-up menu (arrow icon) on the right side of the system tray display widgets that are not in use, or not often used (see Figure 9-33). The Battery and Brightness entry displays a dialog to see battery charges and set screen brightness.

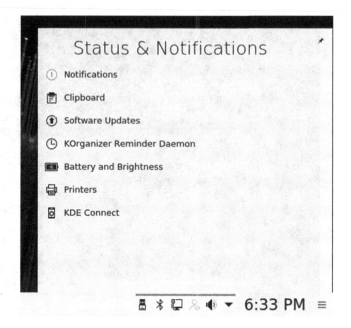

Figure 9-33. *System tray*

To configure the system tray, right-click on the system tray menu (arrow icon) and choose System Tray Settings to open the system tray configuration dialog at the General tab, where you can decide what items to display or entries to make visible or remove (see Figure 9-34). In the Extra Items list, you can check items that you also want displayed on the system tray, such as Printers and Instant Messaging. When you click the Apply button the items are displayed. Items not in use are in the menu. The Entries tab shows how selected items are to be displayed (auto, shown, or hidden).

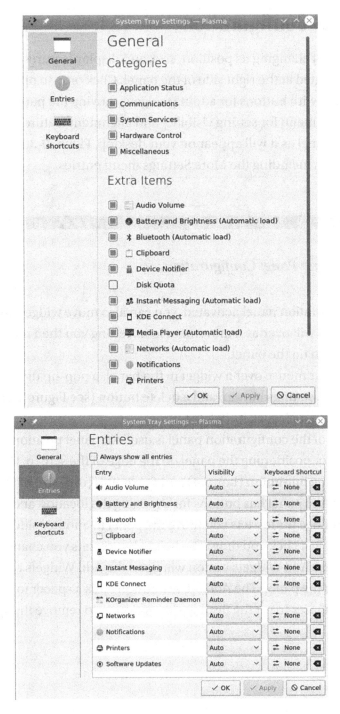

Figure 9-34. *Plasma panel system tray settings*

Plasma Panel Configuration

To configure a panel, changing its position, size, and display features, you use the panel's toolbox, located at the right side of the panel. Click on it to open an additional configuration panel with buttons for adding widgets, moving the panel, changing its size, and a More Settings menu for setting visibility and alignment features. Figure 9-35 shows the configuration panel as it will appear on your desktop. Figure 9-36 provides a more detailed description, including the More Settings menu entries.

Figure 9-35. *Plasma Panel Configuration*

With the configuration panel activated, you can also move widgets around the panel. Clicking on a widget will overlay a movement icon, letting you then move the widget icon to a different location on the panel.

As you move your mouse over a widget in the panel, a pop-up dialog opens showing the widget's name, a settings button, and a delete button (see Figure 9-35). To remove the widget from the panel, click its delete button.

The lower part of the configuration panel is used for panel position settings. On the left side is a slider for positioning the panel on the edge of the screen. On the right side are two sliders for the minimum (bottom) and maximum (top) size of the panel.

The top part of the panel has buttons for changing the location and the size of the panel. The Screen Edge button lets you move the panel to another side of the screen (left, right, top, bottom). Just click and drag. The height button lets you change the panel size, larger or smaller. The Add Widgets button will open the Add Widgets dialog, letting you add new widgets to the panel. The Add Spacer button adds a spacer to separate widgets. Right-click on the spacer to set the flexible size option or to remove the spacer.

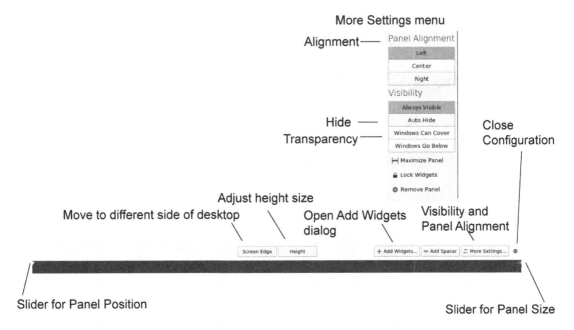

Figure 9-36. *Plasma Panel Configuration details and display features*

The More Setting menu lets you set Visibility and Alignment features. You can choose an AutoHide setting that will hide the panel until you move the mouse to its location. The Windows Can Cover option lets a window overlap the panel. For smaller panels, you can align to the right, left, or center of the screen edge. The More Settings menu also has an entry to remove the panel. Use this entry to delete a panel you no longer want.

When you are finished with the configuration, click the red x icon the upper-right side.

Desktop Effects

Desktop effects can be enabled on the System Settings Desktop Effects tab in the Desktop Behavior dialog in the Workspace section (System Settings ➤ Desktop Behavior). For virtual desktop switching, you can choose Slide, Fade Desktop, and Desktop Cube Animation (see Figure 9-37). The more dramatic effects are found in the Windows Management section. Desktop Effects requires the support of a capable graphics chip (GPU). You may have to install the proprietary graphics driver (System Settings ➤ Driver Manager).

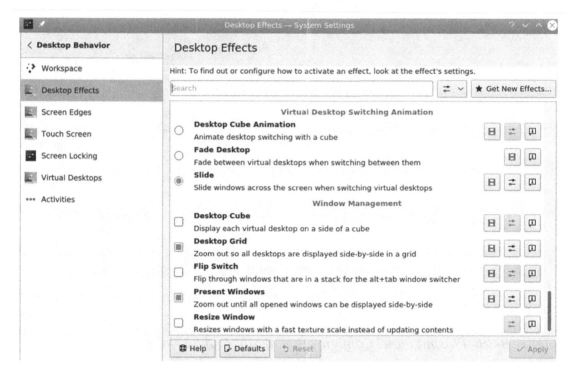

Figure 9-37. *Desktop Effects selection*

Table 9-3. *KWin Desktop Effects Keyboard Shortcuts*

Key	Operation
Alt+Tab	Cover Switch, Thumbnail, or Breeze for open windows
Ctrl+F8	Desktop Grid (use mouse to select a desktop)
Ctrl+F9	Present Windows Current Desktop
Ctrl+F10	Present Windows All Desktops
Ctrl+F11	Desktop Cube (use mouse or arrow keys to move, ESC to exit)

Several windows effects are selected by default, depending on whether your graphics card can support them. A check box is filled next to active effects. If there is a dialog icon to the right of the effects entry, it means the effect can be configured. Click on the icon to open its configuration dialog. Figure 9-38 shows the configuration dialog for the Desktop Grid effect. For several effects, you use certain keys to start them. The more commonly used effects are Cover Switch, Desktop Grid, Present Windows, and Desktop Cube. The keys for these effects are listed in Table 9-3.

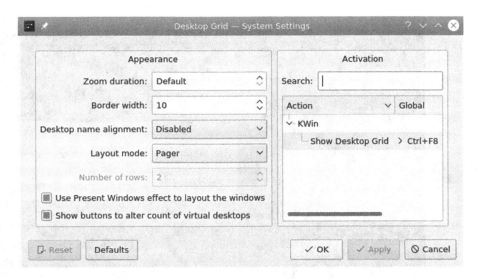

Figure 9-38. *Desktop Effects configuration*

Window switching using Alt+Tab is controlled on the Windows Management dialog's Task Switcher tab, not from Desktop Behavior's Desktop Effects tab. In the Visualization section, you can choose the window switching effect you want to use from the drop-down menu. These include Breeze, Thumbnails, Grid, Cover Switch, and Flip Switch, as well as smaller listings such as informative, compact, text icons, and small icons. The Alt+Tab keys implement the effect you have chosen. Continually pressing the Tab key while holding down the Alt key moves you through the windows. Thumbnails displays windows in a boxed dialog (see Figure 9-39), whereas Cover Switch arranges windows stacked to the sides, and Flip Switch arranges the windows to one side (see Figure 9-40). The default is Breeze, which arranges the window images to the left side of the screen (see Figure 9-39).

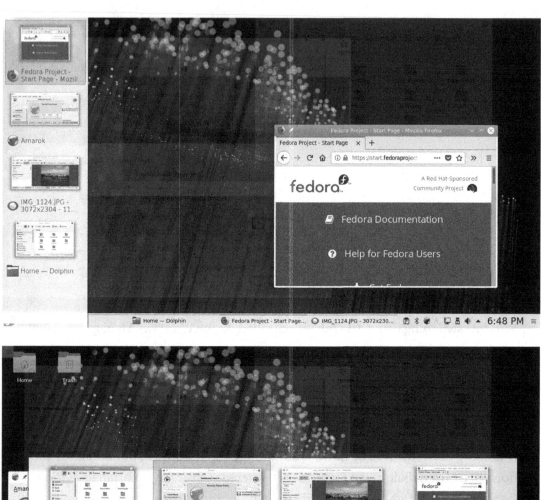

Figure 9-39. Thumbnail and Breeze switch: Use Alt+Tab

The Present Windows effect displays images of the open windows on your screen with the selected one highlighted (see Figure 9-41). You can use your mouse to select another. This provides an easy way to browse your open windows. You can also use Ctrl+F9 to display windows on your current virtual desktop statically and use the arrow key to move between them. Use Ctrl+F10 to display all your open windows across all your desktops. Press the Esc key to return to the desktop.

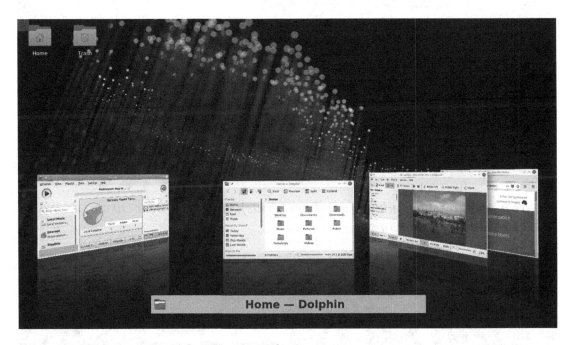

Figure 9-40. *Cover Switch: Use Alt+Tab*

Desktop Grid will show a grid of all your virtual desktops (Ctrl+F8), letting you see all your virtual desktops on the screen at once (see Figure 9-42). You can then move windows and open applications between desktops. Clicking on a desktop makes it the current one. The plus and minus keys allow you to add or remove virtual desktops.

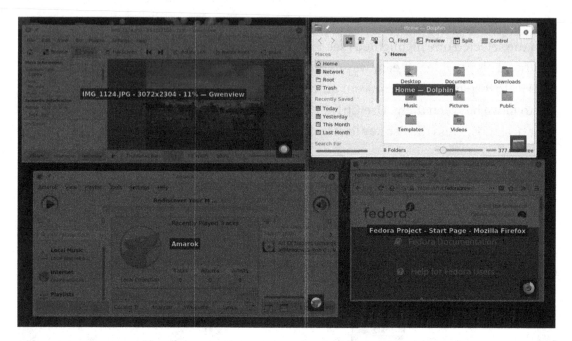

Figure 9-41.   *Present windows (windows effects): Use Ctrl+F9 for current desktop and Ctrl+F10 for all desktops*

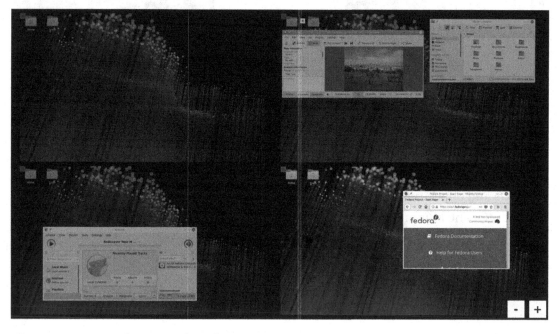

Figure 9-42.   *Desktop Grid: Ctrl+F8*

Desktop Cube will show a cube of all your virtual desktops, letting you move to different desktops around a cube (see Figure 9-43). Stop at the side you want to select. Press Ctrl+11 to start the Desktop Cube. You can then move around the cube with the arrow keys or by clicking and dragging your mouse. Alternatively, if you have a touchpad, you can use a two-finger drag to start and move through the Desktop Cube. When you are finished, press the Esc key to return to the desktop. Desktop Cube Animation will use cube animation whenever you switch to a different desktop using the Desktop Pager.

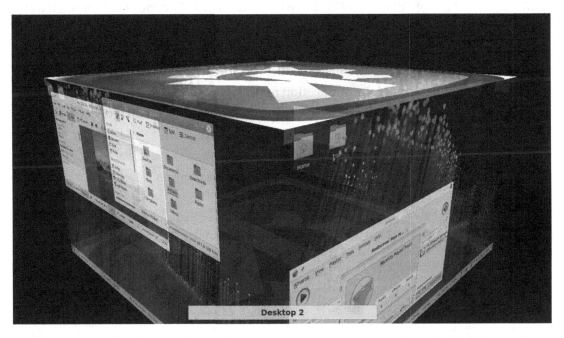

Figure 9-43. *Desktop Cube: Ctrl+F11, drag-mouse, or use the right/left arrow keys (or two-finger drag on a touchpad)*

Plasma File Manager: Dolphin

Dolphin is Plasma's dedicated file manager (see Figure 9-44). A navigation bar shows the current directory either in a browser or edit mode. In the browse mode it shows icons for the path of your current directory, and in the edit mode, it shows the path name in a text-editable box. You can use either to move to different folders and their subfolders. Use the Ctrl+l key or click to the right of the folder buttons to use the edit mode. You can also choose Control ➤ Location Bar ➤ Editable Location. Clicking on the checkmark at the end of the editable text box returns you to the browser mode.

The Dolphin menu bar has been hidden by default. The menus are displayed when clicking the Control button on the right end of the toolbar (see Figure 9-45). You can redisplay the menu bar by choosing Show Menubar from the Control (or View) menu (Ctrl+m). You can hide the menu bar again by choosing Show Menubar from the Settings menu (or pressing Ctrl+m).

You can open a file either by clicking it or by right-clicking it, then choosing the Open With submenu to list applications to open it with. If you want to just select the file or folder, you need to hold down the Ctrl key while you click it. A single click will open the file. If the file is a program, that program starts up. If it is a data file, such as a text file, the associated application is run using that data file. Clicking a text file displays it with the Kate editor, while clicking an image file displays it with the Gwenview image viewer. If Dolphin cannot determine the application to use, it opens a dialog box prompting you to enter the application name. You can click the Browse button on this box to use a directory tree to locate the application program you want.

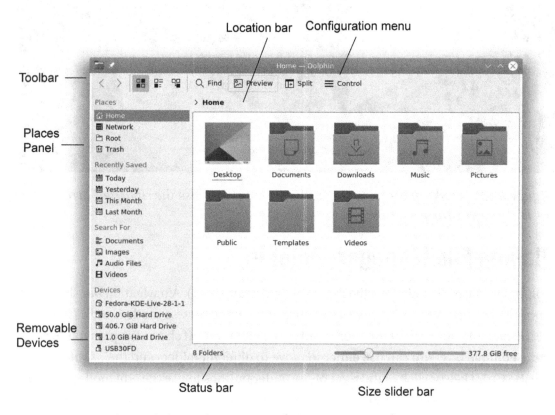

Figure 9-44. *The Dolphin File Manager (Plasma desktop)*

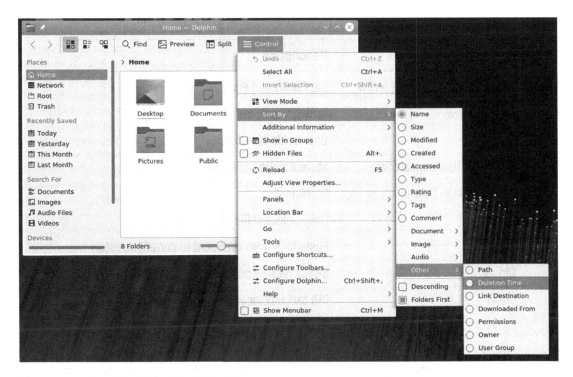

Figure 9-45. *The Dolphin File Manager menus*

Dolphin can display panels to either side (Dolphin refers to these as panels, although they operate more like standalone tabs). The Places panel will show icons for often-used folders like Home, Network, and Trash, as well as removable devices. To add a folder to the Places panel, just drag it there. The files listed in a folder can be viewed in several ways, such as icons, detailed listing (Details), and columns (Control ➤ View Mode menu). See Table 9-4 for keyboard shortcuts.

Table 9-4. *Dolphin File Manager Keyboard Shortcuts*

Keys	Description
Alt+left arrow, Alt+right arrow	Backward and Forward in history
Alt+up arrow	One directory up
Enter	Open a file/directory
Left/Right/Up/Down arrows	Move among the icons
Page Up, Page Down	Scroll fast
Ctrl+c	Copy selected file to clipboard
Ctrl+v	Paste files from clipboard to current directory
Ctrl+s	Select files by pattern
Ctrl+l	URI text box location bar
Ctrl+f	Find files
Ctrl+q	Close window

The Additional Information submenu in the Control menu (or View menu) lets you display additional information about files such as the size, date, type, and comments. Type-specific information can also be displayed such as album, track, and duration for audio files, and word and line counts for documents. You can also display the full path, permissions, and group information (other submenu).

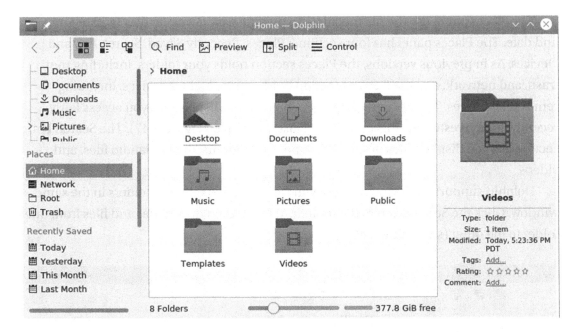

Figure 9-46. *The Dolphin File Manager with sidebars*

Figure 9-47. *The Recently Saved panel of the Dolphin File Manager*

You can display additional panels by selecting them from the Control ➤ Panels submenu. The Information panel displays detailed information about a selected file or folder, and the Folders panel displays a directory tree for the file system. The panels are detachable from the file manager window (see Figure 9-46). Be sure to choose Unlock Panels in the Panels menu to make them detachable.

The Places panel use the file metadata to provide easy access to files by category and date. The Places panel has four sections: Places, Recently Saved, Search For, and Devices. As in previous versions, the Places section holds your folders, including root, trash, and network, and the Devices section holds your attached devices, including removable devices. The Recently Saved section lets you display files you access fairly recently: today, yesterday, this month, and last month (see Figure 9-47). The Search For section lets you displays files of specified types: documents, images, audio files, and videos.

Dolphin supports split views, where you can open two different folders in the same window. Click the Split button in the toolbar. You can then drag folder and files from one folder to the other (see Figure 9-48).

Figure 9-48. *The Dolphin File Manager with split views*

To configure Dolphin, click Configure Dolphin from the Setting menu to open the Dolphin Preferences dialog with tabs for Startup, View Modes, Navigation, Services, Trash, and General (see Figure 9-49). On the Startup tab, you can specify features like the split view and the default folder to start up with. On the View Modes tab, you can set display features for the different display modes (Icons, Details, and Column), like the icon size, font type, and arrangement. The Navigation tab sets features like opening archives as folders. The Services tab is where you specify actions supported for different kinds of files, like play a DVD with Dragon Player, install a true type font file or display image files. The Trash tab lets you configure trash settings like deleting items in the trash after a specified time and setting the maximum size of the trash. The General tab has sub-tabs for Behavior, Previews, Confirmations, and Status Bar. The Behavior tab is where you can enable tooltips and show selection markers. Preview lets you choose which type of files to preview. The image, jpeg, and directories types are already selected. On Confirmations, you can require confirmation prompts for file deletion, moving files to the trash, or closing multiple tabs. On the Status tab, you can choose to show the zoom slider and the amount of free storage.

Figure 9-49. The Dolphin File Manager configuration

Navigating Directories

Within a file manager window, a single-click on a folder icon moves to that folder and displays its file and sub-folder icons. To move back up to the parent folder, you click the back arrow button located on the left end of the navigation toolbar. A single-click on a folder icon moves you down the folder tree, one folder at a time. By clicking the back arrow button, you move up the tree. The Navigation bar can display either the folder path for the current folder or an editable location box where you can enter in a pathname. For the folder path, you can click on any displayed folder name to move you quickly to an upper-level folder. To use the location box, click to the right of the folder path. The Location box is displayed. You can also select Show Full Location in the View ➤ Location Bar ➤ Editable Location menu item (or press Ctrl+L or F6). The navigation bar changes to an editable text box, where you can type a path name. To change back to the folder path, click the checkmark to the right of the text box.

Like a web browser, the file manager remembers the previous folder it has displayed. You can use the back and forward arrow buttons to move through this list of prior folders. You can also use several keyboard shortcuts to perform such operations, like Alt+back arrow to move up a folder, and the arrow keys to move to different icons.

The Copy, Move, Delete, Rename, and Link Operations

To perform an operation on a file or folder, you first have to select it by clicking the file's icon or listing. To select more than one file, hold down the Ctrl key down while you click the files you want. You can also use the keyboard arrow keys to move from one file icon to another.

To copy and move files, you can use the standard drag-and-drop method with your mouse. To copy a file, you locate it by using the file manager. Open another file manager window to the folder to which you want the file copied. Then drag-and-drop the file icon to that window. A pop-up menu appears with selections for Move Here, Copy Here, or Link Here. Choose Copy Here. To move a file to another directory, follow the same procedure, but select Move Here from the pop-up menu. To copy or move a folder, use the same procedure as for files. All the folder's files and subfolders are also copied or moved. Instead of having to select from a pop-up menu, you can use the corresponding keys: Ctrl for copy, Shift for move, and Ctrl+Shift for link (same as for GNOME).

To rename a file, Ctrl+click its icon and press F2, or right-click the icon and select Rename from the pop-up menu. A dialog opens where you can enter the new name for the file or folder.

You can delete a file either by selecting it and deleting it, or placing it in the Trash folder to delete later. To delete a file, select it and then choose the Delete entry in the File menu, File ➤ Delete (also Shift+Del key). To place a file in the Trash folder, drag-and-drop it to the Trash icon on the Places panel, or right-click the file and choose Move To Trash from the pop-up menu. You can later open the Trash folder and delete the files. To delete all the files in the Trash folder, right-click the Trash icon in Dolphin File Manager Places panel and select Empty Trash from the pop-up menu. To restore files in the Trash bin, open the Trash window and right-click on the file to restore and select Restore.

Each file or directory has properties associated with it that include permissions, the filename, and its directory. To display the Properties dialog for a given file, right-click the file's icon and select the Properties entry. On the General tab, you see the name of the file displayed. To change the filename, replace the name there with a new one. Permissions are set on the Permissions tab. Here, you can set read, write, and execute permissions for user, group, or other access to the file. The Group entry enables you to change the group for a file.

Search Bar and Filter Bar

The Dolphin search tool provides a simplified search bar for files and folders. Dolphin also supports a filter bar to search files and folders in the current folder. You can also use the Filter Panel to refine searches by metadata such as type, date, ratings, and tags. For quick access to basic categories and recent use, you can use the Places panel's Recently Accessed and Search For entries, as noted previously.

Search Bar

To search for files, click the Find button on the icon bar to open the search bar, which displays a search text box. You can also choose Find from the Edit menu or press Ctrl+f. The search bar displays a search text box, where you enter the pattern of the file or folder you are searching for. Click the red x button to the left to close the find bar and use the black x button in the text box to clear the search pattern.

Buttons below the search box provide options to qualify the search. The Filename button (the default) searches on the filename. The Content button will search the contents of text files for the pattern. The From Here button searches the user's home folders, and the Everywhere button (the default) searches the entire file system (see Figure 9-50).

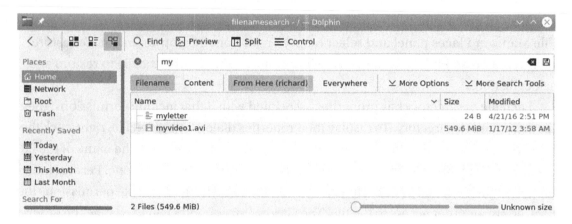

Figure 9-50.   *The Dolphin search bar*

The search results are displayed in the main pane. You can click a file to have it open with its appropriate application. Text files are displayed by the Kate text editor, images by Gwenview, and applications are run. When you are finished searching, click the Close button.

When you pass your mouse over an icon listed in the Query Results, information about it is displayed on the information panel to the right (if the information panel is displayed). Links are shown for adding tags and comments. Right-clicking on this panel lets you open a configure dialog where you can specify what information to display.

The search operation uses the Dolphin implementation of Baloo desktop search. To configure desktop search, choose System Settings ➤ Workspace ➤ Search, File Search tab. On the File Search tab, you can enable or disable file searching and choose folders not to search.

Filter Bar

For a quick search of the current folder, you can activate the Filter bar (Control ➤ Tools ➤ Show Filter Bar or Ctrl+i), which opens a Filter search box at the bottom of the window. Enter a pattern and only those file and directory names containing that pattern are displayed. Click the x button at the right of the Filter box to clear it (see Figure 9-51).

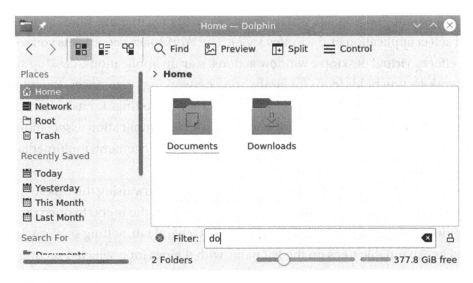

Figure 9-51. *The Dolphin filter bar*

Plasma Configuration: System Settings

With the Plasma configuration tools, you can configure your desktop and system, changing the way it is displayed and the features it supports. The configuration dialogs are accessed on the System Settings window (see Figure 9-52). On Plasma, you can access System Settings from the System Settings entry in the Kickoff Computer or Favorites menus, or from Applications ➤ Settings ➤ System Settings. On the Application Dashboard, you can access it in the Favorites section and in the Settings category.

The System Settings window can be displayed three ways: tree view, icon view, and sidebar view. Use the Configure dialog ➤ General tab to choose the view you want. You can access the Configure dialog from the menu on the sidebar view (upper-left corner) or the Configure button on the icon view (top toolbar). The sidebar view is the current default (see Figure 9-52). The icon view was the default in previous releases (see Figure 9-53). With the sidebar view, System Settings shows an icon list of setting categories arranged in several sections: Appearance, Workspace, Personalization, Network, Hardware, and System Administration (see Figure 9-54). Click an entry to display a new icon list in the sidebar with configuration entries for that category. Selecting an entry shows the configuration settings on the right pane (see Figure 9-55).

The Appearance section lets you set the desktop theme, manage fonts, choose icon sets, and select application and window styles. The Workspace section lets you set desktop effects, virtual desktops, window actions, startup applications, desktop search. The Network section holds icons for configuring networking preferences, Bluetooth connections, and sharing. Personalization lets you set the settings for user management, the date and time, notifications, online accounts, and file/application associations. Hardware lets you set the printer configuration, power management, multimedia devices (sound), your display resolution, and manage drivers.

Alternatively, you can display the System Settings window using the classic tree format. Click the System Settings Configure entry from the menu to open the configuration dialog and select Classic tree on the General tab. Setting sections are displayed as expandable trees on the left pane, with dialogs for a selected section displayed to the right.

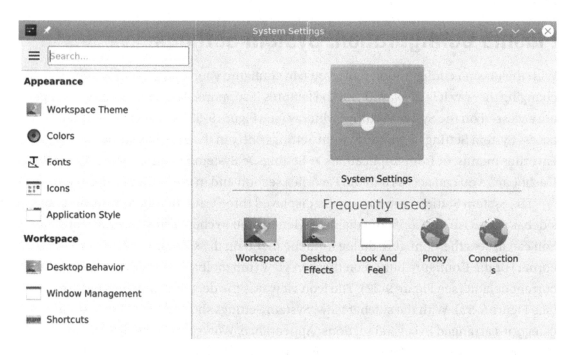

Figure 9-52. *Plasma system settings, sidebar view*

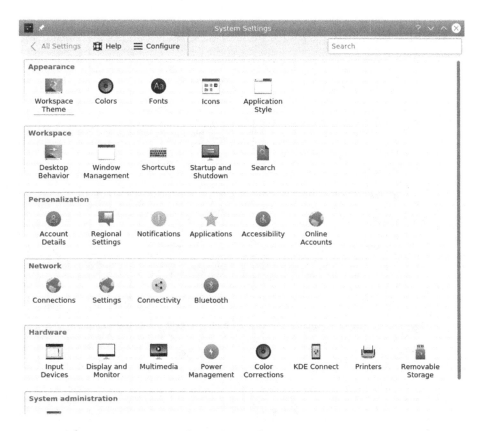

Figure 9-53. *Plasma system settings, icon view*

Figure 9-54. *Plasma system settings, sidebar icon list*

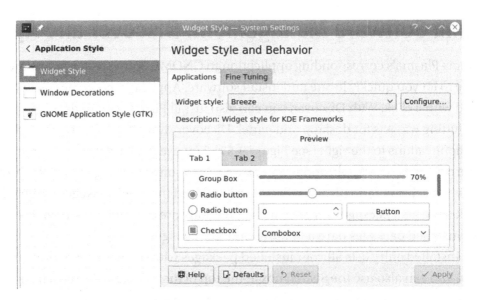

Figure 9-55. *Plasma System Settings ➤ Application Style, Widget Style*

Plasma has administration tools comparable to the Cinnamon and Mate desktops. For example, user management is provided by Kuser, accessible from the System Settings ➤ Account Details (Personalization section), User Manager entry (see Figure 9-56).

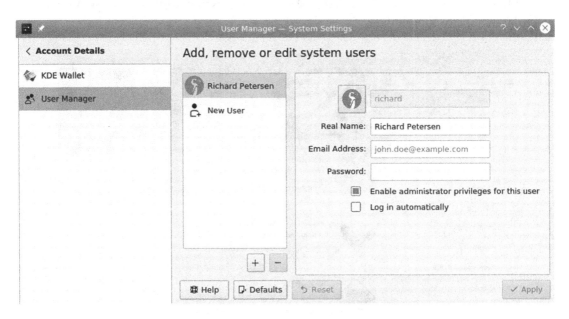

Figure 9-56. *Plasma System Settings ➤ User Manager*

Plasma Software Management: Discover and Apper

Discover is Plasma's corresponding application to GNOME Software. It uses a simple interface to let you quickly locate and install software. Applications can be easily removed with a click. With Discover, you can also install Plasma (KDE) desktop add-ons, including widgets for desktop and panel. Discover shows a sidebar on the left and a list of applications to the right (see Figure 9-57). You use the Discover sidebar to locate software packages. The Applications entry expands to software categories on the sidebar, which, when selected, will display a list of available and installed packages in the right pane. Clicking on a package entry expands it to a software description with an Install button (installed packages have a Remove button; see Figure 9-58).

The Installed entry lists all your installed packages with the Remove button for easy deletion. You can also use the Search box at the top of the sidebar to locate a package. The Settings entry lists your repositories, which you can enable or disable.

The Plasma add-ons entry on the sidebar provides an extensive set of add-ons to different parts of the Plasma desktop. There are categories for fonts, themes, icons, window effects, window switching, and wallpapers, among others. You use the Plasma Widgets entry to manage your desktop and panel widgets.

The Application Addons entry lists add-ons for particular applications, such as calendar events for KOrganizer.

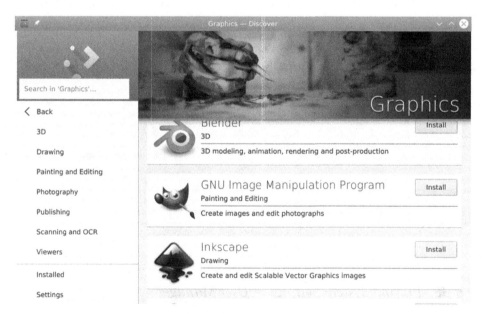

Figure 9-57. *Discover Software Manager*

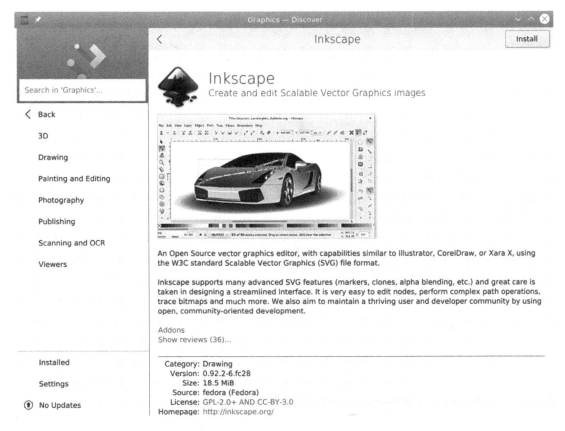

Figure 9-58. *Discover Software Manager, application description*

For software management, you can also use Apper, which replaced KPackagekit software manager. It is not installed by default. Similar to GNOME PackageKit, it lets you search on filenames and descriptions. The Apper dialog shows a toolbar and two sections of icons: Lists and Categories (see Figure 9-59).

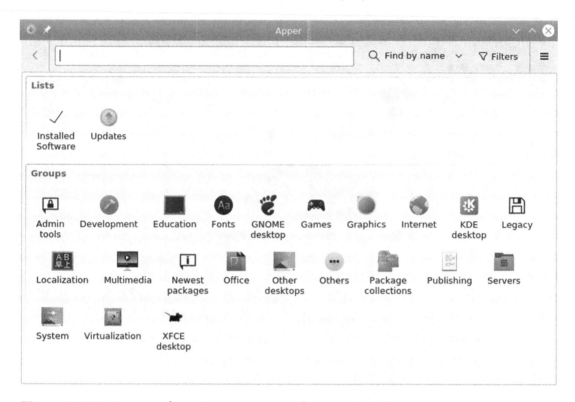

Figure 9-59. *Apper software manager: package categories*

The toolbar at the top shows a search box with a menu to qualify the search, along with filters (installed or new packages). A Pending Changes button shows the packages you have decided to install or remove. The configuration button lists a History and Settings. Use Settings to configure Apper. The Lists section has icons for Installed Software and Updates. Use Updates to update your applications and Installed Software to see what software is installed.

CHAPTER 10

Shells

The *shell* is a command interpreter that provides a line-oriented interactive and noninteractive interface between the user and the operating system. You enter commands on a command line. They are interpreted by the shell and then sent as instructions to the operating system (interactive). The command-line interface is accessible from GNOME and KDE through a terminal window. You can also place commands in a script file, to be consecutively executed much like a program (non-interactive). This interpretive capability of the shell provides for many sophisticated features. For example, the shell has a set of file-expansion characters that can generate filenames. The shell can redirect input and output, as well as run operations in the background, freeing you to perform other tasks.

Several different types of shells have been developed for Linux: the Bourne-Again shell (BASH), the Korn shell, the TCSH shell, and the Z shell. All shells are available for your use, although the BASH shell is the default. You need only one type of shell to do your work. Fedora Linux includes all the major shells, although it installs and uses the BASH shell as the default. If you use the command-line shell, you will be using the BASH shell, unless you specify another. This chapter discusses the BASH shell, which shares many of the same features as other shells.

You can find out more about shells at their respective websites, as listed in Table 10-1. In addition, a detailed online manual is available for each installed shell. Use the man command and the shell's keyword to access them—bash for the BASH shell, ksh for the Korn shell, tsch for the TSCH shell, and zsh for the Z shell. For example, the command man bash will access the BASH shell online manual.

391

© Richard Petersen 2018
R. Petersen, *Beginning Fedora Desktop*, https://doi.org/10.1007/978-1-4842-3882-0_10

Table 10-1. *Linux Shells*

Shell	Website
`www.gnu.org/software/bash`	BASH website, with online manual, FAQ, and current releases
`www.gnu.org/software/bash/` `manual/bash.html`	BASH online manual
`www.zsh.org`	Z shell website, with referrals to FAQ and current downloads
`www.tcsh.org`	TCSH website, with detailed support, including manual, tips, FAQ, and recent releases
`www.kornshell.com`	Korn shell site with manual, FAQ, and references

Note   You can find out more about the BASH shell at `www.gnu.org/software/` `bash`. A detailed online manual is available on your Linux system, using the `man` command with the `bash` keyword.

The Command Line

The Linux command-line interface consists of a single line into which you enter commands with any of their options and arguments. From GNOME or KDE, you can access the command-line interface by opening a terminal window. Should you start Linux with the command-line interface, you will be presented with a BASH shell command line when you log in.

By default, the BASH shell has a dollar sign ($) prompt, but Linux has several other types of shells, each with its own prompt (such as % for the C shell). The root user will have a different prompt, the #. A shell *prompt,* such as the one shown following, marks the beginning of the command line:

$

At the prompt, you can enter a command, along with options and arguments. For example, with an -l option, the ls command will display a line of information about each file, listing such data as its size and the date and time it was last modified. In the following example, the user enters the ls command, followed by a -l option. The dash before the -l option is required. Linux uses it to distinguish an option from an argument.

```
$ ls -l
```

If you wanted only the information displayed for a particular file, you could add that file's name as the argument, following the -l option.

```
$ ls -l mydata
-rw-r--r-- 1 chris weather 207 Feb 20 11:55 mydata
```

Tip Some commands can be complex and take some time to execute. If you mistakenly execute the wrong command, you can interrupt and stop it with the interrupt key (press Ctrl+c).

You can enter a command on several lines by typing a backslash (\) just before you press Enter. The backslash "escapes" the Enter key, effectively continuing the same command line to the next line. In the next example, the cp command is entered on three lines. The first two lines end in a backslash, effectively making all three lines one command line.

```
$ cp -i \
mydata \
/home/george/myproject/newdata
```

You can also enter several commands on the same line, by separating them with a semicolon (;). In effect, the semicolon operates as an execute operation. Commands will be executed in the sequence in which they are entered. The following command executes an ls command followed by a date command:

```
$ ls ; date
```

You can also conditionally run several commands on the same line with the && operator. A command is executed only if the previous command is true. This feature is useful for running several dependent scripts on the same line. In the next example, the ls command runs only if the date command is successfully executed.

```
$ date && ls
```

Tip   Commands can also be run as arguments on a command line, using their results for other commands. To run a command within a command line, you encase the command in back quotes.

Command-Line Editing

The BASH shell, which is your default shell, has special command-line editing capabilities that you may find helpful as you learn Linux (see Table 10-2). You can easily modify commands you have entered before executing them, moving anywhere on the command line and inserting or deleting characters. This is particularly helpful for complex commands.

Table 10-2. *BASH Command-Line Editing Operations*

Movement Command	Operation
Ctrl+f, right-arrow	Moves forward a character
Ctrl+b, left arrow	Moves backward a character
Ctrl+a or Home	Moves to beginning of line
Ctrl+e or End	Moves to end of line
Alt+f	Moves forward a word (not on terminal window)
Alt+b	Moves backward a word
Ctrl+l	Clears screen and places line at top
Editing Command	**Operation**
Ctrl+d or Del	Deletes character cursor is on
Ctrl+h or Backspace	Deletes character before the cursor
Ctrl+k	Cuts remainder of line from cursor position
Ctrl+u	Cuts from cursor position to beginning of line
Ctrl+w	Cuts previous word
Ctrl+c	Cuts entire line and starts a new one

(continued)

Table 10-2. (*continued*)

Editing Command	Operation
Alt+d	Cuts the remainder of a word
Alt+Del	Cuts from the cursor to the beginning of a word
Ctrl+y	Pastes previous cut text
Alt+y	Pastes from set of previously cut text
Ctrl+y	Pastes previous cut text
Ctrl+v	Inserts quoted text; used for inserting control or meta (Alt) keys as text, such as Ctrl-b for backspace or Ctrl-t for tabs
Alt+t	Transposes current and previous word
Alt+l	Lowercases current word
Alt+u	Uppercases current word
Al+-c	Capitalizes current word
Ctrl+Shift+_	Undoes previous change

You can press Ctrl+f or use the right arrow key to move forward a character, or the Ctrl+b or left arrow key to move back a character. Ctrl+d or Del deletes the character the cursor is on, and Ctrl+h or Backspace deletes the character preceding the cursor. To add text, you use the arrow keys to move the cursor to where you want to insert text and type the new characters.

You can even cut words with the Ctrl+w or Alt+d keys and then press the Ctrl+y keys to paste them back in at a different position, effectively moving the words. As a rule, the Ctrl version of the command operates on characters, and the Alt version works on words, such as Ctrl+t to transpose characters, and Alt+t to transpose words. At any time, you can press Enter to execute the command. For example, if you make a spelling mistake when entering a command, rather than reentering the entire command, you can use the editing operations to correct the mistake. The actual associations of keys and their tasks, along with global settings, are specified in the /etc/inputrc file.

The editing capabilities of the BASH shell command line are provided by Readline. Readline supports numerous editing operations. You can even bind a key to a selected editing operation. Readline uses the /etc/inputrc file to configure key bindings.

This file is read automatically by your /etc/profile shell configuration file when you log in. Users can customize their editing commands by creating an .inputrc file in their home directory (this is a dot file). It may be best to first copy the /etc/inputrc file as your .inputrc file and then edit it. The /etc/profile will first check for a local .inputrc file before accessing the /etc/inputrc file. You can find out more about Readline in the BASH shell reference manual at www.gnu.org/manual/bash.

Command and Filename Completion

The BASH command line has a built-in feature that performs command and filename completion. Automatic completions can be affected by pressing the Tab key. If you enter an incomplete pattern as a command or filename argument, you can press the Tab key to activate the command and filename completion feature, which completes the pattern. A directory will have a forward slash (/) attached to its name. If more than one command or file has the same prefix, the shell simply beeps and waits for you to press the Tab key again. It then displays a list of possible command completions and waits for you to add enough characters to select a unique command or filename. For situations in which you know multiple possibilities are likely, you can just press the Esc key instead of two Tabs. In the next example, the user issues a cat command with an incomplete filename. When the user presses the Tab key, the system searches for a match and, when it finds one, fills in the filename. The user can then press Enter to execute the command.

```
$ cat pre <tab>
$ cat preface
```

The automatic completions also work with the names of variables, users, and hosts. In this case, the partial text has to be preceded by a special character, indicating the type of name. A listing of possible automatic completions follows:

> Filenames begin with any text or /.
>
> Shell variable text begins with a $ sign.
>
> Username text begins with a ~ sign.
>
> Hostname text begins with a @.
>
> Commands, aliases, and text in files begin with normal text.

Variables begin with a $ sign, so any text beginning with a dollar sign is treated as a variable to be completed. Variables are selected from previously defined variables, such as system shell variables. Usernames begin with a tilde (~). Hostnames begin with a @ sign, with possible names taken from the /etc/hosts file. For example, to complete the variable HOME given just $HOM, simply press a Tab key.

```
$ echo $HOM <tab>
$ echo $HOME
```

If you entered just an H, then you could press the Tab key twice to see all possible variables beginning with H. The command line is redisplayed, letting you complete the name.

```
$ echo $H <tab> <tab>
$HISTCMD $HISTFILE $HOME $HOSTTYPE HISTFILE $HISTSIZE $HISTNAME
$ echo $H
```

You can also specifically select the kind of text to complete, using corresponding command keys. In this case, it does not matter what kind of sign a name begins with.

For example, pressing Alts+~ will treat the current text as a username. Pressing Alt+@ will treat it as a hostname, and Alt+$, as a variable. Pressing Alt+! will treat it as a command. To display a list of possible completions, press the Ctrl+x key with the appropriate completion key, as in Ctrl+x+$ to list possible variable completions. See Table 10-3 for a complete listing.

Table 10-3. *Command-Line Text Completion Commands*

Command (Ctrl+r for Listing Possible Completions)	Description
Tab	Automatic completion
Tab Tab or Esc	Lists possible completions
Alt+/, Ctrl+r+/	Filename completion, normal text for automatic
Alt+$, Ctrl+r+$	Shell variable completion, $ for automatic
Alt+~, Ctrl+-r+~	Username completion, ~ for automatic
Alt+@, Ctrl+r+@	Hostname completion, @ for automatic
Alt+!, Ctrl+r+!	Command-name completion, normal text for automatic

History

The BASH shell keeps a history list of your previously entered commands. You can display each command, in turn, on your command line by pressing the up arrow key. Press the down arrow key to move down the list. You can modify and execute any of these previous commands when you display them on the command line. The list of history command is kept in your `.bash_history` file.

Tip The ability to redisplay a command is helpful when you have already executed a command you had entered incorrectly. In this case, you would be presented with an error message and a new, empty command line. By pressing the up arrow key, you can redisplay the previous command, make corrections to it, and then execute it again. This way, you don't have to enter the whole command again.

History Events

In the BASH shell, the *history* utility keeps a record of the most recent commands you have executed. The commands are numbered, starting at 1, and a limit exists to the number of commands remembered. The default is 500. The history utility is a kind of short-term memory, keeping track of the most recent commands you have executed. To see the set of your most recent commands, type `history` on the command line and press Enter. A list of your most recent commands is then displayed, preceded by a number. Table 10-4 lists the different commands for referencing the history list.

```
$ history
1 cp mydata today
2 vi mydata
3 mv mydata reports
4 cd reports
5 ls
```

Table 10-4. *History Commands and History Event References*

History Command	Description
Ctrl+n or down arrow	Moves down to the next event in the history list
Ctrl+p or up arrow	Moves up to the previous event in the history list
Alt+<	Moves to the beginning of the history event list
Alt+>	Moves to the end of the history event list
Alt+n	Forward search, next matching item
Alt+p	Backward search, previous matching item
Ctrl+s	Forward search history, forward incremental search
Ctrl+r	Reverse search history, reverse incremental search
fc *event-reference*	Edits an event with the standard editor and then executes itOptions: -l lists recent history events; same as history command -e editor event-reference invokes a specified editor to edit a specific event
History Event Reference	
!*event num*	References an event with an event number
!!	References the previous command
!*characters*	References an event with beginning characters
!?*pattern*?	References an event with a pattern in the event
!-*event num*	References an event with an offset from the first event
!*num-num*	References a range of events

Each of these commands is technically referred to as an event. An *event* describes an action that has been taken—a command that has been executed. The events are numbered according to their sequence of execution. The most recent event has the highest number. Each of these events can be identified by its number or beginning characters in the command.

The history utility lets you reference a former event, placing it on your command line so that you can execute it. The easiest way to do this is to use the up arrow and down arrow keys to place history events on the command line, one at a time. You need not display the list first with history. Pressing the up arrow key once places the last history event on the command line. Pressing it again places the next history event on the command line. Pressing the down arrow key places the previous event on the command line.

You can use certain control and meta keys to perform other history operations, such as searching the history list. A meta key is the Alt key, and the Esc key on keyboards that have no Alt key. The Alt key is used here. Pressing Alt+< will move you to the beginning of the history list; Alt+n will search it. Ctrl+s and Ctrl+r will perform incremental searches, displaying matching commands as you type in a search string.

Tip   If more than one history event matches what you have entered, you will hear a beep, and you can then enter more characters to help uniquely identify the event.

You can also reference and execute history events using the ! history command. The ! is followed by a reference that identifies the command. The reference can be either the number of the event or a beginning set of characters in the event. In the next example, the third command in the history list is referenced first by number and then by the beginning characters:

```
$ !3
mv mydata reports
$ !mv my
mv mydata reports
```

You can also reference an event using an offset from the end of the list. A negative number will offset from the end of the list to that event, thereby referencing it. In the next example, the fourth command, vi mydata, is referenced using a negative offset and then executed. Remember that you are offsetting from the end of the list—in this case, event five—up toward the beginning of the list, event one. An offset of 4 beginning from event five places you at event two.

```
$ !-4
vi mydata
```

To reference the last event, you follow it with an !, as in !!. In the following example, the command !! executes the last command the user executed—in this case, ls:

```
$ !!
ls
mydata today reports
```

You can also perform a search of the listing of previous commands by entering Ctrl-r on the command line. You are prompted to enter a pattern for a search.

```
$ (revrse-isarch) 'vi' : vi mydata
```

Filename Expansion: *, ?, [ ]

Filenames are the most common arguments used in a command. Often, you will know only part of the filename, or you will want to reference several filenames that have the same extension or begin with the same characters. The shell provides a set of special characters that search out, match, and generate a list of filenames. These are the asterisk, the question mark, and brackets (*, ?, and [ ]). Given a partial filename, the shell uses these matching operators to search for files and expand to a list of filenames found. The shell replaces the partial filename argument with the expanded list of matched filenames. This list of filenames can then become the arguments for commands such as ls, which can operate on many files. Table 10-5 lists the shell's file-expansion characters.

Table 10-5. *Shell Symbols*

Common Shell Symbol	Execution
Enter	Executes a command line.
;	Separates commands on the same command line.
`command`	Executes a command as part of another command, using the command's output as a parameter to the primary command.
$(command)	Executes a command and uses the output of that command in whatever statement or command it is used in.
[]	Matches on a class of possible characters in filenames.
\	Quotes the following character; used to quote special characters.
|	Pipes the standard output of one command as input for another command.
&	Executes a command in the background.
!	References a history command.

(*continued*)

Table 10-5. (*continued*)

File-Expansion Symbol	Execution
*	Matches on any set of characters in filenames.
?	Matches on any single character in filenames.
[ ]	Matches on a class of characters in filenames.
Redirection Symbol	**Execution**
>	Redirects the standard output to a file or device, creating the file if it does not exist and overwriting the file if it does exist.
>!	The exclamation point forces the overwriting of a file if it already exists.
<	Redirects the standard input from a file or device to a program.
>>	Redirects the standard output to a file or device, appending the output to the end of the file.
Standard Error-Redirection Symbol	**Execution**
2>	Redirects the standard error to a file or device.
2>>	Redirects and appends the standard error to a file or device.
2>&1	Redirects the standard error to the standard output.

Matching Multiple Characters

The asterisk (*) references files beginning or ending with a specific set of characters. You place the asterisk before or after a set of characters that form a pattern to be searched for in filenames.

If the asterisk is placed before the pattern, filenames that end in that pattern are searched for. If the asterisk is placed after the pattern, filenames that begin with that pattern are searched for. Any matching filename is copied into a list of filenames generated by this operation.

In the next example, all filenames beginning with the pattern doc are searched for and a list is generated. Then all filenames ending with the pattern day are searched for and a list is generated. The last example shows how the * can be used in any combination of characters.

```
$ ls
doc1 doc2 document docs mydoc monday Tuesday
$ ls doc*
doc1 doc2 document docs
$ ls *day
monday tuesday

$ ls m*d*
monday
$
```

Filenames often include an extension specified with a period and followed by a string denoting the file type, such as .c for C files, .cpp for C++ files, or even .jpg for JPEG image files. The extension has no special status and is only part of the characters making up the filename. Using the asterisk makes it easy to select files with a given extension. In the next example, the asterisk is used to list only those files with a .c extension. The asterisk placed before the .c constitutes the argument for ls.

```
$ ls *.c
calc.c main.c
```

You can use * with the rm command to erase several files at once. The asterisk first selects a list of files with a given extension, or beginning or ending with a given set of characters, and then it presents this list of files to the rm command to be erased. In the following example, the rm command erases all files beginning with the pattern doc:

```
$ rm doc*
```

Use the * file-expansion character carefully and sparingly with the rm command. The combination can be dangerous. A misplaced * in an rm command without the -i option could easily erase all the files in your current directory. The -i option will first prompt you to confirm whether the file should be deleted.

Matching Single Characters

The question mark (?) matches only a single incomplete character in filenames. Suppose you want to match the files doc1 and docA, but not the file called document. Whereas the asterisk will match filenames of any length, the question mark limits the match to one extra character. The following example matches files that begin with the word doc, followed by a single differing letter:

```
$ ls
doc1 docA document
$ ls doc?
doc1 docA
```

Matching a Range of Characters

Whereas the * and ? file-expansion characters specify incomplete portions of a filename, the brackets ([ ]) enable you to specify a set of valid characters to search for. Any character placed in the brackets will be matched in the filename. Suppose you want to list files beginning with doc but ending only in 1 or A. You are not interested in filenames ending in 2 or B, or any other character. Here is how it is done:

```
$ ls
doc1 doc2 doc3 docA docB docD document
$ ls doc[1A]
doc1 docA
```

You can also specify a set of characters as a range, rather than listing them one by one. A dash placed between the upper and lower bounds of a range of characters selects all characters in that range. The range is usually determined by the character set in use. In an ASCII character set, the range "a–g" will select all lowercase alphabetic characters from *a* through *g*, inclusive. In the next example, files beginning with the pattern doc and ending in characters 1 through 3 are selected. Then, those ending in characters B through E are matched.

```
$ ls doc[1-3]
doc1 doc2 doc3
$ ls doc[B-E]
docB docD
```

You can combine the brackets with other file-expansion characters to form flexible matching operators. Suppose you want to list only filenames ending in either a .c or .o extension but no other extension. You can use a combination of the asterisk and brackets: * [co]. The asterisk matches all filenames, and the brackets match only filenames with extension .c or .o.

```
$ ls *.[co]
main.c  main.o  calc.c
```

Matching Shell Symbols

At times, a file-expansion character is actually part of a filename. In these cases, you have to quote the character by preceding it with a backslash (\) to reference the file. In the next example, the user must reference a file that ends with the ? character, called answers?. The ? is, however, a file-expansion character and would match any filename beginning with "answers" that has one or more characters. In this case, the user quotes the ? with a preceding backslash to reference the filename.

```
$ ls answers\?
answers?
```

Placing the filename in double quotes will also quote the character.

```
$ ls "answers?"
answers?
```

This is also true for filenames or directories that have whitespace characters such as the space character. In this case, you can either use the backslash to quote the space character in the file or directory name or place the entire name in double quotes.

```
$ ls My\ Documents
My Documents
$ ls "My Documents"
My Documents
```

Generating Patterns

Although not a file-expansion operation, {} is often useful for generating names that you can use to create or modify files and directories. The braces operation only generates a list of names. It does not match on existing filenames. Patterns are placed in the braces and separated with commas. Any pattern placed in the braces will be used to generate a version of the pattern, using either the preceding or following pattern, or both. Suppose you want to generate a list of names beginning with doc, but ending only in the patterns ument, final, and draft. Here is how it is done:

```
$ echo doc{ument,final,draft}
document docfinal docdraft
```

Because the names generated do not have to exist, you could use the {} operation in a command to create directories, as follows:

```
$ mkdir {fall,winter,spring}report
$ ls
fallreport springreport winterreport
```

Standard Input/Output and Redirection

The data in input and output operations is organized like a file. Data input at the keyboard is placed in a data stream arranged as a continuous set of bytes. Data output from a command or program is also placed in a data stream and arranged as a continuous set of bytes. This input data stream is referred to in Linux as the standard input, while the output data stream is called the standard output. A separate output data stream is reserved solely for error messages; it is called the standard error.

Because the standard input and standard output have the same organization as that of a file, they can easily interact with files. Linux has a redirection capability that lets you easily move data in and out of files. You can redirect the standard output so that instead of displaying the output on a screen, you can save it in a file. You can also redirect the standard input away from the keyboard to a file, so that input is read from a file instead of from your keyboard.

When a Linux command is executed that produces output, this output is placed in the standard output data stream. The default destination for the standard output data stream is a device—in this case, the screen. Devices, such as the keyboard and screen, are treated as files. They receive and send out streams of bytes with the same organization as that of a byte-stream file. The screen is a device that displays a continuous stream of bytes. By default, the standard output will send its data to the screen device, which will then display the data.

For example, the `ls` command generates a list of all filenames and outputs this list to the standard output. Next, this stream of bytes in the standard output is directed to the screen device. The list of filenames is then printed on the screen. The `cat` command also sends output to the standard output. The contents of a file are copied to the standard output, whose default destination is the screen. The contents of the file are then displayed on the screen. Table 10-6 lists the different ways you can use the redirection operators.

Table 10-6. *The Shell Operations*

Command	Execution
Enter	Executes a command line.
;	Separates commands on the same command line.
command\opts args	Enters a backslash before a carriage return, to continue entering a command on the next line.
`` `command` ``	Executes a command.
Special Characters for Filename Expansion	**Execution**
*	Matches on any set of characters.
?	Matches on any single characters.
[ ]	Matches on a class of possible characters.
\	Quotes the following character; used to quote special characters.

(continued)

Table 10-6. (*continued*)

Redirection	Execution
command > *filename*	Redirects the standard output to a file or device, creating the file if it does not exist and overwriting the file if it does exist.
command < *filename*	Redirects the standard input from a file or device to a program.
command >> *filename*	Redirects the standard output to a file or device, appending the output to the end of the file.
command 2> *filename*	Redirects the standard error to a file or device.
command 2>> *filename*	Redirects and appends the standard error to a file or device.
command 2>&1	Redirects the standard error to the standard output in the Bourne shell.
command >& *filename*	Redirects the standard error to a file or device in the C shell.
Pipe	**Execution**
command | *command*	Pipes the standard output of one command as input for another command.

Redirecting the Standard Output: > and >>

Suppose that instead of displaying a list of files on the screen, you would like to save this list in a file. In other words, you would like to direct the standard output to a file rather than the screen. To do this, you place the output redirection operator, the greater-than sign (>), followed by the name of a file on the command line, after the Linux command. In the following example, the output of the ls command is redirected from the screen device to a file:

```
$ ls -l *.c > programlist
```

The redirection operation creates the new destination file. If the file already exists, it will be overwritten with the data in the standard output. You can set the noclobber feature to prevent overwriting an existing file with the redirection operation. In this case, the redirection operation on an existing file will fail. You can overcome the noclobber feature by placing an exclamation point after the redirection operator. You can place the noclobber command in a shell configuration file to make it an automatic default operation. The following example sets the noclobber feature for the BASH shell and then forces the overwriting of the oldarticle file if it already exists:

```
$ set -o noclobber
$ cat myarticle >! oldarticle
```

Although the redirection operator and the filename are placed after the command, the redirection operation is not executed after the command. In fact, it is executed before the command. The redirection operation creates the file and sets up the redirection before it receives any data from the standard output. If the file already exists, it will be destroyed and replaced by a file of the same name. In effect, the command generating the output is executed only after the redirected file has been created.

In the next example, the output of the ls command is redirected from the screen device to a file. First the ls command lists files, and in the next command, ls redirects its file list to the listf file. Then the cat command displays the list of files saved in listf. Notice that the list of files in listf includes the listf filename. The list of filenames generated by the ls command includes the name of the file created by the redirection operation—in this case, listf. The listf file is first created by the redirection operation, then the ls command lists it along with other files. This file list output by ls is then redirected to the listf file, instead of being printed on the screen.

```
$ ls
mydata intro preface
$ ls > listf
$ cat listf
mydata intro listf preface
```

Errors occur when you try to use the same filename for an input file for the command and for the redirected destination file. In this case, because the redirection operation is executed first, the input file, because it exists, is destroyed and replaced by a file of the same name. When the command is executed, it finds an input file that is empty.

You can also append the standard output to an existing file using the >> redirection operator. Instead of overwriting the file, the data in the standard output is added at the end of the file. In the next example, the myarticle and oldarticle files are appended to the allarticles file. The allarticles file will then contain the contents of both myarticle and oldarticle.

```
$ cat myarticle >> allarticles
$ cat oldarticle >> allarticles
```

The Standard Input

Many Linux commands can receive data from the standard input. The standard input itself receives data from a device or a file. The default device for the standard input is the keyboard. Characters typed on the keyboard are placed in the standard input, which is then directed to the Linux command. Just as with the standard output, you can also redirect the standard input, receiving input from a file rather than the keyboard. The operator for redirecting the standard input is the less-than sign (<). In the next example, the standard input is redirected to receive input from the `myarticle` file, rather than the keyboard device (use Ctrl+d to end the typed input). The contents of `myarticle` are read into the standard input by the redirection operation. Then the `cat` command reads the standard input and displays the contents of `myarticle`.

```
$ cat < myarticle
hello Christopher
How are you today
$
```

You can combine the redirection operations for both standard input and standard output. In the next example, the `cat` command has no filename arguments. Without filename arguments, the `cat` command receives input from the standard input and sends output to the standard output. However, the standard input has been redirected to receive its data from a file, while the standard output has been redirected to place its data in a file.

```
$ cat < myarticle > newarticle
```

Pipes: |

You may encounter situations in which you have to send data from one command to another. In other words, you may want to send the standard output of a command to another command, rather than to a destination file. Suppose you want to send a list of your filenames to the printer to be printed. You need two commands to do this: the `ls` command to generate a list of filenames and the `lpr` command to send the list to the printer. In effect, you have to take the output of the `ls` command and use it as input for the `lpr` command. You can think of the data as flowing from one command to another. To form such a connection in Linux, you use what is called a *pipe.* The *pipe operator*

(|, the vertical bar character) placed between two commands forms a connection between them. The standard output of one command becomes the standard input for the other. The pipe operation receives output from the command placed before the pipe and sends this data as input to the command placed after the pipe. As shown in the next example, you can connect the `ls` command and the `lpr` command with a pipe. The list of filenames output by the `ls` command is piped into the `lpr` command.

```
$ ls | lpr
```

You can combine the `pipe` operation with other shell features, such as file-expansion characters, to perform specialized operations. The next example prints only files with a `.c` extension. The `ls` command is used with the asterisk and `.c` to generate a list of filenames with the `.c` extension. Then this list is piped to the `lpr` command.

```
$ ls *.c | lpr
```

In the preceding example, a list of filenames was used as input. What is important to note is that pipes operate on the standard output of a command, whatever that might be. The contents of whole files or even several files can be piped from one command to another. In the following example, the `cat` command reads and outputs the contents of the `mydata` file, which are then piped to the `lpr` command:

```
$ cat mydata | lpr
```

Linux has many commands that generate modified output. For example, the `sort` command takes the contents of a file and generates a version with each line sorted in alphabetic order. The `sort` command works best with files that are lists of items. Commands such as `sort` that output a modified version of its input are referred to as *filters*. Filters are often used with pipes. In the next example, a sorted version of `mylist` is generated and piped into the `more` command for display on the screen. The original file, `mylist`, has not been changed and is not sorted. Only the output of `sort` in the standard output is sorted.

```
$ sort mylist | more
```

The standard input piped into a command can be more carefully controlled with the standard input argument (-). When you use the dash as an argument for a command, it represents the standard input.

Values from UNIX Commands: Back Quotes

Although you can create variable values by typing in characters or character strings, you can also obtain values from other commands. To assign the result of command to a variable, you first need to execute the command. If you place a command in back quotes on the command line, that command is first executed and its result becomes an argument on the command line. In the case of assignments, the result of a command can be assigned to a variable by placing the command within back quotes to first execute it. The back quotes can be thought of as a kind of expression consisting of a command to be executed whose result is then assigned to the variable. The characters making up the command itself are not assigned. In the next example, the command `ls *.c` is executed and its result is then assigned to the variable `listc`. `ls *.c` generates a list of all files with an `.c` extension. This list of files will then be assigned to the `listc` variable.

```
$ listc=`ls *.c`
$ echo $listc
main.c prog.c lib.cs
```

You could also use the **$(**command**)** operation to the same effect.

```
$ listc=$(ls *.c)
$ echo $listc
main.c prog.c lib.cs
```

You need to keep in mind the difference between single quotes and back quotes. Single quotes treat a command as a set of characters. Back quotes force execution of the UNIX command. There may be times when you accidentally enter single quotes, when you mean to use back quotes. In the following first example, the assignment for the `lscc` variable has single quotes, not back quotes, placed around the `ls *.c` command. In this case, `ls *.c` are just characters to be assigned to the variable `lscc`. In the second example, back quotes are placed around the `ls *.c` command, forcing evaluation of the command. A list of filenames ending in `.c` is generated and assigned as the value of `lscc`.

```
$ lscc='ls *.c'
$ echo $lscc
ls *.c

$ lscc=`ls *.c`
$ echo $lscc
main.c  prog.c
```
412

Linux Files

You can name a file using any letters, underscores, and numbers. You can also include periods and commas. Except in certain special cases, you should never begin a filename with a period. Other characters, such as slashes, question marks, or asterisks, are reserved for use as special characters by the system and should not be part of a filename. Filenames can be as long as 256 characters. Filenames can also include spaces, although to reference such filenames from the command line, be sure to encase them in quotes. On a desktop such as GNOME or KDE, you do not have to use quotes. A filename cannot have the same name as a subdirectory within the same directory. Directories are treated as type of file.

You can include an extension as part of a filename. A period is used to distinguish the filename proper from the extension. Extensions can be useful for categorizing your files. You are probably familiar with certain standard extensions that have been adopted by convention. For example, C source code files always have a `.c` extension. Files that contain compiled object code have an `.o` extension. You can make up your own file extensions. The following examples are all valid Linux filenames. Keep in mind that to reference the name with spaces on the command line, you have to encase it in quotes, for example, "New book review."

```
preface
chapter2
9700info
New_Revisions
calc.c
intro.bk1
New book review
```

Special initialization files are also used to hold shell configuration commands. These are the hidden, or dot, files, which begin with a period. Dot files used by commands and applications have predetermined names, such as the `.mozilla` directory used to hold your Mozilla data and configuration files. Recall that when you use `ls` to display your filenames, the dot files will not be displayed. To include the dot files, you must use `ls` with the `-a` option.

The `ls -l` command displays detailed information about a file. First, the permissions are displayed, followed by the number of links, the owner of the file, the name of the group to which the user belongs to, the file size in bytes, the date and time the file was last modified, and the name of the file. Permissions indicate who can access the file: the user, members of a group, or all other users. The group name indicates the group permitted to access the file object. The file type for mydata is that of an ordinary file. Only one link exists, indicating the file has no other names and no other links. The owner's name is chris, the same as the login name, and the group name is weather. Other users probably also belong to the weather group. The size of the file is 207 bytes, and it was last modified on February 20 at 11:55 a.m. The name of the file is mydata.

If you want to display this detailed information for all the files in a directory, simply use the ls -l command without an argument.

```
$ ls -l
-rw-r--r-- 1 chris weather 207 Feb 20 11:55 mydata
-rw-rw-r-- 1 chris weather 568 Feb 14 10:30 today
-rw-rw-r-- 1 chris weather 308 Feb 17 12:40 monday
```

All files in Linux have one physical format, a byte stream, which is simply a sequence of bytes. This allows Linux to apply the file concept to every data component in the system. Directories are classified as files, as are devices. Treating everything as a file allows Linux to organize and exchange data more easily. The data in a file can be sent directly to a device, such as a screen, because a device interfaces with the system using the same byte-stream file format used by regular files.

This same file format is used to implement other operating system components. The interface to a device, such as the screen or keyboard, is designated as a file. Other components, such as directories, are themselves byte-stream files, but they have a special internal organization. A directory file contains information about a directory, organized in a special directory format. Because these different components are treated as files, they can be said to constitute different *file types*. A character device is one file type. A directory is another file type. The number of these file types may vary according to your specific implementation of Linux. Five common types of files exist, however: ordinary files, directory files, first-in first-out (FIFO) pipes, character device files, and block device files. Although you may rarely reference a file's type, it can be useful to know when searching for directories or devices.

Although all ordinary files have a byte-stream format, they may be used in different ways. The most significant difference is between binary and text files. Compiled programs are examples of binary files. However, even text files can be classified according to their different uses. You can have files that contain

C programming source code or shell commands, or even a file that is empty. The file could be an executable program or a directory file. The Linux file command helps you determine what a file is used for. It examines the first few lines of a file and tries to determine a classification for it. The file command looks for special keywords or special numbers in those first few lines, but it is not always accurate. In the following example, the file command examines the contents of two files and determines a classification for them:

```
$ file monday reports
monday: text
reports: directory
```

If you have to examine the entire file byte by byte, you can do so with the od (octal dump) command, which performs a dump of a file. By default, it prints every byte in its octal representation. However, you can also specify a character, decimal, or hexadecimal representation. The od command is helpful when you have to detect any special character in your file or if you want to display a binary file.

The File Structure

Linux organizes files into a hierarchically connected set of directories. Each directory may contain either files or other directories. In this respect, directories perform two important functions. A directory holds files, much like files held in a file drawer, and a directory connects to other directories, like a branch in a tree is connected to other branches. Because of the similarities to a tree, such a structure is often referred to as a *tree structure.*

The Linux file structure branches into several directories, beginning with a root directory, /. Within the root directory, several system directories contain files and programs that are features of the Linux system. The root directory also contains a directory called home that contains the home directories of all the users in the system. Each user's home directory, in turn, contains the directories the users have made for their own use. Each of these can also contain directories. Such nested directories branch out from the user's home directory. Table 10-7 lists the basic system directories.

Table 10-7. *Standard System Directories in Linux*

Directory	Function
/	Begins the file system structure, called the root.
/home	Contains users' home directories.
/bin	Holds all the standard commands and utility programs.
/usr	Holds those files and commands used by the system; this directory breaks down into several subdirectories.
/usr/bin	Holds user-oriented commands and utility programs.
/usr/sbin	Holds system administration commands.
/usr/lib	Holds libraries for programming languages.
/usr/share/doc	Holds Linux documentation.
/usr/share/man	Holds the online man files.
/var/spool	Holds spooled files, such as those generated for printing jobs and network transfers.
/sbin	Holds system administration commands in the system.
/var	Holds files that vary, such as mailbox files.
/dev	Holds file interfaces for devices such as the terminals and printers (dynamically generated by udev; do not edit).
/etc	Holds system configuration files and any other system files.
/sys	The sysfs file system listing configuration information for all the devices on your system.
/proc	An older process file system listing kernel information, including device information.

Home Directories

When you log in to the system, you are placed within your home directory. The name given to this directory by the system is the same as your login name. Any files you create when you first log in are organized within your home directory. Within your home directory, you can create more directories. You can then change to these directories and store files in them. The same is true for other users on the system. Each user has a home directory, identified by the appropriate login name. Users, in turn, can create their own directories.

You can access a directory either through its name or by making it your working directory. Each directory is given a name when it is created. You can use this name in file operations to access files in that directory. You can also make the directory your working directory. If you do not use any directory names in a file operation, the working directory will be accessed. The working directory is the one from which you are currently working. When you log in, the working directory is your home directory, which usually has the same name as your login name. You can change the working directory by using the cd command to move to another directory.

Pathnames

The name you give to a directory or file when you create it is not its full name. The full name of a directory is its *pathname.* The hierarchically nested relationship among directories forms paths, and these paths can be used to identify and reference any directory or file uniquely or absolutely. Each directory in the file structure can be said to have its own unique path. The actual name by which the system identifies a directory always begins with the root directory and consists of all directories nested below that directory.

In Linux, you write a pathname by listing each directory in the path, separated from the last by a forward slash. A slash preceding the first directory in the path represents the root. The pathname for the chris directory is /home/chris. If the chris directory has a subdirectory called reports, then the entire pathname for the reports directory would be /home/chris/reports. Pathnames also apply to files. When you create a file within a directory, you give the file a name. The actual name by which the system identifies the file, however, is the filename combined with the path of directories from the root to the file's directory. As an example, the pathname for monday is /home/chris/reports/monday (the root directory is represented by the first slash). The path for the monday file consists of the root, home, chris, and reports directories and the filename monday.

Pathnames may be absolute or relative. An *absolute pathname* is the complete pathname of a file or directory beginning with the root directory. A *relative pathname* begins from your working directory; it is the path of a file relative to your working directory. The working directory is the one you are currently operating in. Using the previous example, if chris is your working directory, the relative pathname for the file monday is reports/monday. The absolute pathname for monday is /home/chris/reports/monday.

The absolute pathname from the root to your home directory can be especially complex and, at times, even subject to change by the system administrator. To make it easier to reference, you can use the tilde (~) character, which represents the absolute pathname of your home directory. You must specify the rest of the path from your home directory. In the next example, the user references the monday file in the reports directory. The tilde represents the path to the user's home directory, /home/chris, then the rest of the path to the monday file is specified, as follows:

```
$ cat ~/reports/monday
```

System Directories

The root directory that begins the Linux file structure contains several system directories that contain files and programs used to run and maintain the system. Many also contain other subdirectories with programs for executing specific features of Linux. For example, the directory /usr/bin contains the various Linux commands that users execute, such as lpr. The directory /bin holds system level commands.

Managing Directories: mkdir, rmdir, ls, cd, and pwd

You can create and remove your own directories, as well as change your working directory, with the mkdir, rmdir, and cd commands. Each of these commands can take as its argument the pathname for a directory. The pwd command displays the absolute pathname of your working directory. In addition to these commands, the special characters represented by a single dot, a double dot, and a tilde can be used to reference the working directory, the parent of the working directory, and the home directory, respectively. Taken together, these commands enable you to manage your directories. You can create nested directories, move from one directory to another, and use pathnames to reference any of your directories. Those commands commonly used to manage directories are listed in Table 10-8.

Table 10-8. *Directory Commands*

Command	Execution
mkdir *directory*	Creates a directory.
rmdir *directory*	Erases a directory.
ls -F	Lists the directory name with a preceding slash.
ls -R	Lists the working directory as well as all subdirectories.
cd *directory*	Changes to the specified directory, making it the working directory. cd without a directory name changes back to the home directory:$ cd reports
pwd	Displays the pathname of the working directory.
directory /*filename*	A slash is used in pathnames to separate each directory name. In the case of pathnames for files, a slash separates the preceding directory names from the filename.
..	References the parent directory. You can use it as an argument or as part of a pathname:$ cd ..$ mv ../larisa oldarticles
.	References the working directory. You can use it as an argument or as part of a pathname:$ ls .
~/*pathname*	The tilde is a special character that represents the pathname for the home directory. It is useful when you have to use an absolute pathname for a file or directory:$ cp monday ~/today
j *pattern*	Use the autojump command to quickly jump to a frequently used directory using a matching pattern.
jumpstat	Statistics showing frequently used directories accessible with autojump.

Creating and Deleting Directories

You create and remove directories with the mkdir and rmdir commands. In either case, you can also use pathnames for the directories. In the next example, the user creates the directory reports. Then the user creates the directory articles, using a pathname.

```
$ mkdir reports
$ mkdir /home/chris/articles
```

If the intervening parent directories in a pathname do not yet exist, you can have them created automatically with the **-p** option. In the following example, the intervening parent subdirectories project/newproject, indicated by the pathname, do not yet exist. Using the -p option creates them automatically, creating the project, newproject, and proposals subdirectories. Without the -p option, you would receive an error stating the directories do not exist.

```
$ mkdir -p  /home/chris/project/newproject/proposal
```

You can remove a directory with the rmdir command followed by the directory name. In the following example, the user removes the directory reports with the rmdir command:

```
$ rmdir reports
```

To remove a directory and all its subdirectories, you use the rm command with the -r option. This is a very powerful command and could be used to erase all your files. You will be prompted for each file. To remove all files and subdirectories without prompts, add the -f option. The following example deletes the reports directory and all its subdirectories:

```
rm -rf reports
```

Displaying Directory Contents

You have seen how to use the ls command to list the files and directories in your working directory. To distinguish between file and directory names, however, you must use the ls command with the -F option. A slash is then placed after each directory name in the list.

```
$ ls
weather reports articles
$ ls -F
weather reports/ articles/
```

The ls command also takes as an argument any directory name or directory pathname. This enables you to list the files in any directory without first having to change to that directory. In the next example, the ls command takes as its argument the name of a directory, reports. Then the ls command is executed again, only this time, the absolute pathname of reports is used.

```
$ ls reports
monday tuesday
$ ls /home/chris/reports
monday tuesday
$
```

Moving Through Directories

The cd command takes as its argument the name of the directory to which you want to move. The name of the directory can be the name of a subdirectory in your working directory or the full pathname of any directory on the system. If you want to change back to your home directory, you need to enter only the cd command by itself, without a filename argument.

```
$ cd reports
$ pwd
/home/chris/reports
```

As a complement to the cd command, you can use the autojump command. Install the autojump package. autojump keeps a record of your frequently accessed directories. You can then use the j command with a partial-matching pattern to quickly jump (cd) to that directory.

```
$ j rep
$ pwd
/home/chris/reports
```

Jumpstart keeps a database of your cd operations and uses it to determine the directory you want. The jumpstat command displays the ranked directories.

Referencing the Parent Directory

A directory always has a parent (except, of course, for the root). For example, in the preceding listing, the parent for reports is the chris directory. When a directory is created, two entries are made: one represented with a dot (.), and the other with double dots (..). The dot represents the pathnames of the directory, and the double dots represent the pathname of its parent directory. Double dots, used as an argument in a command, reference a parent directory. The single dot references the directory itself.

You can use the single dot to reference your working directory, instead of using its pathname. For example, to copy a file to the working directory retaining the same name, the dot can be used in place of the working directory's pathname. In this sense, the dot is another name for the working directory. In the next example, the user copies the weather file from the chris directory to the reports directory. The reports directory is the working directory and can be represented with a single dot.

```
$ cd reports
$ cp /home/chris/weather .
```

The .. symbol is often used to reference files in the parent directory. In the next example, the cat command displays the weather file in the parent directory. The pathname for the file is the .. symbol (for the parent directory), followed by a slash and the filename.

```
$ cat ../weather
raining and warm
```

You can use the cd command with the .. symbol to step back through successive parent directories of the directory tree from a lower directory.

Listing, Displaying, and Printing Files: ls, cat, more, less, and lpr

One of the primary functions of an operating system is the management of files. You may be required to perform certain basic output operations on your files, such as displaying them on your screen or printing them. The Linux system provides a set of commands that perform basic file-management operations, such as listing, displaying, and printing files, as well as copying, renaming, and erasing files. These commands are usually made up of abbreviated versions of words. For example, the ls command is a shortened form of "list" and lists the files in your directory. The lpr command is an abbreviated form of "line print" and will print a file. The cat, less, and more commands display the contents of a file on the screen. Table 10-9 lists these commands with their different options. When you log in to your Linux system, you may want a list of the files in your home directory. The ls command, which outputs a list of your file and directory names, is useful for this. The ls command has many possible options for displaying filenames according to specific features.

Displaying Files: cat, less, and more

You may also have to look at the contents of a file. The cat and more commands display the contents of a file on the screen. The name cat stands for "concatenate."

$ cat mydata
computers

The cat command outputs the entire text of a file to the screen at once. This presents a problem when the file is large, because its text quickly speeds past on the screen. The more and less commands are designed to overcome this limitation, by displaying one screen of text at a time. You can then move forward or backward in the text at your leisure. You invoke the more or less command by entering the command name, followed by the name of the file you want to view (less is a more powerful and configurable display utility).

$ less mydata

When more or less invoke a file, the first screen of text is displayed. To continue to the next screen, you press the f key, the spacebar, or PageUp keys. To move back in the text, you press the b or PageDown keys. You can quit at any time by pressing the q key.

Table 10-9. *Listing, Displaying, and Printing Files*

Command or Option	Execution
ls	Lists file and directory names.
cat *filenames*	Used to display a file. It can take filenames for its arguments. It outputs the contents of those files directly to the standard output, which, by default, is directed to the screen.
more *filenames*	Displays a file screen by screen. Press the spacebar to continue to the next screen and the q key to quit.
less *filenames*	Also displays a file screen by screen. Press the spacebar to continue to the next screen and the q key to quit.
lpr *filenames*	Sends a file to the line printer to be printed; a list of files may be used as arguments. Use the -P option to specify a printer.
lpq	Lists the print queue for printing jobs.
lprm	Removes a printing job from the print queue.

Printing Files: lpr, lpq, and lprm

With the printer commands, such as lpr and lprm, you can perform printing operations such as printing files or canceling print jobs (see Table 10-9). When you have to print files, use the lpr command to send files to the printer connected to your system. In the following example, the user prints the mydata file:

$ lpr mydata

If you want to print several files at once, you can specify more than one file on the command line after the lpr command. In the following example, the user prints the mydata and preface files:

$ lpr mydata preface

Printing jobs are placed in a queue and printed one at a time in the background. You can continue with other work as your files print. You can see the position of a particular printing job at any given time with the lpq command, which gives the owner of the printing job (the login name of the user who sent the job), the print job ID, the size in bytes, and the temporary file in which it is currently held.

If you have to cancel an unwanted printing job, you can do so with the lprm command, which takes as its argument either the ID number of the printing job or the owner's name. It then removes the print job from the print queue. For this task, lpq is helpful, as it provides you with the ID number and owner of the printing job you must use with lprm.

File and Directory Operations: find, cp, mv, rm, and ln

As you create more and more files, you may want to back them up, change their names, erase some of them, or even give them added names. Linux provides several file commands that you can use to search for, copy, rename, or remove files (see Table 10-11). If you have a large number of files, you can also search them to locate a specific one. The commands are shortened forms of full words, consisting of only two characters. The cp command stands for "copy" and copies a file; mv stands for "move" and renames or moves a file; rm stands for "remove" and erases a file; and ln stands for "link" and adds another name for a file, often used as a shortcut to the original. One exception to the two-character rule is the find command, which performs searches of your filenames to find a file. All these operations can be handled by the GUI desktops, such as GNOME and KDE. To quickly search for a file, you can use the **locate** command. The locate command reads from a database of file locations compiled daily by updatedb.

Searching Directories: find

Once a large number of files has been stored in many different directories, you may have to search them to locate a specific file, or files, of a certain type, as well as directories. The find command enables you to perform such a search from the command line. The find command takes as its arguments directory names, followed by several possible options that specify the type of search and the criteria for the search. It then searches within the directories listed and their subdirectories for files that meet these criteria. The find command can search for a file by name, type, owner, and even the time of the last update (see Table 10-10).

```
$ find directory-list -option criteria
```

Table 10-10. *The find Command*

Command or Option	Execution
find	Searches directories for files according to search criteria. This command has several options that specify the type of criteria and actions to be taken.
-name *pattern*	Searches for files with the pattern in the name.
-lname *pattern*	Searches for symbolic link files.
-group *name*	Searches for files belonging to the group name.
-gid *name*	Searches for files belonging to a group according to group ID.
-user *name*	Searches for files belonging to a user.
-uid *name*	Searches for files belonging to a user according to user ID.
-mtime *num*	Searches for files last modified num days ago.
-context *scontext*	Searches for files according to security context (SELinux).
-print	Outputs the result of the search to the standard output. The result is usually a list of filenames, including their full pathnames.

(continued)

Table 10-10. (*continued*)

Command or Option	Execution
-type *filetype*	Searches for files with the specified file type. File type can be b for block device, c for character device, d for directory, f for file, or l for symbolic link.
-perm *permission*	Searches for files with certain permissions set. Use octal or symbolic format for permissions.
-ls	Provides a detailed listing of each file, with owner, permission, size, and date information.
-exec *command*	Executes *command* when files are found.

The -name option has as its criteria a pattern and instructs find to search for the filename that matches that pattern. To search for a file by name, you use the find command with the directory name, followed by the -name option and the name of the file.

$ **find** *directory-list* -name *filename*

The find command also has options that merely perform actions, such as outputting the results of a search. If you want find to display the filenames it has located, you simply include the -print option on the command line, along with any other options. The -print option instructs find to write to the standard output the names of all the files it locates. (You can also use the -ls option instead to list files in the long format.) In the next example, the user searches for all the files in the reports directory with the name monday. Once located, the file, with its relative pathname, is printed.

$ find reports -name monday -print
reports/monday

The find command prints the filenames using the directory name specified in the directory list. If you specify an absolute pathname, the absolute path of the found directories will be output. If you specify a relative pathname, only the relative pathname is output. In the preceding example, the user specified a relative pathname, reports, in the directory list. Located filenames were output beginning with this relative pathname. In the next example, the user specifies an absolute pathname in the directory list. Located filenames are then output using this absolute pathname.

$ find /home/chris -name monday -print
/home/chris/reports/monday

Should you need to find the location of a specific program or configuration file, you could use `find` to search for the file from the root directory. Log in as the root user and use / as the directory. This command searches for the location of the `more` command and files on the entire file system: `find / -name more -print`.

Searching the Working Directory

If you want to search your working directory, you can use the dot in the directory pathname to represent it. The double dots represent the parent directory. The next example searches all files and subdirectories in the working directory, using the dot to represent the working directory. If your working directory is your home directory, this is a convenient way to search through all your own directories. Notice that the located filenames that are output begin with a dot.

```
$ find . -name weather -print
./weather
```

You can use shell wildcard characters as part of the pattern criteria for searching files. The special character must be quoted, however, to avoid evaluation by the shell. In the next example, all files (indicated by the asterisk, *) with the `.c` extension in the `programs` directory are searched for and then displayed in the long format, using the `-ls` action:

```
$ find programs -name '*.c' -ls
```

Locating Directories

You can also use the `find` command to locate other directories. In Linux, a directory is officially classified as a special type of file. Although all files have a byte-stream format, some files, such as directories, are used in special ways. In this sense, a file can be said to have a file type. The `find` command has an option called `-type` that searches for a file of a given type. The `-type` option takes a one-character modifier that represents the file type. The modifier that represents a directory is a d. In the following example, both the directory name and the directory file type are used to search for the directory called `travel`:

```
$ find /home/chris -name travel -type d -print
/home/chris/articles/travel
$
```

File types are not so much different types of files as they are the file format applied to other components of the operating system, such as devices. In this sense, a device is treated as a type of file, and you can use find to search for devices and directories, as well as ordinary files. Table 10-10 lists the different types available for the find command's -type option.

You can also use the find operation to search for files by ownership or security criteria, like those belonging to a specific user or those with a certain security context. The -user option lets you locate all files belonging to a certain user. The following example lists all files that the user chris has created or owns on the entire system. To list those only in users' home directories, you use /home for the starting search directory. This would find all those in a user's home directory, as well as any owned by that user in other user directories.

```
$ find / -user chris -print
```

Copying Files

To make a copy of a file, you simply give cp two filenames as its arguments (see Table 10-11). The first filename is the name of the file to be copied—the one that already exists. This is often referred to as the source file. The second filename is the name you want for the copy. This will be a new file containing a copy of all the data in the source file. This second argument is often referred to as the destination file. The syntax for the cp command follows:

```
$ cp source-file destination-file
```

In the following example, the user copies a file called proposal to a new file called oldprop:

```
$ cp proposal oldprop
```

You could unintentionally destroy another file with the cp command. The cp command generates a copy by first creating a file and then copying data into it. If another file has the same name as the destination file, that file is destroyed, and a new file with that name is created. By default, Fedora configures your system to check for an existing copy by the same name (cp is aliased with the -i option). To copy a file from your working directory to another directory, you have to use that directory name as the second argument in the cp command. In the next example, the proposal file is overwritten by the newprop file. The proposal file already exists.

```
$ cp newprop proposal
```

You can use any of the wildcard characters to generate a list of filenames to use with cp or mv. For example, suppose you need to copy all your C source code files to a given directory. Instead of listing each one individually on the command line, you could use an * character with the .c extension to match on and generate a list of C source code files (all files with a .c extension). In the following example, the user copies all source code files in the current directory to the sourcebks directory:

```
$ cp *.c sourcebks
```

Table 10-11. *File Operations*

Command	Execution
cp *filename* *filename*	Copies a file. cp takes two arguments: the original file and the name of the new copy. You can use pathnames for the files to copy across directories.
cp -r *directory* *directory*	Copies a subdirectory from one directory to another. The copied directory includes all its own subdirectories.
mv *filename* *filename*	Moves (renames) a file. The mv command takes two arguments: the first is the file to be moved. The second argument can be the new filename or the pathname of a directory. If it is the name of a directory, then the file is moved to that directory, changing the file's pathname.
mv *directory* *directory*	Moves directories. In this case, the first and last arguments are directories.
ln *filename* *filename*	Creates added names for files referred to as links. A link can be created in one directory that references a file in another directory.
rm *filenames*	Removes (erases) a file. Can take any number of filenames as its arguments. Literally removes links to a file. If a file has more than one link, you must remove all of them to erase a file.

If you want to copy all the files in a given directory to another directory, you could use * to match on and generate a list of all those files in a cp command. In the next example, the user copies all the files in the props directory to the oldprop directory. Notice the use of a props pathname preceding the * special characters. In this context, props is a pathname that will be appended before each file in the list that * generates.

```
$ cp props/* oldprop
```

You can, of course, use any of the other special characters, such as ., ?, or [ ]. In the following example, the user copies both source code and object code files (.c and .o) to the projbk directory:

```
$ cp *.[oc] projbk
```

When you copy a file, you can give the copy a name that is different from the original. To do so, place the new filename after the directory name, separated by a slash.

```
$ cp filename directory-name/new-filename
```

Moving Files

You can use the mv command either to rename a file or move a file from one directory to another. When using mv to rename a file, you simply use the new filename as the second argument. The first argument is the current name of the file you are renaming. If you want to rename a file when you move it, you can specify the new name of the file after the directory name. In the following example, the proposal file is renamed with the name version1:

```
$ mv proposal version1
```

As with cp, it is easy for mv to erase a file accidentally. When renaming a file, you might accidentally choose a filename already used by another file. In this case, that other file will be erased. The mv command also has an -i option that checks first to see if a file with that name already exists.

You can also use any of the special characters to generate a list of filenames to use with mv. In the following example, the user moves all source code files in the current directory to the newproj directory:

```
$ mv *.c newproj
```

If you want to move all the files in a given directory to another directory, you can use * to match on and generate a list of all those files. In the following example, the user moves all the files in the reports directory to the repbks directory:

```
$ mv reports/* repbks
```

Copying and Moving Directories

You can also copy or move whole directories at once. Both cp and mv can take as their first argument a directory name, enabling you to copy or move subdirectories from one directory into another (see Table 10-11). The first argument is the name of the directory to be moved or copied, and the second argument is the name of the directory within which it is to be placed. The same pathname structure used for files applies to moving or copying directories.

You can just as easily copy subdirectories from one directory to another. To copy a directory, the cp command requires you to use the -r option, which stands for "recursive." It directs the cp command to copy a directory, as well as any subdirectories it may contain. In other words, the entire directory subtree, from that directory on, will be copied. In the next example, the travel directory is copied to the oldarticles directory. Now two travel subdirectories exist, one in articles and one in oldarticles.

```
$ cp -r articles/travel oldarticles
$ ls -F articles
/travel
$ ls -F oldarticles
/travel
```

Erasing Files and Directories: The rm Command

As you use Linux, you will find the number of files you use increases rapidly. Generating files in Linux is easy. Applications such as editors, and commands such as cp, can easily be used to create files. Eventually, many of these files may become outdated and useless. You can then remove them with the rm command. The rm command can take any number of arguments, enabling you to list several filenames and erase them all at the same time. In the next example, the file oldprop is erased:

```
$ rm oldprop
```

Be careful when using the rm command, because it is irrevocable. Once a file is removed, it cannot be restored (there is no undo). With the -i option, you are prompted separately for each file and asked whether you really want to remove it. If you enter y, the file will be removed. If you enter anything else, the file is not removed. In the next example, the rm command is instructed to erase the files proposal and oldprop. The rm command then asks for confirmation for each file. The user decides to remove oldprop but not proposal.

```
$ rm   -i proposal oldprop
Remove proposal? n
Remove oldprop? y
$
```

Links: The ln Command

You can give a file more than one name using the ln command. You might do this because you want to reference a file using different filenames to access it from different directories. The added names are often referred to as *links*. Linux supports two different types of links, hard and symbolic. Hard links are literally another name for the same file, whereas symbolic links function like shortcuts referencing another file. Symbolic links are much more flexible and can work over many different file systems, while hard links are limited to your local file system. Furthermore, hard links introduce security concerns, as they allow direct access from a link that may have public access to an original file that you may want protected. Links are usually implemented as symbolic links.

Symbolic Links

To set up a symbolic link, use the ln command with the -s option and two arguments: the name of the original file and the new, added filename. The ls operation lists both filenames, but only one physical file will exist.

```
$ ln -s original-filename added-filename
```

In the next example, the today file is given the additional name weather. It is just another name for the today file.

```
$ ls
today
$ ln -s today weather
$ ls
today weather
```

You can give the same file several names by using the ln command on the same file many times. In the next example, the file today is assigned the names weather and weekend:

```
$ ln -s today weather
$ ln -s today weekend
$ ls
today weather weekend
```

If you list the full information about a symbolic link and its file, you will find that the information displayed is different. In the next example, the user lists the full information for both lunch and /home/george/veglist, using the ls command with the -l option. The first character in the line specifies the file type. Symbolic links have their own file type, represented by an l. The file type for lunch is l, indicating it is a symbolic link, not an ordinary file. The number after the term "group" is the size of the file. Notice that the sizes differ. The size of the lunch file is only 4 bytes. This is because lunch is only a symbolic link—a file that holds the pathname of another file—and a pathname takes up only a few bytes. It is not a direct hard link to the veglist file.

```
$ ls -l lunch /home/george/veglist
lrw-rw-r-- 1 chris group 4 Feb 14 10:30 lunch
-rw-rw-r-- 1 george group 793 Feb 14 10:30 veglist
```

To erase a file, you have to remove only its original name (and any hard links to it). If any symbolic links are left over, they will be unable to access the file. In this case, a symbolic link would hold the pathname of a file that no longer exists.

Hard Links

You can give the same file several names by using the `ln` command on the same file many times. To set up a hard link, you use the `ln` command with no `-s` option and two arguments: the name of the original file and the new, added filename. The `ls` operation lists both filenames, but only one physical file will exist.

```
$ ln original-filename added-filename
```

In the next example, the `monday` file is given the additional name `storm`. It is just another name for the `monday` file.

```
$ ls
today
$ ln monday storm
$ ls
monday storm
```

To erase a file that has hard links, you must remove all its hard links. The name of a file is actually considered a link to that file; hence, the command `rm` removes the link to the file. If you have several links to the file and remove only one of them, the others stay in place, and you can reference the file through them. The same is true even if you remove the original link—the original name of the file.

CHAPTER 11

Additional Desktops

Several alternative desktops are available for use on Fedora. Table 11-1 lists several popular alternative desktops that you can use for Fedora. You can use these desktops as additional ones that you can install on your Fedora system. At the login screen, the Sessions menu lets you choose which desktop you want to use, just as with Plasma. You can install them from with the `dnf install` command and the desktop name. Some can also be installed with the Packages or Dragora software managers. Look for the meta package with `desktop` in the name, such as `xfdesktop` and `cinnamon-desktop`. Such meta packages will download the entire collection of packages for that desktop interface. The desktops have their own desktop spin ISO images, which you can download and burn onto a DVD or USB. They also operate as Live Workstation DVD/USBs. The spins can be downloaded from the Fedora Spins download page at `https://spins. fedoraproject.org`.

Table 11-1. *Additional Desktops*

Website	Description
`https://xfce.org/`	Xfce desktop. Simple lightweight desktop.
`https://lxde.org/`	LXDE desktop. Small desktop for low-power systems.
`https://spins.fedoraproject.org/ soas/`	Sugar on a Stick (SoaS) desktop. Education desktop for children.
`https://mate-desktop.org/`	MATE desktop. Enhanced GNOME 2 desktop interface.
`https://cinnamon.linuxmint.com/`	Cinnamon desktop. Mint desktop base on GNOME 3 with both GNOME 2 and GNOME 2 features.

© Richard Petersen 2018
R. Petersen, *Beginning Fedora Desktop*, https://doi.org/10.1007/978-1-4842-3882-0_11

You can also install specialized desktops such as those with a custom set of selected applications for Science, Astronomy, Games, or Graphics. The specialize desktops are available at the Fedora Labs website: `https://labs.fedoraproject.org/`. A list of these specialized desktops is shown in Table 11-2.

Table 11-2. *Fedora Labs Desktops*

Website	Description
`https://labs.fedoraproject.org/` `en/astronomy/`	Astronomy: device control tools, astronomy simulation and mapping
`https://labs.fedoraproject.org/` `en/design-suite/`	Design Suite: tools for multimedia and publishing projects
`https://labs.fedoraproject.org/` `en/games/`	Games: sample of games available for Fedora
`https://labs.fedoraproject.org/` `en/jam/`	JAM: for musicians; create, edit, and produce music
`https://labs.fedoraproject.org/` `en/python-classroom/`	Python Classroom: Python instruction
`https://labs.fedoraproject.org/` `en/robotics/`	Robotics Suite: Robotic open source software
`https://labs.fedoraproject.org/` `en/scientific/`	Scientific: Science open source research support tool (graphs, data analysis, math computation)
`https://labs.fedoraproject.org/` `en/security/`	Security Lab: tools for security testing and instruction

The Xfce Desktop

Xfce is a lightweight desktop designed to run fast without the kind of overhead required for full-featured desktops such as KDE and GNOME. You can think of it as a window manager with desktop functionality. It includes its own file manager and panel, but the emphasis is on modularity and simplicity. Like GNOME, Xfce is based on GTK+ GUI tools. The desktop consists of a collection of modules, such as the thunar file manager, `xfce4-panel` panel, and the `xfwm4` window manager. Keeping with its focus on simplicity, Xfce features only a few common applets on its panel. Its small scale makes it appropriate for laptops or dedicated systems that have no need for complex overhead found in other desktops. Xfce is useful for desktops, such as multimedia desktops, designed for just a few tasks or for computers with limited capabilities, such as older computers. You can find out more about Xfce at `https://xfce.org/`.

To install Xfce as an alternative desktop on a system, install the `xfdesktop` package.

You can also use Xfce as a Live DVD, which you can download from `https://spins.fedoraproject.org/`.

The Xfce Live DVD is available in 32-bit and 64-bit versions, such as `Fedora-Xfce-Live-x86_64-28-1.1.iso`. You can then burn the DVD and run it as a Live DVD. Click the Install icon to install an Xfce-based Fedora system on your computer. Double-click the Install icon to install an LXDE-based Fedora system on your computer. Follow the same basic steps for installing Fedora as for the Fedora Live DVD. The Installation Summary screen shows items for Installation Destination, Date & Time, and Keyboard. Be sure to choose the disks to install on and to check the time zone. Once installed, you use the GDM login screen to log in.

The desktop displays icons for your home directory, file system, and trash (see Figure 11-1). Xfce displays a top and bottom panel. The top panel will have buttons for an applications menu at the left. From this menu, you can access any Fedora software applications, along with Fedora administration tools. To the right of the menu is the task bar, showing buttons for open windows. The left side of the panel shows workspace switcher, time and date, network connections (Network Manager), and the session menus displaying the user name. The session menu has entries for shut down, log out, lock screen, suspend, and switch user. The bottom panel has icons for hide/show desktop, terminal, file manager, web browser, applications finder, and a directory menu for your home folder.

You can add more items by clicking the panel and selecting Add New Items. This opens a window with several applets, such as the clock, workspace switcher, applications menu, and launcher. The launcher applet lets you specify an application to start and choose an icon image for it. To move an applet, right-click it and choose Move from the pop-up menu. Then move the mouse to the new insertion location and click.

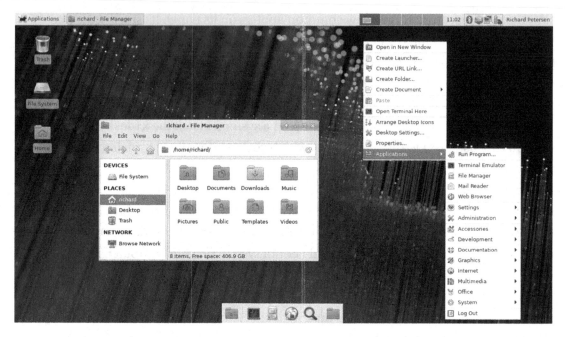

***Figure 11-1.** Xfce desktop*

Xfce file manager is called *Thunar*. The file manager will open a side pane in the shortcuts view that lists entries not only for the home directory but also for your file system, desktop, and trash contents. The File menu lets you perform folder operations, such as creating new directories. From the Edit menu, you can perform tasks on a selected file, such as renaming the file or creating a link for it. You can change the side pane view to a tree view of your file system by selecting from the menu bar View ➤ Side Pane ➤ Tree (Ctrl+t). The Shortcuts entry changes the view back (Ctrl+b).

To configure the Xfce interface, you use the Xfce Settings Manager, accessible from the Applications menu at Settings ➤ Settings Manager. It will be the first entry. This opens the Settings window, which shows icons for your desktop, display, panel, and appearance, among others (see Figure 11-2). Use the Appearance tool to select themes, icons, and toolbar styles (Settings). The Panel tool lets you add new panels and control features, such as fixed for freely movable and horizontally or vertically positioned.

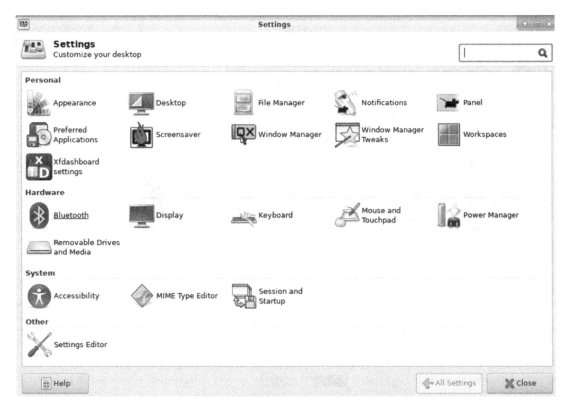

Figure 11-2. *The Xfce Settings Manager*

To configure the desktop, select the Desktop icon in the Settings window or right-click the desktop and select Desktop Settings from the pop-up menu (you can also select Settings ➤ Desktop). This opens the Desktop window, from which you can select the background image, control menu behavior, and set icon sizes (see Figure 11-3).

Figure 11-3. Xfce Desktop configuration

Note   You can also access applications and desktop settings by right-clicking the desktop background to display the desktop menu.

The LXDE Desktop

LXDE (Lightweight X11 Desktop Environment) is another small desktop designed for use on minimal or low-power systems such as laptops, netbooks, or older computers. To install LXDE as an alternative desktop on a system, select the LXDE desktop package on Packages.

You can also use LXDE as a Live DVD, which you can download from
`https://spins.fedoraproject.org/`.

The LXDE Live DVD is available in 32-bit and 64-bit versions, such as `Fedora-LXDE-Live-x86_64-28.1.1.iso`. You can then burn the DVD and run it as a Live DVD. Double-click the Install icon to install an LXDE-based Fedora system on your computer. Follow the same basic steps for installing Fedora as for the Fedora Workstation Live DVD. The Installation Summary screen shows items for Installation Destination, Date & Time, and Keyboard. Be sure to choose the disks to install on and to check the time zone.

The desktop displays a single panel at the bottom with application applets to the right, followed by the windows task bar and system applets (see Figure 11-4). From the Fedora Applications menu, you can access any applications.

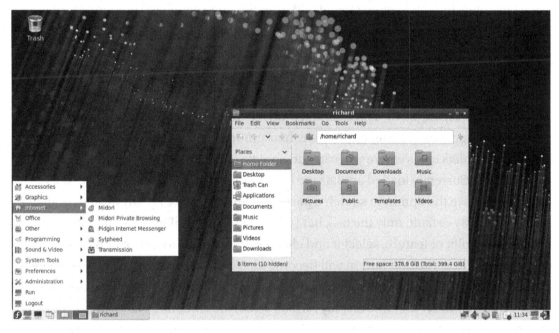

Figure 11-4. *LXDE desktop*

The panel shows applets for the Fedora applications menu, the PC-Man file manager, the terminal window, minimize windows, desktop pager, and window list. On the right side of the panel are the network connection monitor, and the system tray with Network Manager, volume control, clipboard, clock, lock desktop, and the logout button (see Figure 11-5).

Figure 11-5. *LXDE bottom panel*

The logout entry on the Fedora applications menu, and the logout button on the right side of the panel, open a dialog with buttons for logout, shutdown, suspend, hibernate, and reboot.

LXDE uses the PC-Man file manager, as shown in Figure 11-4. The button bar performs browser tasks such as moving backward and forward to previously viewed folders. The Home button moves you to your home folder. The folder button with the yellow star will open tabs, allowing you to open several folders in the same window. The side pane has a location (Places) and directory tree view. You can switch between the two using the button at the top of the pane. You can also choose from the View ➤ Side Pane menu.

To configure your panel, right-click the panel and select Panel Settings. This opens the Panel Preferences window with tabs for Geometry, Appearance, Panel Applets, and Advanced (see Figure 11-6). The Geometry tab lets you set the position and size of the panel. The Appearance tab lets you set the background, theme, and font for the panel. The Panel Applets tab is where you can add applets to the panel. The applets are referred to as plugins. Currently loaded applets are listed, along with format features such as spaces. You have the option to stretch a particular applet to take up any available space on the panel. By default, only the task bar (Window List) is configured to do this. To remove an applet or feature, select it and click the Remove button. If an applet or feature can be configured, the Edit button will become active when you select the applet. You can then click the Edit button to open the applet's configuration dialog. This will vary among applets. To set the time display format, select the clock and click Edit to open the Digital Clock settings dialog. Applets settings can also be edited directly from the panel. Right-click the applet and choose the Settings entry, such as Digital Clock Settings for the digital clock applet.

Figure 11-6. *LXDE's Panel Preferences and plugins*

To add a new applet to the panel, click the Add button to open the Add Plugin to Panel window, which will list all available applets and panel features like spaces and separators. Select the one you want and click the Add button (see Figure 11-6, right).

To configure the desktop, right-click anywhere on the desktop and choose Desktop Settings from the pop-up menu. This opens the Preferences window with tabs for Appearance and Advanced (see Figure 11-7). The Appearance tab lets you set the background and font. The Advanced tab lets you display window manager menus.

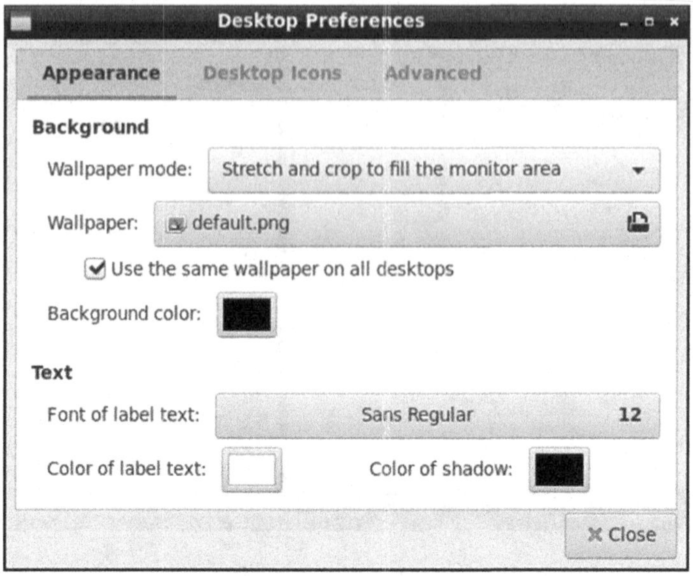

Figure 11-7. *LXDE's Desktop Preferences dialog*

The MATE Desktop

The MATE desktop is designed to be very simple, with a single panel and desktop icons.
You can download the Fedora MATE DVD from https://spins.fedoraproject.org/.
To install MATE as an alternative desktop on a system, install the mate-desktop package.
On the MATE desktop, the panel appears as a long bar across the bottom of the screen.
It holds menus, program launchers, and applet icons. You can display the panel
horizontally or vertically, and have it automatically hide to show you a full screen.

The MATE desktop continues the development of the older GNOME 2 interface
(see Figure 11-8), providing an enhanced version of GNOME 2 based on GTK+. Most
operations can be performed using the Applications, Places, and System menus. There
is both a top and a bottom panel. The top-right panel holds applets for sound, Network
Manager, and the date. The bottom panel holds the windows task bar and the pager
for workspaces. MATE uses a different file manager from GNOME, called Caja, but it
operates much like a GNOME 2 file manager. The file manager window has sidebars with
places and tree views. You can use the File, Edit, View, and Go menus to perform most
operations. There is a home button and computer button for the home folder and for a
computer window, respectively. The desktop also displays icons for both the computer
window and the home folder. The computer window shows all your devices.

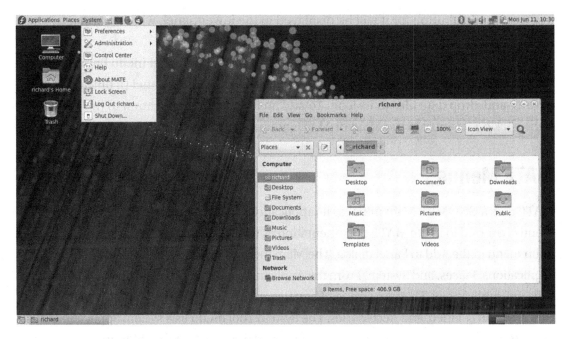

Figure 11-8. *MATE desktop (GNOME 2)*

On the left side of the top panel is the button for the main menu. To the right of the panel are system tools such as icons for the Network Manager, Update Manager, Power, sound volume, and the clock. With this menu, you can access places and applications. On the bottom panel to the left is the Show Desktop button, which hides your open windows, followed by the Window List applet, which shows button for open windows. To the right is the workspace switcher and the trash.

The remainder of the screen is the desktop, where you can place folders, files, and application launchers. You can use a click-and-drag operation to move a file from one window to another or to the desktop. A click and drag on a file icon with the Ctrl key held down will copy a file. Your home directory is accessed from the Home Folder icon on the desktop. Double-clicking it opens a file manager window for your home directory. A right-click anywhere on the desktop displays a desktop menu with which you can align your desktop icons and create new folders.

To quit the desktop, you use the Quit entry in the menu. Clicking on it opens a menu with options to Suspend, Hibernate, Restart, and Shut Down.

From a user's point of view, the desktop interface has four components: the desktop, the panels, the main menu, and the file manager. You have a single panel displayed, used for menus, application icons, and managing your windows. When you open a window,

445

a corresponding button for it will be displayed in the lower panel, which you can use to minimize and restore the window.

To start a program, you can select its entry from the Main panel menu bar menus or the MATE menu. You can also click its application icon in the panel (if one appears) or drag-and-drop data files to its icon. To add an icon for an application to the desktop, right-click on its entry in the Main or MATE menu and select Add to Desktop.

MATE Menus

MATE uses a GNOME 2 Main menu as its applications menu on the top panel. The Main menu is referred to in the MATE documentation as the MATE Panel menu bar, and as the Main menu in the Add to Panel dialog. The Main menu is a menu bar that has three menus: Applications, Places, and System. From the Applications menu, you can access your installed software applications. They are arranged by category with submenus for Internet, Graphics, Office, Sound & Video, and Accessories. The System Tool menu lists system applications such as the terminal, Log file viewer, the dconf Editor, and the MATE System Monitor.

From the Places menu, you can access your home and Desktop folders, along with any bookmarks you have set up. You can also access recent documents. The Computer entry opens a file manager window showing your file systems and attached devices. The network entry lets you access shared systems on your network. With Connect to Server, you can set up an FTP connection. The MATE Search Tool lets you quickly search for files on your home folder, file system, bookmarked folders, or a specified folder.

On the System menu you can access Administration tools from the Administration submenu, and Preferences dialogs from the Preferences submenu. The Preferences submenu has submenus for Hardware, Internet and Network, Look and Feel, and Personal, which corresponds to the sections of the Control Center. You can also access the Welcome dialog and the Control Center. There are also entries to log out, shut down, and lock your system. The Help entry opens the MATE desktop help dialog, with detailed documentation on the MATE desktop.

MATE Panels

The panel is the main component of the MATE interface. Through it, you can start your applications, run applets, and access desktop areas. You can think of the MATE panel as a type of tool you can use on your desktop. You can have several MATE panels displayed on your desktop, each with applets and menus you have placed in them. In this respect,

MATE is flexible, enabling you to configure your panels any way you want. The MATE panel work the same as the GNOME 2 panel. You can easily add applets to the panel, along with application launchers.

MATE uses the traditional GNOME 2 top and bottom panels by default, though you can add more. The top panel applets for the Main Menu (MATE Main menu bar), a launcher for the Firefox Web browser, and several system applets (see Figure 11-22). The system applets display buttons for the Bluetooth, Network Manager, volume control, the power manager, the clock, and shutdown. If you are using the MATE menu (advanced menu), a single Menu button is shown.

The bottom panel has applets for the menu, the window list on the left, and the workspace switcher (see Figure 11-9).

Figure 11-9. *MATE panel*

Caja File Manager

The Caja file manager supports the standard features for copying, removing, and deleting items as well as setting permissions and displaying items. The program name for the file manager is caja. When you click the Home folder icon on the desktop or the Home folder entry on the MATE menu Places section, a file manager window opens showing your home folder. The file manager window displays several components, including a menu bar, a main toolbar, and a side pane (see Figure 11-10). The side pane works like the sidebar in the Nemo and Nautilus (Files) file managers, but with a menu, like the file manager in GNOME 2. The file manager window's main pane (to the right) displays the icons or listing of files and sub-folders in the current working folder. When you select a file and folder, the status bar at the bottom of the window displays the name of the file or folder selected and for files the size, and for folders the number of items contained. The status bar also displays the remaining free space on the current file system.

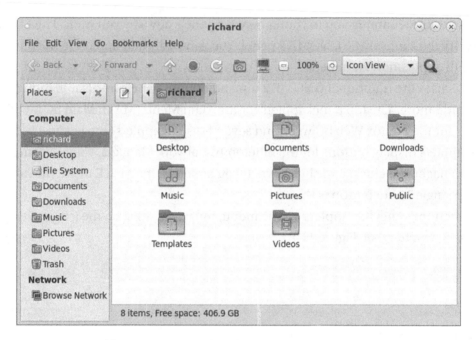

Figure 11-10. Caja file manager with sidebar

Control Center and Preferences

Both Preference and Administration tools can be accessed either from the MATE or Main menus or from the Control Center (see Figure 11-11). You can access the Control Center from the System section on the MATE menu, and from the Main menu's System menu. The Control Center opens a window listing the different applications by section: Personal, Hardware, Administration, Look and Feel, and Internet and Network. Icons for the tools are displayed. Single-click on an icon to open it. The Control Center also has a dynamic search capability. A side pane holds a filter search box and links for the groups. As you enter a pattern in the Filter search box, matching applications appear at the right. Commonly used applications can be listed under Common Tasks. If you want an application to be started when your system starts, you can right-click on its icon and choose Add to Startup Programs to add it directly to the Startup Applications dialog. Several of the tools are administration applications such as Software Boutique, Backups, Users and Groups, and Printers. Others are GNOME preferences used for MATE, such as Appearance, About Me, Screensaver, and Keyboard.

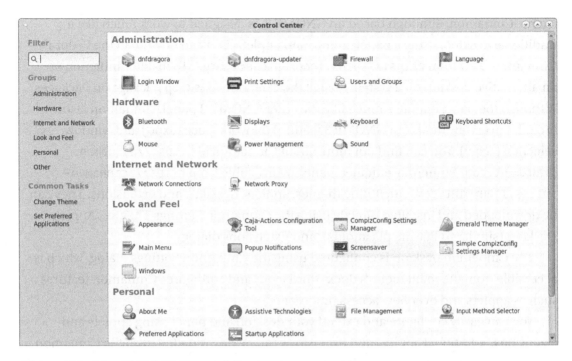

Figure 11-11. *GNOME Control Center*

You can configure different parts of your MATE interface using tools listed in the Preferences menu on the MATE and Main menus, and from the Control Center. MATE provides several tools for configuring your MATE desktop.

The keyboard shortcuts configuration (Keyboard Shortcuts) lets you map keys to certain tasks, like mapping multimedia keys on a keyboard to media tasks like play and pause. Just select the task and then press the key. There are tasks for the desktop, multimedia, and window management. In the window management section, you can also map keys to perform workspace switching. Keys that are already assigned will be shown.

The Windows configuration (Windows, in Look and Feel) is where you can enable features like window roll-up (Titlebar Action), window movement key, and mouse window selection.

The Cinnamon Desktop

The Cinnamon desktop is based on GNOME and was developed for the Linux Mint distribution (see Figure 11-12). It uses a variation of the GNOME 3 window manager (Mutter) called Muffin and a variation of the GNOME 3 nautilus file manager called

Nemo. Cinnamon, although based on GNOME 3, is designed to work much like a traditional desktop, using a panel, menu, and applets. You can download the Fedora Cinnamon DVD from `https://spins.fedoraproject.org/`. To install Cinnamon as an alternative desktop on a system, install the `cinnamon-desktop` package on Packages. Although the panel operates much like the older GNOME 2 panel, Cinnamon also includes overview modes (a GNOME 3 feature) for workspace (expo) and window selection (scale). You can find out more about Cinnamon at `https://cinnamon.linuxmint.com`. Numerous enhancements are available from `https://cinnamon-spices.linuxmint.com/`, including themes, applets, desklets, and extensions. They can be downloaded and installed directly using the Cinnamon Settings Themes, Applets, Desklets (similar to Plasma plasmoids), and Extensions dialogs.

The Cinnamon desktop is configured using the Cinnamon Settings dialog, which is accessible from the main menu's dock (third icon) and configures Cinnamon features such as applets and overview access (hot corner).

You can easily configure and extend your desktop and panel using applets and extensions. Additional applets and extensions can be downloaded from the Cinnamon website. The Cinnamon Settings dialogs for applets and extensions have links to those pages.

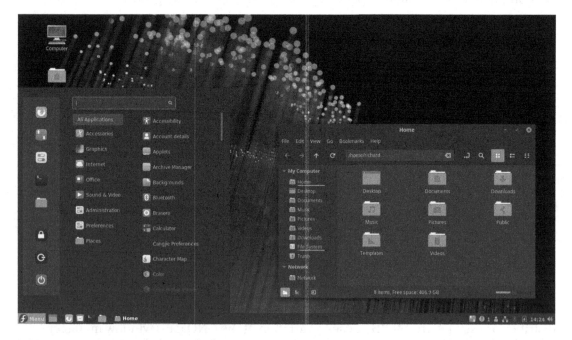

Figure 11-12. *Cinnamon desktop*

Cinnamon Panels

The Cinnamon desktop features a bottom panel with buttons for menus, applications, and the windows task bar (see Figure 11-13). On the right side of the panel are buttons for Network Manager, sound, power, notifications, and calendar menus. On the left side are buttons for the Cinnamon menu, show desktop, Firefox, Thunderbird mail, the terminal window, and the home folder.

Figure 11-13. *Cinnamon's bottom panel*

Panel configuration tasks such as adding applications, selecting applets, setting up menus, and creating new panels are handled from the Panel pop-up menu. Just right-click on the empty space on your panel (the middle) to display a menu with entries for Settings, Troubleshoot, Panel Edit mode, and Panel settings. The pop-up menu lists an additional entry for Add Applets to the Panel. From Settings, you can access commonly used Cinnamon settings such as Applets, Themes, and Menu. From Troubleshoot, you can restart Cinnamon or restore its defaults. You can also turn on the Panel Edit mode, which allows you to change the position of any button on the panel. Using the Cinnamon Settings panel dialog, you can change the position of the panel to the top of the screen or have two panels as GNOME 2 did. You can also change the panel size.

Clicking the Add Applets to the Panel entry opens the Cinnamon Settings ➤ Applets dialog (see Figure 11-14). Click to select an applet and then use the button bar at the bottom to perform a task. The plus button installs an applet and the minus button removes it from the desktop. The x button deletes it from your system. Some applets can be configured and will have a configuration button (gears image). A large number of additional applets can be added that are supported by third-party developers. These are listed on the Download tab. The Sort by menu lets you sort the listing by name, score (most popular), and date (latest). Click on the applet's download button to perform the download it.

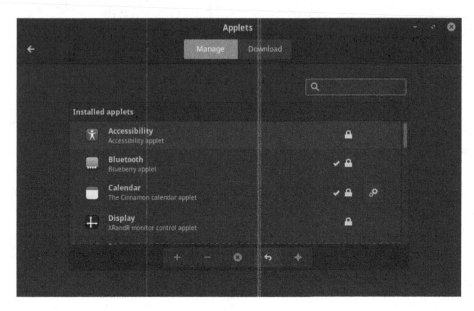

Figure 11-14. *Cinnamon's applets settings*

Cinnamon Settings

Clicking the System Setting button on the main menu's favorites (third icon) opens the System Settings dialog showing all your Cinnamon desktop configuration tools (see Figure 11-15).

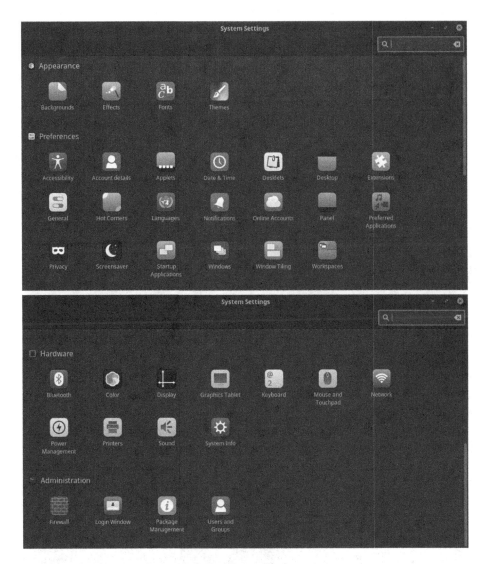

Figure 11-15. *Cinnamon's System Settings dialog*

Cinnamon Menus

The main menu displays three columns of applications and functions
(see Figure 11-16). The first column is a dock that shows icons of favorite applications
and session tasks. These include the Firefox web browser, Dragora software manager,
System Settings, the terminal window, your home folder, lock screen, logout, and
poweroff (last icon). The third icon opens the Cinnamon System Settings dialog. The
second column lists categories for all your applications, as you move through the

categories; the third column shows a listing of all the applications in that category. You can also search for applications and files using the search box at the top of the second column. The results of the search are displayed in the third column.

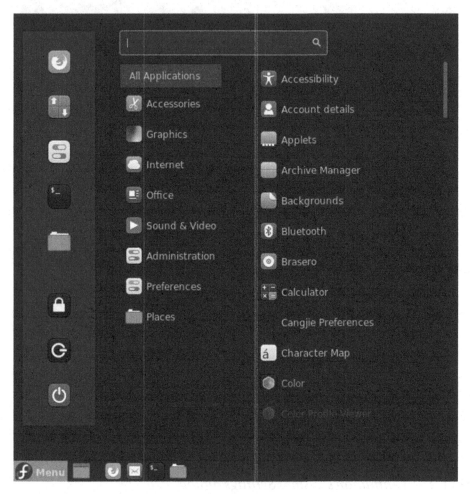

Figure 11-16. *Cinnamon's main menu and favorites*

Cinnamon Workspaces

Workspaces are accessed on Cinnamon from the Expo overview, which you activate by moving your mouse to the top-left corner of the desktop. This opens a workspace switcher displaying your workspaces (see Figure 11-17) (be sure to enable Expo on Hot Corners). Click on a workspace to change to it. A plus button to the right adds new workspaces. When you pass your mouse over a workspace, a close button appears in the upper-right corner, which you can use to remove the workspace. You can move windows from one workspace to another by clicking and dragging them. You can also rename a workspace, by clicking on the text box for its name and entering a new one. To leave the workspace switcher, click a workspace you want to move to, or move the mouse to the hot corner, to return to your current workspace.

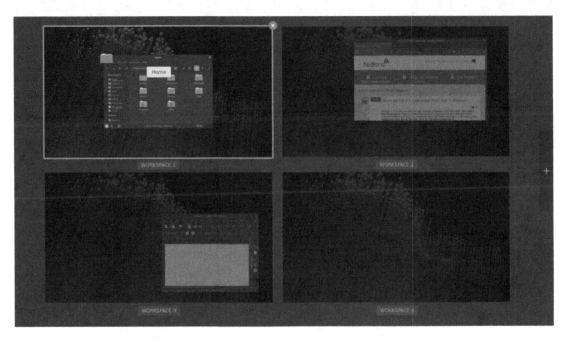

Figure 11-17. *Cinnamon workspace switcher overview*

You configure access to the workspace switcher (Expo overview) using the Cinnamon Settings Hot Corners dialog (see Figure 11-18). The corners in Hot Corners are not enabled by default. Click an entry to enable it. The top-left corner is set to workspace selection by default, and the top-right corner is set to window selection (Scale overview). With window selection, thumbnails of your open windows are displayed, and you choose the one you want.

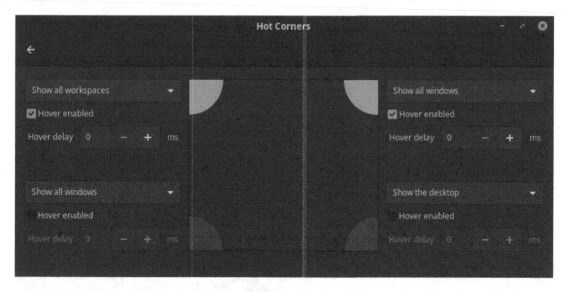

Figure 11-18. *Cinnamon Settings Hot Corners*

You can also enable the Scale and Expo applets, which display buttons for the scale and expo overviews. These buttons let you switch to the window selection overview or the window switcher overview from the panel, as shown here:

Cinnamon File Manager

The Cinnamon file manager, Nemo, works much like previous GNOME file managers, with home and computer buttons and buttons for the icon, list, and compact views (see Figure 11-19). It is based on the GNOME 3 file manager but restores much of the functionality found in the older file manager releases. File, Edit, View, and Go menus let you perform most functions, much like earlier versions of GNOME. The sidebar works much like the current GNOME file manager. Right-clicking an entry in the sidebar lets you open it in a new window or tab. The button before the find button lets you toggle to a location text box view, where you can enter a folder path name. The Computer window (Computer entry in the Go menu) displays your devices.

Figure 11-19. Cinnamon file manager (Nemo)

The LXQT Desktop

LXQT is another small desktop designed for use on minimal or low-power systems such as laptops, netbooks, or older computers. To install LXQT as an alternative desktop on a system, select the LXQT desktop package on Packages.

You can also use LXQT as a Live DVD, which you can download from `https://spins.fedoraproject.org/`.

The LXQT Live DVD is available in 32-bit and 64-bit versions, such as `Fedora-LXQt-Live-86_64-28.1.1.iso`. You can then burn the DVD and run it as a Live DVD. Double-click the Install icon to install an LXQT-based Fedora system on your computer. Follow the same basic steps for installing Fedora as for the Fedora Live DVD. The Installation Summary screen shows items for Installation Destination, Date & Time, and Keyboard. Be sure to choose the disks to install on and to check the time zone.

The desktop displays a single panel at the bottom with system applications like the clock and Dragora software manager to the right (see Figure 11-20). From the Fedora Applications menu on the left, you can access any applications. Next to the menu is a workspace switcher, Quicklaunch plugin, and a task bar for open windows. You can drag any application entry in the menu to the Quicklaunch plugin to have its icon displayed on the panel.

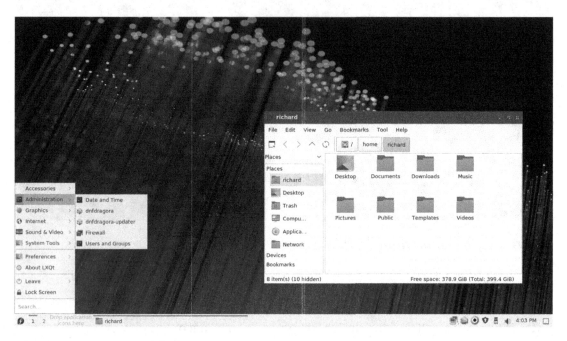

Figure 11-20. *LXQT desktop*

The panel shows applets for the Fedora applications menu, the PC-Man file manager, the terminal window, minimize windows, desktop pager, and window list. On the right side of the panel are the network connection monitor, and the system tray with Network Manager, volume control, clipboard, clock, lock desktop, and the logout button (see Figure 11-21).

Figure 11-21. *LXQT bottom panel*

The logout entry on the Fedora applications menu, and the logout button on the right side of the panel, open a dialog with buttons for logout, shutdown, suspend, hibernate, and reboot.

LXQT uses the PC-Man file manager, as shown in Figure 11-20. The button bar performs browser tasks such as moving backward and forward to previously viewed folders. The Home button moves you to your home folder. The folder button with the yellow star will open tabs, allowing you to open several folders in the same window. The side pane has a location (Places) and directory tree view. You can switch between the two using the button at the top of the pane. You can also choose from the View ➤ Side Pane menu.

To configure your panel, right-click the panel and select Configure Panel. This opens the Configure Panel window with tabs for Panel and Widgets (see Figure 11-22). The Panel tab lets you set the position and size of the panel, the background, and the autohide option. The Widgets tab is where you can add plugins (applets) to the panel. Currently loaded applets are listed. To add a plugin, click in the plus button to the right, which opens the Add Plugins dialog. To remove an applet, select it and click the minus button. If a plugin is configured, the edit button (menu button to the right) will become active when you select the plugin. You can then click the edit button to open the plugin's configuration dialog. This will vary among applets. Plugin settings can also be edited directly from the panel. Right-click the plugin and choose the Configure entry.

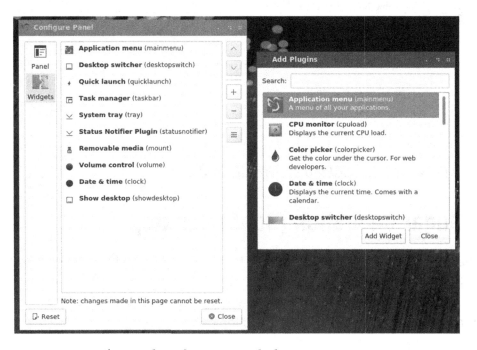

Figure 11-22. *LXQT's Panel Preferences and plugins*

To configure the desktop, right-click anywhere on the desktop and choose Desktop Settings from the pop-up menu. This opens the Preferences window with tabs for General and Advanced (see Figure 11-23). The Advanced tab lets you display window manager menus.

Figure 11-23. *LXQT's Desktop Preferences dialog*

The Sugar on a Stick (SoaS) Desktop

The Sugar on a Stick (SoaS) learning platform is designed for OLPC (One Laptop per Child) computers.

To install Sugar on an installed Fedora system, select the Sugar Desktop Environment package in the Package Collection category on Packages.

As a separate Live USB spin, the Fedora 28 OLPC desktop has been integrated into the Sugar on a Stick (SoaS) project at `https://wiki.sugarlabs.org/go/Sugar_on_a_Stick`.

You can find out more about the Fedora spin of Sugar on a Stick at `https://spins.fedoraproject.org`.

The Sugar on a Stick live ISO image is available in 32-bit and 64-bit versions, such as `Fedora-SoaS-Live-x86_64-28-1.1.iso`. You can then burn the image to a USB drive.

The Sugar on a Stick project also provides a creation kit that you can use to create your own customized Sugar on a Stick system.

The Sugar desktop initially displays a panel with a circular favorites menu (see Figure 11-24). Each icon will start a simple application, including a calculator, text editor, chat, a moon description, terminal window, web browser, and log. The top panel has buttons on the right for the circular favorites menu, or the list version.

To quit Sugar, pass your mouse over your person image at the center of the main screen and leave it there, or right-click the person image. A pop-up menu will appear with the Shutdown, Restart, and My Settings entries.

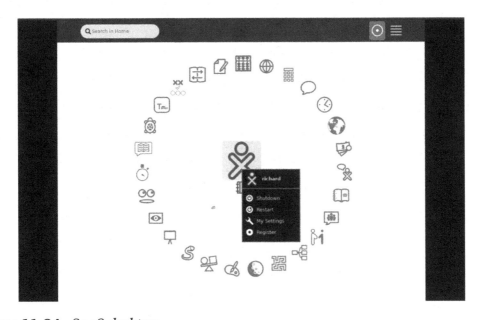

Figure 11-24. *SoaS desktop*

PART IV

Administration

CHAPTER 12

Fedora System Tools

Fedora provides several helpful system tools for monitoring, disk management, logs, and security (see Table 12-1).

Table 12-1. *Fedora System Tools*

Package Name	Application	Description
system-config-selinux	SELinux Management	Manages and configures SELinux policy
gnome-system-monitor	System Monitor	GNOME System Monitor
gnome-system-log	System Log	GNOME system log viewer
gnome-terminal	Terminal	GNOME terminal window
baobab	Disk Usage Analyzer	Baobab Disk Usage Analyzer
gnome-disk-utility	Palimpsest Disk Utility	Palimpsest DeviceKit disk manager
sealert	SELinux Troubleshooter	setroubleshoot, SELinux alert browser
gnome-power-statistics	Power Statistics	Power usage

Performance Analysis Tools and Processes

Linux treats each task performed on your system as a process, which is assigned a number and a name. You can examine these processes as well as start and stop them. Fedora provides several tools for examining processes as well as your system performance (see Table 12-2). Easy monitoring is provided by the GNOME System Monitor. Other tools are also available, such as the KDE System Monitor. Several utilities were designed to be used on a shell command line, displaying output in text lines.

© Richard Petersen 2018
R. Petersen, *Beginning Fedora Desktop*, https://doi.org/10.1007/978-1-4842-3882-0_12

Table 12-2. *Performance Tools*

Performance Tool	Description
vmstat	Performance of system components
top	Listing of most CPU-intensive processes
free	Listing of free RAM memory
sar	System activity information
iostat	Disk usage
GNOME System Monitor	System monitor for processes and usage monitoring (System ➤ Administration ➤ System Monitor)
KDE System Monitor	KDE system monitor for processes and usage monitoring
Frysk	Monitoring tool for system processes

GNOME System Monitor

The GNOME System Monitor displays system information and monitors system processes (Utilities ➤ System Monitor). It has three tabs: Processes, Resources, and File Systems (see Figure 12-1). The Resources tab displays graphs for CPU History, Memory and Swap History, and Network History. If your system has a multi-core CPU, the CPU History graph shows the usage for each CPU. The Memory and Swap Memory graph shows the amount of memory in use. The Network History graph displays the amount of sent and received data, along with totals for the current session.

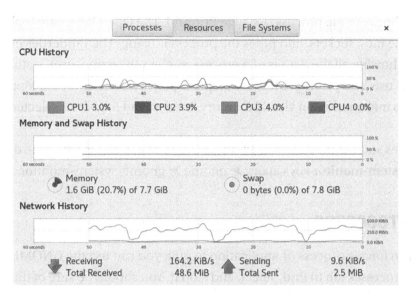

Figure 12-1. *GNOME System Monitor*

Note   System information, such as the Fedora release, hardware information, and system status, is available on the System Settings ➤ Details ➤ About tab.

The File Systems tab lists your file systems, including where they are mounted, their type, and the amount of disk space used and how much is free. You can sort the list by any category. Device, directory, and type names are listed alphabetically. Total, free, available, and used space can be sorted numerically in ascending or descending order. Double-clicking on a file system entry will open that file system in a file manager window.

The Processes tab lists your processes, letting you sort and search processes. You can use field buttons to sort by name (Process Name), process ID (ID), percentage of use (%CPU), and memory used (Memory), among others. The menu (right side of the menu bar) lets you select all processes, just your own (My Processes), or active processes. You can stop any process by selecting it and then clicking the End Process button (lower-right corner) or by right-clicking on it and choosing End. You can right-click a process entry to display a menu with actions you can take on the selected process, such as stopping (Stop), ending (End), killing (Kill), and continuing a process (Continue), as well as changing the priority of the process (Change Priority). The Open Files entry opens a dialog listing all the files, sockets, and pipes the process is using. The Properties entry displays a dialog showing all the details of a process, such as the name, user, status, memory use, CPU use, and priority. Memory Maps display, selected from the Memory Maps entry, shows information on virtual memory, inodes, and flags for a selected process.

Display features such as the colors used for CPU graphs can be set using the dconf editor's gnome-system-monitor keys at org ➤ gnome ➤ gnome-system-monitor.

Managing Processes

Should you have to force a process or application to quit, you can use the GNOME System Monitor Processes tab to find, select, and stop it. You should be sure of the process you want to stop. Ending a critical process could cripple your system.

Application processes will bear the name of the application, and you can use those to force an application to quit. Ending processes manually is usually preformed for open-ended operations that you are unable to stop normally. In Figure 12-2, the Firefox application has been selected. Clicking the End Process button on the lower left will force the Firefox web browser to end (you can also right-click the entry and select End from the menu). Clicking on the button at the lower left displays the properties for a selected process (see Figure 12-2). The menu button on the upper right shows display options such as active, all, your processes, and processes arranged in expandable trees showing their dependencies. The search button, also on the upper right, opens a search box letting you search for a process.

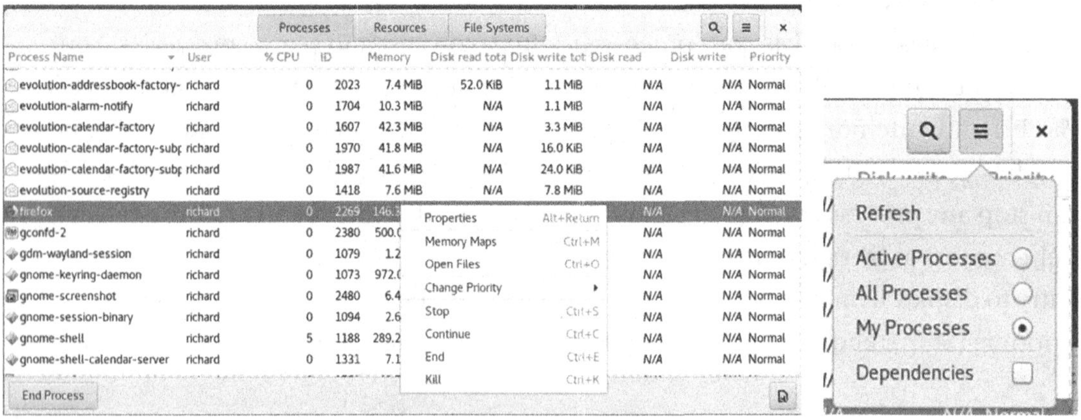

Figure 12-2. *GNOME System Monitor, Processes tab*

You can also use the pkill command with a process name or a process ID to end a process. To use a process name, enter the process name with the -n option for the most recent process for that name.

```
pkill -n firefox
```

You can also use the kill command in a terminal window to end a process. The kill command takes as its argument a process ID. Be sure you obtain the correct one. Entering the incorrect process ID could also cripple your system. Use the ps command to display a process ID. You can search for a process using the -C or -aux options. The ps command with the -C option searches for a particular application name. The -o pid= option displays only the process ID, instead of the process ID, time, application name, and tty. Once you have the process ID, you can use the kill command, with the process ID as its argument, to end the process.

```
$ ps -C firefox -o pid=
5555
$ kill 5555
```

One way to ensure the correct number is to use the ps command to return the process number directly as an argument to a kill command. The process is then stopped by first executing the ps command to obtain the process ID for the firefox process (back quotes), and then using that process ID in the kill command to end the process. The -o pid= option displays only the process ID.

```
kill `ps -C firefox -o pid=`
```

To search for a process using a pattern, you can use a ps command with the -aux option to list all processes and pipe the output to a grep command with a specified pattern. The following command lists all X Window System processes:

```
ps -aux | grep 'firefox'
```

You can obtain just the process IDs with the pidof command.

```
pidof  firefox
```

KDE System Monitor

The KDE System Monitor is accessible on the KDE desktop from System ➤ System Monitor and on the GNOME desktop from the Applications ➤ System Tools ➤ System Monitor. This tool allows you to monitor the performance of your own system as well as remote systems. KDE System Monitor can provide simple values or detailed tables for various parameters. A System Load tab provides graphical information about CPU and memory usage, and a Process Table tab lists current processes using a tree format to show dependencies. You can design your own monitoring tabs with worksheets, showing different types of values you want to display and the form you want to display them in, like a bar graph or digital meter. The Sensor Browser pane is an expandable tree of sensors for information like CPU System Load or Memory's Used Memory. There is a top entry for each host you are connected to, including your own, localhost. To design your own monitor, create a worksheet and drag and drop a sensor onto it.

Glances

Glances is a comprehensive system monitoring tool run from the command line in a terminal window with the glances command. It shows detailed resource use for the system, network, disk, file system, sensors, and processes (see Figure 12-3). It also warns you of any critical alerts. The system section covers detailed memory, CPU, swap and load usage. The network section shows the activity on each network device. The Disk I/O section lists your storage devices and their read/write usage. The File Sys section shows all your partitions and how much memory is used. The Sensors section shows the temperature detected by your sensors such as those for CPU, GPU, and the ambient temperature. The Tasks section lists your active processes by CPU usage, showing memory used, pid, user and the command. Press q to end your glances session.

Glances is organized into modules that you can disable to show only a limited set of reports. For example, if you are not interested in the disk I/O reports, you can disable the diskio module with the --disable-diskio option. See the glances man page for a compete list of module options you can use.

```
glances -- disable-diskio.
```

There are also several runtime commands you can use to show and hide modules, such as **f** to toggle the file system reports on and off, **d** to toggle disk I/O, **n** for network stats, **s** for showing sensors, and **p** to sort processes by name.

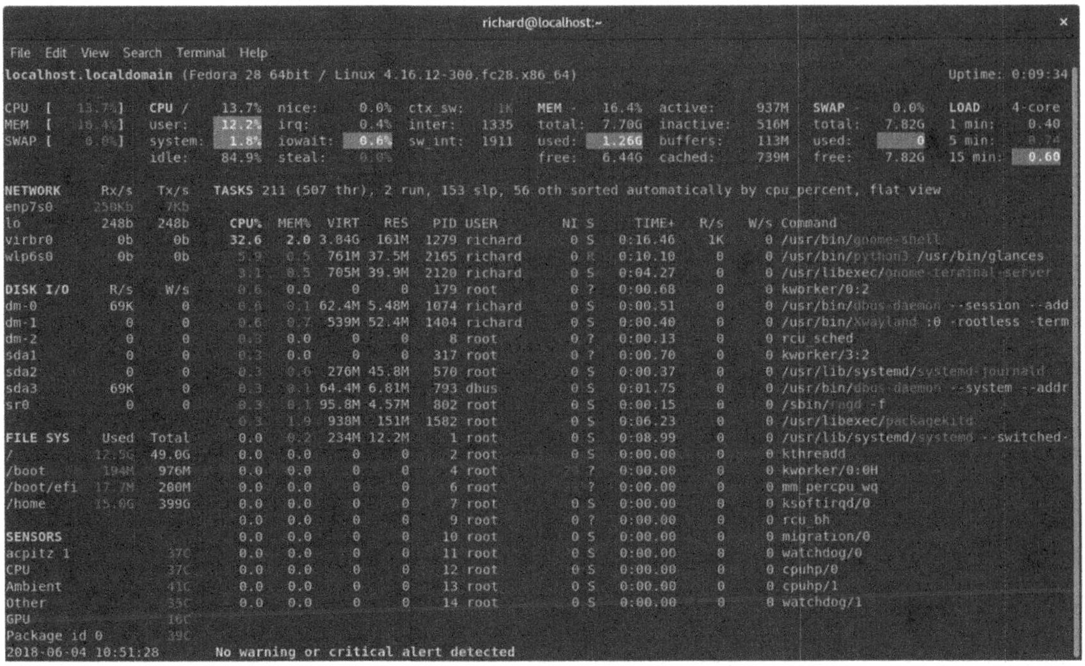

Figure 12-3. *Glances System Monitor*

vmstat, free, top, iostat, dstat, and Xload

From a terminal window, you can use tools such as vmstat, free, top, and iostat to monitor your system (systat package). The vmstat command outputs a detailed listing indicating the performance of different system components, including CPU, memory, I/O, and swap operations. A report is issued as a line with fields for the different components. If you provide a time period as an argument, it repeats at the specified interval, usually a few seconds. The top command provides a listing of the processes on your system that are the most CPU intensive, showing what processes are using most of your resources. The listing is in real time and updated every few seconds. Commands are provided for changing a process's status, such as its priority.

The free command lists the amount of free RAM memory on your system, showing how much is used and how much is free, as well as what is used for buffers and swap memory. Xload is an X Window System tool showing the load, CPU, and memory, iostat displays your disk usage, and sar shows system activity information.

Frysk

Frysk is a specialized complex monitoring tool for system processes. With Frysk you can set up very specific monitoring tasks, focusing on particular applications and selecting from a set of observer processes to provide information about exit notification, system calls, and execution. You can also create your own customized observers for processes. Find out more about Frysk at `http://sourceware.org/frysk`.

Terminal Window Administrative Access: sudo and sudo su

The terminal window allows you to enter Linux commands on a command line (Utilities ➤ Terminal). It also provides you with a shell interface for using shell commands instead of your desktop. The command line is editable, allowing you to use the Backspace key to erase characters on the line. Pressing a key will insert that character.

The terminal window is often used to run administrative tasks. First, log in as the root user, using the `sudo` command. You are prompted to enter your password. You can then run administrative-level commands, such as `dnf` to install packages or `nano` to configure system files.

Should you have several commands to run, you could log in at the root user directly using the `sudo` command in combination with the `su` command.

```
sudo su
```

The terminal prompt then changes to the root user and the current directory (see Figure 12-4). The `cd` command will move you to the root user directory. See Chapter 3 for details on using and configuring the terminal window.

```
                        richard@localhost:~                    ×

 File  Edit  View  Search  Terminal  Help
[richard@localhost ~]$ sudo su
[sudo] password for richard:
[root@localhost richard]# pwd
/home/richard
[root@localhost richard]# cd
[root@localhost ~]# pwd
/root
[root@localhost ~]#
```

Figure 12-4. *Terminal window*

Schedule Tasks

Scheduling regular maintenance tasks, such as backups, can be managed either by using the systemd timers or by the cron service. The systemd timers are systemd files that run service files. Check the man page for systemd.timers for a detailed description of timers. They have the extension .timer. A timer file will automatically run a corresponding service file that has the same name. For example, the dnf-automatic.timer will run the dnf-automatic.service file. The timer file only contains scheduling information. Its filename determines which service file to run. It is possible to designate a different service file with the Unit directive in the timer file. If you want to run a command-line operation for which there is no service file, you can create your own with an ExecStart entry for that command.

The timer files have a timer section in which you define when the service file is run. There are options that are relative to certain starting points like when system booted up, and the OnCalendar option that that reference calendar dates. The OnCalendar option uses calendar event expressions as defined on the systemd.time man page. A calendar even expression consists of a weekday, year, month, and time. The time is specified in hour, minute, and second, separated by colons. A range of weekdays is separated by two periods, and specific weekdays by commas. Leaving out the year or month selects any year or month. The following references weekdays in May at 2 pm.

OnCalendar=Mon..Fri 05 14:00

You can create timer files and place them in the /etc/systemd/system directory. If you also have to set up a service file for it, you can place it in the same directory. To activate a timer be sure to enable it with systemctl. If you created a service file, be sure to enable that also.

You can still use the older cron service to schedule tasks. The cron service is implemented by the cron daemon that constantly checks for certain actions to take. These tasks are listed in the crontab file. The cron daemon constantly checks the user's crontab file to see if it is time to take these actions. Any user can set up a crontab file. The root user can set up a crontab file to take system administrative actions, such as backing up files at a certain time each week or month.

Creating cron entries can be a complicated task, using the crontab command to make changes to crontab files in the /etc/crontab directory. Instead, you can use several desktop cron-scheduler tools to easily set up cron actions. Two of the more useful tools are KCron and GNOME Schedule, the latter which creates an easy-to-use interface for creating scheduled commands.

On KDE you can use the KDE Task Scheduler (KCron) to set up user- and system-level scheduled tasks (install the kdeadmin package). You access the Task Scheduler on the System Settings window, System Settings ➤ Task Scheduler (System Administration section). The Task Scheduler window will list your scheduled tasks. Click the New Task button to open a New Task window in which you can enter the command to run, add comments, and then specify the time in months, days, hours, and minutes from simple arranged buttons. On the Task Scheduler window, you can select a task and use the side buttons to modify it, delete the task, run it now, or print a copy of it. For tasks using the same complex commands or arguments, you can create a variable and then use that variable in a command. Variables are listed in the Environment Variables section. To use a variable in a scheduled task, precede its name with the $ character when you enter the command. Entering just the $ symbol in the Command text box will display a drop-down list of predefined system variables you can use, such as $PATH and $USER.

System Logs, journals, and journald

Various system logs for tasks performed on your system are stored and managed by the journald logging daemon. In effect, logs are now considered to be journals accessible by a systemd daemon, journald. From the command line (terminal window), you can use the journalctl command to access messages. The -f option displays the last few messages and is equivalent to displaying the last few messages in the old /var/log/messages file. The following command lists the last few messages:

```
journalctl -f
```

To see logs from the last system startup (boot), you use the -b option.

```
journalctl -b
```

To see messages for a particular service, you use the -u option and the name of the unit's service file, such as samba.service. The following lists the messages for the Samba server.

```
journalctl -u samba.service
```

With the --since and --until options, you can further specify a time.

```
journalctl -u samba.service --since=12:00
```

If you want, you can still install and run the older rsyslogd, which stores message in the /var/log/messages file.

GNOME Logs and System Log

To view these logs you can use GNOME Logs, Utilities ➤ Logs (GNOME Logs on GNOME Software or the gnome-logs package on Packages). A sidebar lists different log categories: Important, All, Applications, System, Security, and Hardware. Selecting one displays the log in the right pane (see Figure 12-5). A search button on the top right opens a search box, in which you can search for messages in the selected log, modifying the search by field and time. A save button on the top right lets you save the logs to a file. Logs queries the journald daemon for log reports using journalctl.

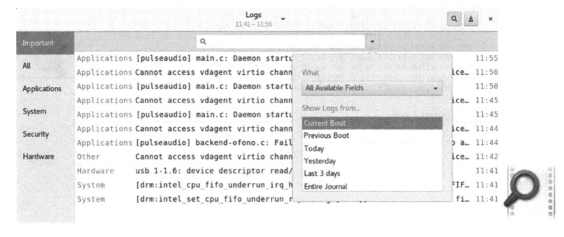

Figure 12-5. *GNOME logs*

You can also use the GNOME Log File Viewer to view these logs (Utilities ➤ System Log). Install System Log on GNOME Software or the gnome-system-log package on Packages. A sidebar lists the different logs. Selecting one displays the log in the right pane (see Figure 12-6). A search button on the top right opens a search box, in which you can search for messages in the selected log. A menu button on the top right lets you perform tasks such as zooming, copying, selecting, and filtering. The System Log queries the journald daemon for log reports using journalctl.

The Wayland display server currently does not allow root access by default to graphical tools, such as gnome-system-log. Many of these older graphical administration tools were designed for the older Xorg server and have not been updated for the Wayland server. A workaround uses the xhost command to add an access control for the root user to the local user. In a terminal window, enter the following command to enable root access through the display server. You have to re-enter this command with each new login session.

xhost +si:localuser:root

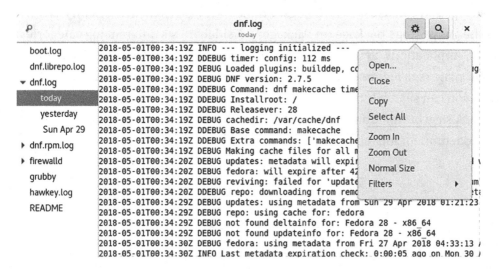

Figure 12-6. *System Log*

Disk Usage Analyzer

The Disk Usage Analyzer lets you see how much disk space is used and available on all your mounted hard disk partitions. You can access it from Utilities ➤ Disk Usage Analyzer. It will also check all LVM and RAID arrays. Usage is shown in a simple graph, letting you see how much overall space is available and where it is. On the Scan dialog, you can choose to scan your home folder (Home Folder, your entire file system (disk drive icon), an attached device like a USB drive, or a specific or remote folder (see Figure 12-7).

Figure 12-7. *Disk Usage Analyzer: Scan dialog*

To scan a folder or device, click the folder or device entry. When you scan a folder or the file system, the disk usage for your folder is analyzed and displayed. Each file system is shown with a graph for its usage, as well as its size and the number of top-level folders and files. Then the folders are shown, along with their size and contents (see Figure 12-8).

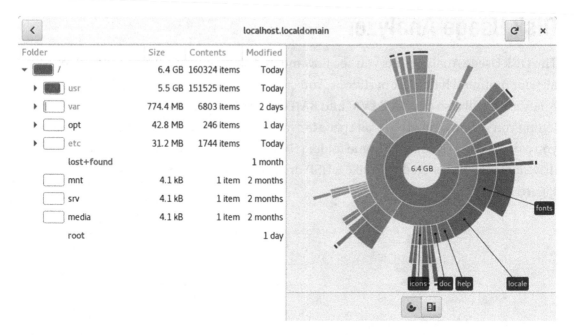

Figure 12-8. *Disk Usage Analyzer*

A representational graph for disk usage is displayed on the right pane. The graph can be either a Ring Chart or a Treemap. The Ring Chart is the default. Choose the one you want from the buttons on the lower right. For the Ring Chart, directories are shown, starting with the top-level directories at the center and moving out to the subfolders. Passing your mouse over a section in the graph displays its folder name and disk usage, as well as all its subfolders. The Treemap chart shows a box representation, with greater disk usage in larger boxes, and subfolders encased within folder boxes.

Virus Protection

Though viruses are rare on Linux, especially on Fedora, which has advanced security features such as SELinux, they can still occur. As a precaution you can install the free and open source Clam Anti-Virus virus protection software (www.clamav.net). On Gnome Software choose ClamTK or, for KDE, KlamAV. Choose clamav, clamav-filesystem, clamav-lib, clamav-update, clamav-data, on either ClamTK (clamtk package, GNOME) or KlamAV (KDE) frontends. For ClamTK, install using the dnf command. Once installed, you can access it as ClamTK. With ClamTK, you can scan specific files and directories, as well as your home directory (see Figure 12-9). Searches can be recursive, including subdirectories. You have the option to also check dot configuration files. Infected files are quarantined. The ClamTK dialog has four sections: Configuration, History, Updates, and Analysis. Updates can be automatic or manual. Click the Help button on the upper right to open the ClamTK Virus Scanner documentation with details on scanning updates and settings.

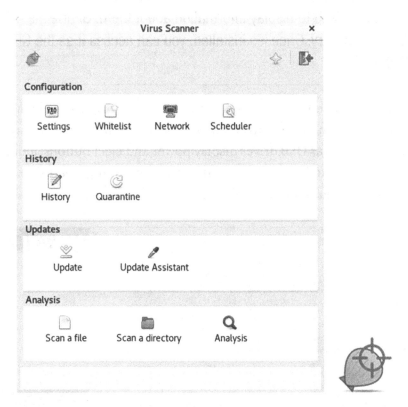

Figure 12-9. *The clamtk tool for ClamAV virus protection*

You can also install the `clamav-milter` and `clamav-scanner` packages, which work with your email application, to detect viruses.

Disk Utility and Udisks

Disk Utility is a Udisks supported user configuration interface for your storage media, such as hard disks, USB drives, and DVD/CD drives (`gnome-disk-utility` package, installed by default). Tasks supported include disk labeling, mounting disks, disk checks, and encryption. You can also perform more advanced tasks, like managing RAID and

LVM storage devices, as well as partitions. Disk Utility is accessible via Utilities ➤ Disk Utility. Users can use Disk Utility to format removable media like USB drives. Disk Utility is also integrated into GNOME Files, letting you format removable media directly.

Note You can use GParted (GNOME Partition Editor) to create and remove your hard disk partitions, and to display information about them. GParted is available from the EPEL repository. Once it's installed, you can access it as the GParted Partition Editor.

The Disk Utility window shows a sidebar with entries for your storage media (see Figure 12-10). Clicking on an entry displays information for the media on the right pane. Removable devices such as USB drives display power and eject buttons, along with a task menu with an entry to format the disk. If you are formatting a partition, like that on removable media, you can specify the file system type to use.

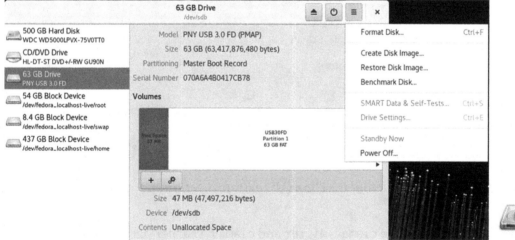

Figure 12-10. *Disk Utility*

If you select a hard disk device, information about the hard disk is displayed on the right pane at the top, such as the model name, serial number, size, partition table type, and SMART status (Assessment) (see Figure 12-11). Click the menu button to display a menu on the upper right with tasks you can perform on the hard drive: Format, Benchmark, and SMART Data.

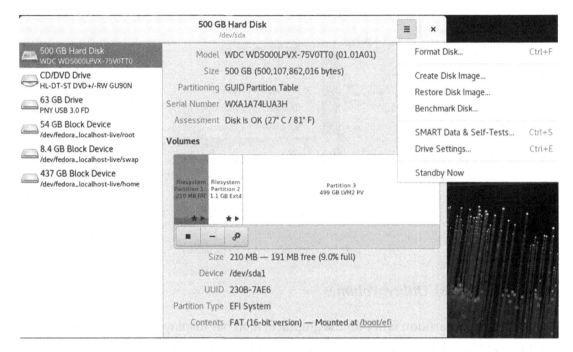

Figure 12-11. *Disk Utility, hard drive*

The Volumes section on the hard disk pane shows the partitions set up on the selected hard drive (see Figure 12-12). Partitions are displayed in a graphical icon bar, which displays each partition's size and location on the drive.

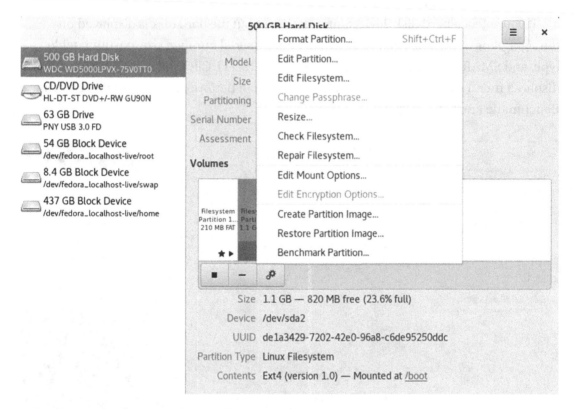

Figure 12-12. *Disk Utility, Volumes*

Clicking on a partition entry on the graphical icon bar displays information about that partition such as the file system type, device name, partition label, and partition size. The Contents entry tells if a partition is mounted. If in use, it displays a Mounted At: entry with a link consisting of the path name where the file system is mounted. You can click on this path name to open a folder with which you can access the file system. The button bar below the Volumes images provides additional tasks you can perform, such as unmounting a file system (square button) and deleting a partition (minus button). From the More Tasks menu, you can choose entries to change the partition label, type, and mount options. Certain partitions, like extended and swap partitions, display limited information and have few allowable tasks.

For more detailed hardware information about a hard drive, you can click on the SMART Data and Tests entry from the task menu in the upper right. This opens a SMART data dialog with hardware information about the hard disk (see Figure 12-13) including temperature, power cycles, bad sectors, and the overall health of the disk. The Attributes section lists SMART details such as the Read Error Rate, Spinup time, temperature, and write error rate. Click the switch on to enable the tests, and off to disable testing. Click the Refresh button to manually run the tests. Click the Start Self-Test button to open a menu with options for short, extended, and conveyance tests.

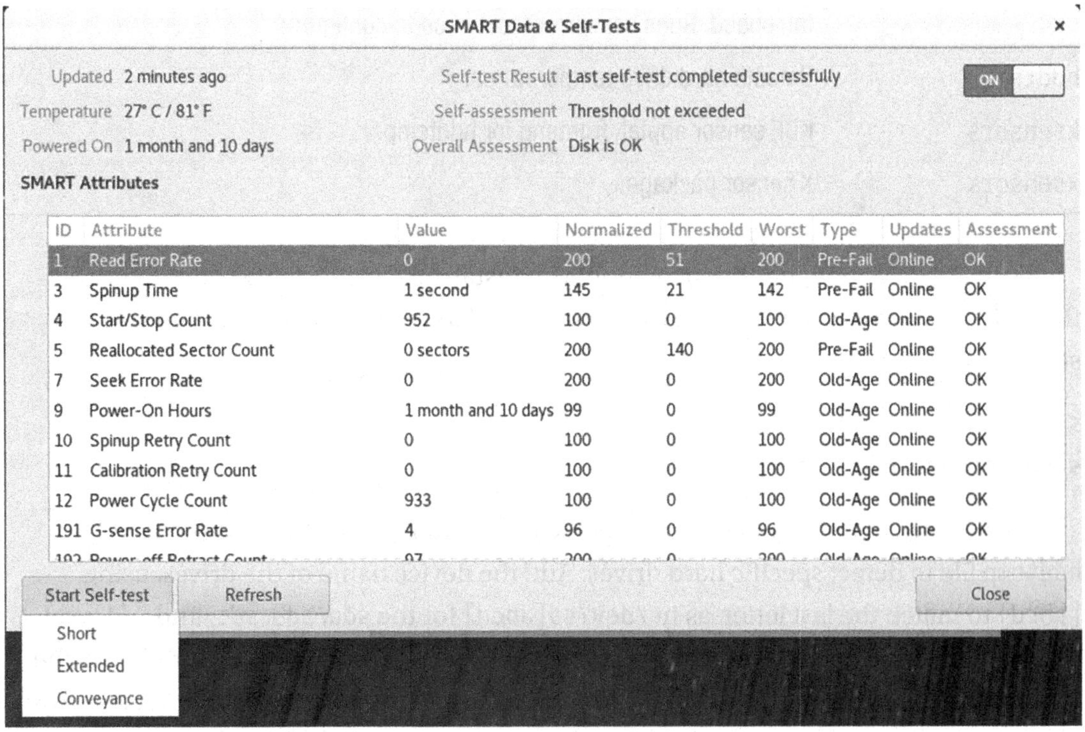

Figure 12-13. *Disk Utility: Hard Disk hardware SMART data*

Hardware Sensors

A concern for many users is the temperature and usage of computer components. You install different software packages to enable certain sensors (see Table 12-3). For the CPU, system, fan speeds, and any other motherboard supported sensors, you use the lm_sensors service. Download and install the lm_sensors package. First, you must configure your sensor detection. In a terminal window, log in as the root user (su) and enter the following (answer yes to the prompts):

```
sudo sensors-detect
```

This service will detect hardware sensors on your computer. It will run as the lm_sensors service.

Table 12-3. *Sensor Packages and Applications*

Sensor Application	Description
lm_sensors	Detects and accesses computer (motherboard) sensors, such as CPU and fan speed. Runs sensors-detect once to configure.
hddtemp	Detects hard drive temperatures.
ksensors	KDE sensor applet, frontend for hddtemp.
xsensors	X sensor package.

For hard drive temperature detection, you install hddtemp. You will have to enable the hddtemp daemon, using the service command as the root user, and then you can start the server.

```
sudo systemctl enable hddtemp
sudo service hddtemp start
```

If your hard disks are not detected, you can to configure the /etc/sysconfig/ hddtemp file to detect specific hard drives. Add the device name of the drives, using [abcd] to match the last letter, as in /dev/sd[abcd] for the sda, sdb, sdc, and sdd hard drives. In the following example, the device name /dev/sd[adcd] was inserted into the HDDTEMP_OPTIONS entry after 127.0.0.1, the localhost IP address used to reference your system.

```
HDDTEMP_OPTIONS="-l  127.0.0.1  /dev/sd[abcd]"
```

To edit the hddtemp file, you must open a terminal window and log in as the root user. Then use an editor such as nano or vi. The nano editor is easier to use. (Press Ctrl+o to save and Ctrl+x to exit; use arrow keys to navigate.)

```
sudo nano /etc/sysconfig/hddtemp
```

On Gnome, you can use Xsensors and two GNOME extensions (Add-ons in GNOME Software), the Hardware Sensors Indicator and Sensors. The extension run as indicator menus at the right side of the top panel, next to the System Status Area menu. Xsensors is a standalone application, which you can access from the Applications overview (see Figure 12-14).

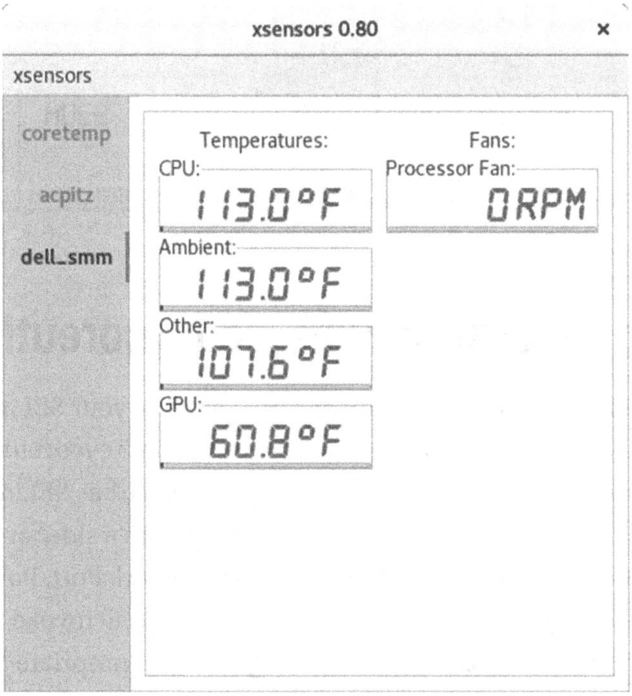

Figure 12-14. *Xsensors*

You can then download and install the ksensors package, the KDE applet for displaying sensor information. On KDE, access Ksensors from Applications ➤ System ➤ Hardware Monitor, where it will appear as an icon on the system tray. Once opened, right-click the KSensors dialog and choose Configure from the pop-up menu to open the KSensors configuration dialog. On the sidebar, choose a sensor category such as Hard Disks, radeon (AMD video card), or nouveau (NVIDIA video card) sensors. On the right pane, you can choose from the Sensors and Preferences tabs. The Preferences tab sets the update frequency and temperature scale. The Sensors tab has subtabs that let you change the name (General), make something visible on the panel (Panel) or dock (Dock), or set an alarm (Alarm). For the System Information tab, a System Panels tab replaces the Sensors tab. It includes subtabs for system information such as CPU Speed and RAM used, which you can make visible and set the tile and colors. To have a temperature displayed on the KSensors panel, but sure to click its visible check box on its Panel tab, and then click on the Apply button. Once configured, click the KSensors icon in the message tray to open the KSensors panel (see Figure 12-15).

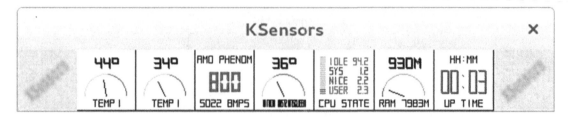

Figure 12-15. *KSensors*

SELinux: Configuration with policycoreutils-gui

With policycoreutils-gui, you can manage and configure your SELinux policies,
although you cannot create new policies. You can install policycoreutils-gui using the
Packages package manager. can access policycoreutils-gui as SELinux Management.
The SELinux Administration window lists several panes with a sidebar menu for Status,
Boolean, File Labeling, User Mapping, SELinux User, Network Port, Policy Module, and
Process Domain (see Figure 12-16). policycoreutils-gui will invoke the SELinux-
management tools, such as sestatus and semanage, with appropriate options to make
configuration changes.

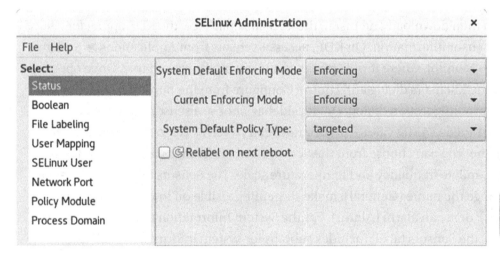

Figure 12-16. *The system-config-selinux, SELinux Management*

The Status pane sets the default and current enforcing modes. Here you can enable or disable SELinux, as well as specify the policy type. By default, the enforcing modes are set to Enforcing. You have the choice of Disable, Permissive, and Enforcing. If you are experiencing difficulties accessing your system, you can set the enforcing modes to Permissive or Disabled. Permissive will allow access, but issue warning messages. Disabled will completely shut down SELinux. The policy is normally targeted, focusing on network services like Samba and Apache. You can download and install more restrictive policies, but you may need a detailed understanding of SELinux to manage them.

This pane also features the relabeling option. Sometimes when you install new server software or update your system, you may need to relabel some of your files and directories. Relabeling will mark the files and directories to correct security access. Check Relabel on Next Reboot to perform the relabeling. It may take some time.

You can also quickly turn the enforcing mode on an off from a terminal window with the setenforce command. The 0 argument turns it off, and the 1 argument turns it on.

```
setenforce 0
```

Use the getenforce command to see what your current enforcement mode is.

```
getenforce
```

Note   Configuration for general SELinux server settings is carried out in the /etc/selinux/config directory. Currently there are only two settings available: the state and the policy. You set the SELINUX variable to the enforcement mode, such as enforcing or permissive, and the SELINUXTYPE variable to the kind of policy you want.

User Mapping shows the mapping of user login names to SELinux users. Initially, there will be two mappings: the root user and the default user.

The Boolean pane lists various options for targeted services, such as web and FTP servers, NFS, and Samba (see Figure 12-17). With these, you can further modify how each service is controlled. There are expandable menus for different services, such as FTP, Apache web server, and Samba. For example, the FTP entry lets you choose whether to allow access to home directories or to NFS transfers.

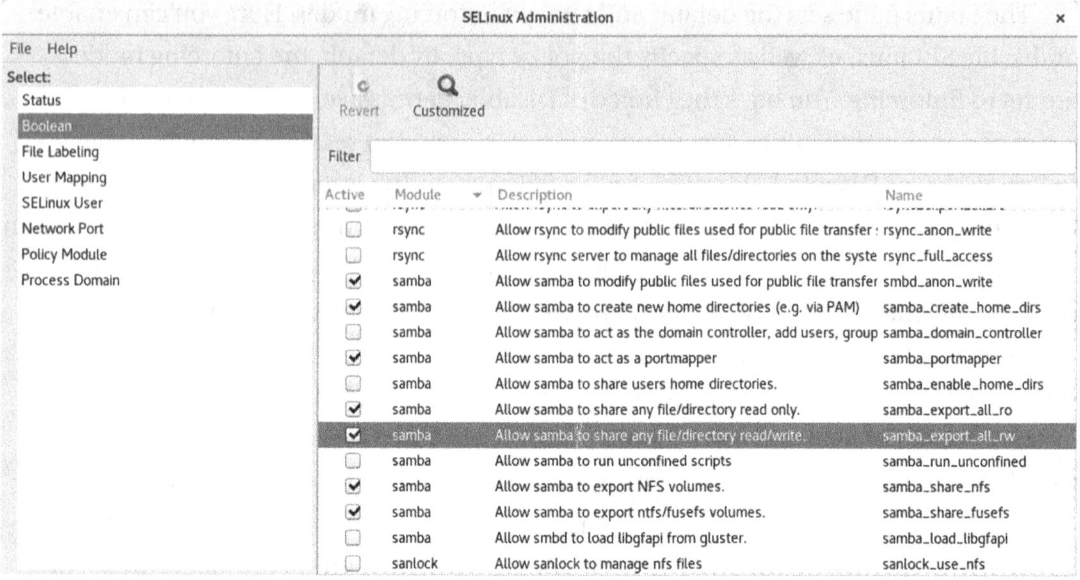

Figure 12-17. *policycoreutils-gui SELinux Boolean pane*

To allow access to many network services, you must not only allow access through your firewall but also through SELinux. The Boolean pane has entries for the different network services. Samba, in particular, has to have its Boolean entries set before you can access Samba shares.

The File Labeling pane will list your system directories and files, showing their security contexts and types. You can edit a file's properties by selecting the entry and then clicking Properties. This displays a dialog with File Name, Type, SELinux Type, and Multi-Level Security (MLS) levels. MLS gives a security level value to resources. Only users with access to certain levels can access the corresponding files and applications. You can change the SELinux type or the MLS level. For a permissive policy, the MLS level will be s0, allowing access to anyone. You can also add or delete entries.

The SELinux Users pane shows the different kinds of SELinux users. Initially, there will be several user types, including root, system_u, and user_u. The root user has full and total administrative access to the entire system. The system_u user allows users to take on administrative access where needed. The user_u user is for normal users. Each entry lists its SELinux user, SELinux prefix, MLS level, MLS range, and SELinux roles. MLS level is the access level (s0 on a permissive policy), and MLS range is the range of access from SystemLow to SystemHigh. A given user has certain roles available. The root user has the system_r, sysadm_r, and staff_r roles, allowing that person system access, administration capability, and staff user access. The `user_u` users also have a `system_r` role, allowing those users to perform system administration, if they have the `root` user password.

The Network Port pane lists the network protocol, the SELinux type, and the MLS security level for ports on your system. Select an entry and click Properties to change the SELinux type or the MLS level for the port. The Group View button will display the SELinux type, along with a list of the ports they apply to. This view does not display the MLS level, as these apply to ports individually.

The Policy Module pane lists the different SELinux policy modules. Here, you will see modules for different applications, such as Thunderbird and Evolution, as well as device service such as USB. Listed also are desktops such as GNOME. The pane allows you to add or remove modules. You can also enable or additional audit rules for a module for logging.

SELinux Troubleshooting and audit2allow

Fedora includes the SELinux troubleshooter, which notifies users of problems that SELinux detects. Whenever SELinux denies access to a file or application, the kernel issues an AVC (Access Vector Cache) notice. These are analyzed by the SELinux troubleshooter to detect problems that users may have to deal with. When a problem is detected, a SELinux troubleshooter notification is displayed in the desktop message tray, along with the troubleshooter icon, as shown here:

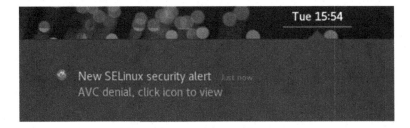

Clicking the icon or notice will open the SELinux troubleshooter window. You can also access it at any time as SELinux Troubleshooter. You can find out more information about SELinux troubleshooter at `https://fedorahosted.org/setroubleshoot/`.

The SELinux troubleshooter window displays the current notice (see Figure 12-18). Use the Next and Previous buttons to page through notices. The number of the displayed notice is shown between the Previous and Next buttons.

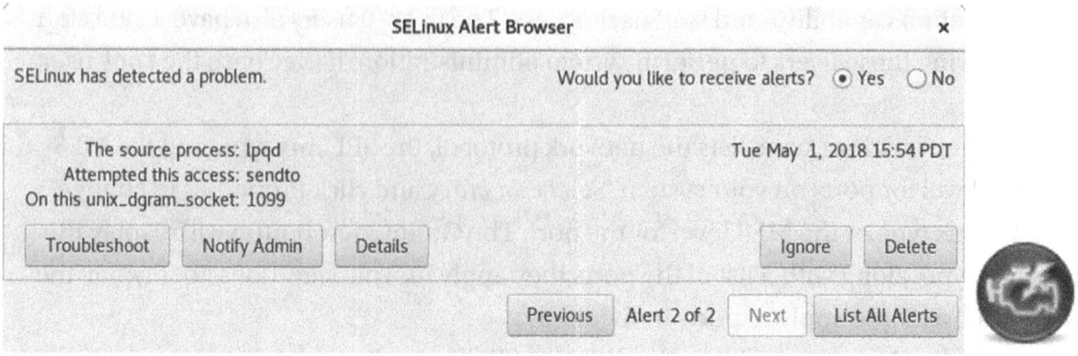

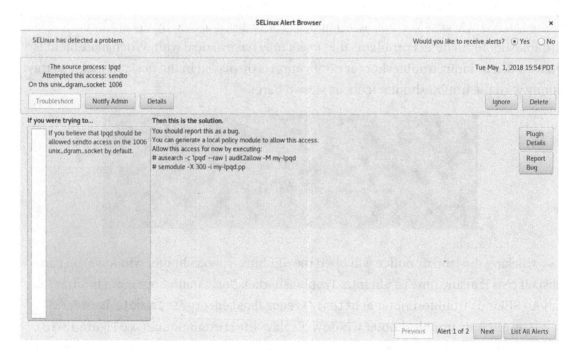

Figure 12-18. *SELinux troubleshooter window*

Clicking the Troubleshoot button displays detailed information about the notice, listing what you may be trying to do and possible solutions (see Figure 12-19). To see a description of the problem and solution in a separate window, click the Plugin Details button to the right of the solution description (see Figure 12-20). For a full description, including policy type, first and last time seen, and the raw audit message, click the Details button at the top left, next to the Notify Admin button (see Figure 12-21).

Figure 12-19. *SELinux troubleshooter, troubleshoot listing*

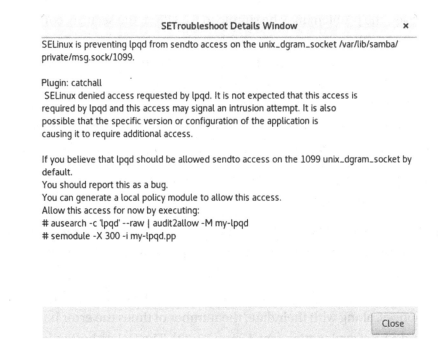

Figure 12-20. *SELinux troubleshooter, plugin details window*

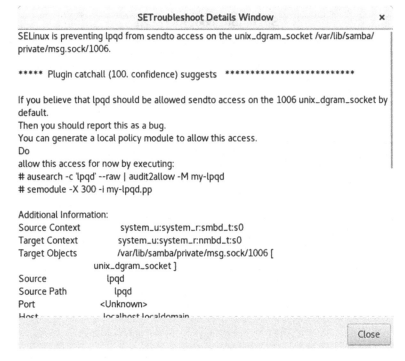

Figure 12-21. *SELinux troubleshooter, full details window*

In many cases, the problem may be simple to fix. Often, the security context of a file has to be renamed to allow access, or access set up to a particular port. In this example, SELinux has to access by the print queue daemon lpqd to the Samba socket (Windows access). The audit2allow and semodule operations are listed as the solution. The audit2allow operation sets the policy, and the semodule operation makes it active. You could open a terminal window, log in as the root user (sudo su), and run the commands. You could copy and paste them to the terminal window from the Details window.

```
ausearch -c 'lpqd' --raw | audit2allow -M my-lpqd
semodule -X 300 -i my-lpqd.pp
```

You could also use the SELinux Management tool to make the changes. In this case, you'd choose the Network Port tab and click the Add button to open the Add Network Port dialog.

To see a full listing of error messages at once, click the List All Alerts button to display a list of alert notices, along with their date, the number of times the error has occurred, its category, and a brief explanation (see Figure 12-22). The Delete button lets you delete alerts.

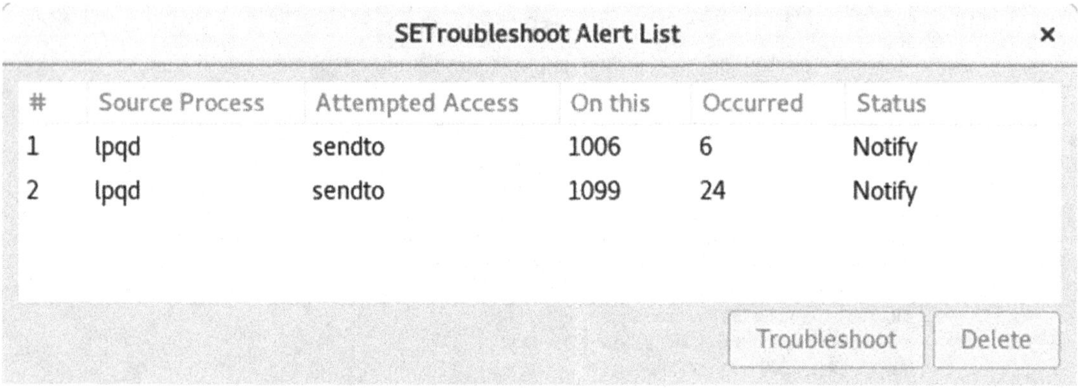

#	Source Process	Attempted Access	On this	Occurred	Status
1	lpqd	sendto	1006	6	Notify
2	lpqd	sendto	1099	24	Notify

SETroubleshoot Alert List ✕

Troubleshoot   Delete

Figure 12-22. *SELinux troubleshooter alert list*

For folders, often the problem is a simple security permission, a security context. For a security context change, you use the chcon command. In the following example, access is granted by Samba to the /mymedia directory.

```
chcon -R -t samba_share_t '/mymedia'
```

More complicated problems, especially ones that are unknown, may require you to create a new policy module, using the AVC messages in the audit log. To do this, you can use the audit2allow command. The command will take an audit AVC message and generate commands to allow SELinux access. The audit log used on Fedora is /var/log/audit/audit.log. This log is output to audit2allow—you then can use its -M option to create a policy module.

```
cat /var/log/audit/audit.log | audit2allow -M local
```

You then use the semodule command to load the module.

```
semodule -i local.pp
```

If you want to first edit the allowable entries, you can use the following code to create a .te file of the local module, local.te, which you can then edit.

```
audit2allow -m local -i  /var/log/audit/audit.log   >  local.te
```

Once you have edited the .te file, you can then use checkmodule to compile the module, then semodule_package to create the policy module, local.pp. Then you can install it with semodule. You first create a .mod file with checkmodule and then a .pp file with semodule_package.

```
checkmodule -M -m -o local.mod local.te
semodule_package -o local.pp  -m local.mod
semodule -i local.pp
```

In the preceding example, the policy module is called local. If you later want to create a new module with audit2allow, you should either use a different name or append the output to the .te file, using the -o option.

CHAPTER 13

System Administration

To make effective use of your Fedora Linux system, you must know how to configure certain features and services. Administrative operations, such as adding users and installing software, can be performed with user-friendly system tools. This chapter discusses basic system administration operations that you need to get your system up and running, as well as to perform basic maintenance, such as adding new users. You can make changes or additions easily, using the administrative tools described in this chapter.

Configuration operations can be performed from a desktop interface, such as GNOME or KDE, or they can be performed using a simple shell command line, on which you type configuration commands. You can also manually access system configuration files, editing them and making entries yourself. Although these tools are accessible from any user account, they can only be managed by users with administrative access. Such users will first be prompted for their user password before they can use them.

Fedora Administrative Tools

On Fedora, administration is handled by a set of administrative tools developed and supported by Fedora, such as those for user management and printer configuration (see Table 13-1). With GNOME, most administration tools have been integrated into GNOME Settings, superseding the older `system-config` tools. For example, the GNOME Settings GNOME Users is the default user management tool, instead of the older `system-config-users`. For printing you can use the GNOME Settings printing tool, instead of `system-config-printer`. The GNOME Settings was covered in Chapter 3, as most of its tools are used for desktop configuration, instead of administration purposes. Tools that have administrative functions, such as the GNOME Users tool, are described in the administrative Chapters (12, 13, and 14). You can access GNOME Settings from the System Status Area dialog as described in Chapter 3 (wrench/screwdriver icon, bottom left).

495

© Richard Petersen 2018
R. Petersen, *Beginning Fedora Desktop*, https://doi.org/10.1007/978-1-4842-3882-0_13

Table 13-1. *Administrative Tools*

Command	Application	Description
GNOME Settings ➤ Details	Date & Time	GNOME Settings date and time configuration tool
firewall-config	Firewall	Configures your network firewall
system-config-printer	Print Settings	Printer configuration tool (older)
GNOME Settings ➤ Devices	Printers	GNOME Settings printer configuration tool
system-config-users	Users & Groups	User and Group configuration tool (older).
GNOME Settings ➤ Details	Users	GNOME Settings user configuration tool
policycoreutils-gui	SELinux Management	SELinux configuration
GNOME Settings	Network and WiFi	GNOME Settings network configuration tools
nm-connections-editor	Network Connections	Network Manager configuration tool (older)

Administrative Access

To perform system administration operations, you must be a user who has administrative access. You can then access administrative tools for specific tasks from any account, temporarily giving you superuser access for just that administrative operation. With administrative access, you can perform tasks such as starting up and shutting down the system, adding or removing users, formatting file systems, and backing up and restoring files, and you may also specify the system's hostname.

Administrative Access from Normal User Accounts

To access an administrative tool, you simply log in to an account that has administrative access and choose the tool you want. A dialog is then displayed that will prompt you to enter your user password. Once you do so, the administrative tool you chose starts up, allowing its functions to have full root user access (see Figure 13-1). The same kind of permission is required for updates and for managing user accounts. When you unlock the Settings ➤ Details ➤ Users tab, you will first be prompted by a dialog for a root user password. For each different administrative tool you start, you must separately enter the root user password.

Figure 13-1. *Administrative access authentication dialog*

Controlled Administrative Access: sudo

The sudo command allows ordinary users to have limited root user administrative access for a specific task. Users can perform a superuser operation without having full root-level control. You can find out more about sudo at https://www.sudo.ws. Administrative users (users with the account type Administrator as specified by Settings ➤ Details ➤ Users) are configured to use sudo automatically. Any user can be directly configured to have sudo access by editing the /etc/sudoers file. With sudo access, a user can use administrative tools as the root user, giving you direct root user access with desktop capabilities.

sudo Configuration

Access with the sudo command is controlled by the /etc/sudoers file. This file lists users and the commands they can run, along with the password for access. If the NOPASSWD option is set, then users will not require a password. ALL, depending on the context, can refer to all hosts on your network, all root-level commands, or all users. To make changes or add entries, you have to edit the file with the special sudo editing command, visudo. This invokes the vi editor to edit the /etc/sudoers file. Unlike a standard editor, visudo will lock the /etc/sudoers file and check the syntax of your entries. You are not allowed to save changes, unless the syntax is correct. Use the vi editing commands to make changes (see Chapter 5). If you want to use a different editor, you can assign it to the EDITOR shell variable.

```
sudo visudo
```

A sudoers entry has the following syntax. The host is a host on your network. You can specify all hosts with the ALL term. The command can be a list of commands, some or all qualified by options such as whether a password is required. To specify all commands, you can also use the ALL term.

```
user    host=command
```

The following gives the user robert full root-level access to all commands on all hosts:

```
robert   ALL = ALL
```

Use vi commands to edit the file. You can move to the root user entry and then press the o command to open a new line. Type the new user entry and then press the Esc key. Press Shift+zz when you've finished editing.

In addition, you can let a user run as another user on a given host. Such alternate users are placed in parentheses before the commands. For example, if you want to give robert access to the mypic host as the user fineart, you use the following:

```
robert mypic = (fineart) ALL
```

By default, sudo will deny access to all users, including the root. For this reason, the default /etc/sudoers file sets full access for the root user to all commands. The ALL=(ALL) ALL entry allows access by the root to all hosts as all users to all commands.

```
root    ALL=(ALL)    ALL
```

To specify a group name, you prefix the group with a % sign, as in %mygroup. This way, you can give the same access to a group of users. The /etc/sudoers file contains samples for a %wheel group.

To give robert access on all hosts to the system-config-users tool, you would use the following:

```
robert ALL=/usr/bin/system-config-users
```

If a user wanted to see which commands he or she can run, that user would use the sudo command with the -l option.

```
sudo -l
```

Using sudo

Once the user is configured, the user can use sudo to run an administrative command. The user precedes the command with the sudo command. The user is then issued a time-sensitive ticket to allow access.

```
sudo date
```

The sudo command becomes very useful when you have to perform an otherwise ordinary task with root user access. This allows you to avoid having to log in as the root user, yet still allows you to have extensive root user access over the system. One very common use is to employ the gedit graphical text editor to edit system configuration files. There is no specific administrative tool to do this, so ordinarily, you would have to log in as the root user to perform this task. With the sudo command, however, you can edit any system configuration file from a normal account. The following example would let you edit the /etc/fstab file, used for automatic file system mounting. Open a terminal window and enter the command. You will be prompted for the user password, then gedit will start as a functional desktop editor.

```
sudo gedit /etc/fstab
```

You could even run the file manager as a sudo operation, allowing the file manager full administrative access from any normal account. The file manager will open to the root user account.

```
sudo files
```

Logging In To the Root User Account Directly: sudo su

There are situations in which you might want to log in directly to the root user account. If you are performing several administrative tasks at once, or if you have to modify configuration files directly, root user account access may work best. The root user is a special account reserved for system management operations with unrestricted access to all components of your Linux operating system. You can log in as the root user from a terminal window or from the command-line login prompt.

sudo su

When logged in as a user with administrative access on the desktop, you can then log in as a root user, using a terminal window and the sudo su command (su stands for switch user). This is helpful if you just need to quickly run a command as a root user. You can use the sudo su command with the root username, or the sudo su command alone (the root username will be assumed). You will be prompted to enter the root user password.

```
sudo su root
password:
```

In the following example, the user logs in as the root user and then runs the nmb script using the service command, which requires root user access.

```
sudo su
password:
service nmb start
```

To exit from a sudo su login operation, when you are finished with that account, simply enter exit.

```
exit
```

If you log in as the root user with the sudo su command in a terminal window, you cannot run desktop applications from that terminal window as the root user. You can, however, run the Leafpad editor from a root user terminal window, allowing you to use leafpad to edit configuration files. Leafpad is a simple desktop editor.

However, the Wayland display server does not allow root access by default to graphical tools, such as Leafpad. Many of these older graphical administration tools were designed for the older Xorg server and have not been updated for the Wayland server. A workaround uses the xhost command to add an access control for the root user to the local user. In the terminal window, enter the following command to enable root access through the display server. You should only have to do this once each time you log in.

```
xhost +si:localuser:root
```

You can then use Leafpad, as shown here, to edit a system configuration file, in this case, /etc/default/grub.

```
sudo su
leafpad /etc/default/grub
```

Note   The su command can actually be used to log in to any user, provided you have that user's password.

Controlled Access with PolicyKit: polkit-1

Designed by the Freedesktop.org project, PolicyKit allows ordinary users and applications access to administration-controlled applications and devices. Currently, it supports several key administrative operations, including Network Manager, Udisks, Packages, Firewall, Samba, and system monitor. Although this could be done with other operations, such as group permissions, PolicyKit aims to provide a simple and centralized interface for granting users access to administration-controlled devices and tools. PolicyKit is used to grant access to shared devices managed by Udisks. This includes most of the devices on your system, including removable ones.

PolicyKit can allow for more refined access. Instead of an all-or-nothing approach, whereby a user has to gain full root-level control over the entire system just to access a specific administration tool, PolicyKit can allow access to specific administrative applications. All other access can be denied. A similar kind of refined control is provided with PAM and sudo, allowing access to specific administrative applications, but administrative password access is still required, and root-level access, though limited to that application, is still granted. You can find out more about PolicyKit at http://hal.freedesktop.org/docs/polkit.

PolicyKit configuration and support is already set up for you. A new version of PolicyKit, polkit-1, is now used for PolicyKit operations. Configuration files for these operations are held in /usr/share/polkit-1. There is, as of yet, no desktop tool available for configuring these settings. The desktop tool polkit-gnome only provides GNOME dialogs for providing authentication, when required by an application or device.

Changing PolicyKit Options

With PolicyKit, administration-controlled devices and applications are set up to communicate with ordinary users, allowing them to request certain actions. If the user is allowed to perform the action, the request is then authorized, and the action is performed.

Difficulties occur if you want to change the authorization setting for certain actions, such as mounting internal hard drives. Currently, you can change the settings by manually editing the configuration files in the /usr/share/polkit-1/actions directory, but this is risky. To make changes, you first must know the action to change and the permission to set. The man page for polkit will list possible authorizations. The default authorizations are allow_any for anyone, allow_inactive for a console, and allow_active for an active console only (user logged in). These authorizations can be set to the following specific values:

auth_admin	Administrative user only, authorization always required
auth_admin_keep	Administrative user only, authorization kept for a brief period
auth_self	User authorization required
auth_self_keep	User authorization required, authorization kept for a brief period
yes	Always allow access
no	Never allow access

You will have to know which PolicyKit action to modify and which file to edit. The action is listed in the PolicyKit dialog, which prompts you to enter the password (expand the Details arrow) when you try to use an application. The File will be the first segments of the action, with the suffix policy attached. For example, the action for mounting internal drives is

org.freedesktop.UDisks2.filesystem-mount-system-internal

Its file is

org.freedesktop.UDisks2.policy

The file is located in the /usr/share/polkit-1/actions directory. Its full pathname is:

/usr/share/polkit-1/actions/org.freedesktop.UDisks2.policy

By default, PolicyKit is configured to require authorization, using the root password before a user can mount an internal hard drive partition. Should you want to allow users to mount partitions without an authorization request, the org.freedesktop.UDisks2.policy file in the /usr/share/polkit-1 directory has to be modified to change the allow_active default for the filesystem-mount-system action from auth_admin_keep to yes. The auth_admin_keep option requires administrative authorization.

502

Enter the following to edit the `org.freedesktop.udisks.policy` file in the `/usr/share/polkit-1/actions` directory with the nano text editor. Be sure to use the `sudo` command for administrative access.

```
sudo nano /usr/share/polkit-1/actions/org.freedesktop.UDisks2.policy
```

If you are configured as a valid `sudo` user in the `/etc/sudoers` file, you can use the `sudo` command instead, which allows you to use desktop editors such as gedit.

```
sudo gedit /usr/share/polkit-1/actions/org.freedesktop.UDisks2.policy
```

Locate the `action` id labeled as

```
<action id ="org.feedesktop.udisks2.filesystem-mount-system">
  <description>Mount a filesystem on a system device</description>
```

This is usually the second action ID. At the end of that action section, you will find the following entry. It will be located within a defaults subsection, `<defaults>`.

```
<allow_active>auth_admin</allow_active>
```

Replace `auth_admin_keep` with yes.

```
<allow_active>yes</allow_active>
```

Save the file. Users will no longer have to enter a password to mount internal partitions.

Note   The System Security Services daemon (SSSD) provides offline access for users relying on remote authentication, such as an LDAP server. The SSSD will cache the authentication method, allowing you to log in offline. Before SSSD, users had to maintain a corresponding local account from which to gain access when offline. SSSD is installed by default. You start it using the `sssd` daemon. Configuration files are located at `/etc/sssd`. See `https://fedorahosted.org/sssd/` for more details.

User (GNOME Settings ➤ Details ➤ Users)

You can configure and create user accounts using the GNOME Users tool accessible from GNOME Settings as Users. Users does not provide any way to control groups. If you want group control and more configuration options, you can use the GNOME Users and Groups application (`system-config-users` package).

You can access GNOME Users from the Details ➤ Users tab on GNOME Settings. The Users tab displays an icon bar at the top showing a list of configured users with arrow buttons to the right and left to move through the list. Figure 13-2 shows information about a selected user. Initially, at the top of the Users tab is an Unlock button. Click on this button to open an authentication dialog, prompting for your password. Once active, you can then change the change the password, account type, icon, or name for the currently selected user. To remove a user, click its Remove User button on the lower right.

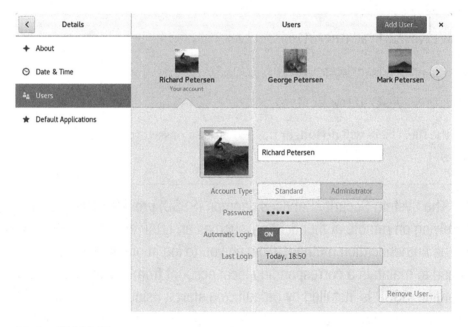

Figure 13-2.   GNOME users

Once authentication is accepted, the Unlock button changes to an Add User button, which you click to add a new user. When you add a new account, the Add User dialog opens, allowing you to set the account type (standard or administrator), the full name of the user, and the username (see Figure 13-3). For the username, you can enter a name or choose from a recommended list of options. You can also choose to set the password at this time. Click the Add button on the upper right to create the user. The new account appears in the icon list of users at the top of the Users tab, showing the name and icon. Selecting the user also shows its account type, language, password, an automatic login option, and the time of the last logon. You can change the account type, language, password, and icon by clicking on their entries.

Figure 13-3. *Add a new user*

The account remains inactive until you specify a password (see Figure 13-4). You can do this when you add the account, or later. You can also change the password for an account. Click the password entry to open the Change Password dialog in which you can enter the new password (see Figure 13-5). On the right side of an empty Password text box, a password generator button is displayed that will generate a password for you when clicked. Once clicked, a generated password is entered the text box and the button disappears, replaced by a checkmark. Deleting the password to show an empty box once again displays the password generator button. Once the password is selected, the account becomes enabled.

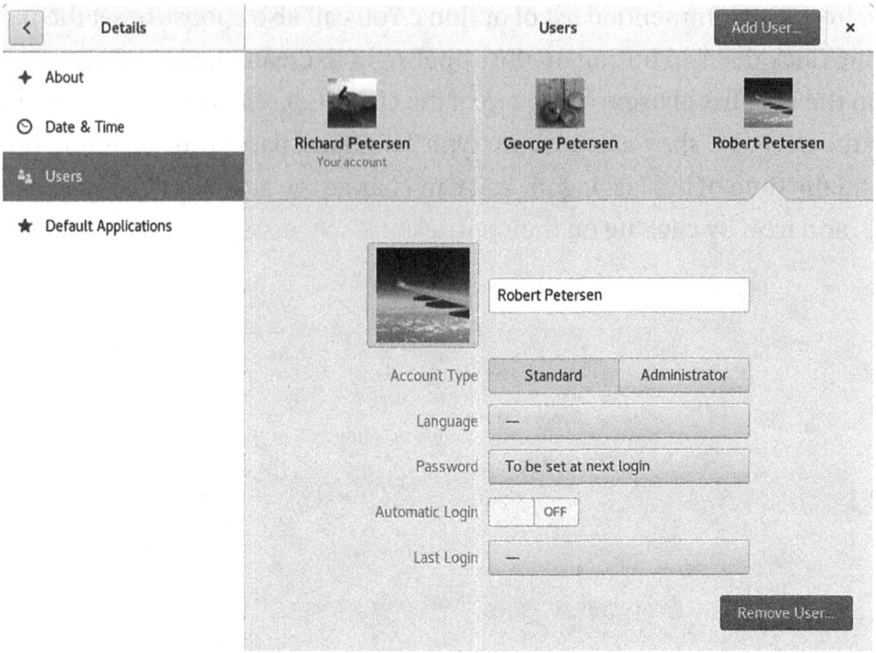

Figure 13-4. *Users, inactive user*

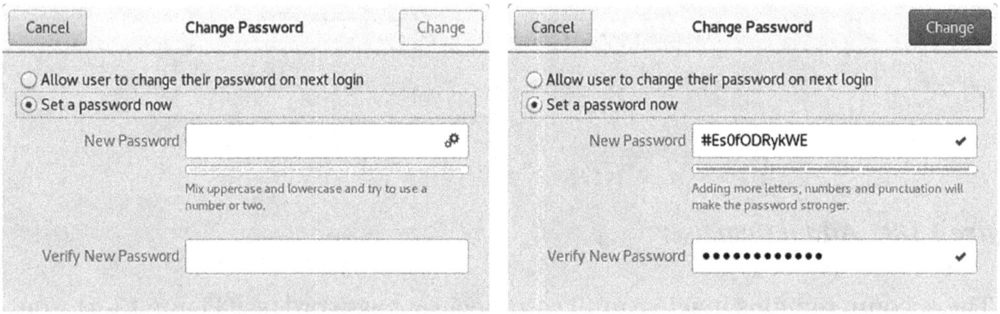

Figure 13-5. *Users, password dialog*

To change the user icon, click the icon image to display a pop-up dialog showing images you can use (see Figure 13-6). You can also take a photo from your web cam (take a photo entry) or select a picture from your Pictures folder (browse for more pictures).

Currently, group configuration is not supported.

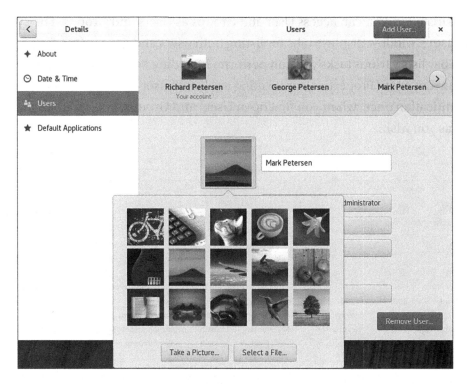

Figure 13-6. *Accounts dialog, Users icon*

Users and Groups Manager: system-config-users

You can also add and manage users by employing the older `system-config-users` application known as Users and Groups. It is not installed by default. You can install it using Packages. Use the package name `system-config-users` to locate it on the Packages application.

The Wayland display server does not allow root access by default to graphical tools, such as `system-config-users`. Many of these older graphical administration tools were designed for the older Xorg server and have not been updated for the Wayland server. A workaround uses the `xhost` command to add an access control for the root user to the local user. In a terminal window, enter the following command to enable root access through the display server. You have to re-enter this command with each new login session in order to use the older Xorg-based administration applications.

```
xhost +si:localuser:root
```

You can then start Users and Groups from Applications ➤ Sundry.

Once installed, you can access User and Groups as Users and Groups. The `system-config-users` window displays tabs for listing both users and groups (see Figure 13-7). A button bar lists various tasks you can perform, including adding new users or groups, editing current ones (Properties), or deleting a selected user or group. You are prompted for authentication once, when you first open Users and Groups. You can then make changes as you wish.

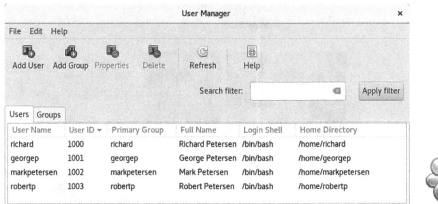

Figure 13-7. Users and Groups: system-config-users

Users and Groups: New Users

To create a new user, click Add User to open a window with entries for the username, password, and login shell, along with options for creating a home directory and a new group for that user (see Figure 13-8).

Figure 13-8. *Users and Groups: Add New User*

Once you have created a user, you can edit its properties to add or change features. Select the user's entry and click Properties. This displays a window with tabs for User Data, Account Info, Password Info, and Groups (see Figure 13-9).

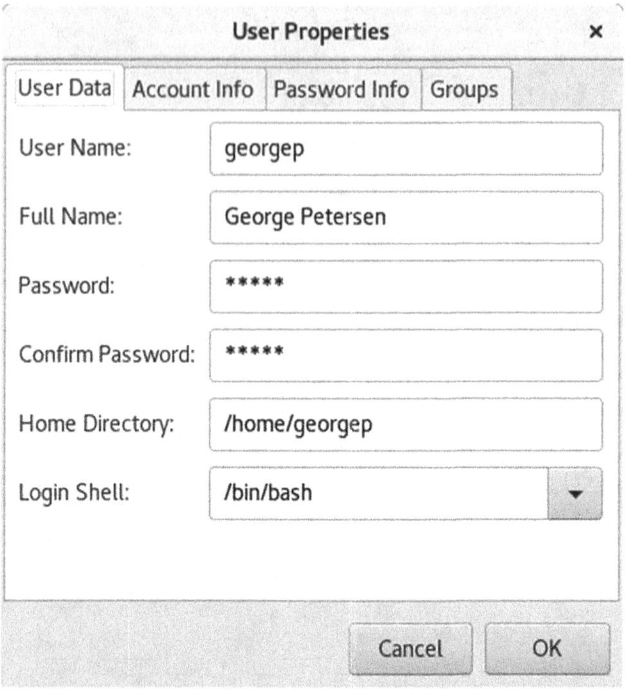

Figure 13-9. *Users and Groups: User Properties window: User Data tab*

On the Groups tab, you can select the groups that the user belongs to, adding or removing group memberships (see Figure 13-10). The Accounts Info tab allows you to set an expiration date for the user, as well as lock the local password. Password Info can enable password expiration, forcing users to change their passwords at certain intervals.

Figure 13-10. *Users and Groups: User Properties window: Adding groups to a user*

Users and Groups: Groups

To add a group, click the Add Group button to open a small window in which you can enter the group name. The new group will be listed in the Groups listing (see Figure 13-11). Groups can be used in file and folder permissions to restrict access to a group of users.

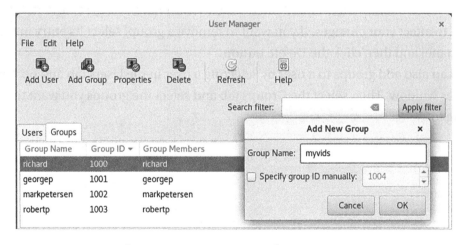

Figure 13-11. *Users and Groups : Groups panel*

To add users as members of the group, select the group's entry and click the Properties button. This opens a window with tabs for Group Data and Group Users. The Group Users tab lists all current users with check boxes (see Figure 13-12). Click the check boxes of the users you want to become members of this group.

Figure 13-12. *Users and Groups: Group Properties: Group Users panel*

If you want to remove a user as a member, click the check box to remove its check. Click OK to affect your changes. If you want to remove a group, select its entry in the Groups panel and then click the Delete button.

You can also add groups to a user by selecting a user in the Users tab and opening its Properties window. Then select the Groups tab and select the groups you want that user to belong to.

Adding and Removing Users with useradd, usermod, and userdel

Linux also provides the useradd, usermod, and userdel commands to manage user accounts. All these commands take in all their information as options on the command line. If an option is not specified, they use predetermined default values. These are command-line operations. To use them on your desktop, you first need to open a terminal window and then enter the commands at the shell prompt with the sudo command.

useradd

With the useradd command, you enter values as options on the command line, such as the name of a user, to create a user account. It then creates a new login and directory for that name using all the default features for a new account.

```
useradd chris
```

The useradd utility first checks the /etc/login.defs file for default values for creating a new account. For those defaults not defined in the /etc/login.defs file, useradd supplies its own. You can display these defaults using the useradd command with the -D option. The default values include the group name, the user ID, the home directory, the skel directory, and the login shell. Values the user enters on the command line will override corresponding defaults. The group name is the name of the group in which the new account is placed. By default, this is other, which means the new account belongs to no group. The user ID is a number identifying the user account. The skel directory is the system directory that holds copies of initialization files. These initialization files are copied into the user's new home directory when it is created. The login shell is the pathname for the particular shell the user plans to use.

The useradd command has options that correspond to each default value. Table 13-2 holds a list of all the options you can use with the useradd command. You can use specific values in place of any of these defaults when creating a particular account. The login is inaccessible until you do. In the next example, the group name for the chris account is set to intro1 and the user ID is set to 578:

```
sudo useradd chris -g intro1 -u 578
```

Once you add a new user login, you need to give the new login a password. Password entries are placed in the /etc/passwd and /etc/shadow files. Use the passwd command to create a new password for the user, as shown here. The password you enter will not appear on your screen. You will be prompted to repeat the password. A message will then be issued indicating that the password was successfully changed.

sudo passwd chris
```
Changing password for user chris
New UNIX password:
Retype new UNIX password:
```

Table 13-2. *Options for useradd and usermod*

Options	Description
-d dir	Sets the home directory of the new user.
-D	Displays defaults for all settings. Can also be used to reset default settings for the home directory (-b), group (-g), shell (-s), expiration date (-e), and password expirations (-f).
-e mm/dd/yy	Sets an expiration date for the account (none, by default). Specified as month/day/year.
-f days	Sets the number of days an account remains active after its password expires.
-g group	Sets a group.
-m	Creates user's home directory, if it does not exist.
-m -k skl-dir	Sets the skeleton directory that holds skeleton files, such as .profile files, which are copied to the user's home directory automatically when it is created; the default is /etc/skel.
-M	Does not create user's home directory.
-p password	Supplies an encrypted password (crypt or MD5). With no argument, the account is immediately disabled.
-r	A Red Hat and Fedora–specific option that creates a system account (one whose user ID is lower than the minimum set in logon.defs). No home directory is created unless specified by -m.
-s shell	Sets the login shell of the new user. This is /bin/bash by default, the BASH shell.
-u userid	Sets the user ID of the new user. The default is the increment of the highest number used so far.

usermod

The usermod command enables you to change the values for any of these features. You can change the home directory or the user ID. You can even change the username for the account. The usermod command takes the same options as useradd, listed in Table 13-2.

userdel

When you want to remove a user from the system, you can use the userdel command to delete the user's login. With the -r option, the user's home directory will also be removed. In the next example, the user chris is removed from the system:

```
sudo userdel -r chris
```

Passwords

One common operation performed from the command line is to change a password. The easiest way to change your password on the GNOME desktop is to use GNOME Users and then select your account. Click the Password entry. The Changing Password dialog opens, in which you enter your current password and then the new password.

Alternatively, you can use the passwd command. If you are using GNOME or KDE, you first must open a terminal window (Terminal). Then, at the shell prompt, enter the passwd command. The command prompts you for your current password. After entering your current password and pressing Enter, you are then prompted for your new password. After entering the new password, you are asked to reenter it. This ensures that you have actually entered the password you intended to enter.

```
$ passwd
Old password:
New password:
Retype new password:
$
```

Administrative users can also use the passwd command to change the password of any user. Precede the command with sudo and add the username whose password you want to change.

```
sudo passwd georgep
```

Display Configuration and Vendor Drivers

Your desktop display is implemented by the X Window System running on the Wayland server. The version used on Fedora is X.org. X.org provides its own drivers for various graphics cards and monitors. You can find out more about X.org at `https://www.x.org/wiki/`.

X.org will automatically detect most hardware. The `/etc/X11/` configuration files will usually hold only keyboard and graphics card information. All other information, such as monitors, will be automatically determined. Should you want to change the screen resolution, use the GNOME Settings ➤ Devices ➤ Displays tab.

As an alternative, you could download and install the drivers and video configuration tools supplied by graphics card vendors such as ATI or NVIDIA. These are provided by RPM Fusion's `nonfree` repository (`http://rpmfusion.org`), when they become available. Due to licensing issues, they are not part of the Fedora repository. Once they are installed, you can use their configurations tools to configure your display. The vendor drivers often provide many more options than the open source X.org drivers, although the X.org drivers tend to be more stable.

The situation is complicated by the fact that Fedora Linux now uses the new Wayland display drivers as the default instead of the X.org drivers. Wayland is the future replacement for X.org but is still under development. Use the following command to see what type of driver you are using.

```
echo $XDG_SESSION_TYPE
```

Though the AMD drives usually work well with Wayland, the NVIDIA drivers are still a work in progress. The Xorg drivers do work, so you would switch to Xorg from Wayland, and install the NVIDIA Xorg drivers.

To use Xorg instead, edit the `/etc/gdm/custom.conf` file and remove the comment character, #, from the following line in the [`daemon`] section.

```
#WaylandEnable=false
```

You can use `nano` to edit it.

```
sudo nano /etc/gdm/custom.conf
```

Because the vendor drivers are designed to work across all distributions, they may conflict with the Fedora X Window System configuration. It is recommended that you use the RPM Fusion packages for the AMD or NVIDIA drivers. These are the same vendor drivers, but with slight configuration modification to ensure Fedora compatibility.

If your X Window System fails to start, you can log in to the command-line interface version (runlevel) by editing your boot loader and placing a 3 at the end of the kernel line. Use the **e** key to edit a line, and **b** to boot when finished.

Bluetooth

Bluetooth is a wireless connection method for locally connected devices such as keyboards, mice, printers, and Bluetooth-capable cell phones. BlueZ is the official Linux Bluetooth protocol and is integrated into the Linux kernel. BlueZ is the official Linux Bluetooth protocol and is integrated into the Linux kernel. The BlueZ protocol was developed originally by Qualcomm and is now an open source project, located at http://www.bluez.org/. It is included in the bluez and bluez-libs packages, among others. Check the BlueZ site for a complete list of supported hardware.

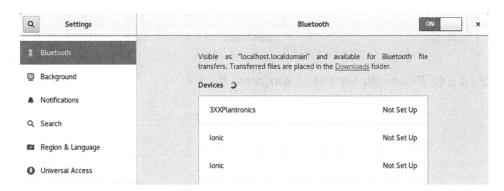

Figure 13-13. *Bluetooth settings (GNOME settings)*

If you have Bluetooth devices attached to your system, a Bluetooth entry is displayed on the system status area menu on the top panel. It will display a message showing the number of connected devices if there are any. Click the entry to display items to turn off Bluetooth and for Bluetooth Settings. Should you turn off Bluetooth, Bluetooth will be disabled, and its entry removed from the system status area menu. Use the Bluetooth Settings dialog, accessible from the Settings dialog, to turn it on again.

The Bluetooth Settings entry in the System Status Area menu to open GNOME Settings to the Bluetooth tab (see Figure 13-13). You can also access Bluetooth tab on GNOME Settings directly. On the Bluetooth settings tab, a Bluetooth switch at the top right lets you turn Bluetooth on or off. Detected devices are listed in the Devices section at the center. Initially, devices are disconnected (see Figure 13-14). Click on a device entry to connect it. A dialog opens with a detected pin number, which you confirm. Then the device configuration dialog is displayed, with a switch to connect or disconnect the device (see Figure 13-15). Pair, type, and address information are also displayed. If the device supports sound, a Sound Setting button is shown, which opens the Sound tab in Settings that displays that device (see Figure 13-16). To remove the device configuration, click the Remove Device button.

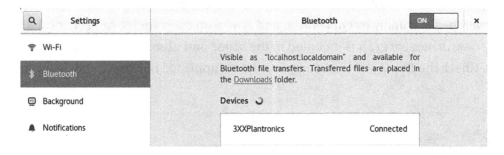

Figure 13-14. *Bluetooth Settings: Connected device*

Figure 13-15. *Bluetooth device configuration*

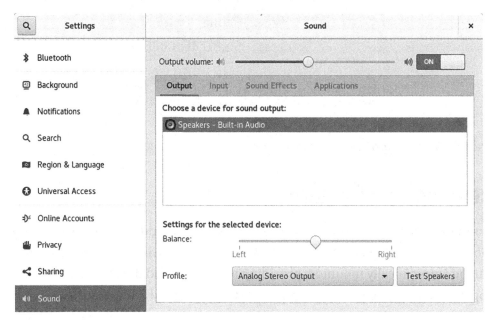

Figure 13-16. *Bluetooth sound*

When connecting to a phone (see Figure 13-17), a pin number is detected and displayed. On the configuration dialog, you can choose to connect or disconnect. If you enable a phone to operate as a mobile phone network device (PAN/NAP), then a new entry appears for the device in the system status area menu, which you can expand to list the entries: Use as Internet Connection and Mobile Broadband Setting. When you click the Use as Internet Connection entry, it will change to a Turn Off entry, once you have connected.

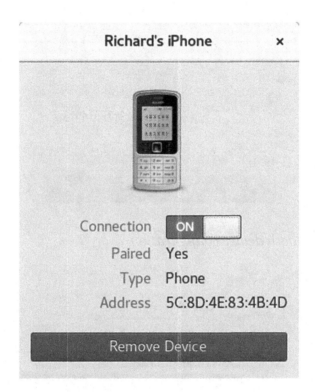

Figure 13-17. Bluetooth for phones

Accessing File Systems

Various file systems can be accessed on Fedora easily. Any additional internal hard drive partitions on your system, both Linux and Windows NTFS, will be automatically detected and can be automatically mounted, providing immediate and direct access from your desktop. In addition, you can access remote Windows shared folders and make your own shared folders accessible.

Access Linux File Systems on Internal Drives

Other Linux file systems on internal hard drives will be detected by Fedora automatically. Icons for them will be displayed by clicking the Other Locations entry of any file manager window's sidebar. Initially, the drive will not be mounted. To mount a file system for the first time, click its icon. You are first prompted to enter your password. Your file system is then mounted. The file system will be mounted under the /media directory and given a folder with the name of the file system label, or, if unlabeled, with the device name. The drive is displayed on the file manager sidebar, with an eject button shown to the right of its entry. To remove the drive, click the eject button for the drive on any file manager window.

Any user with administrative access on the primary console is authorized to mount file systems. You can use the PolicyKit agent to expand or restrict this level of authorization, as well as enabling access for specific users. Users without administrative access are prompted for authentication. Once granted, authentication access will remain in place for a limited time, allowing you to mount other file systems without having to enter your password. These file systems will then be automatically mounted, provided you have left the Remember Authorization checked in the Authenticate window.

Access to Local Windows NTFS File Systems

Linux NTFS (Windows) file system support is installed automatically. Your NTFS partitions are mounted using FUSE, Filesystem in Userspace. The same authentication control used for Linux file systems applies to NTFS file systems. Icons for the NTFS partitions will be displayed by clicking the Other Locations entry of a file manager window's sidebar. Click an entry to mount it. Your NTFS file system is then mounted as a removable device with an eject button appearing in its file manager window. Click the eject button to unmount the device.

The partitions will be mounted under the /run/media directory with their labels used as folder names. If they have no labels, they are given the UUID (Universally Unique Identifier) name as listed in the /dev/disks/by-uuid directory. The UUID is a complex number that uniquely identifies the hard disk device. The NTFS partitions are mounted using ntfs-3g drivers.

Access to Local Network Windows NTFS File Systems

Shared Windows folders and printers on any of the computers connected to your local network are automatically accessible from your Fedora desktop. The DNS discovery service (Avahi) automatically detects hosts on your home or local network and will let you access any of their shared folders directly.

To access the shared folders, click the Other Locations entry of a file manager sidebar (see Figure 13-18). Click the Windows Network icon to see just the Windows machines. However, local systems cannot access your shared folders until you install the Samba sharing server (Samba for Windows systems and NFS for Linux/UNIX systems).

You can also access any shared folder on another Windows host by entering its address in the Connect to Server box at the bottom of the Other Location window. The address of a Windows share always begins with **smb://**. In Figure 3-19, entering the address smb://myshared-data opened the myshared-data shared folder on the richard-asus host.

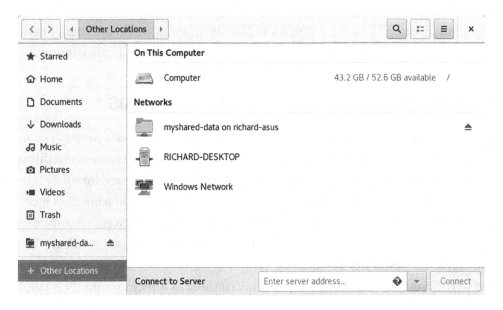

Figure 13-18. *Network places*

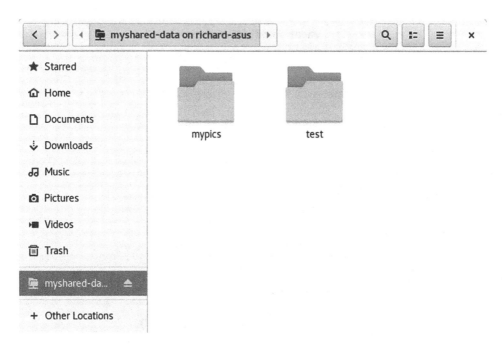

Figure 13-19. *Remote shares*

Permissions on GNOME

On GNOME, you can set a folder or file permission using the Permissions panel in its Properties window (see Figure 13-20).

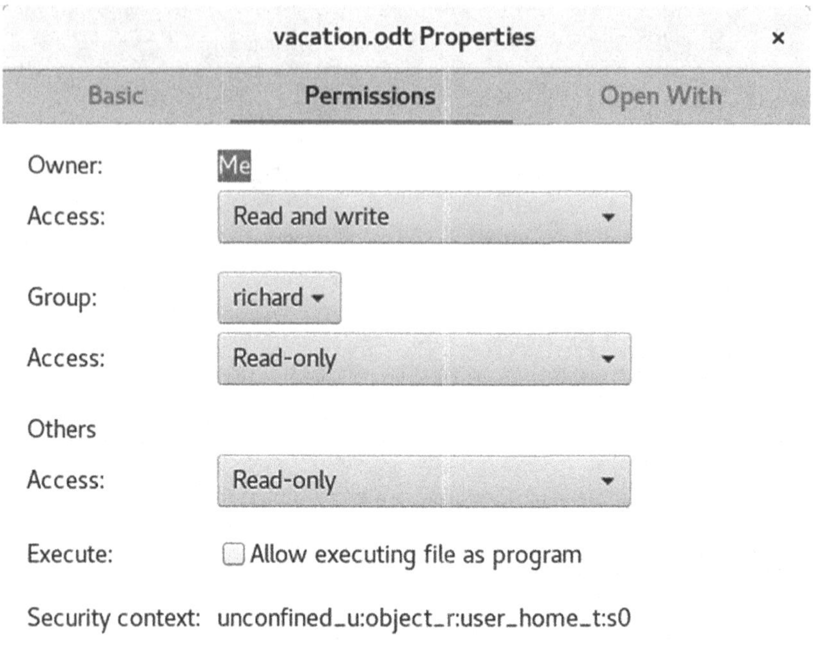

vacation.odt Properties   ×

| Basic | **Permissions** | Open With |

Owner: Me

Access: Read and write   ▼

Group: richard ▾

Access: Read-only   ▼

Others

Access: Read-only   ▼

Execute: ☐ Allow executing file as program

Security context: unconfined_u:object_r:user_home_t:s0

Figure 13-20. *File permissions*

For files, right-click the file icon or entry in the file manager window and select Properties. Then select the Permissions tab. Here you will find menus for read and write permissions, along with entries for Owner, Group, and Others. You can set owner permissions as Read-Only or Read and Write. For the Group and Others, you can also set the None option, denying access. The group name expands to a menu listing different groups; select one to change the file's group. If you want to execute this as an application (say, a shell script), check the Allow Executing File as Program entry. This has the effect of setting the execute permission.

The Permissions tab for folders (directories) Properties dialog operates much the same way, with Access menus for Owner, Group, and Others (see Figure 13-21, left). The Access menu controls access to the folder with options for List Files Only, Access Files, and Create and Delete Files. These correspond to the read, read and execute, and read/write/execute permissions given to folders. The File Access option lets you set permissions for all those files in the folder. They are the same as for files: for the owner, Read or Read and Write. The group and others access menus add a None option to deny access. To set the permissions for all the files in the folder accordingly (not just the folder), click the Change Permissions for Enclosed Files button to open a dialog in which you can specify the owner, group, and others permissions for files and folders in the folder (see Figure 13-21, right).

Note   You can also use the chmod command in a terminal window to change file and folder permissions.

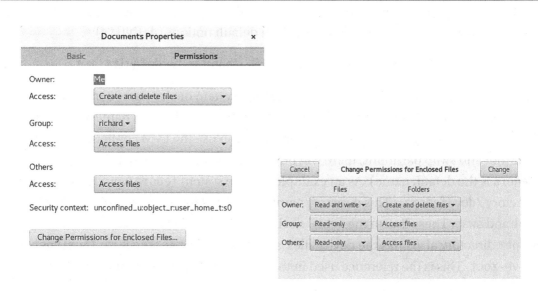

Figure 13-21. *Folder permissions*

Automatic File System Mounts with /etc/fstab

Although most file systems are automatically mounted for you, there may be instances where you require a file system to be mounted manually. Using the mount command, you can do this directly, or you can specify the mount operation in the /etc/fstab file to have it mounted automatically. Make sure your file system is labeled. Fedora uses labels to identify file systems, not device names. If you have to find out the device name of an unlabeled disk, you can use the fdisk command or the GParted tools, to list all your hard disks, their partitions, and their current device names. You can then use the ext2label command to label a file system. GParted is not installed by default but is available on the Fedora Software repository (use Software or Packages to install it).

All file systems are uniquely identified by their UUID. These are listed in the /dev/ disk/by-id directory (or with the sudo blkid command).

sudo blkid

Fedora will use the UUID to identify any unlabeled file system. In the /etc/fstab file, the file system partition devices are listed as a comment and then followed by the actual file system mount operation, using the UUID. The following example mounts the boot file system on a partition identified as 81acc8a9-128a-4860-bae3-999bfee5e0f5 to the /boot directory as an ext4 file system with default options (defaults):

UUID=81acc8a9-128a-4860-bae3-999bfee5e0f5 /boot ext4 defaults 1 1

LVM file systems are already labeled. LVM file system device names are located in the /dev directory with a directory for the volume group and device names within that directory for each logical volume in that group. If you use the LVM configuration for your root and swap partitions, there will be a fedora subdirectory in the /dev directory (fedora is the default name). As an example, the file system fedora would have an LVM directory /dev/fedora/. This directory would hold links for the root and swap volumes, root and swap. These link to the actual device files in the /dev directory. The /dev/ mapper directory also links the device files, such as /dev/mapper/fedora_localhost- -live-root. This is the reference used in the /etc/fstab file to mount the LVM root partition.

```
/dev/mapper/fedora_localhost--live-root    ext4        defaults        1 1
```

If you installed Fedora as fresh install (not an upgrade), you may have to use a mount operation to mount any LVM file systems you had previously. In this case, you would place an entry for the mount operation in the /etc/fstab file. The LVM device name is in the /etc/fstab file. In the following example, the Linux file system labeled mydata1 is mounted to the /mydata1 directory as an ext4 file system type. In addition, an LVM file system, mymedia, is mounted to the /mymedia directory. The logical volume mymedia is part of the logical group, mymedia, which is a directory in the /dev directory, /dev/ mymedia/myvideo.

```
/etc/fstab
UUID=81acc8a9-128a-4860-bae3-999bfee5e0f5 /boot ext4    defaults        1 1
/dev/mapper/fedora_localhost--live-root  /     ext4    defaults        1 1
/dev/mapper/fedora_localhost--live-swap swap   swap    defaults        0 0
/dev/mymedia/myvideo                /mymedia   ext4    defaults        1 1
LABEL=mydata1                       /mydata1   ext4    defaults        1 1
```

To mount manually, use the mount command and specify the type with the -t ext4 option. Use the -L option to mount by label. List the file system first and then the directory name to which it will be mounted. For a NTFS partition, type ntfs. The mount option has the format:

```
mount -t type  filesystem  directory
```

The following example mounts the mydata1 file system to the /mydata1 directory:

```
mount -t ext4  -L mydata1  /mydata1
```

Editing Configuration Files Directly

Although the administrative tools will handle all configuration settings for you, there may be times when you need to make changes by directly editing the configuration files. These are usually text files in the /etc directory or dot files in a user home directory, such as .bash_profile. System configuration files are normally located in the /etc, /usr/share, and /etc/default directories. To change system configuration files, you will need administrative access, requiring you to first log in as the root user. User configuration files are located in dot files in the user's home directory and don't require any administrative access. They can be accessed directly by the user.

You cannot use the gedit text editor to edit system configuration files. Nor can you log in as the root user with the GNOME or KDE desktops. Because you can no longer log in to a desktop user interface as the root user, you must log in through the command-line interface. To edit any of the system-wide configuration files, such as those in the /etc directory, you must first have root user access. This you can specify with the sudo command preceding a command-line editor command. Alternatively, you can use the sudo su command to log in as the root user.

As you can no longer log in to the desktop (unless manually configured) as root, you cannot edit system files with a desktop editor like gedit. Instead, you must use a command-line interface editor like vi, nano, Leafpad, or Emacs. Most command-line editors provide a screen-based interface that makes displaying and editing a file fairly simple. Two standard command-line editors are installed by default on your system, vi and nano. In addition, you can install Leafpad or Emacs. Leafpad is easier to use from a terminal window than nano. It will provide mouse support for menus and for editing. Emacs is much more powerful, but, like vi, is more complex.

The nano editor is a simple screen-based editor that lets you visually edit your file, using arrow and page keys to move around the file. You use control keys to perform actions. Pressing Ctrl+x will exit and prompt you to save the file; pressing Ctrl+o will save it. You start nano with the nano command. To edit a configuration file, you will require administrative access, so you would have to use the sudo command. Figure 13-22 shows the nano editor being used to edit the /etc/default/grub file.

```
sudo nano /etc/default/grub
```

Figure 13-22. *The nano editor and system configuration files*

Unlike system configuration files, user configuration files (dot files) can be changed by individual users directly. To edit user configuration files, you can use a standard editor, such as vi or Emacs, though one of the easiest ways to edit them is to use the gedit editor on the GNOME desktop.

For gedit, user configuration files do not show up automatically. Dot files (hidden files) like .bash_profile have to be chosen from the file manager window, not from the gedit open operation. First, configure the file manager to display dot files. Open any file manager window and, from the View menu, click the Show Hidden Files entry. All your user configuration files will be displayed. Usually you can then just double-click the file to open it in the gedit text editor. Alternatively, you can right-click the file and select Open with Text Editor from the pop-up menu (see Figure 13-23). Gedit will let you edit several files at once, opening a tabbed pane for each. You can use gedit to edit any text file, including ones you create yourself.

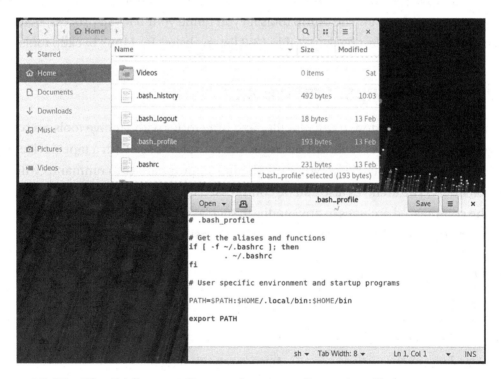

Figure 13-23. *The Gedit text editor and user configuration files*

> **Note**   Be careful when editing your configuration files. Editing mistakes can corrupt your configurations. It is advisable to make a backup of any configuration files you are working on first, before making major changes to the original.

Backup Management: rsync, Déjà Dup, and Amanda

Backup operations have become an important part of administrative duties. Several backup tools are provided on Linux systems, including Amanda and the traditional dump/restore tools, as well as the `rsync` command for making individual copies. Déjà Dup is a frontend for the duplicity backup tool, which uses `rsync` to generate backup archives. Amanda provides server-based backups, letting different systems on a network back up to a central server. The dump tools let you refine your backup process, detecting data changed since the last backup. Table 13-3 lists websites for Linux backup tools.

Individual Backups: archive and rsync

You can back up and restore particular files and directories with archive tools such as `tar`, restoring the archives later. For backups, `tar` is usually used with a tape device. To automatically schedule backups, you can schedule appropriate `tar` commands with the `cron` utility. The archives also can be compressed for storage savings. You can then copy the compressed archives to any medium, such as a DVD, USB drive, or tape. On GNOME, you can use File Roller to create archives easily (Archive Manager).

Table 13-3. *Backup Resources*

Websites	Application
`http://rsync.samba.org`	`rsync` remote copy backup
`http://amanda.org`	Amanda network backup
`http://dump.sourceforge.net`	Dump and restore tools
`https://launchpad.net/deja-dup` `www.nongnu.org/duplicity`	Déjà Dup frontend for duplicity, which uses `rsync` to perform basic backups

If you want to remote-copy a directory or files from one host to another, making a particular backup, you can use rsync, which is designed for network backups of particular directories or files, intelligently copying only those files that have been changed, rather than the contents of an entire directory. In archive mode, it can preserve the original ownership and permissions, provided corresponding users exist on the host system. The following example copies the /home/george/myproject directory to the /backup directory on the host rabbit, creating a corresponding myproject subdirectory. The -t specifies that this is a transfer. The remote host is referenced with an attached colon, rabbit:.

```
rsync -t /home/george/myproject   rabbit:/backup
```

As a precaution, you could first perform a dry run to see what actions your rsync operation will perform. Use the -n option to perform the dry run and add the -v option for details (verbose).

```
rsync -nvt /home/george/myproject   rabbit:/backup
```

If, instead, you wanted to preserve the ownership and permissions of the files, you would use the -a (archive) option. Adding a -z option will compress the file. The -v option provides a verbose mode.

```
rsync -avz   /home/george/myproject   rabbit:/backup
```

A trailing slash on the source will copy the contents of the directory, rather than generating a subdirectory of that name. Here the contents of the myproject directory are copied to the george-project directory:

```
rsync -avz   /home/george/myproject/   rabbit:/backup/george-project
```

The rsync command is configured to use the SSH remote shell by default. You can specify it or an alternate remote shell to use with the -e option. For secure transmission, you can encrypt the copy operation with ssh. Either use the -e ssh option or set the RSYNC_RSH variable to ssh.

```
rsync -avz -e ssh   /home/george/myproject   rabbit:/backup/myproject
```

As when using rcp, you can copy from a remote host to the one you are on.

```
rsync -avz   lizard:/home/mark/mypics/   /pic-archive/markpics
```

You can also run `rsync` as a server daemon. This will allow remote users to sync copies of files on your system with versions on their own, transferring only changed files, rather than entire directories. Many mirror and software FTP sites operate as `rsync` servers, letting you update files without having to download the full versions again. Configuration information for `rsync` as a server is kept in the `/etc/rsyncd.conf` file. On Fedora, `rsync` as a server is managed through `systemd`, using the `/lib/systemd/system/rsyncd.service` file, which starts `rsync` with the `-daemon` option. You can enable it with the `systemctl` command.

```
sudo systemctl enable rsyncd.service
```

You can then start and stop it with the `service` command in a terminal window. Be sure to use the `sudo` command.

```
sudo service rsyncd start
```

Deja Dup

Deja Dup is a frontend for the duplicity backup tool, which uses `rsync` to generate backup archives (`http://www.nongnu.org/duplicity/`). Once installed, you can access Deja Dup from Utilities ➤ Backups.

The `deja-dup` settings dialog shows tabs for Overview, Folders to Save, Folders to Ignore, Storage Location, and Scheduling (see Figure 13-24). A switch at the top right of the dialog allows you to turn automatic backups on and off. The Overview tab provides information about your backup configuration with buttons to restore from a backup and to manually perform a backup, as well as the time of the next scheduled backup.

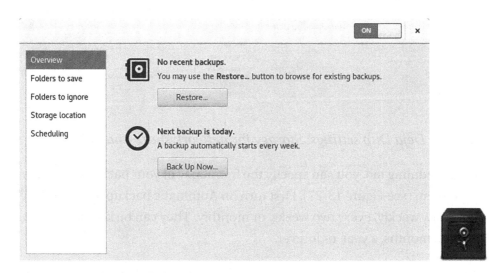

Figure 13-24. *Overview of Deja Dup settings*

The Folders to Save tab lets you specify folders you want to back up and folders to ignore (see Figure 13-25). Click the plus button (+) at the bottom of the folders list to add a new folder for backup. Do the same to specify folders to ignore. The minus button removes folders from the list. Your home folder has been added already. The Folders to Ignore tab specifies folders you do not want to back up. The Downloads and Trash folders are selected initially.

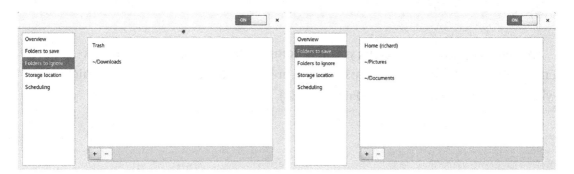

Figure 13-25. *Deja Dup settings: Folders to save and ignore*

The Storage Location tab lets you specify a location to store your backups (see Figure 13-26). You can choose different locations, such as a network server, a cloud account, or a local folder. Choose the one you want from the Backup location menu. With each choice, you are prompted for the appropriate configuration information.

Figure 13-26. *Deja Dup settings: Storage for network share and Local folder*

On the Scheduling tab, you can specify the frequency of your backups and how long to keep them (see Figure 13-27). First turn on Automatic backup. Backups can be performed daily, weekly, every two weeks, or monthly. They can be kept for a week, month, several months, a year, or forever.

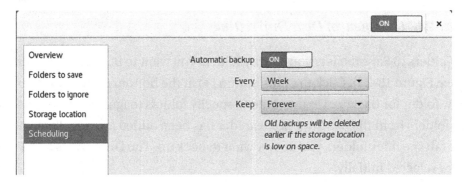

Figure 13-27. *Deja Dup settings: Backup times*

When you perform a backup, you are prompted to back up with or without encryption. For encrypted backups, you are prompted to enter a password, which you will need to restore the files (see Figure 13-28).

Figure 13-28. *Deja Dup backup: Encryption*

When restoring, you are prompted to specify the location you are backing up from, the backup date to restore from, and whether to restore to the original location or a specific folder (see Figure 13-29).

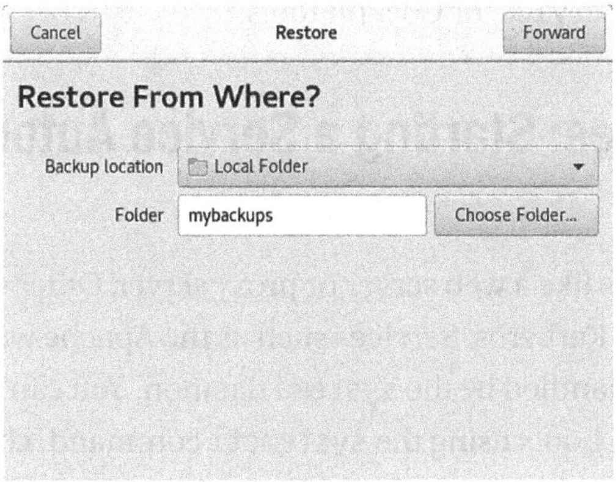

Figure 13-29. *Deja Dup restore*

Amanda

To back up hosts connected to a network, you can use the Advanced Maryland Automatic Network Disk Archiver (Amanda) to archive hosts. Amanda uses `tar` tools to back up all hosts to a single host operating as a backup server. Backup data is sent by each host to the host operating as the Amanda server, where they are written out to a backup medium such as tape. With an Amanda server, the backup operations for all hosts become centralized in one server, instead of each host having to perform its backup. Any host that has to restore data simply requests it from the Amanda server, specifying the file system, date, and filenames. Backup data is copied to the server's holding disk and from there to tapes. Detailed documentation and updates are provided at `http://amanda.org`.

Managing Services

You can select certain services to run and the special target (runlevel) at which to run them. Most services are servers like a web server or FTP server. Other services provide security, such as SSH or Kerberos. You can decide which services to use with the `chkconfig`, `systemctl`, `service`, or Cockpit tools.

Enabling Services: Starting a Service Automatically at Boot

Most services are servers like a web server or proxy server. Other services provide security, such as SSH or Kerberos. Services such as the Apache web server, Samba server, and the FTP server are handled by the `systemd` daemon. You can decide which services to start when the system boots using the `systemctl` command. `chkconfig`, `service`, and Cockpit are simply frontends to the `systemctl` command.

To have a service start up at boot, you need to first enable it using the `systemctl` tool as the root user. Use the `enable` command to enable the service. The following commands enable the `vsftpd` server and the Samba server (`smb`). The `systemctl` command uses the service's service configuration file located in the `/lib/systemd/system` directory.

```
sudo systemctl enable vsftpd
sudo systemctl enable smb
```

Managing Services Manually

Use the start, stop, and restart commands with systemctl to manually start, stop, and restart a service. The enable command starts a service automatically. You can choose to start it manually when you wish using the start command. You can stop and restart a service any time using the stop and restart commands. The condrestart command starts the server only if it is already stopped. Use the status command to check the current status of a service.

```
sudo systemctl start vsftpd
sudo systemctl restart vsftpd
sudo systemctl condrestart vsftpd
sudo systemctl stop vsftpd
sudo systemctl status vsftpd
```

You can also use the service command and Cockpit to start, stop, or restart a service. These are simply frontends for the systemctl command that performs the actual operation using systemd.

```
sudo service start vsftpd
```

Cockpit

The Cockpit management console (under development by Red Hat) provides a web interface for managing both system administration and Internet servers on your system, as well as servers on your network (http://cockpit-project.org). The web interface works best on a desktop system (Fedora workstation). You can use it to manage your system resources, including services, storage, and networking. Once you install Cockpit, be sure to enable it with systemd, which then allows access by your firewall for both Cockpit and HTTPS. The package name is cockpit.

```
sudo dnf install cockpit
sudo systemctl start cockpit
sudo firewall-cmd --permanent --add-service=cockpit
```

You can access Cockpit using a web browser and accessing port 9090 on your local system, localhost:9090. If you install on the workstation, a Cockpit icon is displayed on the Applications Overview. You click it to open Cockpit in your default browser.

The Cockpit page initially prompts you for your username and password. It then shows a listing of the systems on your network. Upon clicking one, you will see links on the left side for administration categories such as system administration, services, networking, and storage. Click on the services link to manage your services. Then click the System Services tab to list the enabled and disabled service, including the network services such as the Apache Web server and the vsftpd FTP server (see Figure 13-30). Click on a service to open a page where you can manage service. Buttons to the right show the current status. Clicking on an arrow button to the right displays a menu for actions you may want to take, such as stopping or restarting a service. If you disable a service, it is moved down to the disabled list. Enabling a service moves it up to the enabled list.

Figure 13-30. *Services: Cockpit*

Cockpit dynamically updates with systemctl. Should you make changes in a terminal window using systemctl, the changes are immediately shown on Cockpit.

chkconfig

To configure a service to start up automatically when the system boots, you also can use the chkconfig tool, which runs on a command line. The chkconfig command uses the on and off options to select and deselect services for startup.

```
sudo chkconfig smb on
```

The chkconfig tool has been modified to work with systemd. You can use chkconfig to turn services on or off (enable or disable). Though chkconfig can turn the systemd service on or off, it was still designed for use by System V services. chkconfig with the --list option lists only System V services, which may not be valid. The reset command does not work with systemd services.

You use the on option to have a service enabled, and the off option to disable it.

```
sudo chkconfig httpd on
sudo chkconfig httpd off
```

The service Command

The service command is now simply a frontend for the systemctl command, which performs the actual operation using systemd. The service command cannot enable or disable services. It only performs management operations such as stop, restart, and status. To start and stop services manually, you can use either Cockpit or the service command. With the service command, you enter the service name with the stop argument to stop it, the start argument to start it, and the restart argument to restart it. The service command is run from a Terminal window. You will have to first log in as the root user, using the sudo command, or use the sudo command if configured. The following will start the smb Samba service.

```
sudo service smb start
```

In Fedora, the systemd version of the service command actually invokes the systemctl command to run the service's systemd .service unit file in /lib/systemd/system. If a service is not enabled, systemd will enable it. You can perform the same operations as the service command, using the systemctl command. The following is the equivalent of the previous command.

```
sudo systemctl start smb
```

Printing

This section covers the printing-configuration tools: the GNOME Printers tool (GNOME Settings ➤ Devices ➤ Printers) and the older system-config-printer tool (Sundry ➤ Print Settings). Most printers are detected for you automatically. You can use the GNOME Settings Printers tool to turn them on or off and access their print queues. As an alternative, you can still use the older system-config-printer. Both are frontends for the Common UNIX Printing System (CUPS), which provides printing services (www.cups.org).

When you attach a local printer to your system for the first time, the GNOME Printers tool automatically detects the printer and installs the appropriate driver. A message appears briefly in the message tray, indicating that a new printer has been detected. The printer is then listed in both the GNOME Printers tool and in the older `system-config-printer`. If the detection fails, you can use the GNOME Printers tool, accessible from GNOME Settings ➤ Devices, to set up your printer.

KDE provides support for adding and configuring CUPS printers through the KDE System Settings➤ Printer Configuration dialog. Select the Printer Configuration icon under Hardware. USB printers that are automatically detected will be listed in the KDE Printer Configuration dialog.

Printers can be local or remote. Both are referenced using Universal Resource Identifiers (URI). URIs support both network protocols used to communicate with remote printers and device connections used to reference local printers.

Remote printers are referenced by the protocol used to communicate with them, including `ipp` for the Internet Printing Protocol used for UNIX network printers, `smb` for the Samba protocol used for Windows network printers, and `lpd` for the older LPRng UNIX print servers. Their URIs are similar to a web URL, indicating the network addresses of the system the printer is connected to.

```
ipp://mytsuff.com/printers/queue1
smb://guest@lizard/myhp
```

For attached local printers, the URI will use the device connection and the device name. The `usb:` prefix is used for USB printers; `parallel:` is used for older printers connected to a parallel port; `serial:` is used for printers connected to a serial port; and `scsi:` is used for SCSI-connected printers. For a locally attached USB printer, the URI would be something like the following:

```
usb://Canon/S330
```

GNOME Printers: GNOME Settings ➤ Devices

The GNOME Printers tool is accessible from the GNOME Settings ➤ Devices ➤ Printers tab. It lists installed printers, letting you configure them and access their job queues (see Figure 13-31). If no printers are detected, an Add button is displayed on the tab, which you can use to detect your printer. To detect additional printers, you can click the Add button. The Printers tab will list entries for detected and configured printers. A printer entry displays the printer name, model, status, a jobs button with the number of jobs, and a configuration button (gear icon). The jobs button to open a dialog listing active jobs for this printer (see Figure 13-32). For each job entry there are buttons to the right to pause or remove the job.

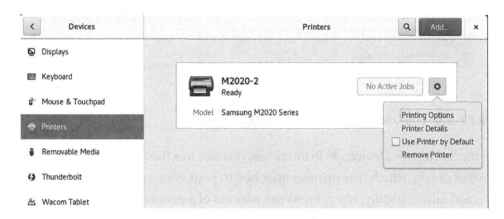

Figure 13-31. *GNOME Settings ➤ Devices ➤ Printers tab*

To configure a printer, click the configure button (gear icon) to display a menu with entries for the printer's options, details, default, and removal (see Figure 13-33). Choosing the Use Printer by Default makes it your default printer. The Remove Printer entry removes the printer configuration from your system. The Printer Details entry opens a dialog with printer's details, such as the name, location, address, and driver. There are buttons for selecting a driver from a search, database, or a PPD file. Clicking on the Printing Options entry opens the printer's options dialog (see Figure 13-33). You can configure printer features, such as page setup, image quality, and color. The Advanced tab lets you set specialized options, such as contrast, ink type, and saturation.

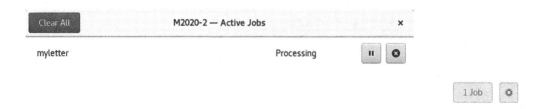

Figure 13-32. *GNOME Printers: Jobs*

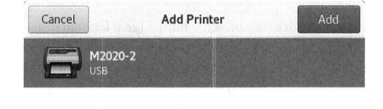

Figure 13-33. *GNOME Printers: Details and Options*

On the Settings ➤ Devices ➤ Printers tab, you can use the Add button to open the Add Printer dialog, which lists printers attached to your system (see Figure 13-34). They are detected automatically. If you know the address of a printer on your network, you can enter it in the search box at the bottom to have it detected and displayed.

Figure 13-34. *GNOME Printers: Add printer*

Remote Printers

To install a remote printer that is attached to a Windows system or another Linux system running CUPS, you specify its location using special URL protocols. For another CUPS printer on a remote host, the protocol used is `ipp`, for Internet Printing Protocol, whereas for a Windows printer, it would be `smb`. Older UNIX or Linux systems using LPRng would use the `lpd` protocol.

Be sure your firewall is configured to allow access to remote printers. On the Public Services tab (Zones tab) in `firewall-config` (Sundry ➤ Firewall), be sure that the Samba and IPP services are checked. Samba allows access for Windows printers, and IPP allows access for Internet Printer Protocol printers usually found on other Linux systems. There will be entries for the Samba client and server, as well as for the IPP client and server.

Shared Windows printers on any of the computers connected to your local network are automatically accessible once configured. Supporting Samba libraries are already installed and will let you access directly any of shared Windows printers. Should you want to share a printer on your Ubuntu computer with users on other computers, you must install Samba and have the Server Message Block services enabled, using the `smb` and `nmb` daemons. The Samba service should be enabled by default. If not, you can enable it using the `systemctl` command as the root user. Open a terminal window (Terminal) and then enter a `sudo systemctl` command for the `smb` and `nmb` servers with the `enable` command.

```
sudo systemctl enable nmb
sudo systemctl enable smb
```

On the GNOME Settings ➤ Devices ➤ Printers tab, click the Add button to open the Add Printer dialog that lists the printers attached to your system. If you know the address of a printer on your network, you can enter it in the search box at the bottom to have it detected and displayed. Remote systems that may have printers are also listed. Normally, these require authentication. Select the system you want to access and click the Authenticate button to open a dialog prompting you for a password.

Once you're granted access, the printers available on that system are listed (see Figure 13-34). To add a printer, select it and then click the Add button. This opens the Select Printer Driver dialog, from which you choose the manufacturer and then the printer model (see Figure 13-35).

Print Settings: system-config-printer

You can also use the older `system-config-printer` tool to edit a printer configuration or to add a remote printer. You can install the `system-config-printer` package, Printer Settings on GNOME Software. This utility enables you to select the appropriate driver for your printer, as well as set print options, such as paper size and print resolutions. You can configure a printer connected directly to your local computer or a printer on a remote system on your network. You can start `system-config-printer` by clicking the Print Settings icon from the Applications overview, Sundry subview. A Print Settings window is displayed, showing icons for installed printers. As you add printers, icons for them are displayed in the Print Settings window (see Figure 13-35).

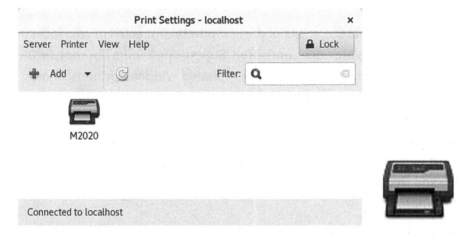

Figure 13-35.   *system-config-printer*

To see the printer settings, such as printer and job options, access controls, and policies, double-click the printer icon or right-click and select Properties. The Printer Properties window opens with six tabs: Settings, Policies, Access Control, Printer Options, Job Options, and Ink/Toner Levels (see Figure 13-36).

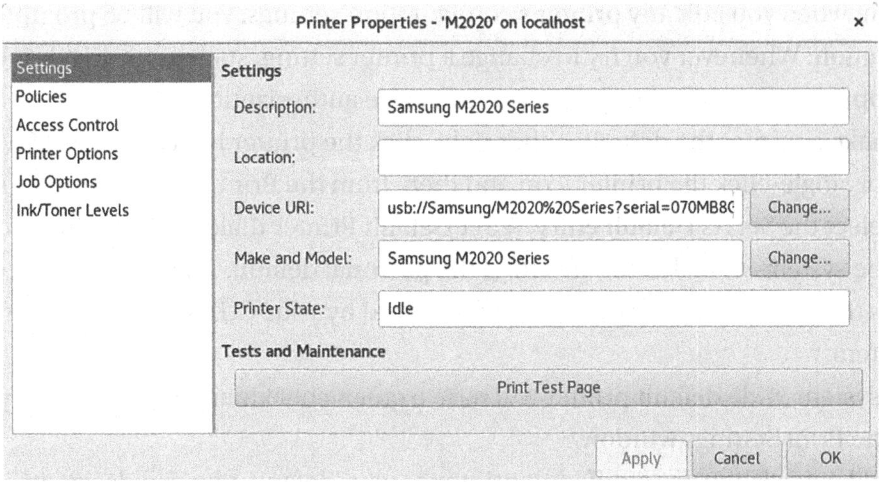

Figure 13-36. *system-config-printer: Printer Properties dialog*

The Print Settings window Printer menu lets you rename the printer, enable or disable it, and make it a shared printer. Select the printer icon and then click the Printer menu. The Delete entry will remove a printer configuration. Use the Set As Default entry to make the printer a system-wide or personal default printer. There are also entries for accessing the printer properties and viewing the print queue.

The Print Settings icon menu is accessed by right-clicking the printer icon. If the printer is already a default, there is no Set As Default entry. The Properties entry opens the printer properties window for that printer.

The View Print Queue entry opens the Document Print Status window, which lists the jobs for that printer. You can change the queue position as well as stop or delete jobs. From the toolbar, you can choose to display printed jobs and reprint them. You will be notified if a job should fail.

To check the server settings, select Settings from the Server menu. This opens a new window showing the CUPS printer server settings. The Common UNIX Printing System (CUPS) is the server that provides printing services (`www.cups.org`).

To select a particular CUPS server, select the Connect entry in the Server menu. This opens a Connect to CUPS Server window with a drop-down menu listing all current CUPS servers from which to choose.

To add, edit, or remove printers requires root-level access. You have to enter your root user password (set up initially during installation) to edit a printer configuration, add a new printer, or remove an old one. For example, when you try to access the printer server settings, you will be prompted to enter the root user password.

Again, when you edit any printer's configuration settings, you will be prompted for authorization. Whenever you try to change a printer setting, such as its driver or URI, you are prompted to enter the root password for device authorization.

To make a printer the default, either right-click the printer icon and select Set As Default or single-click the printer icon and then, from the Print Settings window's Printer menu, select the Set As Default entry. A Set Default Printer dialog opens with options for setting the system-wide default or setting the personal default. The system-wide default printer is the default for your entire network served by your CUPS server, not just your local system.

The system-wide default printer will have a green checkmark emblem on its printer icon in the Print Settings window.

Should you wish to use a different printer as your default, you can designate it as your personal default. To make a printer your personal default, select the entry Set as My Personal Default Printer in the Set Default Printer dialog. A personal emblem, a heart, will appear on the printer's icon in the Print Settings window.

If you have more than one printer on your system, you can make one the default by clicking the Make Default Printer button in the printer's properties Settings pane.

The Class entry in the New menu lets you create a printer class. You can access the New menu from the Server menu or from the New button. This feature lets you select a group of printers to print a job, instead of selecting just one. That way, if one printer is busy or down, another printer can be automatically selected to perform the job. Installed printers can be assigned to different classes.

To edit an installed printer, double-click its icon in the Print Settings window or right-click and select the Properties entry. This opens a Printer Properties window for that printer. A sidebar lists the configuration tabs. Click one to display that tab. There are configuration entries for Settings, Policies, Access Control, Printer Options, Job Options, and Ink/Toner Levels.

To install a new printer, choose the Server ➤ New ➤ Printer menu entry or click the Add button on the toolbar (see Figure 13-37). A New Printer window opens and displays a series of dialog boxes from which you select the connection, model, drivers, and printer name with location.

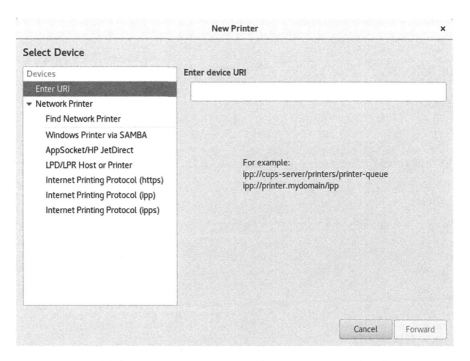

Figure 13-37. *system-config-printer: New Printer dialog*

You can also use `system-config-printer` to set up a remote printer on Linux, UNIX, or Windows networks. When you add a new printer or edit one, the New Printer/ Select Devices dialog will list possible remote connection types. When you select a remote connection entry, a pane will be displayed in which you can enter configuration information.

The location is specified using special URI protocols. For another CUPS printer on a remote host, the protocol used is `ipp`, for Internet Printing Protocol, whereas for a Windows printer, it is `smb`. Older UNIX and Linux systems using LPRng use the `lpd` protocol.

CHAPTER 14

Network Configuration

Network configuration is managed by Network Manager. Network configuration differs, depending on the kind of connection you have, such as a wired connection (Ethernet), a DSL modem, or a wireless connection. The GNOME Settings Wi-Fi and Network tabs are the primary network configuration tools for Fedora, which can be used to configure all your network connections manually. You can configure a variety of network connections, including wired settings, DSL, and WiFi, for the IPv4 and IPv6 protocols. Table 14-1 lists several different network configuration tools.

Network Information: Dynamic and Static

Most networks now support dynamic configuration using either the older Dynamic Host Configuration Protocol (DHCP) or the new IPv6 protocol and its automatic address configuration. In this case, you need only check the DHCP or automatic entry in most network configuration tools. For DHCP, a DHCP client on each host will obtain network connection information from a DHCP server serving that network. IPv6 generates its addresses directly from the device and router information, such as the device hardware MAC address.

© Richard Petersen 2018
R. Petersen, *Beginning Fedora Desktop*, https://doi.org/10.1007/978-1-4842-3882-0_14

Table 14-1. *Fedora Network Configuration Tools*

Network Configuration App	Description
Network Manager	Automatically configures wireless and wired network connections. Can also manually edit them.
GNOME Settings WiFi	GNOME Settings WiFi configuration tab (Settings ➤ Wi-Fi).
GNOME Settings Network	GNOME Settings Network configuration tab, used for wired, VPN, and Proxy connections (Settings ➤ Network).
nm-connection-editor	Network Connections: the older Network Manager configuration utility.
kde-plasma-networkmanagement	KDE version of Network Manager.
firewall-config	Sets up a network firewall using FirewallD server.
system-config-firewall	Sets up a network firewall using IPtables.
wvdial	PPP modem connection, enter on a command line.
wconfig	Wireless connection, enter on a command line.

If you have a static connection (no DHCP or IPv6 support), you have to provide connection information such as your IP address and DNS servers. If you are using a DSL dynamic, ISDN, or modem connection, you will also have to supply provider, login, and password information, whether your system is dynamic or static. You may also have to supply specialized information, such as DSL or modem compression methods or a dial-up number. You can obtain most of your static network information from your network administrator or ISP (Internet service provider).

User and System-Wide Network Configuration: Network Manager

Network Manager will automatically detect your network connections, both wired and wireless. It is the default method for managing your network connections. Network Manager uses the automatic device detection capabilities of udev to configure your connections. Should you instead have to configure your network connections manually, you would use the GNOME Settings Wi-Fi and Network tabs.

Network Manager is user specific. When a user logs in, it selects the network connection preferred by that user. For wireless connections, the user can choose from a list of current possible connections. For wired connections, a connection can be started automatically, when the system starts up. Initial settings will be supplied from the system-wide configuration.

Configurations can also be applied system-wide to all users. When editing or adding a network connection, the edit or add dialog displays an Available to All Users check box in the lower-left corner. Click this check box and then click the Apply button to make the connection configuration system-wide. A PolicyKit authentication dialog will first prompt you to enter your root password.

Network Manager can configure any network connection. This includes wired, wireless, and all manual connections. Network Interface Connection (NIC cards) hardware is detected using udev. udev is the userspace device manager that manages your devices, both fixed and removable. Information provided by Network Manager is available to other applications over D-Bus.

With multiple wireless access points for Internet connections, a system could have several different network connections to choose from, instead of a single-line connection such as DSL or cable. This is particularly true for notebook computers that access different wireless connections at different locations. Instead of manually configuring a new connection each time one is encountered, the Network Manager tool can automatically configure and select a connection to use.

By default, an Ethernet connection will be preferred, if available. For wireless connections, you will have to choose the one you want.

Network Manager is designed to work in the background, providing status information for your connection and switching from one configured connection to another, as needed. For initial configuration, it detects as much information as possible about the new connection.

Network Manager operates as a daemon with the name NetworkManager. If no Ethernet connection is available, Network Manager will scan for wireless connections, checking for Extended Service Set Identifiers (ESSIDs). If an ESSID identifies a previously used connection, then it is automatically selected. If several are found, then the most recently used one is chosen. If only a new connection is available, the Network Manager waits for the user to choose one. A connection is selected only if the user is logged in. If an Ethernet connection is later made, the Network Manager will switch to it from wireless.

The NetworkManager daemon can be turned on or off, using the systemctl command as the administrative user.

```
sudo systemctl start
sudo systemctl stop
```

Network Manager Manual Configuration Using GNOME Network

The GNOME Network configuration is available on GNOME Settings and you can use it to configure all your network connections manually. Automatic wireless and wired connections were covered in Chapter 3. On the GNOME Settings dialog there is a Wi-Fi tab for wireless configuration and a Network tab for wired, VPN, and proxy configurations (see Figure 14-1). On the Wi-Fi tab, an Airplane Mode switch and a list of visible wireless connections are listed to the right. The currently active connection will have a checkmark next to its name. On the top-right bar is a switch for turning wireless on and off. A menu to the right of the switch list entries for connections to hidden networks, turning on your computer's WiFi hotspot capability, and listing previously accessed WiFi networks.

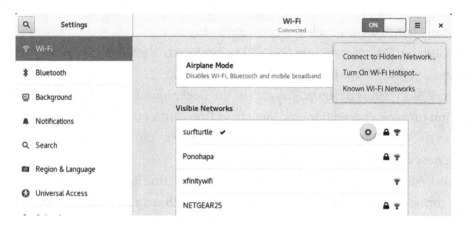

Figure 14-1. *WiFi (GNOME settings)*

Selecting an entry in the Visible Networks list will create a gear button for it, which you can click to open the network configuration dialog with tabs for Details, Security, Identity, IPv4, IPv6, and Reset. The Details tab shows strength, speed, security methods, IP and hardware addresses, routes, and the DNS server IP address. To edit the connection manually, you use the Security, Identity, and IP tabs. The Security tab displays a menu from which you can choose a security method and a password (see Figure 14-2).

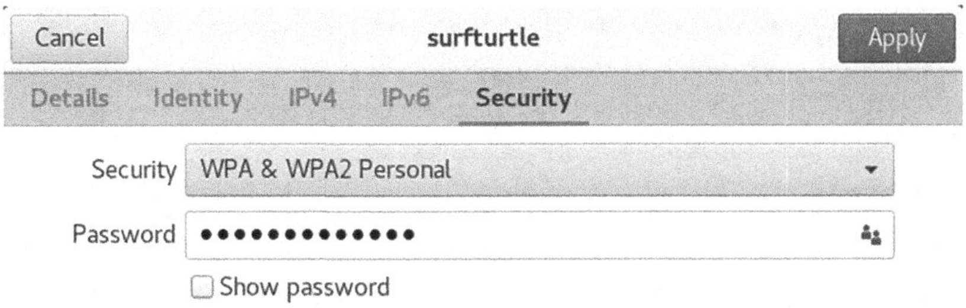

Figure 14-2. *WiFi (GNOME settings): Security tab*

On the Identity tab, you can specify the SSID name (see Figure 14-3).

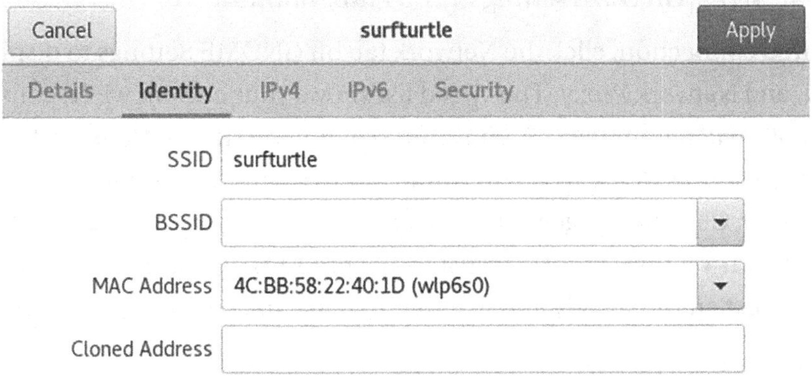

Figure 14-3. *WiFi (GNOME settings): Identity tab*

On the IPv4 Settings tab, a switch allows you to turn the IP connection on or off. There are sections for addresses, the DNS servers, and routes. An Addresses menu lets you choose the type of connection you want. By default, it is set to Automatic. If you change it to Manual, new entries appear for the address, netmask, and gateway (see Figure 14-4). On the IPv6 tab, the netmask is replaced by prefix. You can turn off Automatic switches for the DNS and Routes sections to make them manual. The DNS section has a plus button to let you add more DNS servers.

Cancel		surfturtle		Apply
Details	Identity	**IPv4**	IPv6	Security

IPv4 Method   ○ Automatic (DHCP)   ○ Link-Local Only

⦿ Manual   ○ Disable

Addresses

Address	Netmask	Gateway	
			⊗

DNS   Automatic `ON`

Separate IP addresses with commas

Routes   Automatic `ON`

Address	Netmask	Gateway	Metric	
				⊗

Figure 14-4. *WiFi (GNOME settings): IPv4 tab, manual*

For a wired connection, click the Network tab on GNOME Settings to display lists for Wired, VPN, and Network Proxy. The Wired list shows your current wired connections with on and off switches for each. A plus button at the top right of the Wired list lets you add more wired connections. Next to a connection's switch a gear button is displayed (see Figure 14-5). Clicking the gear button opens a configuration dialog with tabs for Details, Identity, IPv4, IPv6, and Security (see Figure 14-6). On the Details tab, you can choose to connect automatically and whether to make the connection system-wide.

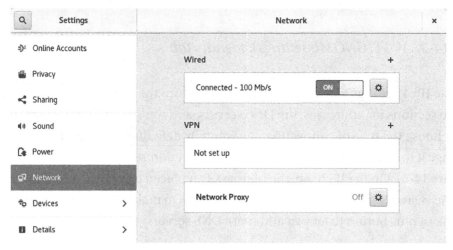

Figure 14-5. *Network (GNOME settings)*

Figure 14-6. *Network (GNOME settings)*

You can use the Security, Identity, and IP tabs to manually configure the connection. The Security tab lets you turn on 802.1x security and choose an authentication method, as well as provide a username and password (see Figure 14-7).

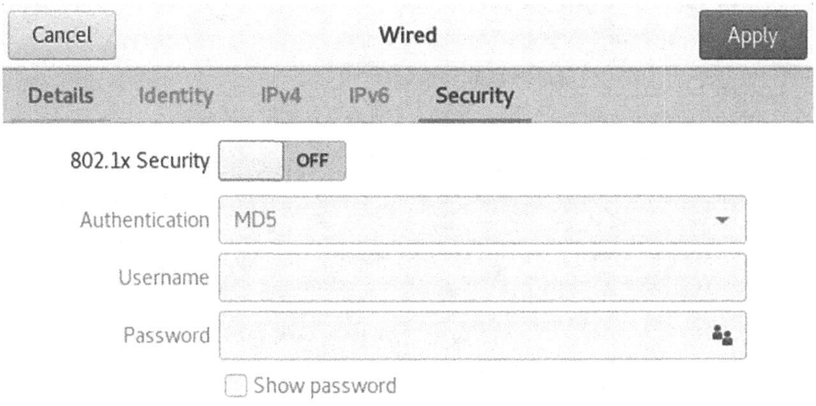

Figure 14-7. *Network (GNOME settings): Security tab*

On the Identity tab, you can set the name, choose the hardware address, set the MTU blocks (see Figure 14-8).

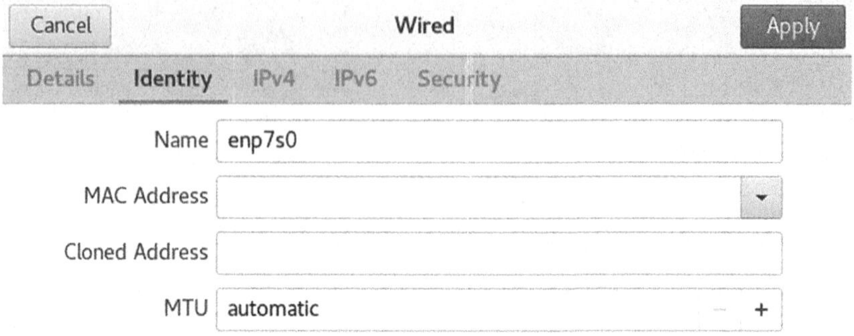

Figure 14-8. *Network (GNOME settings): Identity tab*

On the IP tab, a switch allows you to turn the connection on or off. The tab has sections for addresses, DNS servers, and routes. DNS and Routes have a switch for automatic. Turning the switch off allows you to manually enter a DNS server address or routing information. From the Method set of options at the top, you can also choose to make the connection automatic, manual, link-local, or to disable it. When the connection is set to manual, new entries appear that let you enter the address, netmask, and gateway (see Figure 14-9). On the IPv6 tab, the netmask entry is replaced with a prefix entry.

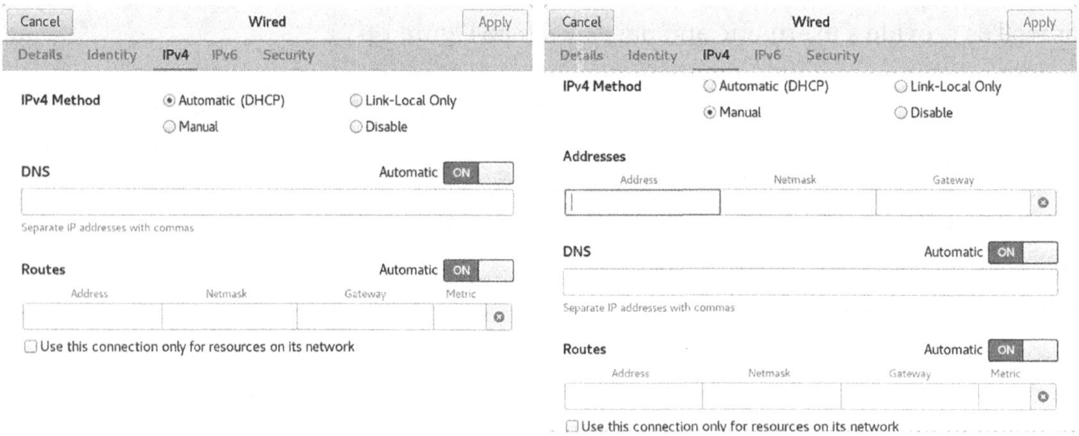

Figure 14-9. *Network (GNOME settings): IPv4 tab*

For VPN connections, click the plus button at the top right of the VPN list to open an Add VPN dialog. The dialog lists supported VPN connection types, such as Point-to-Point or OpenVPN (see Figure 14-10). The Bond, Bridge, and VLAN entries open the Network Connections dialogs for those connections.

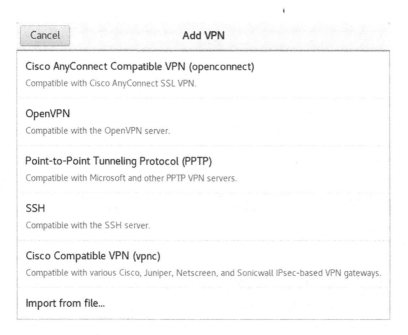

Figure 14-10. *Network (GNOME settings): new connections and VPN connections*

You can then configure the VPN connections from the Add VPN dialog, which shows three tabs: Identity, IPv4, and IPv6 (see Figure 14-11). The IP tabs are the same as for wireless and wired configuration dialogs. On the Identity tab, you can enter the name, gateway, and authentication information. Click the Advanced button for detailed connection configuration.

Several VPN services are available. The PPTP service for Microsoft VPN connections is installed by default. Other popular VPN services include OpenVPN, Cisco Concentrator, and Openswan (IPSec). Network Manager support is installed using the corresponding Network Manager plugin for these services. The plugin packages begin with the name network-manager. To use the openvpn service, first install the openvpn software along with the network-manager-openvpn plugin. For Cisco Concentrator-based VPN, use the network-manager-vpnc plugin. Openswan uses the network-manager-openswan plugin.

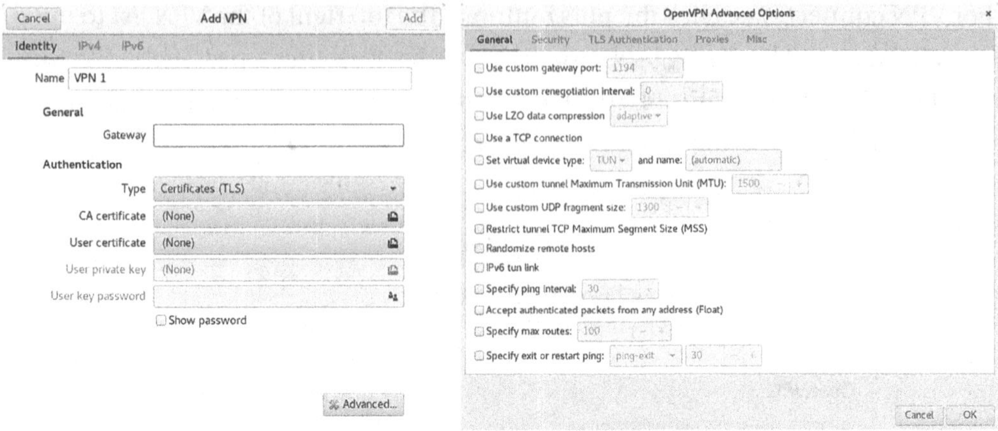

Figure 14-11. *Network (GNOME settings): OpenVPN connection*

Managing Network Connections with nmcli

The nmcli command is NetworkManager command-line interface command. Most
network configuration tasks can be performed by nmcli. The nmcli command manages
NetworkManager through a set of objects: general (g), networking (n), radio (r),
connection (c), device (d), and agent (a). Each can be referenced using the full name
or a unique prefix, such as con for connection or dev for device. The unique prefix can
be as short as a single character, such as g for general, c for connections, or d for device.
See Table 14-2 for a list of the objects and commonly used options. The nmcli man page
provides a complete listing with examples.

The general object shows the current status of NetworkManager and what kind of
devices are enabled. You can limit the information displayed using the -t (terse) and -f
(field) options. The STATE field shows the connection status, and the CONNECTIVITY field
shows the connection.

```
$ nmcli general
STATE        CONNECTIVITY  WIFI-HW  WIFI     WWAN-HW  WWAN
connected    full          enabled  enabled  enabled  enabled
$ nmcli -t -f STATE general
connected
```

The connection object references the network connection and the show option displays that information. The following example displays your current connection.

```
nmcli connection show
```

You can use c instead of connection and s instead of show.

```
$ nmcli c s
NAME        UUID                                  TYPE            DEVICE
enp7s0      f7202f6d-fc66-4b81-8962-69b71202efc0  802-3-ethernet  enp7s0
AT&T LTE 1  65913b39-789a-488c-9559-28ea6341d9e1  gsm             --
```

As with the general object, you can limit the fields displayed using the -f option. Table 14-2 only lists the name and type fields.

Table 14-2. *The nmcli Objects*

Object	Description
general	NetworkManager status and enabled devices. Use the terse (-t) and field (-f) options to limit the information displayed.
networking	Manage networking, use on and off to turn networking on or off, and connectivity for the connection state.
radio	Turns on or off the wireless networking (on or off). Can turn on or off specific kinds of wireless: wifi, wwan (mobile broadband), and wimax. The all option turns on or off all wireless.
connection	Manage network connections. show List connection profiles. With --active showing only active connections. up Activate a connection. down Deactivate a connection. add Add a new connection, specifying type, ifname, con-name (profile). modify Edit an existing connection; use + and - to add new values to properties. edit Add a new connection or edit an existing one using the interactive editor. delete Delete a configured connection (profile). reload Reload all connection profiles. load Reload or load a specific profile.

(*continued*)

Table 14-2. (*continued*)

Object	Description
device	Manage network interfaces (devices).
	status Display device status.
	show Display device information.
	connect Connect the device.
	disconnect Disconnect the device.
	delete Delete a software device, such as a bridge.
	wifi Display a list of available WiFi access points.
	wifi rescan Rescan for and display access points.
	wifi connect Connect to a WiFi network; specify password, wep-key-type, ifname, bssid, and name (profile name).
	wimax List available WiMAX networks.
agent	Run as a Network Manager secret agent or polkit agent.
	secret As a secret agent, nmcli listens for secret requests.
	polkit As a polkit agent, it listens for all authorization requests.

```
$ nmcli -f name, type c s
NAME        TYPE
enp7s0      802-3-ethernet
AT&T LTE 1  gsm
```

Adding the --active option will only show active connections.

```
nmcli c s --active
```

To start and stop a connection (like ifconfig does), use the up and down options.

```
nmcli con up enp7s0.
```

Use the device object to manage your network devices. The show and status options provide information about your devices. To check the status of all your network devices, use the device object and status options:

```
nmcli device status
DEVICE  TYPE      STATE         CONNECTION
enp7s0  ethernet  connected     enp7s0
wlp6s0  wifi      disconnected  --
lo      loopback  unmanaged     --
```

You can abbreviate device and status to d and s.

```
nmcli d s
```

You also use the device object to connect and disconnect devices. Use the connect or disconnect options with the interface name (ifname) of the device, in this example, enp7s0. With the delete option, you can remove a device.

```
nmcli device disconnect enp7s0
nmcli device connect enp7s0
```

To turn networking on or off, you use the networking object and the on and off options. Use the connectivity option to check network connectivity. The networking object alone tells you if it is enabled or not.

```
$ nmcli networking
enabled
```

```
$ nmcli networking on
```

```
$ nmcli networking connectivity
full
```

Should you want to just turn on or off the WiFi connection, you would use the radio object. Use wifi, wwan, and wimax for a specific type of WiFi connection and the all option for all of them. The radio object alone shows WiFi status of all your WiFi connection types.

```
$ nmcli radio
WIFI-HW   WIFI   WWAN-HW   WWAN
enabled   enabled   enabled   enabled
```

```
$ nmcli radio wifi on
```

```
$ nmcli radio all off
```

561

nmcli Wired Connections

You can use nmcli to add connections, just as you can with the desktop NetworkManager tool. To add a new static connection use the connection object with the add option. Specify the connection's profile name with the con-name option, the interface name with the ifname option, and the type, such as Ethernet. For a static connection, you would add the IP address (ipv4 or ipv6), and the gateway address (gw4 or gw6). For a DHCP connection simply do not list the IP address and gateway options. The profile name can be any name. You could have several profile names for the same network device. For example, for your wireless device, you could have several wireless connection profiles, depending on the different networks you want to connect to. Should you connect your Ethernet device to a different network, you would simply use a different connection profile that you have already set up, instead of manually reconfiguring the connection. If you do not specify a connection name, one is generated and assigned for you. The connection name can be the same as the device name as shown here, but keep in mind that the connection name refers to the profile and the device name refers to the actual device.

```
$ nmcli c s
NAME        UUID                                    TYPE             DEVICE
enp7s0      f7202f6d-fc66-4b81-8962-69b71202efc0    802-3-ethernet   enp7s0
```

For a DHCP connection, specify the profile name, connection type, and ifname. The following example creates an Ethernet connection with the profile name my-wired.

```
nmcli con add con-name my-wired type ethernet ifname enp7s0
```

For a static connection, add the IP (ip4 or ip6) and gateway (gw4 or gw6) options with their addresses.

```
nmcli con add con-name my-wired-static ifname enp7s0 type ethernet ip4
192.168.1.0/24 gw4 192.168.1.1
```

In most cases, the type is Ethernet (wired) or WiFi (wireless). Check the nmcli man page for a list of other types, such as gsm, InfiniBand, VPN, VLAN, WiMAX, and Bridge.

You can also add a connection using the interactive editor. Use the edit instead of the add option, and specify the con-name (profile) and connection type.

```
nmcli con edit type ethernet con-name my-wired
```

To modify an existing connection, use the modify option. For an IP connection, the property that is changed is referenced as part of the IP settings, in this example, ip4. The IP properties include addresses, gateway, and method (ip4.addresses, ip4.gateway, and ip4.method).

```
nmcli con mod my-wired ip4.gateway 192.168.1.2
```

To add or remove a value for a property, use the + and - signs as a prefix. To add a DNS server address, you would use +ip4.dns. To remove one, use -ip4.dns.

```
nmcli con mod my-wired +ip4.dns 192.168.1.5
```

You can also modify a connection using the interactive editor. Use the edit instead of the modify option with the connection name.

```
nmcli con edit enp7s0
```

You are then placed in the interactive editor with an nmcli> prompt and the settings you can change are listed. The help command lists available commands. Use the describe command to show property descriptions.

Use print to show the current value of a property and set to change its value. To see all the properties for a setting, use the print command and the setting name. Once you have made changes, use the save command to effect the changes.

```
print ipv4
print ipv4.dns
print connection
set ipv4.address 192.168.0.1
```

The connection edit command can also reference a profile using the id option. The Name field in the connection profile information is the same as the ID. Also, each profile is given a unique system UUID, which can also be used to reference the profile.

Once you are finished editing the connection, enter the quit command to leave the editor.

nmcli Wireless Connections

To see a list of all the available WiFi connections in your area, you use the wifi option with the device object. You can further qualify it by interface (if you have more than one) by adding the ifname option, and by BSSID adding the bssid option.

```
nmcli device wifi
```

To connect to a new WiFi network, use the `wifi connect` option and the SSID. You can further specify a password, wep-key-type, key, ifname, bssid, name (profile name), and if it is private. If you do not provide a name (profile name), nmcli will generate one for you.

```
nmcli dev wifi connect surfturtle password mypass wep-key-type wpa ifname
wlp6s0 name my-wireless1
```

To reconnect to a WiFi network for which you have previously set up a connection, use the `connection` object with the `up` command and the `id` option to specify the profile name.

```
nmcli connection up id my-wireless1
```

You can also add a new wireless connection using the `connection` object and the `wifi` type with the `ssid` option.

```
nmcli con add con-name my-wireless2 ifname wlp6s0 type wifi ssid ssidname
```

Then, to set the encryption type, use the **modify** command to set the `sec.key-mgmt` property. For the passphrase, set the `wifi-sec.psk` property.

```
nmcli con mod my-wirless2 wifi-sec.key-mgmt wpa-psk
nmcli con modify my-wireless2 wifi-sec.psk mypassword
```

Network Manager Manual Configuration Using Network Connections

You can also use the older Network Connections utility (`nm-connection-editor`) to edit any network connection. You may have to run it from a terminal window. It is not installed by default. Established connections are listed, with at toolbar at the bottom for adding, removing, and editing network connections (see Figure 14-12). Your current network connections should already be listed.

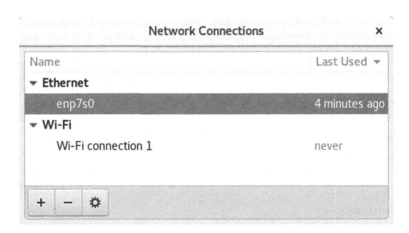

Figure 14-12. *Network configuration (nm-connection-editor)*

When you add a connection, you can choose its type from a drop-down menu. The menu organizes connection types into three categories: Hardware, Virtual, and VPN. Hardware connections cover both wired (Ethernet, DSL, and InfiniBand) and wireless (WiFi, WiMAX, and Mobile Broadband) connections. VPN lists the supported VPN types, such as OpenVPN, PPTP, and Cisco. You can also import a previously configured connection. Virtual supports VLAN and Bond virtual connections.

Configuration editing dialogs display a General tab from which you can make your configuration available to all users and automatically connect when the network connection is available. You can also choose to use a VPN connection and specify a firewall zone.

Editing an Ethernet connection opens an Editing window. The Create button on the Choose a Connection Type dialog is used to add a new connection and opens a similar window, with no settings. The Ethernet tab lists the MAC hardware address and the MTU. The MTU is usually set to automatic. The standard default configuration for a wired Ethernet connection uses DHCP. Connect automatically will set up the connection when the system starts up. There are seven tabs—General, Ethernet, 8.02.1x Security, DCB, Proxy, IPv4 Settings, and IPv6 Settings. The IPv4 Settings tab lets you select the kind of wired connection you have. The manual configuration entries for an IPv4 connection are shown in Figure 14-13. Click the Add button to enter the IP address, network mask, and gateway address. Then enter the address for the DNS servers and your network search domains. The Routes button will open a window in which you can manually enter any network routes.

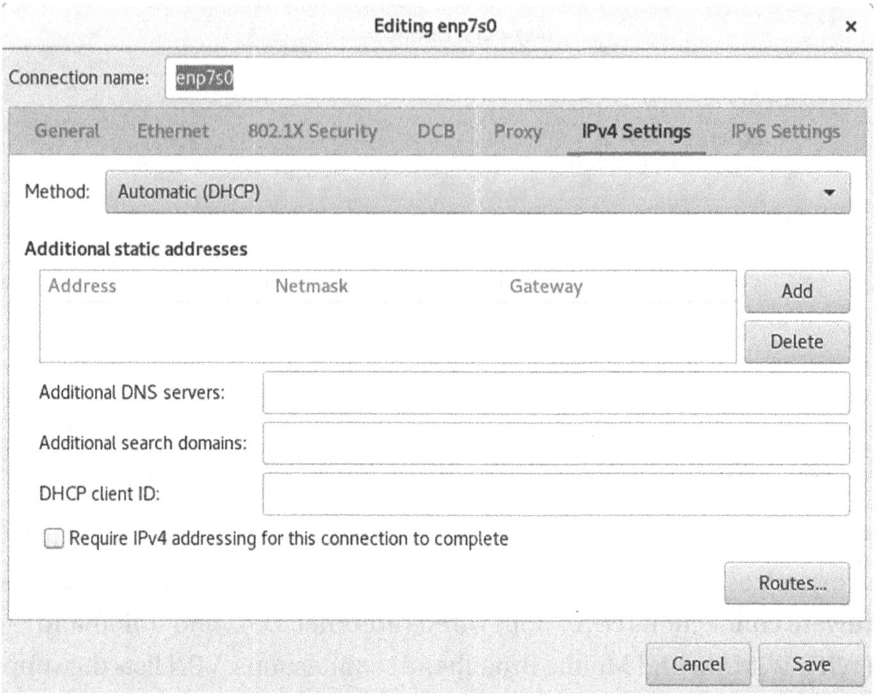

Figure 14-13. *IPv4 wired configuration (nm-connection-editor)*

For a wireless connection, you enter wireless configuration data, such as your ESSID, password, and encryption method. For wireless connections, you choose WiFi or WiMAX as the connection type. The Editing Wi-Fi connection window opens with tabs for general configuration, your wireless information, security, proxy, and IP settings (see Figure 14-14). On the Wi-Fi tab, you specify your SSID, along with your mode and MAC address.

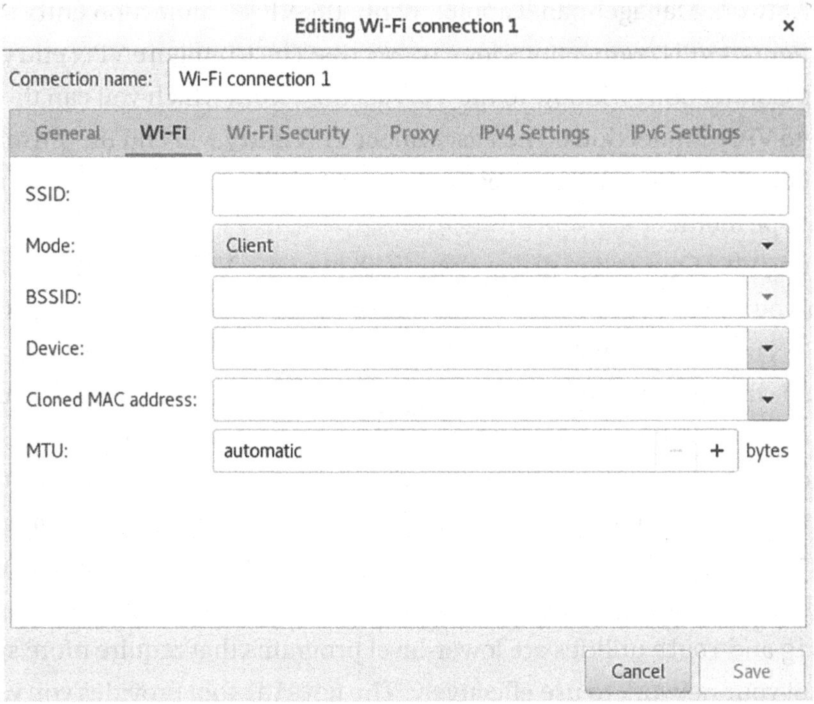

Figure 14-14. *Wireless configuration (nm-connection-editor)*

On the Wi-Fi Security tab, you enter your wireless connection security method. The commonly used method, WEP, is supported, along with WPA personal. The WPA personal method only requires a password. More secure connections, such as Dynamic WEP and Enterprise WPA, are also supported. These will require much more configuration information, such as authentication methods, certificates, and keys.

For a new broadband connection, choose the Mobile Broadband entry in the connection type menu. A 3G wizard starts up to help you set up the appropriate configuration for your particular 3G service. Configuration steps are listed on the left pane. If your device is connected, you can select it from the drop-down menu on the right pane.

Once a service is selected, you can further edit the configuration by clicking its entry in the Mobile Broadband tab and clicking the Edit button. The Editing window opens with tabs for Mobile Broadband, PPP, IPv4, and IPv6 settings. On the Mobile Broadband tab, you can enter your number, username, and password. Advanced options include the APN, Network, and PIN. The APN should already be entered.

On the Network Manager panel applet menu, the VPN Connection entry submenu will list configured VPN connections for easy access. The Configure VPN entry will open the Network Connections window to the VPN section, from which you can then add, edit, or delete VPN connections. The Disconnect VPN entry will end the current active VPN connection. To add a VPN connection, choose a VPN connection type from the connection type menu.

The Editing VPN Connection dialog opens with two tabs: VPN and IPv4 Settings. On the VPN tab, you enter VPN connection information, such as the gateway address and any additional VPN information that may be required. For an OpenVPN connection, you will have to provide the authentication type, certificates, and keys. Clicking the Advanced button opens the Advanced Options dialog. An OpenVPN connection will have tabs for General, Security, and TLS Authentication. On the Security tab, you can specify the cipher to use.

Networks are configured and managed with the lower-level tools: `ifconfig`, `route`, and `netstat`. The `ifconfig` tool operates from your root user desktop and enables you to configure your network interfaces fully, adding new ones and modifying others. The `ifconfig` and `route` utilities are lower-level programs that require more specific knowledge of your network to use effectively. The `netstat` tool provides you with information about the status of your network connections.

Command-Line PPP Access: wvdial

From the command-line interface, you can use the `wvdial` dialer to set up PPP connections for dial-up modems. The `wvdial` program loads its configuration from the `/etc/wvdial.conf` file. You can edit this file and enter modem and account information, including modem speed and serial device, as well as ISP phone number, username, and password. The `wvdial.conf` file is organized into sections, beginning with a section label enclosed in brackets. A section holds variables for different parameters that are assigned values, such as `username = chris`. The default section holds default values inherited by other sections, so you needn't repeat them.

With the `wvdialconf` utility, you can create a default `wvdial.conf` file automatically; `wvdialconf` detects your modem and sets the default values for basic features. You can then edit the `wvdial.conf` file and modify the phone, username, and password entries with your ISP dial-up information. Remove the preceding semicolon (`;`) to unquote the entry. Any line beginning with a semicolon is ignored as a comment.

```
$ wvdialconf
```

The following example shows the /etc/wvdial.conf file:

```
/etc/wvdial.conf
[Modem0]
Modem = /dev/ttyS0
Baud = 57600
Init1 = ATZ
SetVolume = 0
Dial Command = ATDT

[Dialer Defaults]
Modem = /dev/ttyS0
Baud = 57600
Init1 = ATZ
SetVolume = 0
Dial Command = ATDT
```

To start wvdial, enter the command wvdial, which then reads the connection configuration information from the /etc/wvdial.conf file; wvdial dials the ISP and initiates the PPP connection, providing your username and password, when requested.

```
$ wvdial
```

You can set up connection configurations for any number of connections in the /etc/wvdial.conf file. To select one, enter its label as an argument to the wvdial command, as shown here:

```
$ wvdial myisp
```

Setting Up Your Firewall: firewall-config

You can run your firewall on a standalone system directly connected to the Internet or on a gateway system that connects a local network to the Internet. Most networks now use dedicated routers for Internet access, which have their own firewalls. If, instead, you decide to use a Linux system as a gateway, it will have at least two network connections, one for the local network and an Internet connection device for the Internet.

FirewallD

Fedora27 uses the FirewallD firewall daemon, instead of the older static system-config-firewall. To configure FirewallD, you can use the firewalld-config graphical interface. You can also use firewalld-cmd command from the command line. To set up your firewall, run firewall-config (Sundry ➤ Firewall; see Figure 14-15). The firewall is configured using zones displayed on the Zones tab. To configure a particular service, use the Services tab.

With firewall-config you can configure either a Runtime configuration or Permanent configuration. Select one from the Configuration drop-down menu. The Runtime configuration shows your current runtime setup, whereas a Permanent configuration does not take effect until you reload or restart. If you want to edit your zones and services, you need to choose the Permanent configuration. This view displays a zone toolbar for editing the zone, at the bottom of the zones scroll box, and edit, add, and remove buttons on the Services tab for managing service protocols, ports, and destination addresses.

Additional tabs can be displayed from the View menu for configuring ICMP types, whitelists, and for adding firewall rules directly (direct configuration).

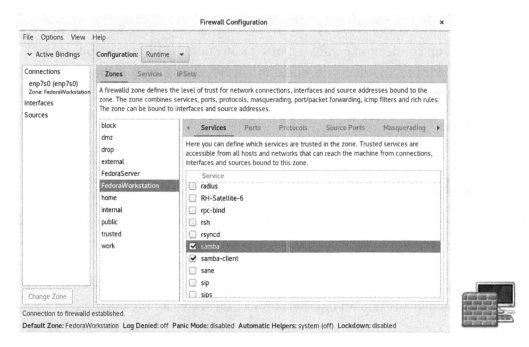

Figure 14-15. *firewall-config: runtime configuration*

A firewall configuration is set up for a given zone, such as a home, work, internal, external, or public zone. Zones provide an added level of protection by the firewall. They divide the network protected by the Firewall into separate segments, which can only communicate as permitted by the firewall. In effect, zones separate one part of your network from another. Each zone has its own configuration. Zones are listed in the Zones scroll box on the left side of the `firewall-config` window (see Figure 14-16). Select the one you want to configure. The `firewall-config` window opens to the default, Public. You can choose the default zone from the System Default Zone dialog, which you open from the Options menu as Change Default Zone.

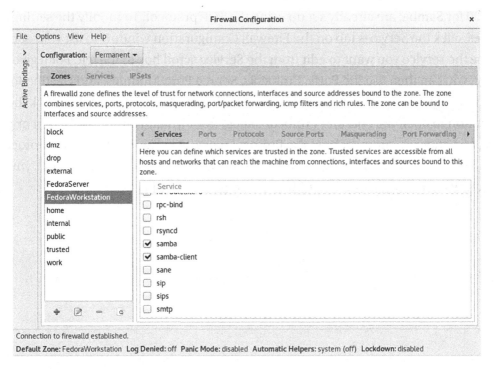

Figure 14-16. *firewall-config: permanent configuration*

If you choose Permanent Configuration from the Configuration menu, a toolbar for zones is displayed below the Zones scroll box, as shown in Figure 14-16. The + button lets you add a zone; the – button removes a zone. The pencil/page button lets you edit a zone. The add and edit buttons open the Base Zone Settings dialog, in which you enter or edit the zone name, version, description, and the target. The default target is `ACCEPT`. Other options are `REJECT` and `DROP`. The Load Zone Defaults button (yellow arrow) loads default settings, removing any you have made.

Each zone, in turn, can have one or more network connections. From the Options menu, choose Change Zones of Connections to open the Network Connections dialog, from which you can add a network connection.

For a given zone, you can configure services, ports, masquerading, port forwarding, interfaces, rich rules, sources, and ICMP filter. The features many users want to change are the services. A Linux system is often used to run servers for a network. If you are creating a strong firewall but still want to run a service such as a web server, an FTP server, or SSH encrypted connections, you must specify it in the Services tab.

For a selected service, you can specify service settings such as the ports and protocols it uses, any modules, and specific network addresses. Default settings, such as port 139 for Samba, are already set up using the TCP protocol. To modify the settings for services, click the Services tab on the Firewall Configuration window to list your services. Choose the service you want to edit from the Service scroll box to the left. For a given service, you can then use the Ports, Protocols, Source Port, Modules, and Destination tabs to specify ports, protocols, modules, and addresses. On the Ports table, click the Add button to open the Port and Protocol dialog, from which you can add a port or port range, and choose a protocol from the Protocol menu (see Figure 14-17). For protocols needed by all hosts and networks, use the Protocols tab. On the Destination tab, you can enter an IPv4 or IPv6 destination address for the service.

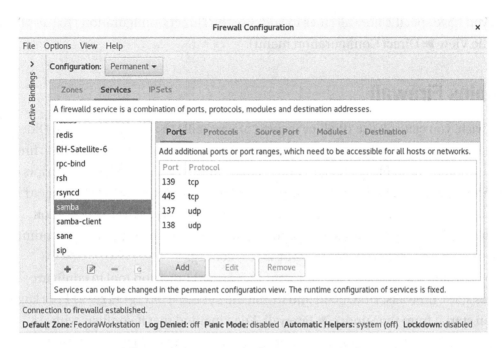

Figure 14-17. *Firewall Configuration dialog: Services tab*

The Ports tab lets you specify ports that you may want opened for certain services, such as BitTorrent. Click the Add button to open a dialog in which you can select the port number, along with the protocol to control (TCP or UDP), or enter a specific port number or range.

If your system is being used as gateway to the Internet for your local network, you can implement masquerading to hide your local hosts from outside access from the Internet. This also requires IP forwarding, which is automatically enabled when you choose masquerading. Local hosts will still be able to access the Internet, but they will masquerade as your gateway system. You would select for masquerading the interface that is connected to the Internet. Masquerading is available only for IPv4 networks, not IPv6 networks.

The Port Forwarding tab lets you set up port forwarding, channeling transmissions from one port to another, or to a different port on another system. Click the Add button to add a port, specifying its protocol and destination.

The ICMP Filters tab allows you to block ICMP messages. By default, all ICMP messages are allowed. Blocking ICMP messages makes for a more secure system. Certain types of ICMP messages are often blocked, as they can be used to infiltrate or overload a system, such as the ping and pong ICMP messages.

If you have specific firewall rules to add, use the Direct Configuration tab (displayed from the View ➤ Direct Configuration menu).

IPtables Firewall

If you wish, you can still use IPtables instead of FirewallD to manage firewalls. Older customized firewall configurations may still want to use the older IPtables static firewall. IPtables systemd unit files manage static IPtables rules, much like System V scripts did in previous releases. The `iptables` command keeps firewall rules in `/etc/sysconfig/iptables`, which is checked for (`ConditionPathExists`). The `iptables` operation runs an `iptables.init` script to start and stop the firewall. The script reads runtime configuration from `/etc/sysconfig/iptables-config`.

You can still use the older `system-config-firewall` desktop tool to configure IPtables static firewalls. Download and install the `system-config-firewall` package. You can start it from the Sundry ➤ Firewall. Keep in mind that it conflicts with FirewallD. You will have to stop and disable `firewallD` before you can use `system-config-firewall`.

```
sudo systemctl stop firewalld
sudo systemctl disable firewalld
```

To set up your firewall, run `system-config-firewall` (Sundry ➤ Firewall). It should be the second firewall icon. The top button bar has buttons for a Firewall Wizard, Apply Button to Effect Any Changes, Reload to Restore Your Saved Firewall, and Disable and Enable buttons (see Figure 14-18). You can enable or disable your firewall with the Enable and Disable buttons. If the Firewall is active, only the Disable button can be used, and vice versa.

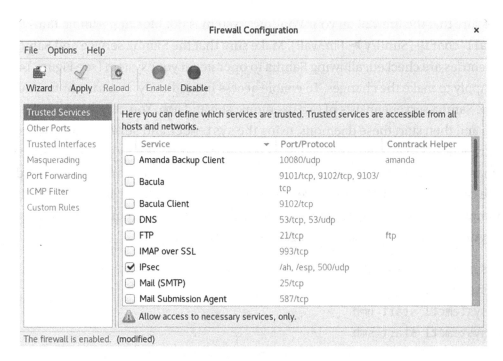

Figure 14-18. system-config-firewall (IPtables)

Setting Up Windows Network Access: Samba

Most local and home networks include some systems working on Microsoft Windows and others on Linux. You may be required to let a Windows computer access a Linux system or vice versa. If you want to allow other Windows users to access folders on your Fedora desktop, you will have to install and configure the Samba server.

Note   See the section in Chapter 3 called "Shared Network Access for Windows Samba: (Samba)" to learn how you can access shared folders from GNOME and from Windows. With the transition from SMB1 to SMB3 (Server Message Block), the file manager desktop browsing no longer works. You have to set up access to shared folders directly.

Be sure that Samba is installed and enabled. Open Packages and click the Server entry or search for samba. Install the samba and samba-client packages. Selecting samba for installation will automatically select any needed dependent packages.

Be sure that the firewall on your Windows system is not blocking Samba. Run `firewall-config` (Sundry ➤ Firewall). Make sure that the Samba service and Samba client entries are checked, allowing Samba to operate on your system (see Figure 14-16). Click Apply to make the changes. To enable access immediately, restart your firewall.

The Samba server consists of two daemons: smb and nmb. You may first have to enable and then start these daemons, using the `systemctl` and `service` commands as the root user. Open a terminal window (Terminal), access the root user with the `su` command, and then enter a `systemctl` command for the smb and nmb servers with the `enable` command to enable the server. Finally, use the `systemctl` command with the `start` option to start it. Once enabled, the server should start automatically whenever your system starts up. Samba is managed by `systemd`.

```
sudo systemctl enable nmb
sudo systemctl enable smb
sudo systemctl start nmb
sudo systemctl start smb
```

Also, make sure that Samba access is permitted by SELinux (`system-config-selinux`). Use the SELinux Management tool and on the Boolean tab and enable Samba access (see Figure 14-16). There are several Samba entries. To share folders, Windows folders, and NFS folders, you would check the following:

```
Allow samba to share any file/directory read/write
Allow samba to export ntfs/fusefs volumes
Allow samba to export NFS volumes
```

Should you receive a security alert, you can change the Samba SELinux file context manually, using the `chcon` and `semanage` commands. The commands to enter will be listed in the Fix Command section of the security alert's Show Full Error Output scroll window. The Samba share directory's SELinux file context is set to `samba_share_t`. The `semanage` command preserves the change through relabeling. In the following example, the SELinux file context for the `/mymedia` share is set:

```
sudo chcon -R -t samba_share_t '/mymedia'
sudo semanage fcontext -a  -t samba_share_t '/mymedia'
```

Network Analysis Tools

Several applications are available on Linux to let you monitor your network activity. Graphical applications like Wireshark provide detailed displays and logs to let you analyze and detect network usage patterns. Other tools like ping, netstat, nmap, and traceroute offer specific services (see Table 14-3). Tools like ping, traceroute, nmap, and netstat can be run individually on a command line (Terminal window).

Table 14-3. *Network Tools*

Network Information Tool	Description
ping	Detects whether a system is connected to the network.
finger	Obtains information about users on the network.
who	Checks which users are currently online.
whois	Obtains domain information.
host	Obtains network address information about a remote host.
traceroute	Tracks the sequence of computer networks and hosts your message passes through.
wireshark	Protocol analyzer to examine network traffic.
netstat	Real-time network status monitor.
tcpdump	Captures and saves network packets.
nmap	Network Mapper, network discovery and security.

Predictable and Unpredictable Network Device Names

Network devices now use a predictable naming method that differs from the older naming method. Names are generated based on the specific device referencing the network device type, its hardware connection and slot, and even its function. The traditional network device names used the eth prefix with the number of the device for an Ethernet network device. The name eth0 referred to the first Ethernet connection on your computer. This naming method was considered unpredictable as it did not accurately reference the actual Ethernet device. The old system relied on probing the network driver at boot, and if your system had several Ethernet connections, the names could end up being switched, depending on how the startup proceeded. With the current version of systemd udev, the naming uses a predictable method that specifies a particular device. The predictable method references the actual hardware connection on your system.

The name used to reference predictable network device names has a prefix for the type of device followed by several qualifiers, such as the type of hardware, the slot used, and the function number. Instead of the older unpredictable name like eth0, the first Ethernet device is referenced by a name like enp7s0. The interface name enp7s0 references an Ethernet (en) connection, at PCI slot 7 (p7), with the hotplug slot index number 0 (s0). wlp6s0 is a wireless (wl) connection, at PCI slot 6 (p6), with the hotplug slot index number 0 (s0). virvb0 is a virtual (vir) bridge (vb) network interface. Table 14-4 lists predictable naming prefixes.

Unlike the older unpredictable name, the predictable name will most likely be different for each computer. Predictable network names, along with alternatives, are discussed at:

https://www.freedesktop.org/wiki/Software/systemd/PredictableNetwork
InterfaceNames/

The naming is carried out by the kernel and is described in the comment section of the kernel source's systemd/src/udev/udev-bultin-net_id.c file.

Table 14-4. *Network Interface Device Naming*

Name	Description
en	Ethernet
sl	Serial line IP (slip)
wl	wlan, wireless local area network
ww	wwan, wireless wide area network (mobile broadband)
p	PCI geographical location (pci-e slot)
s	Hotplug slot index number
o	Onboard cards
f	Function (used for cards with more than one port)
u	USB port
i	USB port interface

The directory /sys/devices lists all your devices in subdirectories, including your network devices. The path to the devices progresses through subdirectories named for the busses connecting the device. To quickly find the full path name, you can use the /sys/class directory instead. For network devices, use /sys/class/net. Then use the ls -l command to list the network devices with their links to the full pathname in the /sys/devices directory (the ../.. path references a cd change of up two directories [class/net] to the /sys directory).

```
$ cd /sys/class/net
$ ls
enp7s0  lo  wlp6s0
$ ls -l
total 0
lrwxrwxrwx 1 root root 0 Feb 19 12:27 enp7s0 -> ../../devices/pci0000:00/00
00:00:1c.3/0000:07:00.0/net/enp7s0
lrwxrwxrwx 1 root root 0 Feb 19 12:27 lo -> ../../devices/virtual/net/lo
lrwxrwxrwx 1 root root 0 Feb 19 12:28 wlp6s0 -> ../../devices/pci0000:00/00
00:00:1c.2/0000:06:00.0/net/wlp6s0
```

So the full path name in the /sys/devices directory for enp7s0 is:

/sys/devices/pci0000:00/0000:00:1c.3/0000:07:00.0/net/enp7s0

You can find the PCI bus slot used with the lspci command. This command lists all your PCI connected devices. In this example, the PCI bus slot used is 7, which is why the PCI part of the name enp7s0 is p7. The s part refers to a hotplug slot, which in this example is s0.

```
$ lspci
06:00.0 Network controller: Qualcomm Atheros QCA9565 / AR9565 Wireless
Network Adapter (rev 01)
07:00.0 Ethernet controller: Realtek Semiconductor Co., Ltd. RTL8101/2/6E
PCI Express Fast/Gigabit Ethernet controller (rev 07)
```

Devices have certain properties defined by udev, which manages all devices. Some operations, such as systemd link files, make use these properties. The ID_PATH, ID_NET_NAME_MAC, and INTERFACE properties can be used to identify a device to udev. To display these properties, you use the udevadm command to query the udev database.

With the info and -e options, properties of all active devices are displayed. You can pipe
(|) this output to a grep command to display only those properties for a given device.
In the following example, the properties for the enp7s0 device are listed. Preceding the
properties for a given device is a line, beginning (^) with a P and ending with the device
name. The .* matching characters match all other intervening characters on that line,
^P.*enp7s0. The -A option displays the specified number of additional lines after that
match, -A 22.

```
$ udevadm info -e | grep -A 22 ^P.*enp7s0
P: /devices/pci0000:00/0000:00:1c.3/0000:07:00.0/net/enp7s0
E: DEVPATH=/devices/pci0000:00/0000:00:1c.3/0000:07:00.0/net/enp7s0
E: ID_BUS=pci
E: ID_MM_CANDIDATE=1
E: ID_MODEL_FROM_DATABASE=RTL8101/2/6E PCI Express Fast/Gigabit Ethernet
   controller
E: ID_MODEL_ID=0x8136
E: ID_NET_DRIVER=r8169
E: ID_NET_LINK_FILE=/lib/systemd/network/99-default.link
E: ID_NET_NAME_MAC=enx74e6e20ec729
E: ID_NET_NAME_PATH=enp7s0
E: ID_OUI_FROM_DATABASE=Dell Inc.
E: ID_PATH=pci-0000:07:00.0
E: ID_PATH_TAG=pci-0000_07_00_0
E: ID_PCI_CLASS_FROM_DATABASE=Network controller
E: ID_PCI_SUBCLASS_FROM_DATABASE=Ethernet controller
E: ID_VENDOR_FROM_DATABASE=Realtek Semiconductor Co., Ltd.
E: ID_VENDOR_ID=0x10ec
E: IFINDEX=2
E: INTERFACE=enp7s0
E: SUBSYSTEM=net
E: SYSTEMD_ALIAS=/sys/subsystem/net/devices/enp7s0
E: TAGS=:systemd:
E: USEC_INITIALIZED=1080179
```

For certain tasks, such as renaming, you many need to know the MAC address. You can find this with the ip link command, which you can abbreviate to ip l. The MAC address is before the brd string. In this example, the MAC address for enp7s0 is 74:e6:e2:0e:c7:29. The ip link command also provides the MTU (Maximum Transmission Unit) and the current state of the connection.

$ **ip link**

```
1: lo: <LOOPBACK,UP,LOWER_UP> mtu 65536 qdisc noqueue state UNKNOWN
mode DEFAULT group default qlen 1 link/loopback 00:00:00:00:00:00 brd
00:00:00:00:00:00
2: enp7s0: <BROADCAST,MULTICAST,UP,LOWER_UP> mtu 1500 qdisc fq_codel state
UP mode DEFAULT group default qlen 1000 link/ether 74:e6:e2:0e:c7:29 brd
ff:ff:ff:ff:ff:ff
3: wlp6s0: <BROADCAST,MULTICAST> mtu 1500 qdisc noop state DOWN mode
DEFAULT group default qlen 1000 link/ether 4c:bb:58:22:40:1d brd
ff:ff:ff:ff:ff:ff
```

Index

© Richard Petersen 2018
R. Petersen, *Beginning Fedora Desktop*, https://doi.org/10.1007/978-1-4842-3882-0

F